MASTERING EXCELLENCE:

A Leader's Guide to Aligning Strategy, Culture, Customer Experience & Measures of Success

To my good friend. Marty for with great appreciation your support as I wrote this. Best wishes.

Library of Congress Cataloging-in-Publication Data

Lawton, Robin L.

Mastering Excellence: A Leader's Guide to Aligning Strategy, Culture, Customer Experience & Measures of Success.

Includes index (pp. 325-328)

ISBN: 0998420808
ISBN 978-0-9984208-0-6 (acid-free paper)
1. Excellence. 2. Leadership. 3. Cultural change. 4. Strategy. 5. Voice of the customer. 6. Management system.
7. Customer-centered. I. Title.

Published in the United States by C3 Excellence Publishing.

www.C3Excellence.com

C3 Excellence Mission: Promote the widespread, successful adoption of customer-centered culture (C3) principles and practices.

Other books by Robin L. Lawton include the following:

Creating a Customer-Centered Culture: Leadership in Quality, Innovation and Speed (1993)

The Change Agent's Guide to Radical Improvement (2002) with Ken Miller

Leadership: Helping Others to Succeed (2014) with Dr. Warren Bennis, Representative Pat Schroeder, Senator George Mitchell

A prism makes visible the light we cannot see.
The 8 Dimensions of Excellence creates insights to
make excellence visible and you radiant.

In memory of my mother, Jean, who told me many times,
"If it's worth doing, it's worth doing well,"
and led quietly by example.

CONTENTS

ACKNOWLEDGMENTS

This book and the underlying customer-centered culture system could not have been created without many wonderful customers who gave me the opportunity to learn from them over the past several decades. Many became good friends; some became colleagues. Among those were Bill Nugent at Dartmouth-Hitchcock Medical Center; Bob Hawkesworth at several Alberta government agencies; Bruce Rismiller at Northwest Airlines; Carlton Braun at Motorola; Cindy Matson at California State University; Dale Landry at Southern Alberta Technical Institute; Dar Schwanbeck at Northern Alberta Business Incubator; David Ellerington at Imperial Oil; Hillary Blevins at Girl Scouts; Jack Parsons at American Honda; Jan Magdziasz at two government agencies in Florida; Jennifer Winchester at Jackson County Community College; Judy MacCully at Group Health Cooperative; Julian Tan and Grace Kon at UNI Strategic in Singapore; Karen Lewis at Raytheon; Ken Miller at Missouri Department of Revenue; Kristin Arnold at Extraordinary Team; Kyle Markland at Affinity Plus Credit Union; Laurie Emerson at Vermont Council for Performance Excellence; Linda Logan at Fiscal Foundations; Lisa Powell, Les Beck, and Ben Rogers at Linn County, Iowa; Linda Langston at National Association of Counties; Marty Collins at City of Milwaukee; Mitch Witten at the City of Louisville; Quentin Wilson in the Missouri governor's cabinet; Rob Lass at Mayo Clinic; Ron Marafioti at US Coast Guard; Ted Sawchuk at Meteorological Services of Canada; Seth Pillsbury at HRQMC; Shelley Bowen at BlueCross BlueShield of Kansas City; Stephanie Easthope at Wolters Kluwer Health; Tracy Hatch, Jocelyn Stein, and AnneMarie Burgess at MN Department of Transportation; all of my guest authors who have written chapters at the end of this book, and many others to whom I apologize for inadvertently failing to mention them. Thank you, Masters of Excellence.

The one person who has supported, inspired, collaborated and guided me to bring this book to completion began working with me as my chief operating officer in 2003, the lovely woman who is now my wife, Peggy. Her highly creative mind, wizardry in areas I will never master, and unflagging role as my biggest fan and best friend cannot be overstated. She is my muse.

A USER'S FOREWORD

My first exposure to Customer-Centered Culture (C3) concepts was in an executive workshop Rob gave at my firm about three years ago. At the time, I was an operational-level manager and had seen other attempts to improve my organization's performance. All had very limited success and very little staying power. My first response to hearing about C3 was that it would be one more such effort. It was not long before I began to change my mind, even finding myself one of its most ardent proponents. My transition from skeptic to convert continues stronger than ever. While Rob's message is clearly intended for management at the highest levels, I believe my experience as an operational manager in a large organization has been—and is likely to be—shared by many others like myself.

It's challenging for me to pick the greatest objective element that the C3 system has taught me. As a subjective whole, the result of what I have learned as a student of C3 has a regular and positive impact on the customers for whom I produce things. There are many more customers than I would have thought.

What is less important to me is the C3 process. Many people understand processes. Perform step one through step ten, and you achieve a desired result. That is a good thing, but to me, the process is not the essence of C3. I accept C3 as an articulated value or moral obligation to society, not to be constrained as a description of steps and processes. C3 is far more than that.

I have seen processes take a traditional producer-centered approach, either through education programs or via years of experience. Processes are a by-product of customer demand or satisfaction, not a driver of it. Processes require training; moral principles require education. C3 is a continuous lesson in customer-centered philosophy, language, and practice. The objective is not to train you to be a C3 robot. On the contrary, it forces you to think in a new way. A singular version of a C3 step process is a reduction from and misinterpretation of something much larger. Learn the C3 philosophy, thinking, and language, and apply it as it fits.

Since learning the C3 principles and language, I now often ask others and myself, "What is the product, and who is the customer?" Granted, the customer should be considered before the product is produced, but plenty of legacy products exist that have never considered brokers, fixers, and end users. This is because the traditional product-centered culture I referred to earlier seems to be the dominant culture in business. Once the C3 language is understood and a mental connection is made between products and customers, the C3 foundation is set, and the underlying paradigm of C3 begins to become real. The switch has been flipped. It clicks mentally and naturally. We can then understand that the customer has (or should have) more effect on the product than the product has on the customer. As a result, we naturally should begin to question whether our products create desired outcomes for our customers.

I have found that people are producing products for customers who don't exist. When you make this fact apparent, the immediate reaction is to create doubt about why you are producing that product or who you are trying to satisfy. That doubt causes reflection, redirection, and improvement.

After a few positive customer-product experiences with coworkers, the organization culture begins to change because it is so clear and obvious what is important— the customer. Eventually a customer-centered culture begins to form. It starts as a microculture change at first, but one that rapidly expands to others willing to accept and embrace it. The result of applied C3 logic is a support group of customer-focused individuals who are aware of the products they produce and know who they are producing them for. Naturally the perceptions and attributes of relevant products improve. A product's ability to satisfy is improved because the customer was involved with defining and improving it!

Hidden in the philosophy and language of C3 is a book of moral principles. At its root is consideration for others. It is a social obligation. Its principles and practices can be applied to all things that we intend to have an effect on others. Producer-centered cultures produce synthetic satisfaction (serving oneself), whereas the customer-centered culture produces organic and true satisfaction (serving others).

It seems to me that you should find this book and Rob's first one on the customer-centered culture in the Quality Management section of a bookstore, if there were one, maybe next to Deming, Shewhart, Juran, Ackoff, Crosby, and others. However, the C3 message is void of the usual statistics and rich on relevant, undisputable, and timeless facts. C3 challenges the Deming/Shewhart cycle by adding an element of what to plan for, which really should precede their plan-do-check-act (PDCA) cycle. If we are not considering the customer and his or her desired outcomes, we are unintentionally planning to go out of business.

Chase Mathews
Quality Expert

Some men see things as they are and say, "Why?"
I dream of things that never were and say, "Why not?"
—George Bernard Shaw

CHAPTER 1—INTRODUCTION

My goal with this book is to help you excel, engage, and excite. Leaders like you have high expectations, a vision of the possible and an urgency to improve others' lives. You pursue results previously thought impossible. Your personal charisma might be sufficient enough that others can't help themselves but to follow. If this is you, thank your lucky stars for good genes. For the rest of us mere mortals, leadership is something we tend to learn over time through trial and error. If you want to leverage and advance what you already know and lead with a mastery that makes enterprise transformation easier and more joyful, my hope is that this book will offer a clear path and many answers.

The material here is especially intended for you as a Master of Excellence. Your more traditional role may be an executive change leader, founder of a new business, CEO, initiative champion, consultant to senior management, teacher of best-in-class management practices, or strategic project leader in a complex organization. This book is designed to provide you with a powerful, elegantly simple framework, road map, and new tools. They support your objective to achieve superb organizational performance, customer success, and employee engagement that others would envy. This is not a task that is easy or for the timid. But stunning results are possible, more than compensating for the effort. I couldn't say that with my first book in 1993. The material in this book reflects both the evolution in my own thinking and learning over the intervening twenty-three years plus the experience of many hundreds of organizations and thousands of practitioners who put the underlying ideas into practice.

Reading books on how Steve Jobs, Elon Musk, Sir Richard Branson, John Kennedy, Muhammad Yunus, or other broadly admired leaders achieved success, despite overwhelming challenges, can be highly inspiring. Their stories confirm that effective leaders can transform the seemingly impossible into a new reality. Unfortunately what they did may not appear to be directly transferrable to what we want to do. Our situation is unique, just as theirs were. This is one of the main reasons I have made sure to include many examples from government, health-care, and other noncommercial enterprises. It is important to realize that these ideas and methods are equally effective there and in every other environment where they have been applied.

You may not be starting a new business, leading the exploration of space, eliminating hunger, or even working in a commercial enterprise. In fact, you may not even recognize the hidden and significant opportunities for excellence right under your nose. That situation is very common. Expect to have many hidden opportunities uncovered as you read. The road map described in this book will reveal, define, achieve, and sustain excellence in a knowledge-intensive environment. Though we will talk about what others have done, this book is primarily about what you can accomplish by taking specific actions. I believe your success will hinge on my ability to do at least a few key things:

1. Show how these principles and new practices are both similar to, yet significantly different from, what you already know.

2. Reveal how seemingly small changes are actually paradigm-altering catalysts, causing dramatic and unexpected results.

3. Make the material so interesting and personally relevant that you can't resist applying most of the Leader's Actions for creating a culture of customer-centered excellence.

4. Enable you to experience the taste of an orange, as if for the first time.

How would you describe the taste of an orange to someone who had never even heard of it? You might talk about it as a fruit, where it is grown, its color, how it compares to related citrus fruits, its shape, its chemical and nutritional properties, and its uses. Will the person you told this to now understand the taste of an orange? Sadly, no. In fact, that taste cannot be meaningfully described. It must be experienced. So it is with this material. In other words, I can explain it to you, but I can't understand it for you.

This taste-of-the-orange scenario is precisely the challenge I have had when asked to describe C3 practices. My short answer to "What is C3?" is this: *C3 is a system for aligning the strategic direction and operational practices of an organization to satisfy customer priorities and engage employees to excel.* Those practices involve fully understanding the answers to critically important questions such as the following:

- What we do we do?
- Why do we do it?
- How do we do it well?
- Who we do we do it for?
- What do they want?
- Why do they want it?
- How well do (and could) we deliver on those wants?
- How can success be measured when expectations are squishy and seem immeasurable?
- What are the main barriers to organizational transformation?
- How do we create innovative, sustainable new successes we never thought were possible?
- What are effective ways to win over the nonbelievers?
- How can we enjoy, not just survive, our role as Masters of Excellence?

We may believe we already know the answers and that they are just common sense, just as the orange we aren't familiar with may appear to be like the tangerine we know and love. In both cases, we are likely wrong. Consider that we often talk about common sense when referring to someone who doesn't have it. We will get to the point where we actually have that new common sense. When we do, we'll want to be patient with those not there. They will have to go through some version, albeit with less detail, of the same process that we will pursue for mastery. Only through experiential learning will these answers be revealed. The first step will be to become clear about what we do not know. The goal is to be conscious about what we know, articulating and modeling the practices so others will follow.

C3 is a system for organizational transformation. It rests on four cornerstones:

1. **Philosophy.** This includes a mind-set, paradigm, beliefs, and values. This philosophy is intended to assure customer priorities permeate all our thoughts and actions.

2. **8 Dimensions of Excellence (8DX).** The 8DX graphic depicts a framework that shows the

relationships among three issues of importance to customers and the enterprise (outcomes, products, and processes), the numbered sequence in which they must be addressed for optimum effectiveness, and the elements to include in planning, execution, and measurement.

3. **Measures.** This addresses the purposes of measurement, what the measures should include, and how to translate ambiguous intent (by both customers and leadership) into objective criteria of excellence.

4. **Methodology.** The methodology consists of powerful C3 tools designed for ease of use in any work context, but they are especially suited for those in knowledge-intensive work. They cover topics including strategic planning, voice of the customer (VOC), product design, measurement (satisfaction and balanced scorecards), surveys, Lean process, innovation, and project management (when the solution is unknown). The scientific foundation rests on an interdisciplinary integration from fields including linguistics, sociology, economics, psychology, communications, philosophy, statistics, and chaos theory.

A strong mechanism employed by C3 is the explicit channeling of communication flow among customers, leaders, managers, and individual contributors.[1] This is accomplished through the capture, articulation, understanding, and action to satisfy expectations from the voice of each of those parties:
- Voice of Customer (VOC): expectations about outcomes, products, and processes
- Voice of Leadership (VOL): expectations about intent and organizational direction
- Voice of Management (VOM): interpretation and deployment of VOL
- Voice of Workers (VOW): expectations about the context of work, the products received, and the products to create to satisfy the intent of leadership and satisfy customers' VOC.

There is a very good chance you are already familiar with some of the topics related to this book's content. Specific initiatives, approaches, and tools you may have employed go by names such as Lean, Six Sigma, Malcolm Baldrige Award Criteria, VOC, systems thinking, ISO 9001, theory of constraints, agile enterprise, and so on. Again it is easy to be fooled by what might appear at first to be familiar and, therefore, already well-known. The ingredients for a soufflé and omelet are very similar; the difference in how they are combined and cooked creates significantly different final results.

You are getting new ingredients, a new recipe, and a new picture of the final results you can reasonably expect. The proof is in the eating. One example of a new ingredient that may at first look familiar is called the "Strategic 5 Whys." Many change leaders have learned about a different, but similarly named, 5 Whys technique. It is used to identify the root cause of a problem. That method looks backward in time to identify when a bad result first started to form. The technique has been around for decades and can be helpful to solve past operational issues. It is reactive. The Strategic 5 Whys is future-oriented and looks forward to the results wanted. It identifies the dependencies of specific elements that will increase the likelihood of achieving that result. This method is strategic, predictive, and new. Better yet, it is easy. But it starts with different assumptions and ends with much bigger results. We can say the two approaches are complementary but fundamentally different in purpose, scope, and impact.

Our role as Master of Excellence is to take others where they have not been, where they may be afraid to go, to a place they don't believe is attainable, are uncertain where "there" is or, conversely, can't wait to get started on the adventure. Being effective while leading all these potential followers is a lot easier when we don't make it a solo endeavor. That is true whether we are the supreme leader or a principal

---

[1] See a graphic of this flow in appendix 10.

agent of that person. Our continuous goal as Master of Excellence is to do everything possible to engage many others as allies, intellectually and emotionally. Our success depends on them wanting to go where we want to take them. We want them chomping at the bit to excel and excite customers.

This book will be of benefit if it enables you to achieve new insights, inspire others to articulate and execute your vision of excellence, create objectively measured improvements in organizational performance, increase your enterprise's raving fans, or create heroes. We tend to consider heroes to be those who have done the extraordinary under difficult conditions and at great personal risk. Some of the dramatic changes we will seek certainly carry some risk. The world is rapidly changing around us. So continuing to do what we've always done also has risk. "If it ain't broke, don't fix it" is the mantra for sticking with the status quo. To deny that issues such as customer expectations, technology, social norms, health, environment, and economics are matters that are in constant flux is to court disaster.

It is in our interest to assume everything we have understood to be true is less stable and predictable than we know. That self-imposed uncertainty as we start fosters receptiveness to discovery. The good news is that the changes are not random. We want to seek out and embrace emerging trends. That will require us to question what excellence means and consider the possibility that our current state is inadequate. "If this is the best we can do, we aren't looking hard enough" will be our battle cry. Willingness to leave our comfort zone and seek new insights, results, and practices turns risk into opportunity.

Heroes uniformly view themselves as simply having done what was necessary on behalf of others. They view their actions as normal, that is, what anyone else would have done. Our role as Master of Excellence is to enable those around us to view the extraordinary as normal, achievable, and survivable. That last element differentiates heroes from martyrs. We don't want to be or let others become martyrs in pursuit of our vision. Having a path to victory that avoids minefields should be a handy asset. Welcome to the journey.

CHAPTER 2—THE ROAD MAP

The next page is intended to be your road map, showing how the material in this book is organized. The fuel powering our journey and insights comes from applying the Leader's Actions and C3 tools along the way. If you would like to download an optional electronic version of the Leader's Actions, please see the Mastering Excellence Workbook at http://www.C3Excellence.com.

The 8 Dimensions of Excellence, also referred to as 8DX, is the main graphic describing the framework for addressing excellence. If you are a visual thinker and like to see how all of the key elements in a system are related, you will love the 8DX framework. If you simply want a text version of the recipe for success, the 10 Steps shown on the next page should do the trick (also included as a printable reference with the electronic workbook).

Our strong bias is to *define excellence from the outside in* from the customers' perspective. So we will put especially heavy emphasis on understanding and applying Dimensions 1 through 4. We will use stories and examples to illustrate how the surface simplicity of 8DX can, upon application, reveal hidden depth and power. Excellence can be—and usually is—defined by organizations from the inside out, Dimensions 5 through 8. That is, based on our past personal or industry experiences, biases, and assumptions, we decide within our enterprise what the basis for excellence is.

This is not wrong, just limiting. Our history often determines how we define success and leads us to assume customers will agree. Because customers frequently do not agree, we will shun that as our strategic approach. But there is no need to throw out sustainable practices that have worked well for us up to now.

Wholesale discarding of the past in exchange for the new is neither necessary nor advocated. Sometimes our audience and potential followers can believe we are now on to the new next thing again. They may expect that this, too, shall pass. We can help our cause by reminding the cynical that taking a college math class is not an indictment of previous high school math classes. Learning is progressive and additive, building on what came before. Anything that enables us to add to our strengths and minimize our weaknesses is desired. Embrace it. We just can't be where we want to be by staying where we are. We are going to look at conventional practices from a new perspective that reveals important, overlooked elements that constrain excellence.

10 STEPS TO CUSTOMER-CENTERED EXCELLENCE	POSITION(S) IN THE 8 DIMENSIONS OF EXCELLENCE FRAMEWORK	CHAPTER	LEADER'S ACTIONS
		1 - Introduction	
		2 - The Road Map	
1. Establish the conditions for excellence, transformation & leadership		3 - Getting Results	
		4 - We Shall Overcome	1 - Opportunities with High Potential 2 - The Ready, Reluctant, and Powerful 3 - Indicators of Highly Visible Results
		5 - Where Are We?	4 - C3IQ, a Self-Assessment
		6 - Change Levers and Ambiguity	5 - Confusion Regarding the Customer 6 - Core Values Ambiguity 7 - Alignment of Values with Measures (KPIs) 8 - Crush Vital Lies
		7 - How Did We Get Here?	
		8 - 8 Dimensions of Excellence	9 - Connect Initiatives and Measures with 8DX 9a - Create Missing Measures
2. Articulate strategic & customer-desired outcomes		9 - Customer-Desired Outcomes	10 - Capturing Customer-Desired Outcomes
3. Determine how each outcome will be measured		10 - Reveal and Reduce Mission Confusion	11 - Differentiate Desired and Undesired Outcomes
4. Set numerical goals and due dates		11 - Why, Oh Why?	12 - Strategic 5 Whys
		12 - Connecting the Strategic Dots	13 - The Strategy Map, Part 1
5. Select the critical few products and owners most likely to impact outcome success		13 - Two Key Questions	
		14 - Work as Products	14 - Personal Products
		15 - Evolution of Products	
		16 - What's Service Got To Do With This?	15 - Constraints on Service Excellence 15a- The Value of Answers 15b- Opportunities to Satisfy Customers
		17 - Knowledge Age Products	
		18 - Prioritizing Products	16 - Target Product Selection Matrix (TPSM) 17 - What Is the Target Product? 18 - Excellence Thru Entertainment
		19 - Strategy Map Integration	19 - The Strategy Map, Part 2
6. Identify end user, broker and fixer customers for target products		20 - Customers	20 - Customer Roles and Power

Figure 1—The Road Map

Volume 2 will address the following steps of the 10 Steps to Customer-Centered Excellence:

Step 7: Uncover and measure customers' priority outcome, product, and process expectations
Step 8: Innovate or redesign products to achieve best outcomes
Step 9: Cut the time to produce, acquire, and use products by 80 percent
Step 10: Integrate cultural change levers to sustain, celebrate, and broaden success

The book is divided into two volumes, consistent with the flow of the 10 Steps to Customer-Centered Excellence shown in the Road Map. Volume 1 covers most of what we need to successfully complete in steps 1 through 6. This is where we set the strategic context for excellence, define our direction forward, and prioritize the critical few areas to begin deployment of our Strategy Map. We end by removing all ambiguity concerning who "the customers" are so we can truly sustain our focus on them.

Volume 2 covers steps 7 through 10, with special emphasis on how to uncover and satisfy the heart, mind, and voice of the customer. While we will have covered how to measure success at the enterprise level in volume 1, we now do this at the product/service level, enabling us to consider both new product design and innovation, which better satisfies customers while creating the success we aspire to.

Some of the same principles involved in product design are relevant for process design too. We look at how we can radically transform the process experienced by the customer, as distinct from our equally valid producer desires. Finally we discuss the role of strategic projects to jump-start enterprise transformation and how to accommodate the shift toward a sustainable new culture of excellence without exclusive dependence on projects. While volume 1 is a must-read for the Master of Excellence who is also a strategic leader, volume 2 will support deployment so our direction is sustained and advanced.

There is more than one way to use this book for your journey to sustainable excellence. Consider two extremes:

1. You could read the chapters and pick up a few good ideas without completing any of the Leader's Actions. That would be like driving out to see the Old Faithful geyser and consider that as your trip to Yellowstone National Park. It's certainly worth doing, and thousands of visitors do that every year. But that three hours of steamy excitement is hardly equivalent to experiencing the 300 geysers, 10,000 thermal springs, 290 waterfalls, 50 mammal species, 950 miles of trails, and countless other natural assets contained in the rest of the 9,000 square kilometers of park.

2. Completing every Leader's Action after reading every word in this book would be a bit like hiking every trail in Yellowstone. Both would be highly rewarding but admittedly a tad time-consuming. However, doing it all would put you in that elite number of explorers to do so. It enables you to become a Master of Excellence.

At least as far as this book goes, there is a middle ground that represents "don't miss this" guidance. Apply the Leader's Actions in the order they appear, reading any content in a given chapter necessary for completion. Successful completion of Leader's Actions is where the insight and learning really occurs. They are equivalent to charging up each major trail at Yellowstone. Just keep in mind that doing so without noting the map and warnings about bear, bison, or moose could cause some regret later on the trail. All Leader's Actions are in appendix 1. The critical few in Volume 1 include the following Leader's Actions with the relevant chapters:

4, C3IQ	16, Target Product Selection
13, Strategy Map, Part 1	19, Strategy Map, Part 2
14, Personal Products	20, Customer Roles

This will provide a concise understanding of the road map, create the greatest insights, and have the potential to help you achieve very tangible results with relatively little time and effort. On the other hand, read the entire story and you are likely to discover many gems of content that have unexpected value.

CHAPTER 3—GETTING AMAZING RESULTS

I am often asked what distinguishes organizations that get the biggest, most sustainable results by using the 8DX framework and C3 practices. This question recognizes that some leaders and their organizations will adopt new practices more completely than others do. In fact, many will be excited about a few specific concepts and cherry-pick related C3 tools. Because they actually can get good results by doing that, they can be happy with only partial deployment. I am often disappointed to see that happen because I know so much more is possible without an inordinate effort. But they are satisfied with what I consider a quick fix so I have learned to accept my customers' satisfaction with half a loaf.

The empirical evidence across hundreds of organizations reveals there is an answer to the question regarding the biggest and most lasting results. While I hesitate to reduce the multifaceted transformation process to what may seem like a simplistic answer, the pattern is unmistakable. Those Masters of Excellence who apply the Strategy Map overwhelmingly outperform those who don't and do so with much greater speed and simplicity. This is a discovery I had not expected when I began my C3 work in the mid-1980s. So if no new thinking were necessary, no counterproductive assumptions were in place, and there were no resisters to the dramatic changes you would advocate, then you could just skip the next seven chapters and jump right into applying the Strategy Map. On the other hand, the best seeds still require a prepared field to yield a great harvest. Once the field is prepared, the Strategy Map enables you to define, integrate, and align the following elements:

- The compelling reason to seek transformation (with your vision of the future)
- Prioritized desired outcomes wanted by customers and the enterprise
- Measures of success attached to core values, outcomes, and key products/services
- Numerical goals for performance improvement, tied to specific owners
- Personal relevance to daily work
- Reduction of ambiguity that impedes excellence
- Deliberate use of the six levers for transformation

My early career observation had been that strategic plans were largely a waste of time and money and were rarely worth more than the paper they were printed on, despite having taken months to create. If consultants were involved, the cost to their clients was significant. It was often the case that the only folks who understood what the strategic plan really meant were those directly involved in its development. It rarely involved anyone but the executive team. The employees throughout the organization, who ultimately would enable the plan to be achieved, were usually not invited to contribute to the strategic plan in any formal way. Ditto for customers. So it was not surprising to see the plans miss critically important information such as customer-desired results, have missing or weak linkage between intended outcomes and the daily work employees did, and have little alignment with performance reviews, accountability for results, and rewards/consequences.

Naturally the plans ended up on a shelf or otherwise led to underperformance. Sadly, I continue to see this situation, with strategic plans often little more than glorified to-do lists with milestones of activities to be completed. Such plans confuse moving the ball (in football) or getting players on base (in baseball) with scoring points and winning the series.

Activities without goals are of dubious value. What had not been clear to me was why it had to be this way and how both the process and results could be improved. The first opportunity to test an alternative approach presented itself unexpectedly. What made it unexpected was that a service monopoly, with no obvious competitors and perceived by its customers as holding them hostage, wished to become best in class, innovative, and dramatically improve both customer satisfaction and employee engagement. Why would they bother? Enlightened leadership had a lot to do with it. Let me explain.

I had been invited in the late fall to briefly discuss C3 principles and practices with the late Missouri Governor Mel Carnahan and his cabinet. In our meeting, Governor Carnahan explained he had identified a lengthy list of results that, if achieved, he believed could contribute to "make Missouri the best place to live and work in the nation." I observed that was a bold aspiration, but it seemed at odds with the Missouri state license plate on my rental car. He asked how the license plate was relevant.

I said I understood he wanted Missouri to be the leader, the best among all the states. He agreed. I recalled how the tag line on Missouri plates said "Show-Me State". I suggested that statement was equivalent to saying "prove it to me" and seemed to convey an attitude more like a reluctant follower than a leader. One of his cabinet members said I had understood it correctly. He suggested I might have an even better handle on the way some citizens thought by understanding what their state animal was. I admitted ignorance. He said it is the mule. I replied that those two symbols, the license plate and the mule, showed perfect alignment in a resistant sort of way. But they reflected more of a followership position than the leadership vision the governor was clearly pursuing.

Enjoying the joke, he asked what I would propose to be done. I outlined what could be done and suggested that, upon success, the license plate of the new national leader might more appropriately say the Watch-Me State. With that auspicious start, I began work with the departments most eager to demonstrate leadership and make change occur that would be visible to citizens.

Shortly after that meeting, Quentin Wilson informed me that he believed he might soon be named as the new director of the Missouri Department of Revenue (MODOR) and thought my ideas could be applied there. That department, responsible for tax collecting, motor vehicle licensing, and related issues, was arguably not on any citizens' most-loved list. His predecessor had been of the opinion that they had no competitors and owned their market, so why rock the boat? That was not how Quentin thought. Until the governor said every department was to strive to be the best of breed among sister agencies nationally, there was little or no compelling need to change. The desire to be the best was the kind of thinking that led him to put Quentin, an inspired and determined leader himself, in charge of MODOR the following January.

Quentin shared the good news of his promotion and asked me again if these customer-centered practices could really be applied in government and achieve meaningful results in just the two years the governor had left in his term of office. I assured him it was possible if we followed the 10 Steps.[2] We would want to first draft a new strategic plan framework with participation from citizens (steps 1 through 5). We would begin deploying the plan with a critical few key projects (steps 6 through 10).

Time was of the essence, so the planning session was conducted in March, focusing on customer priorities. Taxpayers representing different audiences, both personal and business, were invited to participate in what would be a three-day planning session.[3] All management and a cross-section of employees also attended. A version of the Strategy Map[4] guided our work.

One priority from citizens that rose to the top during the session was the desire to have tax refunds paid directly into a bank account within one day of the tax return being submitted. This was the VOC. A number of employees commented that such a result was totally unrealistic. It normally took about forty-five days, and if it had been possible to do the job in fewer days, they would already have done so. Furthermore, as one person energetically vented, making whatever changes necessary to satisfy this taxpayer dream would certainly require legislative approval. In her many years with MODOR, she had never seen their legislature approve any major change whose proposal originated from the department. Skepticism reigned, as is normal for most major change efforts.

Quentin reminded them that their first job was to listen to and understand what customers wanted. Employees would be given tools to discover how those desires could best be met. Until they had proven what could not be done, he asked everyone to assume it could be and work toward that result.[5] This was a major shift in mind-set!

The plan was completed in days, and Quentin introduced it to the entire department with his vision to "simplify." That became their rallying cry. Shortly after, key measures of success were identified, emphasizing outcomes relevant to customers, front line employees, and the department.

Four deployment projects were identified. They were chartered,[6] teams were formed, and all were completed within about five months. The teams created highly compelling proposals based on unimpeachable data and customer insights. Some legislative action was required and, to the surprise of many, resulted in approval on the first attempt. Team recommendations immediately began to be implemented. Results within eighteen months included the following:

- The redesign of key products, improving simplicity, time, and taxpayer money[7]
- The reduction of complexity by rescinding 107 rules
- The savings of $2 million on just one project
- The cut in response time by over 80 percent,[8] to pay tax refunds
- A reduction by 50 percent of the wait lines in motor vehicle offices and lifetime licensing costs
- A flood of customer kudos
- A proclamation from the governor, recognizing the impact of C3

---

[2] The 10 Steps are outlined in Chapter 2.

[3] External customers attended only part of this session.

[4] This is addressed in Leader's Actions 13 and 19.

[5] This statement is one anecdote a leader can use to counter Vital Lie 1, discussed shortly.

[6] C3 projects use a special chartering approach, management system, and set of tools described in volume 2.

[7] See the discussion regarding one of the projects in chapters 18 and 20.

[8] Despite what you might think, this impact was achieved primarily through innovative product/service design, not process improvement. We'll discuss this later when addressing service as products.

- The selection of MODOR as the first state agency to win Malcolm Baldrige National Award criteria
- The application of C3's outcomes-driven approach throughout government in an initiative called Show-Me Results, contributing to Missouri state government jumping to rank among the top-five states in the Government Performance Project of *Governing* magazine.

How visible do you think these results were? Thousands of taxpayers were affected. The governor returned much of the savings to taxpayers in the form of individual checks, sent with a note that this was an illustration of his transformation efforts for the state government, newly titled Show-Me Results. Do you suppose this might have had any impact on his subsequent reelection? Then there was the following evidence of early citizen sentiment, typical of the deluge of such comments Quentin received:

> To: dormail@mail.dor.state.mo.us
>
> Subject: TAX FILING & RETURN
>
> *WOW! In over 35 years of filing my Missouri state tax returns I have never had the following occur: I mailed my completed return to you on January 23 and received my refund check on February 2nd. Please accept my congratulations and thanks for whatever you have done to the Department of Revenue to make this happen. One very satisfied resident of the great State of Missouri.*

This is the kind of customer testimonial every Master of Excellence lives for. It makes the effort worthwhile to remove barriers to achieving what some will think is impossible. Someone in the governor's cabinet remembered my suggestion about changing the Missouri license plate slogan from the "Show-Me" to the "Watch-Me" state. They reminded me they had been paying attention by sending the license plate below.

Figure 2—Watch-Me State

The C3 practices and related Show-Me Results initiative endured for more than three changes in governors from both parties over several years. Quentin had begun the transformation process by adding to MODOR's mundane mission of collecting taxes and license fees with his vision to simplify. Being the best among fifty states was part of that vision and the compelling reason to reexamine and radically redesign his agency, engaging "the ready few" first. He solicited priority outcomes from MODOR's customers, using the VOC methodology[9] and conducting dozens of focus groups for their key products. He established measures linked to the organization's key values, outcomes, and core products. Quentin demonstrated what the foundational elements are for a culture of excellence and executed the road map with speed in an enterprise known more for hostages than excited customers and engaged employees.

The MODOR experience has been the pattern for more than twenty years for organizations that start with a customer-centered strategic plan and get the best, most enduring results. They went beyond the

---

[9] See an introduction to the VOC methodology in Chapter 22.

Strategy Map and used many of the C3 tools with employees in project teams. Case 4, discussed in Chapter 11, provides an example of what is possible when an organization creates such a plan without using additional tools. They still got eye-popping results. What we can say for sure is this: if they can do it, you can too! The following are a few comments on what is possible:

> Using this methodology, we identified nine (9) characteristics of the extraordinary experience, along with one or more measure for each one. Our loan closure rate went from 50% to 75% and our customers saved interest expense. The dollar value of those improvements was $8 million/month over what it was five months ago. [Employees] feel like we've invented the better mousetrap.
>
> —CEO/President, Affinity Plus Federal Credit Union

> Product improvement teams have reported significant improvement to our executive leadership in the areas of cost savings, enhanced staff utilization and improved customer success, [including] 450% increase in first time problem diagnosis on a key product that is our number two source of customer calls, 29% reconciliation of delinquent accounts which netted $1.21 million in revenues during the 1st quarter...
>
> —Executive Director, Louisville MSD Utilities

Results like these, plus the cardiac unit that cut discharge times by almost 50 percent, the university that dramatically reduced bureaucracy, the electronics company whose purchasing department saved $13 million in procurement costs in just one year, and several organizations that won top recognition such as the Baldrige National Award, are examples of the kinds of results change leaders like you have achieved. They did it by using just some of what you are going to learn how to apply here. Few have applied it all, so you may not either. Not to worry. If they could achieve awesome and amazing results, you can too. Only one caution: if you take your steady hand off the tiller, you can expect the boat to turn in a direction you had not intended. Keep a firm grip on the new direction we are about to take.

CHAPTER 4—WE SHALL OVERCOME

Our likelihood of achieving outstanding success is dependent on a willingness to consider an entirely new view of the world as seen by customers, a readiness to embrace and apply new insights, persistence in the face of periodic obstacles that look insurmountable, and ceaseless challenging of both our own and others' assumptions about what can or can't be achieved. When we are about to do something new, it will help to anticipate some of the most common obstacles and have a game plan on how we might respond. These common obstacles we will seek to destroy early:

1. The preoccupation with process improvement[10] to the detriment or exclusion of understanding and satisfying customer priorities
2. Vital Lies[11] that perpetuate myths, impeding transformation
3. Ambiguity that causes chaos, confusion, conflict, and underperformance
4. Weak alignment among strategic direction, execution, and customer experience

Why is it that some of the most famous and successful innovators, entrepreneurs, and creators in their fields were young, often didn't finish high school or college, and had limited formal training or traditional experience in the areas in which they ultimately became leaders? One possibility is that they hadn't learned enough to know what couldn't be done. Another is that they had an experience with and insight about a personal unmet need they thought others might share.

One recent example, of many, is a college dropout named Travis Kalanick. You may have heard of the company he cofounded with Garrett Camp, Uber. Just a few other innovative dropouts that come to mind include Thomas Edison, Bill Gates, Mark Zuckerberg, Daniel Ek, Walt Disney, Larry Ellison, Woody Allen, Louis Armstrong, Ray Bradbury, Andrew Carnegie, Winston Churchill, Ray Kroc, Hiroshi Yamauchi, Steve Jobs, and Sir Richard Branson.[12]

No, I'm not anti-education. On the contrary, we live better through continuous learning. But formal learning institutions don't always nurture nontraditional thinking. Earning a degree is sometimes confused with earning an education. I have observed that potential or budding leaders have often achieved

---

[10] Starting with discussion in Chapter 7 on how our process preoccupation began.

[11] See Chapter 6.

[12] Their respective roles include: renowned inventor, CEO and cofounder of Microsoft, CEO of Facebook, CEO and founder of Spotify, pioneer of cartoon films and creator of Disneyland, CEO and founder of Oracle, playwright and actor, jazz musician, CEO and founder of McDonald's, CEO of Nintendo (transforming it from a card game company), CEO and cofounder of Apple, CEO and founder of Virgin Records, which became a conglomerate of over four hundred companies by 2016.

success precisely because they "think different," as the memorable 1997 Apple Computer ad conveyed. The unique perspective and ability to communicate different thinking is part of the soul of a leader. Such uniqueness does not spring from conventional, entrenched, institutionally certified thinking. It can threaten the status quo by suggesting there is another way to interpret what is, another way to accomplish objectives others have labored less successfully to achieve and another way to articulate what the goal even is.

When our voluntary or assigned role is to lead change and obtain new levels of excellence, we are likely to be a threat to others who are comfortable with things as they are. Expect it. Prepare for it. Understand it as the challenge that was so eloquently described five hundred years ago by a famous consultant:

> [T]here is nothing more difficult to carry out, nor more doubtful of success, nor more difficult to handle, than to initiate a new order of things. For the reformer has enemies in all those who profit by the old order, and only lukewarm defenders in all those who would profit by the new order, this lukewarmness arising partly from fear of their adversaries, who have the laws in their favour; and partly from the incredulity of mankind. Who do not truly believe in anything new until they have had actual experience of it. Thus it arises that on every opportunity for attacking the reformer, his opponents do so with the zeal of partisans, the others only defend him half-heartedly, so that between them he runs great danger.

—Niccolò Machiavelli, *The Prince*[13]

Those with power within our organization, discipline, or broader society may be captives of conventional thinking, causing initial resistance to the change we lead. That resistance could be active or passive. Just because we don't hear a version of, "No, I can't. I don't want to. You can't make me," doesn't mean we have support. When I have had clients tell me they want their organization to be more nimble, responsive, and less complex, I often ask for a measure of success we should use as reference. The process cycle time, how long something takes to get something done, is often cited. It is not unusual, upon asking for an improvement goal, to hear that 20 to 30 percent improvement would be great. When I suggest we might aim for 80 percent time reduction, the usual reaction is disbelief, resistance, and statements along the lines that I don't know their business well enough to know that it can't be done. What they don't know is that this result has been achieved far more often than not in every context we've sought it.

When Quentin at MODOR encouraged employees to suspend their disbelief and pursue this level of never-before-attempted excellence that customers would notice, everyone was shocked when we cut 90 percent of the tax refund time and achieved customer love. Evidence in the improvement literature, as well as what I have repeatedly found in my own work, is that many internal organizational processes (referred to in short as "business processes") waste 95 to 99.5 percent of elapsed process time. That is, things hit bottlenecks, sit awaiting some action, get done over, or otherwise are not being worked on productively. Given this pattern, it is no big stretch to think we could cut 80 percent of the total time. But when first confronted with this objective, it can take your breath away. That is just what we want to do, as Masters of Excellence. Take their breath away.

---

[13] I beg the forgiveness of readers of my first book. This quote was used there and is one of a small number of excerpts from that source that I felt compelled to include in this current work.

We can easily encounter experts who are in a position to pass judgment on and discredit our efforts to follow a new path. Their power of certainty can compete with our passion for the possible. The following are a few examples.

The abolishment of pain in surgery is a chimera. It is absurd to go on seeking it today. "Knife" and "pain" are two words in surgery that must forever be associated in the consciousness of the patient. To this compulsory combination we shall have to adjust ourselves.

—Alfred Velpeau, the leading surgeon of his day in Paris, authoring many writings on medicine, obstetrics and gynecology, surgery, and cancer, here decrying the use of anesthesia (1839)

Thomas Edison's ideas of developing an incandescent lamp [are] unworthy of the attention of practical or scientific men.

—Select Committee on Lighting by Electricity, British House of Commons (1879)

I do not look upon any systems of wireless telegraphy as a serious competitor with our cables.

—Sir John Wolfe-Barry, speaking to stockholders of the Western Telegraph Company (1907)

There's no likelihood man can ever tap the power of the atom.

—Robert Millikan, Nobel Prize Winner in Physics (1920)

It is highly unlikely that an airplane, or fleet of them, could ever successfully sink a fleet of Navy vessels under battle conditions.

—Franklin D. Roosevelt, assistant secretary of the navy (1922)

We don't like their sound, and guitar music is on the way out.

—Decca Recording Co., rejecting the Beatles (1962)

There is no reason anyone would want a computer at home.

—Ken Olson, chairman and founder of Digital Equipment Corp., in a presentation at the World Future Society in Boston (1977)

Here are some names you are not likely ever to see in the Forbes 400...Bill Gates.

—*Forbes* magazine (1983)

The internet will soon go spectacularly supernova and in 1996 catastrophically collapse.

—Robert Metcalfe, inventor of Ethernet, in *InfoWorld* magazine (December 1995)

I'd shut it down and give the money back to the shareholders.

—Michael Dell, predicting the demise of Apple Computer in October 1997, which, shortly after, eclipsed Dell Computer in size

With the benefit of hindsight, we might well observe that these experts should have known better than to make such pronouncements. So what do we do when on the receiving end of such dismissals? Others might throw up their hands in despair. As masterful leaders, we will use a clearly articulated approach to do the following:

1. Identify the opportunities with high potential to significantly improve both customer and organizational success (avoiding the low-hanging fruit that can represent quick but insignificant wins);

2. Engage first those individuals with high readiness to pursue new levels of excellence (not necessarily those who need to embrace change or would appear to be best equipped to do so, despite their lack of intrinsic desire); and

3. Seek levels of excellence with high visibility of results that many would consider the epitome of wow!

The 8DX framework helps us right away by satisfying the first of the three criteria for success: identifying high potential opportunities. It forces us to be unambiguous about and focused on the desired results we and our customers want to achieve. This delays our natural tendency to jump right into a problem-solving mode. We'll get to the problems and undesired outcomes we want to reduce, but not before we have a chance to organize them around a prioritized hierarchy of desired outcomes to achieve. Once those outcomes have been defined, we can establish measures of success and numerical, audacious goals. This will clear our mind and free up our energy from distractions. It is the start to making the complex simple. The first step is to take a moment to do the first Leader's Action.

Leader's Action 1: Opportunities with High Potential
(See Appendix 1)

The second criterion involves high readiness. It would be lovely if we could work with, report to, and hire only those who shared the excellence DNA we personally have. However, most of us come into leadership positions within organizations that already exist. We have to work with what we have. It may not be everything we might wish for. If we had a choice between a highly skilled person who has ten things on his or her to-do list that don't include our priorities and a person who is less skilled but desperately eager to help us move the world with our excellence initiative, I have repeatedly found it pays to invite the eager. Yes, that can mean we ignore the reluctant, at least at the beginning of our transformation efforts. An important exception is when the supreme leader we report to is reluctant or initially opposed to our drive for excellence. We ignore that at our peril.

This brings to mind a company that hired a new CEO. The board was very explicit that the CEO's main task was to significantly improve shareholder value. The CEO embarked on a program of selling off parts of the business that would bring in big bags of cash. That cash was then available to distribute to shareholders. Some of the biggest were also board members. Since the CEO's compensation was tied to profitability and cash on hand, he personally did quite well. The fact that thousands of employees lost their jobs and fewer business units existed a few years later was irrelevant. He eventually ran out of parts of the business to sell and left with a wonderful severance package.

Had you and I been working on driving excellence and strengthening a collaborative culture there, we would have done well to realize we were never going to get his buy-in to our efforts. This is a worst-case scenario that can happen. Polishing our résumé and looking for a landing of our own would have been the smart move. Assuming we don't have that situation to deal with, it still is worth remembering that success builds support, engagement, and more success.

We can usually train for skills quicker than turning the disbelievers and devil's advocates into converts. Guiding the ready few and working on the critical few priorities is where we should invest our energies. Once a critical mass of believers and the supportive culture has been established, the desired behaviors, values, and attitudes of our followers can become conditions of employment. Until then, we may very well be leading a guerilla warfare operation and should act accordingly. Even without having selected a target for improvement, it is likely you have a good idea who the top three most ready, best, and brightest are that can help you lead your transformation. Likewise, you probably also know three with great knowledge, talent, or skills but who are unlikely to be eager volunteers for the new challenges you will have in mind. Take a moment to name those in both groups here. We will reexamine them when we discuss deployment.

Leader's Action 2: The Ready, Reluctant, and Powerful
(See Appendix 1)

This brings us to the third criteria for success— high visibility of results. Suppose we and our special operations team have the mission to blow up the enemy that is holed up in caves around a key mountain pass. How visible do we want to be on the way to their stronghold? Right, invisible. How visible do we want it to be when the caves erupt with shooting flames followed by no enemy movement and immense quiet? That combination of stealth on the way to our objective and high visibility of results helps us survive the short term and be there to celebrate heroic results with our followers that others will want to emulate.

This low visibility of effort and high visibility of result is in stark contrast to what we sometimes do when starting a new initiative: pronounce the new, promise what many will believe is unattainable (like previous efforts that fell short) and spend a lot of energy fending off demands and related expectations for instant results. It really is a good thing to announce our intent in broad terms. If everyone is engaged, required to adopt the new practices, and will be well-supported in doing so, communicate that widely as well. A well-articulated strategic plan that is broadly understood and personally relevant to all employees is a good start. Clarity of purpose is essential. Steve Jobs repeatedly told Apple employees to focus on making insanely great products, not insanely great profit.

Once the purpose is clear, providing adequate support to enable execution will be essential. In the absence of such context or working under severe resource constraints, we will want to use results, not pronouncements, to sell our cause. Those results must come from work on the first selected issues. We will do well to keep the details under wraps, except for those in our inner circle of conspirators…er…creative reformers, until we're in a position to say what we did successfully, not just what we intended. Complete the next Leader's Action considering the MODOR story in Chapter 3.

Leader's Action 3: Indicators of Highly Visible Results
(See Appendix 1)

There are lots of options and choices to be made in our pursuit of leadership excellence. It can feel overwhelming. Or it could seem a bit like standing at the North Pole, deciding to go south and knowing that any step will take us there. What a wonderful feeling— to be clear that, no matter what we do, we will be going in the direction we want. Unfortunately going in the general direction can be a far cry from arriving at the destination we envision within our desired time frame. The notion we should just do it can offer hope. Such hope suggests that any action is better than no action. Maybe, but let's not kid ourselves. Hope is not a strategy. If the excellence we seek is what our customers care about, not just what we or others in our industry or profession believe matters, the bad news is that not every path will get us there with economy of effort.

CHAPTER 5—WHERE ARE WE?

Culture determines how we define reality, what is normal, and what is acceptable or not. So it should be no surprise that culture has a direct bearing on the creation, transformation, care, and feeding of excellence. Senior leadership, starting with the single individual at the top and including any others who would be Masters of Excellence, are responsible for what that culture is and what it could be. Let's be clear about what we could mean by culture:

- *An artificial medium containing the nutrients necessary to cultivate bacteria, tissue cells, or other organisms*. This version of culture could be the first thing that comes to mind for a biologist.

- *The quality of an individual viewed by others as being knowledgeable in and adept at practicing the most advanced behaviors and choices representing excellence.* To say one has culture may refer to his or her manners, tastes, social associates, the kind of work and play he or she pursues, or the environment in which he or she does it.

- *The characteristics of a group of people that make them unique by virtue of their shared language, history, customs, beliefs, values, and definitions of intellectual constructs, such as time, space, cause-effect, and power.* Consider this the view of anthropologists, sociologists, politicians, philosophers, and Masters of Excellence.

Despite the differences in these meanings, they can have an unexpected convergence for the Master of Excellence. Whether by design or accident, we already have a culture. That is one answer to where we are. The supreme leader and his or her lieutenants own it, whether they wish to or not, no matter what their past role has been in creating it. The closer we are to being viewed as an agent of that leader, the more we are held responsible for the culture. The history that got us here may not be of our making, but the way we define or redefine that history and our future is within our control.

The story of the Alamo has been told in American school textbooks quite differently than the version told in Mexican schools. Whose story is correct? The victor and the vanquished will have their own different tales.

The Confederate battle flag was removed from government grounds in many US cities and several Southern states in 2015. Simply put, the cultural meaning of that symbol was consciously changed by broad social and political pressure from being an element of proud Southern identity to one of oppression, slavery, and fear no one could be proud of. Cultural symbols can change in meaning. The masterful leader will seize those symbols to either reframe or remake them to achieve the new vision.

The theories of Viennese physician Franz Gall (1758–1828) were the basis for "the only true science of the mind" called phrenology, widely popularized beginning in the 1820s in Europe and spreading in America from the 1830s until the middle of the twentieth century. Proponents believed the shape and bumps of the skull explained character strengths and weaknesses. Anthropologist Samuel Morton in his 1839 book, *Crania Americana*, supported phrenologist views, explaining how the "Teutonic family" of skulls ranked highest on intelligence and the "Negro group" ranked lowest. The redefining of human history in this pseudoscientific manner offered support for slavery and enduring subsequent racial inequities. Beliefs are not science, though they can both offer compelling explanations for our past, current, and anticipated behavior. If we believe verifiable facts will win out, our job is to provide overwhelming evidence.

On a current and scientifically compelling scale, Jared Diamond explains in his 1997 book, *Guns, Germs and Steel*, that genetic superiority of Eurasians and North Africans is not the reason their civilizations survived and conquered others. He convincingly presents a new story with supporting evidence of how differences in technology and power across human societies originated in environmental, geographical, and cultural variation. Written language and resistance to diseases are factors that favored Eurasian civilizations.

As Masters of Excellence, we have a story to tell that is within our control. It may cause us to be personally viewed as the role model or antihero for culturally valued behaviors. Steve Jobs clearly established with his own attire that clothing does not make the man. He valued creative thinking that focused on anticipating what customers would want. His trademark uniform of black turtleneck instead of a suit was a version of a counterculture symbol emulated by his successor and his counterparts at many other innovative technology companies.

Our culture could be a rich medium for growing toxic practices, as life-threatening as anthrax bacteria and Ebola virus. It could be a place for growing new ideas, as life-supporting as mold that produces antibiotics such as penicillin. Changing the story of our culture is not the same as changing the culture itself. The latter is not for the faint of heart but is definitely achievable. Before we take on that task, let's find out where we are and what needs changing. Unlike an IQ test that seeks to evaluate our personal cognitive ability, the C3IQ is intended as an assessment of an organization's behaviors as a customer-centered culture. We start by taking the assessment personally. We'll tie Leader's Actions to those answers throughout the rest of the book. Please complete it before we proceed.[14]

Leader's Action 4: C3IQ, a Self-Assessment
(See Appendix 1)

The total possible score is 125. If you got better than 100, the customer-centeredness of your organization may not require much change. Just to be sure your view of things is the same as what others think, it would be wise to ask at least ten of your colleagues and/or those who report to you to also take the assessment. The larger the number and the more diverse the group taking the assessment, the more likely you are to arrive at the truth about the organization's C3IQ. Uncovering that shared truth is the goal. If everyone gets a 100-plus score, you can confidently conclude there is nothing more to read here. Congratulations! You are already close to the walking-on-water stage of excellence. The rest of us mere mortals will hurry to catch up. The next chart shows the distribution of all scores as of 2016.

---

[14] An electronic, self-scoring version of the assessment is included in the Mastering Excellence Workbook of Leader's Actions available in the store at http://www.C3Excellence.com

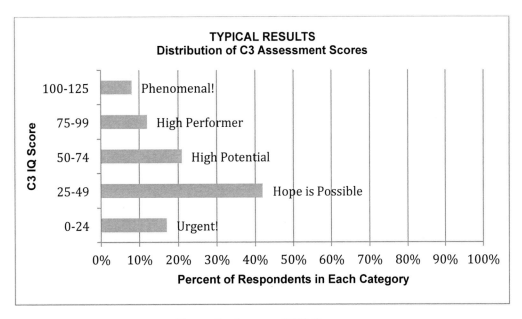

Figure 3—Average C3IQ Scores

The average score is about seventy.[15] I have yet to see a situation where a cross-section of managers and employees representative of the whole organization gets an average score of over 100. At least, not before applying the 8DX Road Map. A pattern worth noting is that, as the rank of respondents rises, so do their scores. That difference can be due to leaders being more optimistic, strategic objectives being less clearly understood as we go down organizational levels, leaders being less knowledgeable than those closest to customers and operations, and/or leadership intent not fully deployed throughout the enterprise. One theme here concerns ignorance and/or ambiguity about how things ought to be. A second relates to alignment between intent and how things really are. Our goal going forward is to create shared understanding and enlightenment while reducing ambiguity that constrains high performance.

With our C3IQ in hand, we now have the answer to where we are regarding three main topics covered by the assessment: strategic direction, customer experience, and excellence. We've also identified opportunities to improve the degree to which the following is observed:

- Priorities of the enterprise, functional groups, and individuals are aligned with each other and with what customers want (items 1–16);

- Agreement exists on shared language and the meaning of key terms such as service, outcomes, and customers (items 3, 9–12);

- Mechanisms are in place for deploying and balancing issues of high importance (items 8, 14–17);

- There is a defined method for uncovering, understanding, and satisfying what customers want, whether those customers are external or internal to the enterprise (items 12–14, 15b, c, f);

- Customers have power to define and drive excellence (items 11–14);[16]

- There is consensus on the criteria for and timing of how celebration or correction will occur (items 7, 17–18); and

- All 8DX are defined and measured (items 2–3, 14–15).

---

[15] This is based on hundreds of organizations completing this assessment before they began applying the C3 concepts and principles outlined in this book.

[16] Contrary to common belief, customers who walk away do not have power. By leaving, they abdicate whatever power they could have. We may only know they weren't happy but not know what would have made them enthusiastic fans.

A C3IQ score of less than 100 is all the evidence we need at the moment that our culture and leadership behaviors could do better to foster excellence. It prepares us to use the 8DX Road Map to get where we want to be. We will connect specific actions that will get us to the top score on each assessment item as we go.[17] Consider either your personal score or the average for your group as the target for all references to C3IQ scores going forward. As we work to raise our C3IQ, there is one more pattern to observe.

Once they fully understand the 8DX framework, many leaders have found that the responses they first made to certain items actually were more optimistic than the reality. This means your scores may go from fives to threes or worse on individual items as we proceed. So have those antidepressants handy to tide you over until you achieve the ecstasy of outstanding leadership. You may find it enlightening to date your assessment so your original responses can be differentiated from a later version, following changes you make when finished with the book. You may also find it helpful to copy the last appendix, intended to be used as a bookmark you will reference throughout your reading. (For an optional electronic version that is printable, see the Mastering Excellence Workbook in the store at http://www.C3Excellence.com.)

To give you a sense of what is possible, the first chart below shows the C3IQ scores of respondents from a specific business before leadership embarked on the transformation process. The second chart is based on the enterprise C3IQ scores eighteen months after the core excellence principles and practices that are outlined in this book were first introduced.

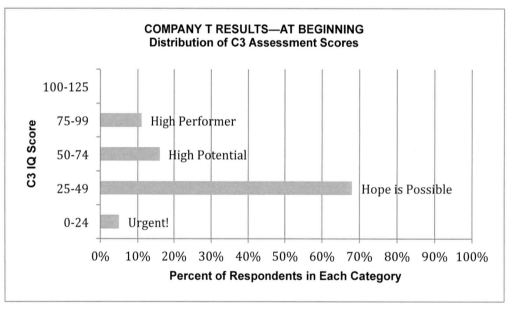

Figure 4—Before the Transformation Began

[17] Leadership actions to reduce ambiguity, using the six levers for cultural transformation, are summarized in appendix 1.

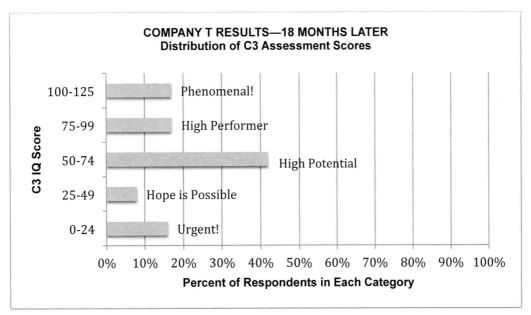

COMPANY T RESULTS—18 MONTHS LATER
Distribution of C3 Assessment Scores

Figure 5—Eighteen Months Later

Among the leadership actions taken to shift the cultural profile to the right, perhaps three had the biggest impact:

- A conscious effort was taken to reduce ambiguity related to language and strategic goals. Cultural change levers and how to reduce ambiguity is central to our discussion next.

- Deployment of ten cross-functional projects was tied to the strategic plan, whose success exceeded all previous project experience at the enterprise.[18]

- A customer satisfaction policy, essential to operationalize customer focus goals, was created.[19]

You may have noticed the urgent responses went up on the second chart. Upon investigation, it turned out some respondents now realized how much room there was for future improvement. They felt the remaining gaps should be attended to now! I can assure you that once you begin the customer-centered transformation process, you can expect impatience with the status quo and slow improvement to become pronounced. Let's view that as a good thing, propelling us forward ever more rapidly.

---

[18] See a succinct description of the C3 project management methods at www.C3Excellence.com.

[19] See Chapter 6.

CHAPTER 6—CHANGE LEVERS AND AMBIGUITY

The Master of Excellence is tempted to pick the single issue we believe stands between us and excellence and then work hard on it. Doing so is a bit like the proverbial blind man who believes the tail of the elephant he is holding is merely a rope. To fully grasp the size and scope of cultural transformation, avoiding a piecemeal approach bound to be ineffective and unsustainable, we need to understand the whole elephant. We can use six main levers to strengthen or change our organizational culture:

1. Language
2. Values
3. Measures
4. Power
5. Assumptions
6. Modeling

Each of these levers represent key sources enabling or constraining excellence. All are capable of being double-edged swords. Each is a lever when consciously used to advance excellence. It can be a constraint when we don't recognize it as a source of ambiguity or conflict. Consider them as levers when we do something with them and as constraints when they do something to us. The challenge for a leader is to transform a constraint into a lever for transformation.

Life is permeated with ambiguity. As a Master of Excellence, we will strategically employ or destroy ambiguity to achieve a specific outcome. To achieve mastery requires us to identify the main sources of ambiguity; recognize when or where it exists; understand how ambiguity affects the organization and those we wish to satisfy; and adopt behaviors, mechanisms, or systems to master its presence or impact.

Ambiguity is a condition with great power to prevent success. Its opposite is certainty. We will use several tools that can make our leadership easier than it otherwise would be. In general, ambiguity that is not used purposefully has a negative effect on the functional excellence of the organization and its people. It is, therefore, an enemy to destroy.[20]

The American Society for Quality (ASQ) conducted a research project with Forbes Insights in 2014, with results published in a report titled "Culture of Quality."[21] The research was accomplished through a global

---

[20] Certainty that springs from fiction, not fact, can also be dangerous. See the information about Vital Lies in this chapter. As Mark Twain said, "It's not what we don't know that gets us into trouble. It's what we know for sure that just ain't so."

[21] http://asq.org/culture-of-quality

survey of over 2,200 executives, managers, and quality professionals, augmented by more in-depth interviews. Several of the study findings, relevant to our discussion about ambiguity, include the following:

- 50 percent said the quality vision is not understood throughout their organization, with only a third saying it is compelling.

- 61 percent said their quality values are clearly stated.

- 48 percent said customer needs are the driver of their quality programs, but only 24 percent said their organizations are effective at identifying just what customer expectations actually are.

- 75 percent of C-suite respondents believed they have a culture of quality, while less than 50 percent with job titles related to quality thought so. The view is rosier for those at the top.

- Less than half (47 percent) said leaders lead by example or otherwise live quality values.

A related ASQ 2013 study found that 51 percent of respondents said there was no agreement on what quality means and there needs to be one.[22] These research results are consistent with research by others and my own firm's empirical observations.

The point is that the evidence causes us to reach the inescapable conclusion that ambiguity in both language and behavior exists in organizations of all kinds worldwide. Roughly half of all employees view it as a problem. I guess the good news is the glass is half-full. We can do much better.

The following discussion is intended only as an introduction to key ambiguity-driven constraints that the six transformation levers can very effectively resolve. Cases and examples throughout the book will offer many illustrations of how these levers work in practice.

1. LANGUAGE

Language as a source of ambiguity. It may seem crystal clear when we say that our organization is or aims to be customer-focused. Yet this is a most problematic statement. We may assume that everyone in the enterprise understands whom the customer in "customer focus" means. We would likely be wrong. The ambiguity can easily defeat our best intentions. Which of the following describes the customer that employees in your organization could have in mind? Circle the relevant numbers below. A customer is one who…

1. buys something from the business;
2. funds or invests in the enterprise;
3. uses any of the enterprise's products;
4. uses a specific product or service;
5. uses but does not buy the product or service;
6. represents others who will use the product;
7. receives and transfers the product to someone else who uses it;
8. regulates production or distribution of the product;
9. modifies the product for someone else's use;
10. is thought of as an entire organization;
11. is thought of only as an individual person;
12. is external to the enterprise;
13. is within the enterprise;

[22] "Discoveries," American Society for Quality, ASQ Global State of Quality Study, 2013, http://asq.org/global-state-of-quality/reports.aspx.

14. is an employee who uses a product that someone else within the enterprise produces;
15. is more important than all other customers;
16. is equal in importance and power with all other customers; or
17. hollers the loudest.

How many of these seventeen parties could be considered customers? _____. If we see that there is no single correct answer, people disagree on the answer but consensus matters, seeking to be customer-focused will be like chasing a snowflake.

It is clear that there are different kinds of roles and conditions under which a person might be a customer. Do you see any ambiguity? If so, it can create conflict, unwanted competition, uncertainty regarding who to listen to, inadvertent deafness to hearing the needs of the most important kind of customers, confusion when a person is one kind of customer in one situation and a different kind in another, disproportionate effort satisfying the wrong customer, and so on. This kind of ambiguity is a prime cause of chaos, confusion, rework, staff dysfunction, and enterprise underperformance. Otherwise, being customer-focused is a wonderful idea.

When there is a user for a product that is different from the buyer, which customer should we focus on? If we say both, we may be assuming each of them has equal power in the design of the product. That is rarely the case when the buyer and user are two different parties. The priorities of the two will be different. It is also no mystery that power tends to follow the money.

Once upon a time not so long ago, if a couple were to go looking for a new car, the salesperson would talk to the male, acting as if his female partner or spouse were invisible. Thankfully, that situation has improved somewhat in North America. When there are conflicting priorities, which party should we satisfy? Saying we will be customer-focused is not precise enough to be helpful.

Some organizations have sources that fund products but don't buy or use them. To complicate matters, a college or university, medical facility, or government agency may get funding from sources that will never personally use the products produced by those recipient enterprises. Is an investor a customer? Not knowing the correct answer can be fatal to the enterprise. When a snack food company sponsors a TV program for preschool children, is the program producer primarily concerned with satisfying the needs of kids or the needs of the sponsor?

Understanding what the correct answer is for the long term offers insight and understanding to one of the main forces underlying the early twenty-first-century upheaval in the media industry. It also explains a key reason for Apple's giant success, as opposed to formidable competitors such as Blackberry, Motorola, IBM, Sony, and others: *unrelenting focus on the end users of its products.*

Using broad-brush terms such as constituents or stakeholders would appear to eliminate ambiguity. Don't these terms include all possible customers? They do, but if the different kinds of customers also differ in power and importance to the success of the enterprise, then we have merely created for ourselves a false sense of clarity. We might think about it this way: all horses are animals, but all animals are not horses. It we aim to ride that horse to excellence, we better make sure we aren't saddling up a goat.

The principles and admonitions of the Baldrige Criteria, ISO 9001[23] family of standards, European Foundation for Quality Management (EFQM), and other systems to achieve both quality and excellence tell us to make customer focus one of our top priorities. If you think those systems have resolved the customer ambiguities, I urge you to research them. I'm afraid you will be disappointed. The same disappointment can occur when we believe the marketing department understands who the customer is. One simple example is the leadership of a car company who believed the buyers of its cars were the most important customers. Those who buy cars from the manufacturer are the dealers. Drivers and passengers got secondary attention. That multiyear mistake cost the company (and others like it) their previously dominant market share position.

Leader's Action 5: Confusion Regarding the Customer
(See Appendix 1)

Language as a lever to advance excellence. If ever there were a time when having a common language would be a good thing, it is when we are leading others to achieve a shared vision of excellence, if not perfection. That time is now. Language functions as a lever when it creates consensus of meaning and purposeful, deployable intent. Language includes written, nonverbal,[24] and symbolic communication. Five specific words are known to create ambiguity and confusion for those who would be Masters of Excellence, as well as for their followers. Those terms can be turned into levers for creating a cohesive culture of excellence in the following chapters:

1. Customer (Chapter 20)
2. Service (Chapter 16)
3. Supplier (Chapter 20)
4. Input (Chapter 18)
5. Output (Chapter 18)

Celebrate language as a lever under your control when such terms are sufficiently unambiguous that we and every employee can personally apply them to his or her own work. We've briefly discussed why the first word here is an obstacle. The remedy, in briefest form, is to understand which of only three possible roles a person can play as a customer (Chapter 20) and always determine which one is relevant and most dominant regarding the specific product under consideration.

2. VALUES

Values as a source of ambiguity. We may find ourselves telling those who follow us that we value teamwork, learning, initiative, innovative thinking, pay-for-performance, family, continuous improvement, customers, and a variety of other motherhood-and-apple pie sentiments. Good for us. If it's not already a habit, practicing all those values all the time can be demanding. Some do it exceptionally well. Many of us are surprised to discover some values can compete or conflict with each other. When that misalignment occurs, we can be surprised again to find the result is fear and the perception that leadership is dishonest or hypocritical. The most commonly stated core values include the following:

- Integrity
- Quality

---

[23] The Baldrige Criteria consists of seven criteria for excellence. ISO 9001 had eight key principles as of 2015. Customer focus was in the top three in both cases.

[24] In our multicultural world, it is more important than ever that we understand how nonverbal behaviors such as shaking one's head, hand/finger gestures, and smiling can carry unintended and undesired meanings in some contexts.

- Efficiency
- Teamwork
- Sustainability
- Financial strength
- Customer satisfaction

Lumber Liquidators stated most of these in their corporate documents and on their website in 2015. For example, the Lumber Liquidators' mission statement is "To deliver quality hardwood flooring at low prices [and be] lean, efficient and sustainable in everything we do…protecting the long-term health of the forests, farms and plantations that are the lifeblood of our business." It "aims to be the industry leader in sustainability because it's good for the environment, and because it's good for the future of our business."[25]

Leadership further stated in their Code of Business Conduct and Ethics,[26] "Lumber Liquidators is committed to dealing fairly and honestly with its customers, suppliers, competitors and employees.

- You must not use false data or manipulate information in a manner to suggest that our products or services have characteristics or comply with specifications when you know that they do not.

- Suppliers should be chosen on the basis of the price, quality, and desirability of their goods and services."

All this looks pretty clear and unambiguous on the surface. But if we scratch a little deeper, it becomes clear which values are of superordinate importance. The US Department of Justice led a multi-agency investigation into Lumber Liquidators' sourcing of sustainable materials. The company pleaded guilty to outlawed practices of logging, acquiring, and selling wood products made from endangered species, and demonstrably destroying the habitat of endangered animals such as Siberian tigers and Amur leopards. The company was not just a violator of the Lacey Act but also the most egregious, intentional corporate offender of sustainability practices to date. It was fined over $13 million in a settlement announced by a Virginia federal court on October 22, 2015. Its CEO had resigned a few months earlier. Their stated core value of sustainability was clearly subordinate to short-term profitability and any related bonuses.

We cannot say here that leadership was deceitful, evil, or corrupt. You might conclude otherwise. What we can say is that there was conflict among core values, and not all were practiced equally. Some managers and employees may very well have felt they were taking actions expected of them, consistent with at least one of the company's core values. The moment employees can pick and choose which of a competing set of values to follow, chaos will reign.

As a Master of Excellence, we have to carefully consider how our stated core values are attached to measures of success (the subject of our next discussed source of ambiguity) and related rewards. We can say with certainty that the presence and size of a reward tied to a core value will always trump a stated value with an absent or lesser reward.

---

[25] The Lumber Liquidators' home page at http://www.lumberliquidators.com/sustainability/sustainability/ (as of March 15, 2016) states, "Our Mission: Since our first store opened, Lumber Liquidators has had a very simple mission: to deliver quality hardwood flooring at low prices.

That isn't just a slogan. It's a guiding principle that affects every facet of our business. Delivering hardwood floors for less requires us to be lean, efficient and sustainable in everything we do. We do this by minimizing our energy and land use; having an efficient supply chain; seeking to work with credible and trustworthy suppliers; avoiding waste; and investing in, and protecting, the long-term health of the forests, farms and plantations that are the lifeblood of our business."

[26] This is an excerpt from Lumber Liquidators' Code of Conduct and Business Ethics on the home page at http://www.lumberliquidators.com/ (as of March 15, 2016).

Masters of Excellence mean what we say and say what we mean. The core values espoused by us, an organization's leaders, make up one of the cornerstones of excellence. We guide desired behavior of members in the culture we lead. To the extent we do that, we engender trust, consistency, brand strength, and loyalty from employees and customers. When we say something is important but encourage or allow practices that conflict with that stated priority, we can easily become a poster child for hypocrisy, derision, and defection. In the Internet age, we cannot hide from who we are perceived to be.

Sadly many examples of stated core values and mission statements are at odds with their organization's practices. We can expect these disconnects to be exposed sooner or later. Let's take the initiative to do the exposing. But do it when you can do the proposing on how to tighten alignment among all our values. True, this is not for the faint of heart. Pairing our critiques of what is with construction of the new makes it easier for those in power to hear us. Consider this a key element of Politics 101.

It is surprising how often we can observe that some value we have said is of great importance has no bridge to guide related behavior. For example, it is common for us to say customer satisfaction is one of our highest priorities while having no customer satisfaction policy. We have plenty of other policies. (This is true for you if there was a score of three or more on the C3IQ item 8.) The purpose of such policies is to operationalize our values and to guide purposeful, consistent behavior. The Master of Excellence will identify where the disconnects could occur and then take action to eliminate them.

Even well-established organizations fostering good leadership practices have fallen victim to weak alignment between values and policy. Such is the case with the International Standards Organization (ISO), a nonprofit body made up of experts representing 163 countries. Their purpose is to develop voluntary, consensus-based, market-relevant international standards that ensure and support quality, safety, efficiency, and innovation. Established in 1947, they have published over 21,000 standards primarily addressing manufacturing and technology. The 2016 revision of ISO 9001 standard on quality management systems states the first of four benefits for having such a system is "the ability to consistently provide products and services that meet customer…requirements." It further states that "top management shall demonstrate leadership and commitment with respect to customer focus."[27]

It sounds good, and it is. This emphasis on customers is a new element in this standard, a sign we interpret as growing enlightenment. However, while the standard goes on to say leadership is responsible for having a quality policy, it is mute on the necessity for a customer satisfaction policy. If the two are be different, we have ambiguity regarding leadership's responsibility.

Wait a minute, you might say. Aren't we splitting hairs here? Isn't seeking good-quality products and services the same as seeking customer satisfaction? Excellent questions, if I do say so myself. Is it possible to have a technically perfect, high-quality product that a customer is not satisfied with? Consider that many products that are now obsolete were, at the time their demise began, of high quality. That would include typewriters, slide rules, carbon paper, eight-track stereo, monocles, steam engines, buggy whips, floppy disks, and much more. In addition, there are many instances where comparable and competing products win over customers due to factors not entirely related to the product.

One of our customer principles offers some explanation: The customer's knowledge of and feelings about the producer will color his or her satisfaction with the product.[28] One of the examples we discuss shortly

---

[27] The first clause (5.1.2) in the Customer Focus section of the 2016 ISO Standard.
[28] See the customer principles in Chapter 20.

concerns airlines. In short, the absence of a customer satisfaction policy in an organization putting that topic high in its list of core values has a major plank missing in their bridge to excellence.

Values as a lever to advance excellence. Our values are expressed in our personal behavior, what we measure, what we tie to rewards or consequences, and the degree to which our policies guide our expression of those values in daily work and relationships with others.

Excellent policies succinctly create alignment between organizational values and behavior. As we've noted, the vast majority of leaders will say customers and their satisfaction are among the most important enterprise priorities. The startling revelation is that few actually have a written policy[29] to deploy that intent. How important, then, can it really be? We can and absolutely must fix that disconnect, using the following guide:

1. When creating or revising a policy, create the bridge(s) among our stated values, intent, and daily behavior.

2. Fully deploy the policy, instituting a method for eliminating ambiguity about the core value (such as who the customer is).[30]

3. Acknowledge that all core values are not of equal importance by communicating which of them is more important than others. It should be clear which value(s) trumps others in the case of conflict among them. Name the vital few.

4. Ensure key values are aligned with key performance indicators (KPIs), rewards, and consequences.

Consider this customer satisfaction policy displayed prominently by a major retailer, "We guarantee customer satisfaction by refund, replacement or return."[31]

Does this policy address a customer's desired or undesired outcomes?[32] Since the intent is to describe the corrective action the company will take when the customer is unhappy with a purchase, its focus is on the latter. In other words, it's actually a customer **dis**satisfaction policy, describing the actions to be taken when dissatisfaction occurs. Compare that to the following policy.

All employees, associates and partners will:
1. Proactively solicit customer needs and expectations.
2. Confirm that we have understood those expectations.
3. Develop, package, deliver, and support our products to meet those expectations.
4. Measure the degree to which our customers' product and outcome expectations are achieved.
5. Never blame the user when he or she cannot make a product or process work. Provide understanding and then help. Assume he or she has done his or her best.
6. Aggressively seek to close any gap between what our customers expect and what they experience.[33]

Figure 6—Sample Customer Satisfaction Policy

---

[29] A policy is not to be confused with an exhortation, slogan, aspiration, or wish. Simply stating we will not discriminate on the basis of gender, ethnic background, religious preference, and other nonjob factors when hiring does not constitute a policy unless it's deployed.

[30] The solution to eliminating ambiguity about the customer is addressed in Chapter 20.

[31] Labeled as Walmart's customer satisfaction policy, this is displayed on the wall at the returns or customer-service desk.

[32] Differentiating between these two kinds of outcomes, referred to as Dimensions 1 and 2, are discussed in chapters 8 and 10.

[33] This was developed by the author and his colleagues for their own use and provided to many of its clients with permission to use.

The first four statements on the sample policy emphasize behavior related to customer-desired outcomes. The last statement covers undesired outcomes, results the organization wants to avoid. In this case, there is also a linkage to how the producer will execute its intent[34] to create satisfaction, both proactively and in response to dissatisfaction.

Policy as Values Deployment. A policy is a broad guide to action, often including an objective, a statement of intent and principles. It is a basis for consistent conduct for those working within an organization. The manner of deployment is spelled out without getting into procedural details. The six policy statements in this case are also constructed in a manner that suggests how measures could support accountability and verify execution. The construction of the policy facilitates policy deployment. We will be describing in much greater detail the mechanisms for applying the policy when discussing the VOC in volume 2.

The enlightened leadership of Linn County, Iowa, decided to transform their organization's culture to focus on customers. They drafted a new strategic plan, defining its mission to "provide all customers the most satisfying products while maintaining sound fiscal management in order to enhance the quality of life [in the county]." Leadership observed the agency had lots of policies but none for customer satisfaction. They wondered whether such a policy could strengthen consistent deployment of their five core values:

1. Communicate openly and effectively.
2. Demonstrate personal integrity and respect for others.
3. Be accountable for our actions and decisions.
4. Recognize valued contributions.
5. Create a supportive, positive work environment.

To answer that question, they were asked to identify which of the six policy statements (shown in figure 7) might be relevant to the first core value and could reduce ambiguity. They found that at least statements 1, 2, and 5 were not only relevant but also gave guidance on how to deploy the value. For the second core value, statements 1, 2, 4, and 5 fitted.

As they worked down the list of core values, they saw that every point in the proposed customer satisfaction policy offered articulated support and behavioral direction for core values that previously had had little. So they adopted the policy, modifying it a bit to suit their unique context. That one policy had a principal role in deploying all of their core values.

Mission statements, strategies, and policies represent intent, what we can call the voice of leadership (VOL). Procedures are designed to carry out that intent with detailed steps to be taken. Those represent the voice of management (VOM). Masters of Excellence strive to create alignment among the VOL, VOM, and VOC, connecting the dots.

Fantasies that leaders all too often communicate to their organizations masquerade as vision and mission statements. "We are the preferred supplier of X" and "Our customers are our highest priority" are two that routinely show up in various ways. They are fantasies when they are not clearly supported and deployed with success. Why is it that companies with trends such as declining market share over multiple years, increasing customer defections, product recalls, complaints ricocheting around social media, technology that is rapidly becoming obsolete, and other indications of failure to perform feel compelled to

---

[34] This is the producer's process, Dimension 8.

put such statements in their key corporate documents?

The most forgiving way to look at the disconnect might be to say leadership is sharing its vision of the future. That could be so if we can see clear evidence in the strategic and business plans that leadership knows what customers want, have measured the degree to which they get it, and have well-developed plans and supporting incentives to deliver. When those little details are missing, we can be sure about at least one thing. We've crossed the fine line between vision and hallucination. We might contrast Vital Lies[35] and hallucination. There is a difference. The first involves statements about the present and past that are not true. Hallucination concerns statements about future intent that are not supported with a clear bridge to get there. There is no medication for this ailment, but there is a treatment plan. It starts with a prescription to practice truth in leadership.

Speaking of treatment plans and incentives reminds me of a values disconnect I've seen a number of times in health care. On the one hand, many health care leaders and professionals are adamant that patient concerns are paramount and their field should not be thought of as a money-oriented business. Facts can suggest otherwise. The US government pays doctors for treating Medicare patients, plus an additional 6 percent of the cost of any drug they administer in their office. If there is more than one drug that could provide comparable results but the drugs differ in cost, which drug should a doctor administer? If we were the patient, I think it would be fair to say we'd like to get the least expensive one. From the ten-year period from 2005 through 2014, the drug-cost portion of health care has increased 17 percent, faster than any other Medicare program segment.[36]

It does look like there is an incentive that works to focus on the money-oriented aspect of health care for at least some in the business. The Centers for Medicare and Medicaid Services (CMS) thought so too. They proposed a two-phase change to begin in 2016. It would pay doctors more for prescribing the drugs shown to be more effective. Imagine that! Among those opposing the idea include doctors' groups, drug producers, and, naturally, their favorite politicians.

Sometimes the truth is scary. Please review the following three mission statements of real competitors. As you do it, let's play "Where's Waldo?" In this version of the game, see if you can find the word "customer" in these statements. What else is a main difference among the following statements?

- **Mission Statement, Airline A:** *To be recognized worldwide as the airline of choice.*

- **Mission Statement, Airline B:** *Airline B is committed to providing every citizen of the world with the highest quality air travel to the widest selection of destinations possible. Airline B will continue to modernize its fleet while maintaining its position as the largest air carrier in the world, with the goal of becoming the most profitable airline. Airline B is the airline that treats everyone with equal care and respect, which is reflected in the way each Airline B employee is respected. Airline B recognizes that its employees are the key to the airline's success and invests in the future of its employees. By investing in tomorrow's technologies and by following a strict adherence towards environmental regulations, Airline B demonstrates its commitment to the world environment.*

- **Mission Statement, Airline C:** *Airline C is dedicated to the highest quality of customer service delivered with a sense of warmth, friendliness, individual pride, and Company Spirit.*

---

[35] The concept and importance of Vital Lies is discussed under assumptions, coming shortly in this chapter, and then applied in Leader's Action 8. A vital lie is a constraining assumption not supported by evidence. Also see appendix 2.

[36] "A Fix for Medicare Drug Spending," *Bloomberg BusinessWeek*, May 31, 2016, 8.

Does it matter that the first two statements don't include the mention of customers? Don't be confused by the reference to "every citizen." Unless every citizen is a customer, that broad brush is a platitude without substance. Could one of those firms be at all related to the YouTube music video released by musician Dave Carroll in 2008 called "United Breaks Guitars"? Yup. It was viewed over three million times in its first ten days and had over fourteen million views by the end of 2014. It was produced after he had spent months attempting, without success, to get the airline to respond to the tossing of his guitar case by baggage handlers, resulting in his guitar getting smashed.[37]

What we see is that the focus of the mission statements differs in points of view. Views can be producer-centered or customer-centered.

Airline C is Southwest Airlines (SWA). Customers consistently ranked SWA in the top two airlines as the most satisfying for more than twenty years. It is not a coincidence that they are the only major US carrier to have had forty-two consecutive years of profitability and 154 consecutive dividends paid. They flew the most passengers annually and had not experienced any layoffs or bankruptcy (as most others previously had) through 2014. In that year, employees received a record of $355 million in profit-sharing (the first in the country to offer such a plan),[38] and investors had their stock value go up over 100 percent in 2014. There are several winners here: customers, employees, investors, and management. There's a big loser, too: their competitors.

Major upheavals in the economy, social fabric, and technology create huge stresses on many organizations. A crisis tends to lower the water level to reveal what had been hidden obstacles to success. Such was the situation with September 11, 2001. Although this dramatic terrorist assault on what was arguably the economic heart of America took only a moment to occur, its intensive fallout played out over several years.

Among the industries hit hardest were airlines. Five US airlines went bankrupt by 2005 and eight by 2011, as shown in the figure below. On the other hand, SWA was one of the few to make a profit in 2002 and had a market capitalization value of $9.11 billion by the fall of that year, bigger than the value of all the other major airlines combined.[39] It is reasonable to conclude again that this triumph in the face of extreme adversity was not a coincidence.

---

[37] "United Airlines shows how not to run your business," *Forbes*, July 24, 2009.

[38] "Southwest Airlines' 41st-consecutive profit sharing payment," *Wall Street Journal*, February 4, 2015.

[39] *BusinessWeek*, August 5, 2002. The other ten totaled $7.82 billion in market cap.

COMPETITOR BANKRUPTCY FILINGS 1990-2011

- Continental: December, 1990
- America West: June, 1991
- US Airways: August 2002
- United: December, 2002
- JetBlue: September, 2002
- Northwest: September, 2005
- Delta: September, 2005
- AirTran: April, 2008
- Alaska Air: November, 2011
- American: November, 2011

Figure 7—Competitors Dive as Southwest Soars

We were talking about how the truth can be scary. It can also be enlightening and inspiring, as we see with SWA and its customers. Most of the legacy carriers as of 2015 advertised ticket prices that were incomplete. The price of the product was really far higher after hidden baggage and other fees were added at check-in. To think that customers are too stupid to notice is the height of arrogance. SWA's advertised prices included the first two bags for free. So maybe it is true that the truth will set you free. I like to think so.

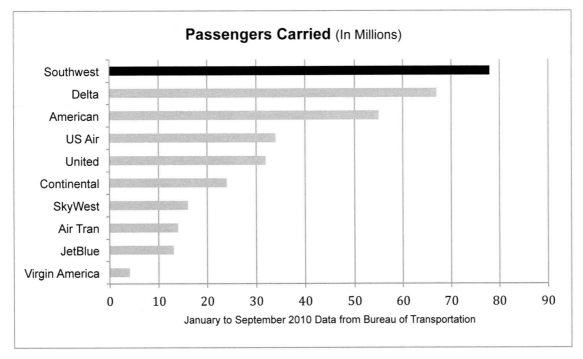

Figure 8—A Nonfinancial Measure of Success

The irony is that the producer-centered carriers who put emphasis on being biggest and most preferred in their mission statements have lost out on both counts to the ones most focused on customers. This picture is not, of course, unique to airlines. It seems to be a universal affliction.

The voice of leadership is dependent on understanding the heart, mind, and voice of customers to remain relevant. A leader who rarely talks with actual users of his or her enterprise's products will not be as effective as possible. That means the VOL must be aligned with the VOC. Entrepreneurs very often start their businesses because of their own experiences as a customer who didn't or couldn't get what they wanted from an existing operation. No one could deny that Herb Kelleher (Southwest Airlines), Steve Jobs (Apple), Sir Richard Branson (Virgin), John Boggle (the Vanguard Group), Elon Musk (Tesla), and other highly successful entrepreneurs stayed exceptionally engaged with customers who used their products.

Effective leaders want and need their intent deployed. When that intent, described in mission statements, core values, and strategic plans is vague, unimaginative, and impersonal, we diminish our opportunity to be inspiring and better than just average. Enter the VOM, who will try to fill any gaps in the VOL with procedures (and related bureaucracy). They will do the best they can to understand the VOL and push their VOM constructively. One test of how well this is done is to ask, when reading a procedure, whether or not it would be viewed by prospective employees as an enticement to join the enterprise. Let's continue our examination of SWA to see how this has worked.

If you have been a passenger on any of the US legacy carriers (American, Delta, or United), you are likely to have experienced shortly after boarding a flight attendant reading (or stating with the same enthusiasm as if reading for the thousandth time) safety instructions over the public address system. On some carriers, this is accomplished by shutting off all the lights and turning on a video cranked to maximum volume to capture your undivided attention. The message involves how to fasten your seatbelt. You have been required by US law to have these in your car since 1968 and then first required to use them in 1984.[40] Perhaps the airline's reminder is just what you need because you don't drive, haven't forced your kids to buckle up, are a slow learner, have a death wish, or have amnesia. The message also tells you how to use the bottom of your seat as a flotation device. The presumption here is you will be flying over water and you will be able to float after falling from the sky in an unplanned dive. You are also reminded not to smoke, how to put on the oxygen mask, where the exit doors are, and so on, and pay strict adherence to all further instructions…or else! I have asked flight attendants on different carriers why they all do this. The stock answer has been that the Federal Aviation Administration (FAA) requires them to do so. But that is not true!

Consider some evidence. First, actually the pilot has the responsibility to make sure passengers know how the seat belts work and fasten them before takeoff. The FAA does not specify exactly what to say or how to do this. Second, how is it that SWA gets away with not using the same standardized, dare we say, condescending, approach as other airlines? It must not be required. Their flight attendants sometimes sing the instructions, tell jokes, do rap or poems, put on skits, and otherwise engage passengers. On SWA, we may very well experience a planeload of passengers giving the flight attendant an enthusiastic ovation after the safety announcement. Does it sound like their safety procedure is in alignment with their mission statement? Does it look like employees are allowed (encouraged or expected) to demonstrate some individuality in how they express company spirit while complying with the law? Does this way of doing things cost as little as the standard industry approach? Have they differentiated themselves? Could their competition copy them and do it too? Yes, yes, a thousand times yes. If SWA can do this and get away with it, one could easily conclude the FAA thinks this is just fine and dandy. They do.

There is one more detail about alignment. The little black book flight attendants refer to for their compelling safety message is pretty much the same across all the legacy carriers. They are rectangular.

---

[40] This is required in every state except New Hampshire.

The SWA one is heart-shaped, perhaps related to the company logo (a winged heart), stock symbol (LUV), and their home airport (Love Field). Flight attendants are supplied with resources such as an entertainment kit with a manual on ways to interact with passengers, called "Life's Just Fun and Games."[41]

One of SWA flight attendants was renowned for engaging his planeload of customers in his use of safety messages delivered in rap. SWA leadership recognized David's creative modeling of their core values. They asked him to deliver the company's financial results to Wall Street analysts the same way. He did and was given a standing ovation.

This would be a good time to see how this issue of alignment among mission, values, policy, and behavior is relevant to your own situation. Consider your C3IQ score for item 8. A score of greater than or equal to three indicates the enterprise has policies covering priorities stated in its mission, core values, and/or strategic plan. That's the good news. I'm not a fan of bureaucratic and unnecessary paperwork, but an organization that says employment must not be based on discriminatory practices is hardly serious about it when there is no policy addressing what behavior is acceptable or unacceptable. The absence of the critical few policies necessary to support core values is a cause of ambiguity and uncertainty. We either mean what we say or we don't. The Master of Excellence will identify which core values have missing or inadequately supportive policies and close the gap(s).

Leader's Action 6: Core Values Ambiguity
(See Appendix 1)

This brings us to C3IQ item number 14. A score of less than or equal to three says a customer satisfaction policy is weak or missing. Sadly this is the norm across the vast majority of enterprises, no matter the industry. If that is your situation, review the six-point policy described above to see if putting a version of it in place could close the gap. This can be an essential step if we want to get to a score of five on items 14, 15a–d and f, and 18. What else should you do next?

My assumption is that you are reading this, at least in part, because you aim to be a truth-teller. Although dissidents often take up this role, one of my favorite leaders in this regard was Mikhail Gorbachev, general secretary of the Soviet Communist Party (1985–1991). Upon coming to power in March 1985, he introduced two strategic programs: perestroika (economic reform) and glasnost (openness). Glasnost is a model for how far-reaching and transformational an engaging truth-telling campaign can be. Key outcomes wanted were modernizing the Soviet Union, adopting democratic practices, and ending the Cold War with the West. Much of that was achieved by 1990. That included the installation of democratic governments in all previous Soviet bloc nations, the end of the Cold War (marked by the destruction of the Berlin Wall and German reunification), and Gorbachev being personally awarded the Nobel Peace Prize.

As with any large-scale change, there were unintended consequences. Two that are notable is that Gorbachev lost his formal national leadership position and the Communist Party's controlling political power over several other eastern European countries was terminated. As he later related, his personal loss of power caused him to see his failure to completely realize everything he set out to do as an enduring regret. He nonetheless did not regret being the catalyst for seismic changes in the growth of democratic society. Like most things in life, the size of the risk is often related to the scope and

---

[41] See SWA's core values, published on its website as of 2016.

magnitude of the contemplated change. For those of us working to be effective leaders, remember the words of Machiavelli from Chapter 1.

None of my client leaders has yet won the Nobel Prize. I do have hope. Many have won significant recognition such as Baldrige National Awards, industry best-in-class recognition, and other acknowledgments of excellence as a direct result of applying C3 practices. The most successful ones all started with a clear statement of strategic intent and an unambiguous path to deployment. Engaging others in that effort is essential to personal survival, no matter where you are in the hierarchy.

3. MEASURES

Measures as a source of ambiguity. A nonprofit community organization, Healthy Start Coalition, had a mission to improve the health of expectant or new mothers and their infants. Most of its funding came from the state in the form of grants. One of the programs set up to improve a new mom's health was a therapist-led smoking-cessation program. Healthy Start contracted with about a dozen psychologists who offered both individualized and group therapy sessions. I asked the executive director how the efficacy of the smoking cessation program was determined. She said they counted graduates, those who finished the programs they had registered for, as successful. Whether or not the prospective or new moms actually stopped smoking was not something they tracked. She said they really had no control over that desired outcome,[42] and that had nothing to do with how funding was obtained. The state paid by the session. Each client could receive up to ten. The more sessions attended by a customer, the greater the money received from the state and paid to contracted therapists.

Based on this description of the organization's practices, which of the following conclusions could we say are true?

- The greater the number of clients who finished the program, the more successful the program.
- Program success was positively correlated with the money spent.
- The more numerous the sessions received, the more benefit a client experienced.
- The more effective a therapist is, the more he or she is paid.
- The more funding received by Healthy Start, the more clients got treatment.
- Based on the number of clients seen, Healthy Start could claim to be more or less effective.

Measures as a lever to advance excellence. We are tempted to answer both true and false to these statements. That reveals ambiguity. The Healthy Start smoking cessation program was a vital resource in the community. Based on how measurement occurred, it would be difficult to unambiguously determine how effective it was. So, yes, I gave you a trick question. This is exactly the kind of scenario many of us discover when looking at the effectiveness of measures to tell us what is really going on.

It is important to recognize that the leadership, management, contracting therapists, and employees had many years of experience and deeply cared about their customers. Many were highly educated. They were smart people. How could such ambiguity be allowed to persist? The same way it does in every organization, through the gradual creation of habit without close scrutiny or testing of underlying assumptions. Our Master of Excellence job is to pull back the curtain of illusion.

I got acquainted with a number of the Healthy Start therapists. One told me it could take as few as one or two sessions to get a mom to stop smoking. I asked how he got such a quick result. He said he routinely

---

[42] See Vital Lie 1, discussed shortly under assumptions and in appendix 3.

would explore in the first meeting with a client if she were both willing and a good subject for hypnosis. For those meeting both criteria, he would immediately put the client into a hypnotic state and provide instruction to quit smoking. He said his success rate could be over 50 percent, but he had never formally measured it. He indicated that he did report how many smoking cessation sessions he delivered and how many moms stopped smoking, so he guessed we could do the math and find out for sure.

We set out to do that, but I asked him to just confirm with me my understanding of what the Healthy Start situation really was. Therapists who used the full ten allotted sessions would get paid the most (whether or not cessation occurred). Therapists like him who achieved smoking cessation in only one session got paid for one session, the least. He said that pretty much summed it up. I asked him if, to his knowledge, any other therapists used hypnosis or any other method that got comparably fast results. Not to his knowledge. I summarized my observations for the executive director:

1. The Healthy Start mission was to achieve the desired outcomes of improved health of mothers and their infants.

2. Smoking cessation could be achieved in as few as one therapeutic session.

3. A client could participate in a maximum of ten sessions without achieving the desired outcome.

4. Healthy Start and its independent therapists were paid based on their activity with clients, not on the results.

5. A therapist who was least effective with a client or took the longest to get results was paid the most; the most effective and fastest therapist was paid the least.

6. Not all therapists practiced the equally effective treatment methods.

7. Therapists who were less effective were not necessarily aware of those who were better, but if they knew, they might be willing to adopt more successful methods.

8. The agency and the state defined success in terms of the number of clients who finished the program they had enrolled in, not on whether the desired outcome had been achieved.

9. Activity, not results, was the basis for therapist compensation. (Put in terms of the 8DX framework described in the next chapter, this is equivalent to paying for work we do as part of Dimension 8 [process] without any consideration for the effect we have on Dimension 1 [customer-desired results].)

The executive director agreed that all this was true. But her hands were tied by the way the state had set up funding. We discussed the fact that her agency created the contracts with therapists. There was no mention of outcome in the contracts. We discussed the possibility that the agency could add a provision to new contracts, requiring therapists to measure the efficacy of their programs, report it to the agency, and seek out alternative practices that improved overall effectiveness. She agreed to try it out.

The executive director suddenly saw that what had been impossible was now possible, that measurement could be aligned with the agency's most important priorities, human resources could be developed consistent with the enterprise mission, the customer experience would be improved, and there was a clear path for compensating excellence that could be replicated in other areas.

The star therapist was asked to introduce his use of hypnosis to the other therapists. They were encouraged to seek new ways to achieve better and faster results since new contracts were going to stipulate that effectiveness, not just activity, would become new expectations for continuing work with the agency. That is, we would put far more emphasis on Dimensions 1 and 5 (customer-desired and producer-desired outcomes, respectively) than on Dimension 8 (the producer's activity). Beyond the obvious improvement for clients and therapists, the agency's capacity to treat a much larger population of prospective clients was greatly enhanced.

The Scope of Things to Measure. The scope of things we can measure ranges from the astronomical to the subatomic. Don't let anyone tell you something can't be measured. Anything can be measured. We may simply need to apply ourselves to create measures that effectively drive excellence with simplicity.

A very common challenge is the appearance that something is immeasurable. It may be true that beauty is in the eye of the beholder. That adage implies that beauty is subjective, as it may be. When we find there is cross-cultural agreement that a particular woman's face is beautiful, that consensus is not chance or the conclusion of one beholder. It turns out that facial beauty is quantifiable, based on the geometric relationships of facial features and those features' relationship to each other. The length of nose and lips in relation to the height and width of the face, respectively, are two such measures. As we learn to translate subjective judgments into objectively measurable characteristics, we transform art into science. That does nothing to diminish artistic and subjective appeal. It does make it possible for a person who is otherwise not an expert in the subjective to become equally competent as an expert on objective criteria and their measures. As a Master of Excellence, it is to our advantage to enable and empower many others to quantify excellence as easily and quickly as possible. We then know what the target is so we can create or replicate it.

The identification and development of the critical few measures of excellence has been applied with vigor in the competitive sports world. Although running as a sport began at least as early as 776 BC when it was the only event in early Olympic Games, it is only relatively recently (the early twentieth century) that intensive data-based study of speed occurred. Early research tended to focus on factors that slowed down runners, such as wind resistance. It's pretty typical of our bias to study root causes of undesired outcomes.

The speed of an Olympic sprinter is not just dependent on impediments, genetics, and experience. Peter Wyand at Southern Methodist University has conducted what some view as the most advanced research into the biomechanics of sprinting. Among his team's findings in 2000 was the discovery that the force with which a runner's foot hit the ground was what separated the winners from the rest. The fastest had a foot impact of five times his body weight, versus three-and-a-half times of average runners.[43] If you were the coach, otherwise known as Master of Excellence, for your running team, would this information be of value?

Much of the material we've covered concerns conflicts regarding the intent of measures and the use of measures to help resolve ambiguity and conflict. Our emphasis has been on measures related to the core values and strategic direction of our enterprise. Thinking about the grandest, most macro sort of related measures suggests a look at things from the national or international level.

Americans are very familiar with the phrase from the US Declaration of Independence, "We hold these truths to be self-evident, that all men are created equal, that they are endowed by their Creator with certain unalienable Rights, that among these are Life, Liberty and the pursuit of Happiness."

Some refer to this pursuit of happiness as the American dream, a core value of the nation. They may be familiar with the roots of this sentiment, attributed to British philosopher John Locke's publication in 1689

---

[43] Dina Fine Maron, "The Secret to Speed," *Scientific American*, August 2016.

of his *Two Treatises of Government*. What most are not familiar with are the national measures that tell us how alive and well those inalienable rights are. Bet you can't name one such measure. We certainly have many national statistics, reported by large agencies on a regular basis. Gross national product (GDP) would be one you have undoubtedly heard about several times in the last year. GDP is the total annual value of all the goods and services produced by a country, plus net income from foreign investments. The US GDP from 1950 to 2016 peaked in the third quarter of 2016. Is a high GDP a measure of happiness or its pursuit? If we look at the political forces and anger by the electorate in 2016, we would have to conclude GDP was not a measure of happiness.

Another country that won its independence from Britain was Bhutan (1947). Nestled in the eastern Himalayas between China and India, Bhutan has taken a different path to happiness and measurement. Bhutan's fourth dragon king, Jigme Singye Wangchuck, coined the term "gross national happiness" (or GNH) in 1972. The intent was to strengthen the country's Buddhist spiritual values in its economic and social development instead of one based on Western values tied to money and property. The GNH philosophy began by resting on four pillars: sustainable development, preservation and promotion of cultural values, conservation of the natural environment, and good governance.

GNH replaced GDP as the measure of national well-being. It is based on six factors measuring levels of GDP— life expectancy, generosity, social support, freedom, and corruption. To be sure, the GNH index has evolved, aided significantly by the development of a policy capable of being deployed. (Recall our related discussion about the need for and power of a customer satisfaction policy earlier in this chapter.)

A revision in 2005, called GNH 2.0, was created by Med Jones, president of the International Institute of Management, leading to many subsequent refinements by others. The original four pillars have now been expanded to eight, and the United Nations introduced the World Happiness Index report in 2011. Thakur Singh Powdyel, Bhutan's minister of education, believes the world has misinterpreted Bhutan's quest. "People always ask how can you possibly have a nation of happy people? But this is missing the point," he says. "GNH is an aspiration, a set of guiding principles through which we are navigating our path towards a sustainable and equitable society. We believe the world needs to do the same before it is too late."[44]

The point is that a core value, whether held by a nation, an enterprise, a department within that enterprise, or an individual, is easily stated but more powerful when measured. It took the tiny nation of Bhutan to model how this could be done at the national and now global level.

One of the values we have seen in our previous enterprise examples, and now internationally, concerns sustainability. President Barack Obama promised to make a cleaner environment a central theme of his presidency. A major barrier to creating appropriate guidelines and regulations supporting sustainability and combating climate change was the need to quantify the social cost of carbon emissions. How could one make a compelling case for more regulation if there were no agreement on its benefits? To make a long story short, President Obama achieved what many thought was impossible. His administration, working collaboratively with businesses, citizens, interest groups, multiple agencies, and a range of experts, came up with a number, the social cost of carbon. This single number is intended to represent all the costs society incurs when we burn fossil fuels. That number is now part of federal regulations.[45] The bottom line is that the impact of one ton of carbon emissions creates a societal cost of $36 in poor health,

---

[44] Annie Kelly, "Gross National Happiness in Bhutan," *The Guardian*, December 1, 2012.

[45] Audie Cornish, "Heard on All Things Considered," *NPR News*, August 17, 2016.

crop failures, weather disasters, lost income, and more. This doesn't sound like much until you add up the millions of tons released each year. And this measure is just a beginning stake in the ground.

The measurement ideal we seek as Masters of Excellence is for there to be a clear line of sight from the most macro of value-related measures to the most micromeasures related to an employee's daily work. The better the alignment, the stronger the measures. So to finish our thinking about the scope of things to measure, it makes sense to take one simple example of measurement at the individual level. There's no need to pick something ridiculously easy. I've said we can measure anything. Admittedly I haven't given you a lot of guidance on exactly how to do that up to this point. We'll begin that process with Leader's Action 9 and get deep into it in volume 2. Perhaps an example of how to measure the squishiest of issues can help. Our technical term of "squishy" means highly subjective. The aim continues to be the use of measures as a lever to reduce ambiguity and strengthen unity of purpose.

As so often happens for those of us who travel a lot, I found myself seated on a plane next to a woman who was eager to chat. Initial pleasantries led to questions about what we each did for work. It turned out we were both authors. She had written several self-help books, two of which had become best-sellers. She indicated the books were about ways to build better interpersonal and intimate relationships, primarily with the reader's significant other or mate. Her readers, based on their letters to her, were mostly women.

I asked if she was aware of improvements her books had made in the lives of her readers. She said readers reported anecdotes about how her books had helped. I asked if she measured the improvement in readers' relationships as a result of reading her books. The question intrigued her, but she didn't see how that would be possible. She wasn't dealing with something simple, like weight loss, after all.

I asked if there would be any desire on her part to measure relationship improvement or provide the readers with a way to do that themselves. She said sure, but that sounded like a pretty complicated task, and she didn't want to get into the survey business. I told her surveys were not necessary, but measurement could still be done, if she wished, and my clients routinely encountered such challenges measuring what seemed at first to be immeasurable issues of great complexity. She asked how that could be done.

I said the first thing to agree on is that a caring relationship is a desired outcome her readers hope to achieve or improve upon. She agreed. The next thing would be to identify possible characteristics of that outcome that could be objectively observed to be present to some degree. She said the whole notion of caring seemed to defy easy measurement. While brainstorming, I asked if any of the following statements might be related:

- Percent of times in a period (hour or day) a person said yes (versus no) to their mate
- Number of minutes spent per day together at meals
- Number of seconds of continuous, unbroken eye contact per period (during a meal, an hour, a day, and so forth), not counting blinks
- Number of total minutes of touch per person per period (hour or day)
- Number of endearments used with the other person per day
- Number of eye contacts accompanied with a smile made per period (before breakfast, during the day, and so forth)
- Number of compliments a person gives per day
- Number of compliments a person receives per day
- Number of complaints a person makes about the other person per day

- Number of minutes spent together in a common hobby or interest per month
- Percent of discretionary income spent on jointly shared interests or hobbies per month
- Percent of time spent alone with the other person

These were just the first dozen possible measures I suggested. After each one, she agreed that they could be signs a relationship was caring (or not) and sounded pretty simple for a reader to track. Remember, these are just what can be measured, not that all should be measured. She said she had never thought of providing such easy-to-measure criteria and would look into how that might be done, in her next book.

So what? How is this story related to excellence? We had been discussing the challenge for us as Masters of Excellence to create a clear line of sight between enterprise core values and the daily behavior of all employees. When we say things like "employees are our greatest asset," what are the measures we have put in place so all managers and supervisors actually act that way? If that is not currently being done, we need to close the gap. Employees who do not feel treated as an asset or don't consciously know to treat others that way are a sign our organization is not as good as we all may wish. If it can be done with a caring intimate relationship, we can do it for caring employee relationships. You now have the principle, a quickie course in the method, and an example to use as reference.

The Master of Excellence looks for ways to assure that what we measure and how we use those measures will (a) align strategic objectives with operational and personal performance,[46] (b) numerically define our core values, (c) recognize success, and (d) correct the causes and apply consequences for failure. An unmeasured priority creates doubt about the importance of what is said to be valued. We use measures to make values and excellence numerically visible. The 8 Dimensions of Excellence will provide a good guide for that practice.

One caution to keep in mind is that some measures do not need to be done and perhaps should not be done indefinitely. It is sad to observe measures, once created, becoming immortal fixtures of the organization. When an effective habit has been established, we need to stop measuring it to death. It is the job of the Master of Excellence to make a sunset law or put other mechanisms in place to end measurement that has achieved its purpose and is no longer necessary. We will pick up this issue of measurement again in Chapter 8.

Measures as a lever to increase failure. Ambiguity is sometimes not the worst result we can experience. There are many examples of values and measures that are very clear, well-aligned, and a disaster to various stakeholders. A case in point is the story of Al Dunlap, the CEO of Scott Paper, beginning in 1994. Like every other employee, Dunlap had performance objectives to meet. One was to increase the company's share value. He did an outstanding job in that department, organizing a restructuring that resulted in 225 percent growth of share value by the following year. Shareholders who sold at the right time in that year clearly won. But then there is the other side of the story. He simultaneously arranged the sale of the company to Kimberly-Clark and the elimination of 35 percent (11,000 employees) of the workforce. Lots of folks lost out.

Dunlap promoted his brilliance with his book, *Mean Business*. It became a best-seller. His practices continued under his role as CEO of Sunbeam, beginning in 1998. By this time, he had a well-established moniker of Chainsaw Al. To make a long story short, he replicated his mean business practices by, among other things, selling off various divisions of Sunbeam and firing thousands. Again, his performance objective, set by the board of directors, was to increase shareholder wealth. That can work for a while, and it did, but when you run out of divisions to sell and employees to do work, the final value of the business is not so hot. He was finally fired. He would claim he did exactly what he was hired to do, and the measures proved his success. Sunbeam never did recover from the image of the firm he created within a few short years, filing for bankruptcy in 2001. Dunlap did win an award, however, from *Time* magazine, as one of the top-ten worst bosses.[47]

One of the many lessons to be learned from this story is that what gets measured gets done. So be careful what you wish for. Another lesson is related not just to measures of success but to the mission of the enterprise. Many of us may have heard (or said ourselves) during our professional careers that the mission of our commercial enterprise is to make a profit. My emphatic response to that is no, no, no! Profit is a mathematical calculation of income minus costs, in its simplest form. It is one of many outcomes an enterprise may seek. Mission is the purpose of the enterprise. Profit may be one measure of success but not *the* measure. If profit truly were the sole purpose of a business, then any business activity that results in profit is justified. That would require the enterprise to have no soul, no moral

---

[46] For a practical guide on how to measure the seemingly immeasurable, please see the eight steps in Chapter 4, Creating a Customer-Centered Culture: Leadership in Quality, Innovation, and Speed.

[47] Dan Fastenberg, "Al Dunlap, Top 10 Worst Bosses," *Time* magazine, October 18, 2010.

compass, no operating ethical behavior, and no benefit for some broader good or audience other than the receipt of money. Prostitution, drug-running, death for hire, and a variety of other pursuits are all just fine. I call that organized crime. The following principles can help us better align our values and measures.

MEASUREMENT PRINCIPLES

1. What we measure is what we value.
2. Anything can be measured.
3. The biggest constraints on what we measure are our Vital Lies.
4. Success is defined by the measures and pace of improvement for each of the 8 Dimensions of Excellence.
5. The higher a person is in an organization, the less likely his or her work is measured.
6. Measure customer-desired outcomes at least as well as undesired outcomes.
7. If a product is worth producing, it is worth measuring.
8. The unit cost, quality, yield, cycle time, rework cost, and satisfaction with every product are key contributors to excellence and can be measured.
9. A measure without a numerical goal for improvement is of limited value.
10. Measurement systems and tools that emphasize reliability over validity can easily create misleading conclusions.
11. Don't tell me what you value; show me what you measure.

Leader's Action 7: Alignment of Values with Measures, KPIs
(See Appendix 1)

4. POWER

Power as a source of ambiguity. The executive director (ED) of a county agency was proudly telling me early in our work together that he had been consciously working to empower his management team. When asked for an example, he said he had told his directors to collaborate on the design of new uniforms for field staff and coordinate it with the new logo and staff car color. The logo had already been determined before he gave them this assignment. His directors, queried separately, confirmed they had been put in charge of these decisions. They also said that uniform and car color were the most important decisions he had allowed them to make independently in the prior year. They did not at all feel empowered.

The result of such "empowerment" practices meant the ED had made it abundantly clear where the source of power was. Since his view of his own benevolence was obviously a Vital Lie, we identified it as one on our short list to destroy. That was done by discussing with his team the issues they felt little control over that they wanted turned over to them. The ED was receptive and agreed to their requests. He was surprised to discover the pace of change began to accelerate noticeably.

When we communicate as leaders that we value teamwork (but don't let teams actually execute decisions they've arrived at through agreed-upon methods), say customers are important (but require no customer input for priority changes that impact them), and assert that employees are empowered (but require multiple approvals for the tiniest of expenditures on essential tools of the job that have already been authorized), we have permitted ambiguity of power to exist. We also foster lack of trust and diminished initiative.

No professional or regulatory body yet mandates adoption of C3 practices. It is a system that is only used by those with sufficient insight to recognize its potential value to the enterprise. You could call it a pull system in the sense that, once begun, many adopters cannot help themselves but follow the natural, organic path C3 pulls them along. I have occasionally encountered a situation where the top leader wants to augment the aspirational nature of C3 and use a more forceful, compulsory approach to get the resisters to change. Those leaders want to use more of a push system to accelerate the transformation pace.

One system I recommend in such cases is the ISO 9001:2015 international standard (referred to as ISO for short here). The intent of ISO and C3 are similar, to advance the interests and success of the enterprise by providing products and services that satisfy its customers. Two main differences between the two systems is that:

1. ISO provides certification to an organization; C3 certifies individuals as Masters of Excellence in specific areas of competency.[48]

2. ISO offers ten broad areas of competence without a prescribed path to achieve it, whereas C3 provides a prescription for mastering excellence.

An example related to our discussion of power can illustrate how these differences play out in real life. The CEO of a company wanted it to continuously practice its top core value of customer satisfaction. Two of his top VPs on the leadership team wanted to be left alone to run manufacturing and engineering, respectively. Observing that the CEO was not willing to expend sufficient personal capital to persuade them, nor replace them with others, I recommended he commit the corporation to becoming ISO 9001 certified. He agreed, brought in an auditor to identify priority compliance issues, and began the certification process. Achieving certification was made mandatory. The CEO and VPs all agreed that any major corrections preventing certification would be owned as the responsibility of one of them, without exception.

The VP for quality soon observed that two serious issues the company needed to correct remained unresolved for several months. Each issue was described in a document called a "corrective action report" and had been assigned to each of the responsible executives. Upon researching the delay in correction, the quality VP found that both corrective actions had been assigned to lower-level employees. Those employees told him they lacked the power to remedy the problems. They had been given responsibility without authority. I'll bet you've observed or experienced this sort of situation more than once in your career.

The quality VP was a Master of Excellence quite familiar with C3 practices. Viewed in terms of the levers we've been discussing, he recognized the problem was rooted in ambiguities of power and language. There had been no agreed-upon definition of responsibility, as there had never been any discussion about it. There was also no description of the power the recipient of a corrective action had to remedy a problem. There was a twofold remedy:

---

[48] See http://www.C3excellence.com for details.

1. Responsibility had to be defined in writing to also carry the requisite authority to fulfill that responsibility. When in doubt, responsibility was always referred up to the manager above the assignee.

2. The quality VP knew he was the owner of all corrective actions initiated, so he had the liberty to provide a new instruction. No corrective action could be assigned to an employee who did not have the commensurate authority to carry out or direct the successful remedy.

This probably sounds like an obvious and simple solution. When we are caught in the middle of swirling ambiguities and the inevitable finger-pointing, the obvious and the simple do not always spring to mind. Recognizing that the source of a problem may be ambiguity and understanding how to change it into a lever can be a new strength for all Masters of Excellence.

Power as a lever to advance excellence. Seek to improve the degree to which we consciously and systematically engage end user customers (including those who are employees), giving them the ability to influence the design of products and processes. In the situation with the corrective actions, the receiving employees had not been asked what they needed to achieve the desired results. There is no substitute for asking them the right questions before or as we begin creating new products. One of the most powerful tools for doing this is addressed in Leader's Action 12 with the Strategic 5 Whys. The full VOC methodology is discussed at length in volume 2. This early dialogue assures that the power to drive excellence is from the outside in.

It is insufficient to seek feedback after we deliver the product since any deficiencies delay and diminish satisfaction and incur correction costs that could have been avoided. We may practice the autocratic power of one, the collaborative power of informal coalitions, or deployment of formal teams. Each form of power has its place. Power is determined by who (a) drives the design of products and processes, (b) selects what behavior gets rewarded, and (c) holds both the authority and capacity to achieve or prevent a specified result.

When there is responsibility without commitment or authority, we may experience the power of none. This easily leads to chaos, confusion, finger-pointing, added costs, and discontent. On the other hand, when initiative is rewarded (or at least not punished), we encourage the courageous to practice what has been called the Jesuit maxim, "It is more blessed to beg forgiveness than ask permission."

5. ASSUMPTIONS AND VITAL LIES

Assumptions as a source of ambiguity. Assumptions can support pursuit of the possible or rejection of what is thought to be impossible. President John Kennedy said in 1961, "This nation should commit itself to achieving the goal, before this decade is out, of landing a man on the moon and returning him safely to the Earth."[49] No one had done that before, so there was no evidence it could be done. That might well have resulted in resistance with many saying it was not possible. His effectiveness as a leader involved making a compelling case that the risk of not pursuing this goal was outweighed by the risk of losing face to the Soviets, who might get there first.

Kennedy focused on the certainty of leadership in space versus the technical ambiguity related to navigation in space. That choice and political will inspired success on both fronts and was achieved in

---

[49] May 25, 1961: JFK's Moon Shot Speech to Congress.

1969. We now call such out-of-the-box, grand aims to achieve the previously unknown as "moon shots." Conversely, the head of 20th Century Fox movie studios, Darryl Zanuck, said in 1946 he believed TV would not be able to hold any market after the first six months. Did his company shape or benefit from the dramatic growth of TV's popularity in the following decade? Not much. This nay-saying, we will refer to and discuss shortly as a Vital Lie. In both of these cases, a leader was sharing his vision of the future he was successful in achieving. One was enabling; the other was constraining. We can use such cases as supporting the adage that one should be careful what one wishes for.

One of the "moon shots" of early 2016 was Mark Zuckerberg's ten-year plan to create the ability to connect every person on the planet. His well-articulated vision for how Facebook would use the technology of virtual/augmented reality and mobile communications using all platforms, video and artificial intelligence, and other technologies was unique among technology companies in its detail, breadth, time frame, and broad communication. Where others may fail to lay out a road map due to uncertainty, Zuckerberg chose to impose a shape to the unknown future and thereby make it less ambiguous.

Assumptions tend to rule us in our personal lives, just as much as in our professional pursuits. We routinely tell our kids, "I know you can do that." We say that even though the kid has never done it before, so we really don't know. But we are hopeful. We may say the same sort of thing to those who report to us. Again, it is with hope. It is well established by educational research that what teachers expect of their students is correlated with the results achieved.

Moon shots and assumptions about what could be are the opposite of Vital Lies. The latter tend to support, at best, justification for current behavior or, at worst, the impossibility of change. When those Vital Lies are never challenged by those of us leading excellence, we are tacitly leaving it up to others to decide when to seek the truth, when to support the truth, and know when it is okay for facts to be uncollected or ignored.

Crush Vital Lies to advance excellence. It is one thing for language to be a source of ambiguity. It is quite another when it is an unrecognized source of disinformation, misdirection, and disempowerment. Such is the case with Vital Lies,[50] which function as barriers to excellence. Our effectiveness as Master of Excellence is dependent on our skill in recognizing when a Vital Lie is stated and used as the basis for inaction and knowing how to destroy it. That ability gives us a big lever to change language, assumptions, values, and measures.

A Vital Lie is a constraining assumption, self-deception, justification, denial, rationalization, myth, or other excuse for not changing.[51] The overall performance of the organization is diminished by Vital Lies in the same way personal well-being is reduced by a thousand cuts. One may be survivable, but many cause death. Ten of the most common are briefly identified here:

1. **We don't have control over that.** This belief gives us permission not to seek change. We are absolved of any responsibility of the issue. The destructive beauty of such a self-fulfilling prophecy is that we can prove it true by inaction. While it is true that meteorologists don't prevent hurricanes, an accurate and timely forecast can minimize loss. We often have more potential for controlling a situation than we may think. The story about Healthy Start Coalition offered an example of how this showed up and what was done to crush it.

---

[50] Playwright Henrik Ibsen coined this term.

[51] These are discussed in-depth with examples and leadership actions to take in appendix 2.

2. **Satisfaction will occur if dissatisfaction declines.** When customer (or employee) complaints decrease, we are easily led to believe satisfaction is improved. Maybe. Or we may just not be asking the right questions or seeing all the evidence. Yes, we may stop inflicting pain on them, but that hardly qualifies as making them feel good. A second assumption embedded here is that we know what satisfaction is, that we have defined it. Dissatisfaction can seem obvious when we hear customers complaining about something as running late. But is the opposite of late on-time? And if it occurred, would it be a source of satisfaction? Just because the plane doesn't crash doesn't mean we are particularly satisfied with the flight. We expect that as the barest of minimums. It is not a satisfier when it lands as expected, though it is definitely a dissatisfier if it doesn't.

3. **We are on the leading edge in our industry.** I once interviewed many directors of boards for the largest firms within a certain industry. Almost to a person, each of them said they believed their firm was on the industry's leading edge. It seemed clear to me that not all of them could be right, unless, of course, they lived in Garrison Keillor's fictitious Lake Wobegon where "all the women are strong, all the men are good-looking and all the children are above average."[52] Believing we are the best might be true but can often breed complacency and arrogance. It discourages critical thinking. Intel's Andy Grove had a passion for destroying innovation-draining complacency and thus created a high performance enterprise. His motto and book share the same name: *Only the Paranoid Survive*. He wanted the assumption to be that someone else was about to overtake Intel. Running more creatively and faster was the only way to stay on top.

4. **Growth in customer demand or market share means customers are happy.** IBM was the dominant producer of personal computers, and Microsoft was king of personal computer software prior to 2000. Were their customers happy? Why did they defect in droves to a much smaller company based in Cupertino, making mobile devices with an alternative operating system?

5. **We know what business we are in.** The popularity and growth of Southwest Airlines from their inception in 1971 is often attributed to their lower-priced flights, their fuel purchasing practices, or standardization on a single aircraft. Those are related to SWA's success but represent a narrow, dangerously incomplete view that is producer-biased. Does that explain how SWA, by 2014, had forty-one years of consecutive profitability and became the largest US carrier in terms of passenger miles? What few of their competitors and industry analysts did not understand, but could easily have discovered, is that successive SWA leaders had created and sustained a business culture that does everything possible to entertain its customers, often in unexpected ways. It's no accident that their trading symbol is LUV and that flight attendants are trained and encouraged to give safety announcements by song, poetry, skit, and joke. Are they an airline or an entertainment enterprise?

6. **We know who our customers are.** We often confuse the people who buy, fund, or regulate with those who use the product or service. Customers are usually a significantly more diverse group than we realize. The ones we are furthest from are the ones we know least well. But those end users are most important to satisfy in the long term. See Chapter 20 for a complete discussion on how to truly determine who our customers are.

7. **Customers don't know what they want.** This belief permits us to (a) not bother asking, and (b) tell them what we think they want. We might call this the "father knows best" belief. It leads us easily to number eight.

8. **We know what customers want.** This may have been true yesterday. A safer bet is to assume we don't know until we check again. Likewise, gun safety begins with the assumption a gun is always loaded until we check. Failing to check can be fatal.

9. **What customers say they expect is what they do want.** This belief has caused untold frustration for leaders sincerely listening for customer priorities. There can be significant differences between what customers expect and what they want. For example, a dental customer may expect pain but not

---

[52] Garrison Keillor was the host of *The Prairie Home Companion* radio variety show (1974–2016) and used this tagline with his stories of the fictitious northern Minnesota town of Lake Wobegon.

want it. Should our aim be to satisfy their expectations or their wants? We can easily shoot for the former and discover that our success does not result in their satisfaction. In addition, customers may not give us an answer to every question we ask. This may be due to their inability to understand our question or their perceived irrelevance of the question. And we may not ask every pertinent question we should have. In general, customers will easily tell us the improvements they want for a product they are already familiar with. Unless we ask, they may not tell us the outcome they are trying to achieve. Improving the product without improving the outcome inevitably leads to customers telling us they didn't get what they really wanted.

10. **Our performance measures confirm our excellence.** An organization can meet or exceed all industry standards, have no product returns, see no customer defections, nor receive any lawsuits filed against it. This does not mean customers love it. A water utility can meet all government regulations but still provide water consumers hate to drink. The danger is interpreting customer capture, retention, and even loyalty as anything close to customer ecstasy. Our measures of success can lead to faulty conclusions. As others have discovered, if we simply torture numbers long enough, they will confess to anything. An organization that believes it is already at the top of its game may see no reason to change a thing. See Vital Lie 4.

Assumptions as a lever to advance excellence. We can listen for and stamp out Vital Lies that inhibit the pursuit of excellence. We can articulate assumptions about what is possible, why it is worth pursuing, and how its pursuit will be encouraged. Assumptions supported by verifiable facts hold up better than unsupported ones. But the leader must also recognize that faith can always trump what appears to be incontrovertible evidence to the contrary. When faith is the only basis for an assumption you wish to change, find another belief in the related body of faith that supports the assumption you wish to have adopted and then assure the supporting evidence is put forth and connected to it. This means that verifiable facts will not persuade those who hold fast to faith, no matter what. The Master of Excellence will do better to find an inconsistency or conflict in the broader faith to justify an alternative view. All faiths include ambiguities and inconsistencies the Master of Excellence can exploit.

Vital Lies obscure and ignore the truth. Competing truths create ambiguity. Success involves the conscious creation of choices that manage, eliminate, or expand ambiguity. A wonderfully insightful book related to this topic is *Finite and Infinite Games: A Vision of Life as Play and Possibility* (1987, 2013) by James Carse. The notion that all of human endeavor can be viewed in the context of playing finite games where the purpose is to win when it ends, or play infinite games with the purpose to keep the game going and win when it never ends, is relevant to Masters of Excellence. Being clear about which game we are playing and whether those around us are playing the same game is pretty handy if we wish mastery of the game.

Leader's Action 8: Crush Vital Lies
(See Appendix 1)

Leaders of a large transportation organization had historically viewed cost savings to build and maintain roads as the key indicators of efficiencies both they and their customers would want. I asked if it were possible to save money on building roads but cause customers to incur many gallons of fuel, hours of time delays, and lost business due to construction sites? They quickly recognized that the party that experienced the savings had a direct bearing on any measures of efficiency. The producer could become more efficient while the customer becomes less efficient.

Challenging Vital Lies will make some people uncomfortable. Too bad. Eliminating the organization's constraining fictions is part of our leadership and Master of Excellence job description. A small change will require little or no discomfort. A big, audacious change that has never been attempted before can make folks uneasy at first. It can also be exciting. The inherent risk of the new can scare the hell out of some while promising a thrilling experience to others. Our role as leader is to search for and engage those ready to embrace the departure from the known. Exposing Vital Lies can be exhilarating for them.

Those who reach the pinnacle of success do not sustain that position by being receptive to a laissez-faire approach to excellence. Although leaders such as Apple's Steve Jobs, Samsung chairman Lee Kun-Hee,[53] Virgin Atlantic's Sir Richard Branson, performer Michael Jackson, Tesla's Elon Musk, Amazon's Jeff Bezos, and Quentin Wilson at MODOR[54] may have been revered by their customers, fans, and others, most were also known for being highly demanding. In some cases, the term "difficult" has been used. It's just that they had no patience with mediocrity and excuses. They were, or still are, passionate perfectionists, and toughness sometimes goes with the territory.

Climbing Mount Everest will be a cold, uncomfortable pursuit much of the way. We wouldn't start on such a trek if the goal weren't worth it. There are observations you and I will make throughout this book that may occasionally upset some readers. Upset is not my goal, but it may be a necessary step in revealing the truth. Yes, I understand that it is my truth and the truth flowing from customers of hundreds of quite varied enterprises. Just as you will do with others, I ask that you suspend your disbelief and try to avoid being defensive when feeling uncomfortable on the journey. The places where discomfort occurs deserve reflection and contemplation. On the other hand, you may finish the book and conclude I have merely provided an argument in support of what you've always believed. That's my hope.

6. MODELING

Modeling as a source of ambiguity. A company made industrial products that each cost several million dollars. The president had communicated his key values, which included "Customer satisfaction is our top priority." His company was about to ship a new model of the product to a first-time customer they had been courting for years. During the final testing, it was discovered that a couple of key components demonstrated intermittent failure. The director for quality put a hold on the shipment of the product until either the sources of the problems could be identified or the customers could replace the components later. The head of production said his group was done with assembly and any replacement parts could not be obtained without missing the agreed-upon ship date. The president released the product for shipment as is. This was not the first time such a scenario had occurred. No communication was made with the customer about the situation prior to shipment. Was the behavior of the president and head of production consistent with the top priority?

Modeling as a lever to advance excellence. I was conducting a workshop for an airline client. About a hundred participants from many of the operational units were in attendance. We were discussing the issues of core values, levers for change, and power. A flight attendant, Jennifer, described a situation that she thought illustrated how the company's systems failed to support some of its stated key values. She had a situation where a customer had spilled his drink on another passenger. The wet passenger was understandably quite upset, but it was clear it was just an accident so the airline had no obligation to do anything but provide some towels so he could dry off. The stickiness would remain. Jennifer, realizing

---

[53] Chairman Lee Kun-Hee declared in 1993 that, to be the leader with consumers, Samsung would have to "change everything except your wife and children." *USA Today*, April 22, 2014.

[54] Quentin Wilson was named director of MODOR in January 1998. He championed the principles and methods outlined here, starting with his one-word strategic vision for his organization, simplify. Those efforts resulted in moving his department from twenty-fifth to number one of fifty states in the nation in only two years, as ranked by *Governing* magazine.

the passenger was going to need a dry cleaner for his suit, took a twenty-dollar bill out of her purse and gave it to the passenger for the cleaning, asking his forgiveness. Jennifer then related how the company had no provision to reimburse her.

Just before Jennifer began telling her story, Bruce, the executive responsible for customer satisfaction and sponsor of the workshop, had stopped by the session and was standing in the back of the room. As she was finishing her story, Bruce walked up toward the front of the room where she was sitting and asked if there had ever been any compensation given to her for handling this situation. She said no. He took his wallet out, pulled out a fifty-dollar bill, and handed it to her, thanking her for what she had done. He then turned to the rest of the room and invited them to follow Jennifer's example, that it was the right thing to do and that he would take on the task of fixing the company's system that hadn't supported Jennifer. He also said that, until the fix occurred, he invited anyone in Jennifer's situation to emulate her and send him the bill. The room erupted in applause. The system was ultimately corrected. Bruce had effectively modeled the behavior he wanted from others and, as luck would have it, had a hundred witnesses.

We are continually demonstrating the behavior we want. Despite what we may have said is important, what we actually do when the chips are down is what matters. The single most important element of modeling is the establishment of trust. Say what we mean without ambiguity and mean what we say with consistent, reliable follow-through. This modeling fosters respect, trust, and confidence in others to pursue results that may not have been thought attainable.

Everything we have addressed in this section on levers is related to our personal behavior. We might sum up what we can do to enhance trust as a Master of Excellence this way:

a. **Tell the truth**. If the truth changes due to new data, direction, and so forth, explain to those involved so they can continue to view you as a source of truth and eliminator of ambiguity.

b. **Challenge Vital Lies**. Ask for the evidence supporting an assumption or conclusion you believe is constraining excellence.

c. **Say what you mean.** Use language that is as unambiguous as possible. Avoid euphemisms.

d. **Reject exceptions to core values and commitments.** Assume that every exception weakens the value or commitment ten times more than every instance in support. Just like a reputation that takes a lifetime to build but a moment to destroy.

e. **Mean what you say**. Do the right thing unequivocally, as defined by core values.

f. **Recognize and reward**. Use every opportunity to reinforce the desired behavior in others.

g. **Visibly follow through**. Always follow through on a commitment in a timely, visible way.

h. **Look for and eliminate ambiguity.** Every instance potentially constrains excellence.

i. **If it's worth doing, it's worth measuring**. A measure without a goal and "done" date is meaningless for advancing excellence.

The six levers we've discussed are rarely used alone. They are inextricably interconnected. Pushing on one will inevitably move others. Similarly, ambiguity or certainty cuts across all six. Knowing the specific places where ambiguity exists gives the Master of Excellence the opportunity to exercise his or her bias for action with focus.

LEADERSHIP PRINCIPLES

1. Leaders envision and embrace as achievable what others think is impossible.

2. It is not enough for a passionate innovator to create the technically possible. Success is dependent on understanding and articulating who wants it and why.

3. Excellence is achieved and sustained when defined by customers, created by engaged employees, measured by management, and rewarded by leaders.

4. Confusion, chaos, conflict, and dysfunction are reduced as certainty replaces ambiguity.

5. Purposeful success will not be fully realized without continuously using all six levers of cultural transformation: language, values, measures, power, assumptions, and modeling.

6. The complexity of cultural transformation is simplified by creating explicit alignment among core values, strategic outcomes, measures of success, and product ownership.

7. The mind and fortitude of an innovator are focused on why we do what we do for specified others.

8. The differences among the four outcomes in the 8DX are as fundamental as differences among the four elements of earth, fire, water, and air.

9. Vital Lies are destroyed with proof the assumptions are false.

10. When we claim something is important but don't measure it, the importance is less than we claim.

11. A core value whose practice is rewarded will be more dominant than a value not tied to reward.

12. Excellence is undermined by failures that carry no consequences.

13. Internal alignment is enabled when every employee can see the relationship between his or her personal products and those at the enterprise level.

14. A core value is alive when a written policy directs and supports its active deployment and related behaviors.

15. The Master of Excellence assures that end users of all products produced everywhere within the enterprise are treated as the definers of excellence and determiners of satisfaction.

16. Those who incorporate entertainment as part of their product offering will be viewed as more excellent and satisfying than those who don't.

17. Language functions as a lever when it creates consensus of meaning and purposeful, deployable intent.

18. Power is determined by who (a) drives the design of products and processes, (b) selects what behavior gets rewarded, and (c) holds both the authority and capacity to achieve or prevent a specified result.

19. Policies can make values visible, actionable, and personally relevant.

20. When you hear a Vital Lie, ask for the evidence that would prove the statement

21. The role of a leader is to identify when there is potential conflict between strategic direction and operational matters and find a way to create consensus.

22. Leaders of customer-centered excellence are totally clear about the difference between customer-desired and undesired outcomes, Dimensions 1 and 2.

23. If pursuing excellence is the goal, we have confused activity with results.

CHAPTER 7—HOW DID WE GET HERE?

To be a Master of Excellence requires us to take a multidimensional path, which includes our ability to discover and strengthen personal characteristics and behaviors that others will want to emulate. It also includes our leadership of organizational practices that are clearly articulated and routinely executed in a manner that creates a self-sustaining culture of excellence. Our emphasis will be especially on the organizational change part of the path with personal behaviors woven in as support.

We can organize our options for transformation by considering some of the most common themes organizational change and improvement initiatives generally pursue: process, people, performance, principles, procedure, profit, policy, and promotion. On the personal behavior side, we've certainly got to address passion, persistence, and power. I have no idea why these topics all start with "p." It's probably just a fluke. There is overlap across these topics, and we'll do our best to appropriately integrate them into one leadership system. We can simplify our starting point by considering three mutually exclusive themes:

- Process (activities)
- Product (deliverables)
- Outcome (purposes)

No buyer's guide objectively evaluates the unimpeachable facts demonstrating the relative effectiveness of these three core themes and their related methods. What we can say for certain is that there is a very strong pattern that reveals which theme has received the most attention, investment, and promotion over the past several decades. Examine the formal names of change initiatives below. Is the focus most frequent on process, product, or outcome?

- Activity-Based Costing (ABC)
- Agile Enterprise
- Business Process Improvement (BPI)
- Business Reengineering
- Change Management
- Clinical Pathways
- Continuous Process Improvement (CPI)
- Customer Service Enhancement
- Cycle Time Reduction
- ISO 9001
- Just-in-Time (JIT)
- Lean (reduction of waste)
- Operational Excellence
- Productivity Improvement
- Six Sigma
- Supply Chain Management
- Teamwork and Collaboration
- Total Quality Management (TQM)
- Value Stream Design and Mapping
- Quality Management System (QMS)

This is not intended to be a complete list of initiatives aimed at helping us improve excellence and competitive position. It does represent many of the most popular in terms of money invested, books written, meetings held, emails sent, and people trained. The pattern is what is important. The most common theme is process. The assumption is that excellence is dependent on how we carry out work. That seems reasonable and intuitive at first glance. Could first appearances be deceiving?

Process is not a bad thing to work on. But it is often inappropriate, insufficient, self-centered, and misguided to make it the overwhelming center of attention it has become. It is possible to have people working in collaborative teams on waste-free processes that are fast and efficient, making products or delivering services few people want. Consider the value of improving the processes for making, distributing, and maintaining products such as the following around the end of the twentieth century by the referenced leaders at the time:

1. Maps by Rand McNally
2. Dial phones by the Bell companies, plus related products such as pay phones, phone booths, and Yellow Pages directories
3. Incandescent bulbs by GE (whose last US plant was closed in September 2010)
4. Cameras and film by Kodak
5. Boom boxes, cassette tapes, Walkman music players, and CDs by Sony
6. Board games such as Monopoly by Milton Bradley
7. Taxi rides by providers such as Yellow Cab
8. Tons of coal by Peabody Energy (who filed for bankruptcy in 2016)

Do newer, innovative organizations give process the same priority as older, more traditional ones? Nope. Outcomes customers want, best achieved by new products and services, drive innovative start-ups. Many entrepreneurs have been unsatisfied customers of traditional products. They start their new businesses as a superior alternative, believing others share those wants. Their focus is on the *whats* (products) and *whys* (outcomes) of customer priorities. When Steve Jobs famously said his computers were intended "for the rest of us," he was not referring to better production processes, the how. When Google's co-CEOs were asked in 2003 what their strategic objective was, they said it was to enable someone looking for an answer to find it among the first three responses received to a search query. A critical element of the Amazon.com Jeff Bezos built is the ability of prospective customers to see product reviews from other customers who bought and used the product. Customers want products and services, not processes. To paraphrase a famous politician, "It's all about the customer, stupid!"

It is important that we avoid thinking that products and customer outcomes are only the domain of commercial innovators. We should be able to agree that every organization has the common mission of giving its customers what they want. Even organizations that function as regulators, arguably forcing upon some customers things they don't want (for the benefit of many others), can carry out their mission in a manner that is more agreeable than it might otherwise be. One secret to success is to competently balance the competing interests of diverse customers. New organizations tend to be very clear about their mission, the product(s) whose use will best support that mission, and the customers it seeks to satisfy. They don't have the baggage and liabilities of the past. The rest of us do have historical baggage that can take some rethinking and hard work to jettison.

The longer an enterprise has existed, the more likely it is that its past successes or practices may be irrelevant to the current age. That history creates an inertia that keeps an organization doing what it always did. A challenge for the well-established organization is to continually reflect on its current and potentially emerging purpose, as wanted by those it serves.

It is relatively easy to keep doing what we've been doing, tweaking how efficiently we do it. That is what we are organized to do. Why is it that the leaders in such diverse businesses such as Yellow Pages phone directories, mainframe computers, board games such as Monopoly, and transistor radios did not become Google, Apple, Microsoft (with Xbox), or Pandora? Masters of Excellence have the mind and fortitude of an innovator, focused first on why we do what we do. It helps a great deal when we can encourage those around us to be actively conscious about and challenging of those whys. Exactly how to do this purposeful focus will be the next area of application to address.

Let's first examine how we got to the present practices. Why has process improvement become such a big deal? The answer is rooted in history, economics, self-interest, and whom we view as the customer.

We could start as far back as the agricultural age, beginning at least ten thousand years ago. But let's not. It is enough to briefly examine the recent history of process improvement starting with the industrial age of the past 250 years or so. The industrial producers achieved success through process improvements led separately by two main contributors, James Watt and Frank Gilbreth.

James Watt (1736–1819) invented a better steam engine around 1769. Watt redesigned the Newcomen steam engine to function in a rotary fashion, a change from its reciprocating motion, and reduced its energy consumption by 80 percent. This and related new designs greatly enhanced the steam engine's broad applicability to grinding, weaving, pumping, locomotion, and other tasks that became the foundation for the industrial revolution.

The steam engine was not a consumer product. The customers were established enterprises wanting to improve—you guessed it—their production processes. Those first users were mine operators and others who used the engines to pump water. As we know, steam engines were quickly incorporated into other new products such as mills, looms, reapers, tractors, ships, and trains. Watt's leadership and outstanding contribution was to design new products that improved the outcomes his customers wanted: greater production volume, speed, yield, and capacity at less energy consumption. Related measures of production success had been well established during the agricultural age,[55] carried over into the industrial age, and are still relevant today. The products Watt's industrial customers produced were largely commodities such as bales of cloth, bushels of wheat, tons of flour, boards, barrels of oil, rifle barrels, deliveries by rail and ship, and so forth.

The main differentiator among commodity products is the price. The price charged is, of course, heavily dependent on the cost to produce it. Reducing the cost can offer a competitive advantage. Any efforts to improve production will include process improvement, that is, how things get made. Consistency is important. Variation in a manufactured item such as a rifle barrel can cause bullets to jam upon firing. The result can be injury or death to the user of the gun. Processes that reduce variation are a good thing. Inserting steam engines into the production process can reduce the cost, production time, and variation while simultaneously increasing volume produced. It is in the interest of the producer to do this, particularly when the objective is to produce huge volumes of a commodity for a mass market.

Frank Gilbreth (1868–1924) was born into the perfect age to address the human side of industrial

---

[55] We consider each age—agricultural, industrial, or knowledge—to be defined by the predominant kind of work in which most people were engaged for personal economic benefit. Each age comes to a close when the labor force for a given geopolitical group (for our purposes, nations) receives personal income by producing a particular kind of product. We will use specific years when the new age begins simply for ease of memory and demarcation. Each such year is chosen by the author due to a specific set of events occurring then, along with phases of human social development generally accepted by historians and other social scientists. The agricultural age began about 10,000 BC, the industrial age was about 1769, and the knowledge age was about 1969.

production. He and his wife, Lillian Moller, studied the labor production process first in construction and then applied his speed work and "one best way" concepts to a wide range of work practices. That systematic process study became the basis for time and motion analysis of manual work. Gilbreth and others such as Frederick Taylor became the drivers of the new field of scientific management. Frank and Lillian's philosophies were popularized in a book, *Cheaper by the Dozen,* by one of their children.

All this effort to improve processes should feel like common sense. But there is a catch. We're no longer in the mass-market industrial age. Sure, some businesses are still there or act as if their one size really fits all. Is it still relevant when more than 85 percent of the current workforce does not personally produce widgets? Not so much. How does process improvement fit with leadership practices when your business uses 3D manufacturing where lot sizes are tiny and products are customized or customizable to the individual user? It is far more important now to understand how customers and employees think, what they believe, and how they work and live. How does traditional process improvement work out for service and knowledge work where every product is in some way unique to the user? Not so well, but we'll address why and what to do about it when discussing process excellence in volume 2.

The idea that process improvement would be financially beneficial to producers of mass-market commodity products is still and will always be relevant. Such improvement satisfies producer self-interest and falls into the eighth of the 8DX covered in the next chapter. That's a good deal for producers but possibly without customers experiencing any benefit. We might view that situation as a glass half-full.

Another answer to how we developed an obsession with process is that formal quality management philosophies, principles, and tools had a rebirth as strong contributors to better business practices in the late twentieth century. A number of industries in the United States had been encountering serious competition from Japanese businesses by the time NBC broadcast a special white paper program in 1980 called, "If Japan Can, Why Can't We?" The essence of the program was to explain how Japan had evolved from a reputation of producing shoddy products to become the source of high-quality and low-cost products American companies had difficulty matching. The program offered the answer to Japan's success as coming from the management philosophy and statistical analysis practices that Dr. Edwards Deming, an American consultant, had brought to Japanese management and manufacturing employees beginning shortly after the end of World War II. General MacArthur introduced Deming to Japanese business leaders as part of the effort to help Japan rebuild after its destruction.

Deming's key teachings, based on those described by Walter Shewhart in his 1931 book on quality control, included the core idea that products should be reproducible identically, without waste, when the production processes were controlled to behave in statistically predictable ways. This message was in stark contrast to the prevailing practice, prior to Shewhart's 1931 book, that quality management primarily consisted of sorting, identifying defective products, and removing them from the production process. Deming criticized American management for maintaining those reactive practices and blaming workers and equipment for production failures and inconsistencies. Deming's insistence that management itself caused 85 percent of the problems[56] was, predictably but unfortunately, not eagerly embraced by many of the very leaders he was addressing.

An increasing number of major US business leaders began studying Deming's methods of statistical process control during the 1980s. Other experts such as Dr. Joseph Juran (1904–2008) and Philip Crosby (1926–2001) published books and taught additional quality management practices that supported

[56] Lloyd Dobbins, "If Japan Can, Why Can't We?" NBC, June 24, 1980.

the idea that poor quality, broadly understood as "things gone wrong," cost business uncounted but significant expenditures and customer dissatisfaction.

Of the two topics, cost and satisfaction, measuring the former was far more relevant to management and became the strong (if not exclusive) emphasis of quality improvement initiatives for decades. Management has traditionally had incentives for reducing costs. Not so for improving customer satisfaction. Cost accounting also has the advantage of being tied to verifiable facts. Satisfaction has traditionally been seen as related to the soft and squishy perceptions of customers. Which of the two topics get more attention in a master's degree in business administration today?

What Deming and his contemporaries did was develop and deliver a number of teachable, repeatable practices. One of his admonitions was that one must guard against the possibility of building consistent, low-cost products that customers do not really want. The whole point to managing quality was to profitably satisfy customers. Implicit was the requirement to figure out exactly what customers want. But how to do that would be assumed to be the province of marketing, product design engineers, or unnamed others and was not a core teaching of these quality gurus.

The result of quality improvement practices in manufacturing that started in the 1980s led directly to the kinds of initiatives shown in the list at the beginning of this chapter. Deming, Shewhart, and many other quality experts did plenty to preach that the superordinate objective of all involved is to produce the right products error-free so customers are highly satisfied and the enterprise thrives. But improvement efforts defaulted to focus on production versus the experience of consumption. Nonetheless, it is easy to observe that quality management practices in manufacturing industries have significantly improved since 1980. Let's celebrate that.

It is important to recognize the workforce has changed significantly since 1980. The vast majority of the twenty-first century labor force does not personally make manufactured widgets. That's why we call this the postindustrialized era. When a single computer application used on a mobile device is created, it is then simply copied millions of times. It doesn't get built repeatedly on a production line. Getting it right the first time means getting it *right the only time*. Ditto for an email, a policy, a phone answer, and so on.

Thinking about this situation can raise a number of questions:

- Is there consensus on what quality means?
- Do we practice a set of teachable, repeatable practices for creating nonmanufactured, service and knowledge-age products of high quality?
- Do current quality management methods apply equally well at service and not-for-profit organizations?
- Are we measuring the cost of poor quality (things gone wrong, rework, or waste) for knowledge products?
- Do we have written designs that describe what quality is for one-of-a-kind knowledge products?
- Is there an incentive or reward system in place for producing low-cost, high-satisfaction products?

The answer to these questions is usually a big fat no. The American Society for Quality (ASQ) is the largest association of quality management professionals in the world with about 80,000 members in over 140 countries. Based in Milwaukee, Wisconsin, the organization publishes journals and books, offers training, sponsors a number of regional and global conferences, and conducts research. ASQ published results of their Global State of Quality Research in 2013. One finding relevant to our discussion here was that there is no consensus on a definition of quality.[57] A reported 50 percent of respondents said there is no one definition, and an equal number said there needs to be one. Hoyer and Hoyer[58] reviewed definitions by many of the great experts, concluding, "Walter A. Shewhart provides the best definition [in his 1931 book] from both an intellectual and practical perspective." The essence of that definition is that quality "is achieved by translating subjective customer wants and values into measurable, objective characteristics, which are realized with minimum variation."[59] Here we are, over eighty years later, still struggling to get consensus among practitioners.

I agree with the conclusion reached by Hoyer and Hoyer that Shewhart's definition continues to be relevant today, and we would do well to use it. Clearly we cannot have quality if we don't know what customers want. Knowing what customers want and consistently thinking like them is a goal we should aspire to. A research study of executives and quality management practitioners in 2014[60] found that only 48 percent of respondents said customer needs are the drivers of their organizations' quality improvement efforts.

In that same study, executives had a far rosier view of how well their organizations were performing on quality than those closest to the customers or the improvement efforts. The results of this research should not be news. The same issues as the ones just discussed have been observed for years and are likely to change very little until our obsession with process is better balanced with customer focus.[61]

We might summarize the research like this:
1. We don't agree on what quality (or excellence, service, or customer) means.
2. We don't use customer priorities as the target to satisfy.
3. Only 24 percent of employees believe their organizations effectively identify what customers want.
4. The higher in the organization we are, the better we feel about our performance.
5. Yikes! Deming and Shewhart must be turning over in their graves.

My assumption is that, if you are a leader, you know darned well there is a significant gap between where your organization is and where both your customers and colleagues think it should be. And you want to close the gaps.

To get a quick sense for where your own organization stands on the above issues, take a look at how you answered the following items on the C3IQ (Chapter 5):
#3: definitions of customer-desired outcomes are in the strategic plan
#10: agreement on what service means
#11: agreement on who the customer is
#13: a defined/practiced method for uncovering customer priorities exists
#15b, d, and f: customer success is defined and measured

Enough about where we are and how we got there. Let's work on getting where we could be.

---

[57] American Society for Quality, "Discoveries," ASQ Global State of Quality Study, 2013, http://asq.org/global-state-of-quality/reports.aspx.

[58] R. W. Hoyer and Brooke Hoyer, "What is Quality," *Quality Progress* (July 2001), 53–62.

[59] Bob Kennedy, "Finding Harmony," *Quality Progress* (November 2014), 18.

[60] ASQ and Forbes Insights, "The Culture of Quality," September 2014.

[61] See related research findings in the discussion about language as a source of ambiguity in appendices 4 and 5.

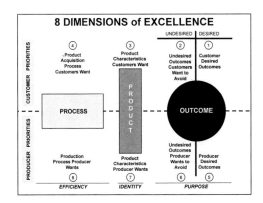

CHAPTER 8—8 DIMENSIONS OF EXCELLENCE (8DX)

Quality and excellence are closely related but do differ. Both treat the customer as the party to be satisfied and the source of the definition for each term. Efforts to improve quality generally define the bull's-eye as better meeting the specified characteristics of a product, as articulated by intended customers. Deviation from the bull's-eye occurs when we observe things gone wrong. Compliance, consistency, and problem-solving have traditionally been strong features of quality management. One way to assure the quality of something is to define and manage the process that enables or prevents us from getting there. Product and process are therefore connected. I strongly contend the definition and improvement of the product's design should occur first. If we are creating a product few want, improving the processes for producing it is a waste of effort.

Excellence means best. It is aspirational, not corrective, in emphasis. It suggests we are elevating the target to a new level. Excellence was a core value of Steve Jobs and continues to be at the top of the core values in the Apple culture. He routinely challenged employees to create "insanely great products." Importantly, customers may not have specified that new level. When excellence is observed and experienced, though, it makes the previously good not good enough. Jim Collins's 2001 book, *Good to Great*, and Tom Peters' 1982 book, *In Search of Excellence*, are consistent with this notion of excellence as distinct from good. One difference between our discussion of excellence in this book versus how Peters and Collins used it is that profitability is not considered here as a qualifying criteria determining whether or not an organization is excellent. It would be a crime to disqualify government, health care, nongovernmental organizations (NGOs), and other not-for-profit enterprises from being termed excellent simply because profit is not their goal or a measure of success. On the other hand, many of the commercial entities we will discuss here as practicing excellence have also been among the top profit performers in their industry. That is not an accident.

The core concepts for building pervasive customer focus were outlined in my first book[62] when I coined the term customer-centered culture (now called C3). We will be building on the principles, tools, and methodology of C3 here.

A company such as Apple epitomizes the culture, leadership, and practices necessary to achieve excellence. There is no evidence Steve Jobs made profitability or volume (at truly enviable levels) principal values to pursue. There is plenty of evidence that every new product, including the overly

---

[62] Robin Lawton, *Creating a Customer-Centered Culture: Leadership in Quality, Innovation and Speed* (Quality Press, Milwaukee, WI, 1993).— Also referred to as the "C3 textbook."

expensive Lisa computer, was an expression of what Jobs defined excellence to be. It was always to be best, whether potential customers were thought able to afford it or not. Apple could have lowered its price to achieve more sales. They would not have reduced its excellence. That same behavior was witnessed when their 5S version of iPhone was introduced into China. The $9 billion in quarterly Chinese sales by the end of that first year (2013) confirms excellence sells. Interestingly sales of the cheaper iPhone 5c did not do so well upon introduction several months later.

Excellence can be defined from either our internal producer perspective (shared by competitors) or by that of our customers (independent of what we think). We will seek to improve the balance between those points of view, but our bias will unabashedly be from the viewpoint of customers. When in the situation where we are the customer, we have 20/20 vision about the truth. The problem is that it is terribly easy when we are on the other side of the phone, the desk, the cash register, the website, and so forth to experience instant amnesia of these customer insights. Self-interest is the explanation for these potentially competing views of reality.

Our goal is to create excellence both as a producer and as our customers would wish it. The 8 Dimensions of Excellence (8DX) framework provides a powerful but easy-to-understand guide for doing that. It is visually described in the graphic below. Since we will be referencing this continuously, please copy the version in appendix 10. It will make a handy bookmark. (For an optional electronic version, see the Mastering Excellence Workbook in the store at http://www.C3Excellence.com.)

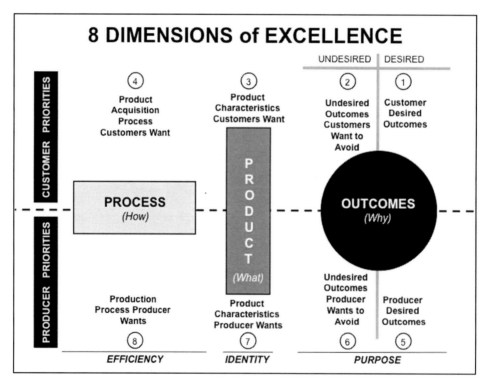

Figure 9—8 Dimensions of Excellence Framework (8DX)

We began in the previous chapter by thinking about leadership improvement practices related to three themes: process, product, and outcome. Consider those topics as synonymous with how, what, and why. The pattern we have observed is that process has received the lion's share of attention for those driving improvement. The 8DX graphic shows there are two dimensions related to process. Consider the change initiatives listed in the last chapter. Do they tend to focus on Dimension 4 or 8? The general consensus is that 8 is the target for improvement, particularly by established enterprises. The version of process that is defined by Dimension 8 has been the primary trend for both profit and not-for-profit organizations for well over a hundred years. That strong pattern means that, as transformation leaders, we can differentiate our established enterprise by addressing Dimension 4 and seeking customer-centered excellence. That is just what our state tax agency client did by working to make the process for acquiring tax refunds much simpler and faster. Cutting 80 percent of that cycle time caused them to jump from a rank of twenty-fifth of fifty states to number one, winning high taxpayer satisfaction.

One of the reasons Amazon.com has become so successful is leadership's obsession with Dimension 4, the customer's acquisition process. A mark of excellence is when you are considered the best on at least one of the Dimensions. Even better is when that excellence is tied to one or more of Dimensions 1 through 4. Such is the case for Amazon, which makes it very easy to determine which of a number of competing products has been most satisfying for users, makes the buying process simple, and makes the delivery process predictable and fast. The company started doing this with products that cost only a few dollars. It has shown what is possible, delivering outstanding customer-centered performance that threatens all retailers who continue the old business model.

New enterprises such as Apple, Google, Amazon, Uber, and Lyft created an immediate leadership position by putting a special emphasis on Dimension 4: how easily and quickly customers can acquire and use the desired product. For Uber and Lyft, the product is a ride. No matter which dimension we work on, we will always do better by starting with Dimension 1, making it the context for all transformation. Mission-driven entities (the Red Cross, Goodwill, or AARP) tend to naturally be oriented to improving Dimension 1. One reason may be that the entity's mission is not so clouded by its connection to money.

We might compare the 8DX framework to economic supply-and-demand thinking. Dimensions 1 through 4 represent issues related to customer demand. Dimensions 5 through 8 are related to supply matters the producer cares about. The framework is a succinct but powerful way to identify the critical few areas we must pursue to achieve excellence. If we focus on all eight Dimensions, excellence will be broadly enhanced. If we improve a few, excellence will be limited. Dimensions 1 through 4 address the customer experience, sometimes referred to as voice of the customer (VOC). These are drivers of satisfaction and include leading indicators of organizational success.

Notice the labeling at the bottom of the 8DX framework: efficiency, identity, and purpose. The numbering of the dimensions shows that we start our focus on the right and then work backward. This assures we are starting with the end in mind. Our leadership effectiveness is greatly enhanced when we can unambiguously define the purpose of our organization in terms of results. Those results are from two distinct perspectives: why our customers want to work with us (Dimensions 1 and 2) and why we exist as an entity (Dimensions 5 and 6). The active word here is "why." Defining our purpose from both points of view enables us to develop measures of success and numerical goals for improvement. We tend to be much more effective in doing this for producer priorities than for customer priorities. We need only look at guidance documents such as the organization's strategic plan, core policies, and KPIs to see how well each of the outcome-related dimensions are currently addressed. It is very common to see Dimension 5 as well-defined, measured, and attached to numerical goals while Dimension 1 is not.

The outcomes we and our customers want are achieved by customers using the products we create. Products refer to what we give others. Our organization's identity is intimately linked to those products. The stronger the link, the stronger our brand. When we think of the Internal Revenue Service, some of their products that immediately come to mind are tax forms, booklets, and refund checks. Similarly, when we hear a reference to the iPhone or iTunes, we immediately think of Apple. Appendectomies and liver transplants could make us think of Mayo Clinic. Bachelor of science degrees in engineering can bring MIT to mind. We can see with these examples that a product is a deliverable that may or may not be directly exchanged for money. When an entity is not the only one we think of when its core products are mentioned, it has a weak brand and may be viewed as having a commodity product. A Lasik procedure is a specific surgical laser eye procedure with a differentiated brand. Ditto for Midas Muffler, which, incidentally, does not produce mufflers. They create muffler repairs. Furthermore, an organization's product could be funded or purchased by parties other than the final end user of it.

An important point is that the relationship between a product and money can be a major cause of confusion. Although iTunes is a product, it is not sold. It is a sort of modern jukebox that contains songs, movies, and other publications that are sold or rented. Many business analysts were confused about the value of iTunes when Apple first made it available. Without iTunes, there was no way to access songs. A similar confusion existed among business investment professionals when Google started up. Their fundamental question: how will Google make money if its answers are free? Implicit in that question was the conclusion that Google had no viable business model and the prudent investor should put his or her money into something that had obvious monetary value. Oops. Wrong call.

As a Master of Excellence, we have to be vigilant to prevent confusing value with money. A product may have far greater value than is evident by the money exchanged for it. There are far more revenue-free products produced by an organization (both in terms of kind and volume) than products that are funded or sold.[63] We'll explore this in some depth.

What might not be obvious at first glance in the 8DX framework is that products are not just created for customers external to our organization. In fact, every externally used product is dependent on many other products that have been produced entirely for use by others within our organization. One of our leadership roles is to *assure clear alignment between a product produced for external consumption and the related products that are designed, produced, delivered, and used internally.* For example, a recipe is a product used by cooks within the bakery to produce chocolate-chip cookies purchased by shoppers. A recipe that is incomplete, inaccessible, complex, or ambiguous can result in inconsistent or poor-quality cookies. We improve cookie excellence by assuring recipe excellence. The highly effective Master of Excellence makes totally clear this relationship among internally consumed products, externally used products, and how they all contribute to create desired outcomes wanted by both end user customers and the enterprise.

Every product can be deemed of high quality when it simultaneously meets the expectations of customers and its producer. Those expectations should be articulated and measured in Dimensions 3 and 7, respectively. Leaders creating a customer-centered culture will assure there is a well-defined method for uncovering, translating, and delivering what customers want. Most organizations have little or no such method articulated and consistently practiced for all products produced by the organization. The absence of such a methodology leads to dangerous assumptions about what customers want. On the other hand, we may do a comparatively good job defining the product characteristics wanted by the

---

[63] This has significant implications for how we measure productivity, at least at the national level. Conventional measures are dependent on having a dollar value of the thing produced, divided by the dollar cost to produce it. When a product has no direct dollar value because it is not purchased, does that mean the labor invested to produce it has no value? The short answer is no. A free "app" that costs nothing but whose use saves you money on something else clearly has value. The challenge is to be more inclusive in how we measure the value of products, addressed in appendix 6.

producer, at least in terms of how our product compares with a competitor's. But is it possible to have a product that compares favorably with its competitors but still dissatisfies customers? Maybe comparing ourselves to other producers (sometimes considered benchmarking) is not the end-all to determining how good we are.

Internally used products tend to get much less attention regarding their design and desired characteristics. For example, we may have measures for priority characteristics of the cookie but little or none on the simplicity, understandability, and accessibility of the recipe. We may periodically audit cookie quality. Do we audit the quality of recipes, specifications, designs, and similar products? When you think something is well-defined, see if objective measures of success exist and are being used to drive excellence. Three of the top-five characteristics customers want for virtually any product generally fall into categories we could label as ease-of-use, timeliness, and certainty. This will be fully explored when we discuss VOC in volume 2.

Only when we are clear about the outcomes and products we are in business to create are we ready to tackle efficiency and process, how we create products. The key word here is "how." As we discussed in Chapter 7, we often charge off to map and improve processes before making sure the intended outcomes and customer-desired product characteristics are defined and measured. The Master of Excellence will avoid that common practice of working on how before thoroughly addressing why and what. Having a wonderfully efficient, inexpensive, and error-free process that creates products customers don't want is a waste of resources. But the mirage of success is beguiling.

The Master of Excellence will use the 8DX framework as a guide for asking questions of his or her people and for providing him or her with succinct, unambiguous, easily applied answers. All enterprise managers should be able to provide the definitions, measures, and current numerical performance related to each of the 8 Dimensions. Their current ability to do that is likely to be highly limited. Our challenge is to dramatically improve that situation. Knowing the kinds of content that go into each Dimension is a step toward helping them do that.

The numbering within the 8DX framework is intentional. Our long-term enterprise viability is most dependent on success in Dimension 1, and in Dimension 8 it is the least. Yet short-term success can be achieved quickly in Dimension 8, creating the illusion of sustainability. The 8DX is as relevant in not-for-profit as in for-profit environments, performing well across diverse cultures. The synopsis here describes each dimension with a few illustrative examples:

1. **Customer-desired outcomes:** These are their ultimate hopes and their purpose for coming to us, such as joy, security, personal time, belonging, good health, wealth, certainty, recognition, fulfillment, and respect. How well (and quickly) they get those results through us reveals our effectiveness.

2. **Undesired outcomes customers want to avoid or eliminate:** This includes loss, death, impoverishment, fear, discomfort, waste (time, money, or effort), frustration, sickness, reduced status, and a host of other unwanted conditions. Guard against the assumption that the reduction of an undesired outcome improves satisfaction; it merely reduces dissatisfaction. The absence of poverty is not necessarily wealth.

3. **Product and service characteristics customers want:** Ease-of-use, accessibility, low cost of ownership, durability, simplicity, and usefulness are the kinds of product characteristics generally wanted. Product refers to a specific deliverable or object that we can give to others, count, and make plural with an "s." All work can be defined as products. All customers are identified by the product(s) they receive.

4. **Product-acquisition process customers want:** This is timely arrival of product requested, no wait or cue time, or ease of acquisition. The product is quickly functional. The customer's priorities for and experience of process should be given at least as much attention as Dimension 8.

5. **Producer-desired outcomes:** This includes leadership, growth, financial strength, market share, mission fulfillment, and brand dominance.

6. **Undesired outcomes producers want to avoid or eliminate**: This includes waste, high turnover, financial loss, customer defection, instability, and conflict.

7. **Product characteristics producers want:** This includes easy to build, low cost to produce, low variability, no maintenance or warranty costs, easy to distribute, and consistent with sustainability.

8. **Process characteristics producers want:** This includes process consistency, simplicity, low variation, high productivity and efficiency, comfortable lead times, high yield, and capacity that matches demand. This is where most improvement efforts focus. A lean, waste-free process for the producer is not necessarily experienced that way by customers.

Values and Initiatives Are Fellow Travelers

Our world is constantly changing. Hitching our wagon to those things that are most stable or constant over time provides stability and predictability. That is an excellent foundation for embarking on innovation and radical change aimed at the constants. Of all of the dimensions, Dimension 1 is most stable over time. The customer's superordinate, ultimate desired outcomes change little, if at all. Is there a time when a customer will not want good health, economic well-being, and so on? We should note that a producer's outcomes, when shared with any of the customer's desired outcomes, will be more constant over time than when those outcomes diverge. On the other hand, some of a producer's strategic desired outcomes, Dimensions 5 and 6, may very well change in priority, perhaps even yearly.

A commercial enterprise might seek differing priorities such as improved profits one year, improved market share another, increased share price another time, or greater sales volume. These are Dimension 5 priorities. You'll notice that Dimension 1 outcomes wanted by customers in the hospitality, computer repair, health-care, financial-services, and government cases we will soon discuss are unlikely to change over time. The specifics related to all the other dimensions, 2 through 8, do change continuously. Knowing that the customer's desired outcome does not change over time can be a powerful lever for driving innovation and predicting the desirability of new products. The product that better achieves a customer's desired outcome has a leg up on becoming a leader.

This is as good a time as any to offer both an example and a prediction of how Dimension 1 can work. A desired outcome for the recording and playback device produced by the Gramophone Company in the late nineteenth century was to enable listeners to "feel like I'm there." That outcome has not changed over the past 150 years, but the products for achieving it has. The companies dominant in the production of products such as the Victrola, phonograph, stereo, radio, boom box, and Walkman were each supplanted by products from other companies that better achieved the unchanging desired outcome regarding musical and recorded programs. Arguably, the iPod was the latest to dominate that field upon introduction in 2001. When iTunes was introduced in 2003, it immediately dominated the retail music industry, selling a million songs in its first week. Walmart had previously been US king in that field.

Sound is only one sense to invoke when attempting to re-create the feeling-like-I'm-there outcome. The first feature film to integrate vision and sound was *The Jazz Singer* in 1927. That same year, Harry

Warner, CEO of Warner Brothers Pictures, responded with, "Who the hell wants to hear actors talk?"[64] That quote illustrates the normal tendency of a leader to be blindsided by a better or more complete solution to satisfying a priority customer-desired outcome.

Apple had, by 2016, done a superb job of advancing the successive approximation of feeling-like-I'm there with new products such as the iPhone and the huge library of apps related to sound and video reproduction. The threat to meet in 2016 was the virtual reality or augmented reality (VR/AR) headsets introduced to a general user audience by Oculus Rift in 2014.[65]

The addition of the three-dimensional experience and 360-degree view of images is simply a predictable, next logical step in satisfying an unchanging customer-desired outcome. If Apple continues its innovation track, we can predict it will incorporate some form of wireless, lightweight, supremely easy to use VR/AR headset integrated with its iPhone and iTunes by the end of 2018. Or it may fall onto the garbage heap of past leaders. New competitors such as Facebook's Oculus Rift, Microsoft's Hololens, HTC's Vive, Samsung's Gear, and Google's Magic Leap were all just a few heavyweights aiming at the same customer-desired outcome in 2016. It's not a fantasy to expect evolution into a more complete version of sight-and-sound immersion. Let's consider a prediction for what comes after that.

We've seen how the migration from monaural sound to stereo to surround to 3-D sound, plus two-dimensional vision to 3-D immersive vision, describes an evolving path of innovation. It is not a stretch to predict that the next iteration will involve the sense of smell. Think of how exciting it would be to record smells of food that could be played back from cooking programs on your iPhone. The range of smell applications is huge. Just the ability to use smell to augment learning and memory could offer a huge advance in education. To say nothing about your ability to record with your phone the sensation of sailing and smell of the ocean you experienced during your Caribbean vacation so you can play it back for friends and family. Want something more mundane? Consider the traffic cop recording that margarita on your breath or the medical lab testing various bodily fluids remotely by capturing their smell.

Achieving and sustaining constancy of purpose and excellence are dependent on our understanding of Dimension 1, the customer's desired outcome. Doing that well prepares us to work backward through the other seven dimensions of excellence, connecting and integrating all the elements.

Our change and transformation initiatives, in addition to KPIs, often reflect our core values, operationalizing them. If we hold efficiency as a high value, we are likely to have established at least one initiative to remove cost and waste, along with measures to gauge improvement. We connected our core values with current measures with Leader's Action 6 and 7. What we did not do then is to determine how our initiatives and measures are aligned with the eight dimensions. That is, to what degree do we have balance in emphasis on all of the dimensions? We'll answer that in the next Leader's Action. A KPI is a numerical measure of success tied to a numerical improvement goal. A measure without a goal is meaningless and a cause of ambiguity concerning our intent. Activities, statements of intent, and binary yes/no checks are not acceptable KPI measures. KPIs will generally be structured in any of the following ways:

1. **The number of occurrences during a period.** This is often a count reflecting volume or frequency. Examples include the number of new customers acquired, the number of requests

---

[64] When told by his brother, Sam Warner, CEO, that the studio was working to develop talking films.

[65] The main difference to consider between VR and AR is that VR blocks out the real world. AR enables the user to be aware of the real world while experiencing the virtual one. The VR experience prompts you to jump out of the way of the oncoming virtual train.

made, the number of deliveries, the number of products produced, or the number of customer complaints.

2. **The relationship of two variables.** This ratio is often stated as a percentage or average. Examples include percentage of customers referring others to you, percentage of customers defecting, percentage of products returned, percentage of deliveries made by promised date, average minutes to find the answer on the website, percentage profit (income over expense), or percentage yield (number of cases work when was done right the first time compared with all work done).

3. **The monetary value of something occurring during a period.** Examples include the dollar value of products sold, the dollar unit cost per product produced, the dollar cost of rework, or the dollar cost of delays imposed on customers.

Until we achieve mastery over all the C3 concepts, it is easy to confuse outcomes, topics, and measures. The following table gives examples of common topics, sometimes referred to as measures (which they are not). We show examples of measures that could be used and numerical improvement goals we might attach to them.

Examples of Outcome Topics (not measures)	Sample Measures	Sample Goals
1. Growth in customer acquisition	Number of first-time buying customers last month	Greater than or equal to 20
2. Fast response to customers	Number of minutes from customer initiation of request to complete answer received	Less than 2 minutes • Average for all requests per month • For all requests
3. Reduction in customer complaints	Number of complaints	10 percent reduction from previous month
4. Cost reduction to produce	Dollar cost per unit produced	5 percent reduction from prior quarter
5. Quality improvement	Number of hours of rework Dollar cost of rework Percent done right first time Dollar warranty costs incurred	Less than two hours of rework per month Less than $100 rework cost Greater than or equal to 99 percent right the first time Less than 0.001 percent of sales per month
6. Customer satisfaction	Percent of five-star ratings (of five) Percent of new customers due to referrals	Greater than or equal to 90 percent of ratings are five stars (of five) Greater than 5 percent of new customers due to referrals

Figure 10—Translating Outcomes into Measures

Leader's Action 9: Connect Initiatives and Measures with the 8 Dimensions
(See Appendix 1)

Leader's Action 9a: Create Missing Measures
(See Appendix 1)

Executive Summary: 8 Dimensions

1. Initiatives directing change, improvement, productivity, quality, excellence, and related topics have historically focused on how we do work, Dimension 8. It is possible to improve internal processes without customers experiencing any benefit.

2. What we measure is what we value, despite what we may tell ourselves.

3. If excellence is said to be an enterprise value, we will have published numerical goals to achieve within a defined period. Based on Leader's Actions 7 and 9, how well are our measures aligned with what we value?

4. A balanced scorecard can only be considered balanced if all 8 Dimensions are well measured.

5. The virtues of understanding, defining, and measuring Dimension 1 are many:

   - It is the only one of the eight that is stable over time.

   - It is a strong driver for both excellence and innovation.

   - The absence of Dimension 1 definition makes it very likely there will be no related measures of success or goals.

   - It is positive and aspirational, not focused on deficiencies.

   - It propels strategic direction and invites innovation.

   - It infuses all other dimensions and enterprise initiatives with customer focus.

   - It supports the development of leading indicators.

   - It provides a durable context and broad scope for directing quality improvement initiatives that address Dimensions 3, 7, and 8 via standards (for example, ISO 9001) and methods (for example, Lean, Six Sigma, balanced scorecards, continuous improvement, and so on).

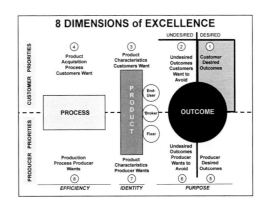

CHAPTER 9—CUSTOMER-DESIRED OUTCOMES

Dimension 1 is defined by the outcomes or results our customers want to achieve when they come to us. Think of their desired outcomes as the ultimate purpose they have in mind. These are often not verbalized, yet they expect us to know what their outcomes are. And we ought to. Verbalized or not, we're going to be held responsible for achieving them. Any failure in our doing so should be assumed to degrade the customer's experience and give competitors a potential advantage. Let's use the insight and expertise we already have as customers to consider the outcomes we personally desire when working with organizations in each of the following industries: hospitality, field service, health care, financial service, or government.

The purpose for providing industry-specific examples is to illustrate how broadly you can apply the ideas and methods we cover. Every example should offer insights that will be personally relevant for you, no matter your specific circumstances. The various examples are intended to give a three-dimensional picture of what outcomes are, how they can be easily confused without the necessary definitional rigor, and what the ramifications of performing well or not can be. The Leader's Actions toward the end of each case are intended to be quick, easy, and personally relevant. They will provide insights you would not otherwise obtain.

CASE 1: SLEEPY DEFINITION OF SUCCESS

We've all had many occasions to travel for work or business. Think of your own experience staying overnight in a hotel prior to a business meeting the next morning. What is the most important outcome, the ultimate result you hope to achieve from that overnight stay? Our research over thirty years has found the absolutely most important priority business travelers have from that stay is a good night's sleep. When asked what matters most, this priority is named within seconds.[66] It doesn't require any thought. No matter what else happens, our customer experience is less than satisfactory if we don't sleep well. This should not be a breakthrough revelation. Remember, this refers to Dimension 1, a customer-desired outcome that does not change. So is this what hotels are working to improve? Maybe, but the evidence suggests otherwise.

You've undoubtedly noticed that the hospitality industry is obsessed with determining how satisfied we are with our stay. In North America, they assess our satisfaction primarily through surveys. You will notice that there is a survey in virtually any room in which you've stayed. Or they send an email after our

---

[66] An example of the actual question asked is, "A satisfying overnight stay is one that results in _____?"

stay, asking for our feedback. Take a close look at the survey questions asked by one of the United States' largest privately held international hotel chains, shown below. Do you see the question on a good night's sleep?

ACTUAL CUSTOMER SURVEY

	Yes	No
1. If in the area again, would you be willing to return to this hotel?		

2. How would you rate our staff spirit:	Poor	Average	Excellent
a. Front desk receptionist			
b. Housekeeping staff			
c. Telephone operators			
d. Room service servers			
e. Restaurant servers			
f. Lounge servers			
g. Recreation staff			

3. How would you rate our:
a. Front desk services			
b. Check-in efficiency			
c. Check-out efficiency			
d. Telephone services			

4. How would rate our guest room:
a. Cleanliness of bedroom			
b. Condition of bedroom			
c. Cleanliness of bathroom			
d. Condition of bathroom			

5. How would you rate the working condition of the:
a. Television			
b. Heating/air conditioning			
c. Internet access			
d. Water temperature/pressure			
e. Lighting-bedroom			
f. Lighting-bathroom			

6. If you used any of the following, how would you rate our:
a. Breakfast service			
b. Lunch service			
c. Dinner service			
d. Lounge service			
e. Room service			

7. How many times have you been to this hotel in the last 12 months?
8. How many times have you stayed at a different hotel brand in the past 12 months?
9. How did you hear about us? (Word of mouth, advertising, travel agent, corporate policy, other)

10. What is the purpose of your trip? (Business, pleasure, convention)
11. How likely are you to recommend this hotel to others?

Figure 11—Actual Hotel Customer Survey

That's right. There is no question about sleep! Is there any question on the list that offers the possibility of identifying a more important outcome than sleep? The consensus among thousands of respondents is no! Please consider that all of our discussion about hotels here can just as easily be applied to hospitals and other industries. How difficult would it be to ask any of the following questions:

- How many hours did you sleep last night?

- How many hours had you hoped to sleep?
- How many hours a night do you sleep at home, on average?
- If you were interrupted in your sleep, which of the following was a cause? (Provide options along with an "other" option to fill in.)

Those are low-tech questions, easily asked and easy to record for analysis and potential action. They could be on the survey or asked at checkout. For those with a technology bent at the time this book was published, we might ask guests at check-in if they wear an iWatch, Fitbit, or comparable high-tech wristband that monitors sleep. If yes, we could ask them to report not just the hours slept but also the number of hours spent in deepest sleep. Now we'll get both quantity and quality of sleep if we retrieve that information at checkout or on a written survey. If the guest doesn't wear such a sleep tracking device, could we loan one (perhaps to every tenth customer to keep costs down but still get excellent data)? When was the last time such an offer was made to you at check-in? Could it be a differentiator for the hotel? Could this also be relevant for hospitals and their patients?

One prediction I feel very confident making is that personal data collected by wearable devices will soon begin augmenting and then replacing satisfaction surveys such as what hotels currently use. Such devices are quite capable of capturing biometric, motion, video, audio, environmental, and related data at the real-time personal level. Some industry analysts use the term "big data" to include the capture of customer behavior through various kinds of observation. This practice will grow and become more intensive, with many in a customer role allowing or welcoming that to occur (either by tacit or active approval). In general, it is essential to also capture perception data such as what surveys collect when it is augmented by objective data and vice versa. Capturing subjective data without objective validation gives us incomplete understanding of an issue. It is also a mistake to collect objective customer data and then impose meaning on it without interaction with the customer that can provide insights that are otherwise elusive.

Considering just the simple hotel survey at it stands today, the first thing on our minds might be to wonder why no sleep question is asked. There are several possible reasons frequently suggested:

1. They've already designed the hotel and your room to give you a terrific sleep and are confident you are getting it.

2. Hotel management doesn't care and doesn't have a clue about customers' priorities.

3. Getting a good night sleep is not within their control, so there is no point in asking about it.

4. The survey questions are standardized by an independent research company and applied across all hotels for comparison purposes to rank relative customer experience.

5. There is an unspoken policy to avoid asking questions related to satisfaction if the asking could raise customer expectations or lead to assumed performance commitments.

6. It is too hard to get meaningful information.

We will examine each answer regarding hotels, but there is a very good chance the discussion will apply equally to many other enterprises. See how many of the issues are relevant to your own organization's key product, its customers, their desired outcomes, and internal organization behavior. It is important to recognize that the leadership, management, and employees are likely to have many years of experience and deeply care about their customers, and many are highly educated. They are smart people. But they are probably not looking at things from the customer's perspective as we are doing here.

First, it is possible everything related to a good night's sleep has been designed into your room and environs. The check-in and checkout processes referenced in the survey questions above have also likely been designed with certain characteristics in mind. Why ask about those and not about sleep? To assume we've slept well would seem the height of arrogance.

Second, I have found no evidence that the criteria to become a manager of either a specific hotel or the entire chain includes being either uncaring or stupid. On the contrary, managers generally point to many things they do to make guests happy. One piece of evidence offered is the satisfaction policy of a one-night refund if the guest is not satisfied. That policy is actually aimed at Dimension 2, intending to minimize an undesired outcome. It is more appropriate to call it a dissatisfaction policy. The policy may describe the intent and behavior of the business when it learns a customer is unhappy. This is not a bad thing to do but is insufficient (at the least) and possibly misguided to boot. Where is the policy that describes what the enterprise will do to proactively assure the customer is happy, particularly with their top priorities? In fact, both hotels and hospitals have a wealth of policies covering all manner of issues, but few have a sleep policy. A couple of chapters could easily be written on this topic. Suffice it to say, sleep complaints and the relationship of insomnia to general health, work performance, and safety have been heavily researched. The Master of Excellence will aggressively seek to close the gap between what we know and what we are doing about it.

A proactive way to address satisfaction can include finding out before the customer arrives what the desired outcome is for the stay. Both the timing and manner of inquiry are important. Customers are routinely asked for credit-card information, a moderately invasive question they tolerate. With care, the hotel could find out the purpose for the stay and the intended outcomes. Let's be clear that a stay on the wedding night may not have sleep at the top of the outcome priorities. The reserving party may not tell either. Balancing inquiry and privacy is important and learnable. When the reservations lady at the Marriott in Kauai asked me if there were a special occasion related to my reservation, I told her it was to celebrate the honeymoon with my new bride. She offered congratulations and said they would work on getting us a nice view of the ocean. The surprise awaiting us in the room was the general manager's congratulatory personal note with a complementary bottle of champagne, chilling in an ice bucket. That really impressed us. The view was great too. The feather-free room was prepared as my account profile had requested. All of these thoughtful touches helped immediately begin inducing a sense of relaxation, mitigating the stresses of travel to get there from halfway around the world. One thing we should understand is that different kinds of customers can rank desired outcomes differently. So maybe hotel personnel do care but just don't routinely think about customer-desired outcomes.

Third, the absence of a sleep question in the survey is based on the assumption the hotel really can't control sleep. If we believe that assumption is true, what improvement action will we take? None! We would be absolved of any responsibility to even give it a second thought. We would assume it will be a waste of time and effort to try. A look at the evidence could offer some insight into the validity of the assumption. It is well-established by sleep experts and hotel customers alike that stimulating any of our five senses—sound, sight, smell, taste, and touch—could affect sleep quality. Does the hotel have any control over these sources of stimulation? Let me share a few observations.

Perhaps we've all had similar experiences with hotel rooms. All of mine have had windows. All my windows have had some kind of blinds or curtains. The usual curtains slide left or right, coming together in the middle to close. Most curtains are difficult to close fully. Maybe they were just fine when first installed, but then they got washed once. Just like some of my T-shirts, they shrank and don't quite come together any more. That might not be a problem by itself, but all my windows seem to face east. This becomes clear when the sun comes up, slides through that crack in the curtains, and lands right on my pillow. The frequency with which this has happened leads me to conclude that the folks who design the hotel rooms are descendants of those who designed Stonehenge. You couldn't do it by chance. If ever there were proof the hotels have control over a good night's sleep, this is it. The leaders of the Crown Plaza hotels decided to act on this insight and routinely started providing large spring clips (like those used to close bags of potato chips) so customers could clip the curtains together. They also provided foam earplugs, lavender linen spray for relaxation, and a CD containing a guided progressive relaxation tutorial ending with a white noise audio loop. Their questions on sleep satisfaction got high marks. Probably just a fluke.

We could run through the other sleep prevention conditions such as banging doors, grit or sticky stuff that adheres to your feet on the way to the middle-of-night bathroom visit, and tap water that smells and tastes unlike the bottled water thoughtfully offered in the room as an expensive alternative. It's not that these experiences are from cheap motel dives. Your experience probably includes similar instances, and they aren't that rare as to excuse them. You know darn well the hotel has control over them all. It probably won't add much to tell you about the time I heard singing around bedtime and, after fruitlessly trying to find the source, called the front desk. The clerk immediately gave the explanation. An opera company was in town, and most of its members were staying in this hotel. It turns out the hotel had randomly placed them in rooms around the facility. Not, mind you, in one wing or floor of the hotel. The clerk informed me I was not the only caller who wasn't an enthusiastic opera fan at bedtime. But the situation was something they claimed they could not control. Who assigned the customers to their rooms? Wasn't that hotel staff?

The statement, "We can't control that," should always be considered a Vital Lie until proven otherwise. A Vital Lie is a constraining assumption, self-deception, justification, denial, rationalization, myth, or other excuse for not changing. Vital Lies are beliefs that factual evidence does not support. Achieving excellence demands that we challenge and work to eliminate Vital Lies. They stifle innovation and pursuit of the possible while sustaining the status quo. As a Master of Excellence hearing this statement from anyone in your organization, treat it as the unverified assumption it is. Ask for the evidence that would prove the statement true. If there is none, you have just uncovered your first instance of identifying the most frequent of all Vital Lies.[67]

The fourth explanation for excluding sleep questions from the hotel's satisfaction survey has some basis to it. There are research outfits that make a business of selling data comparing how customers rate competitors. If the purpose is to determine how well one does in satisfying those customers and what priorities to improve, it helps to be asking the right questions, not just the same questions. When no hotels ask about how well customers slept, the things that did get asked will be assumed to be the drivers of a satisfying experience.

The fifth explanation assumes the organization is attempting to limit its risk. Not asking about sleep avoids making an implicit promise that a good sleep will be assured. To believe the customer might have that expectation only if we ask about it is, when you think about it, pretty absurd. Who are we kidding?

The sixth explanation offers a self-fulfilling prophecy. What we really do by failing to ask customers about

---

[67] The playwright Henrik Ibsen coined the term "Vital Lies." He used it in reference to the beliefs we hold dear that are not subjected to close enough scrutiny to reveal the truth. See appendix 3 for illustrations and in-depth discussion of ten common Vital Lies.

their highest priorities is invoke what we could call a "don't ask, don't tell" policy. That is, when we don't ask, they don't tell us. But don't think they aren't going to hold us accountable and tell many others how well we performed.

Once upon a time,[68] the White House commissioned a study on customer satisfaction. One finding was that 96 percent of dissatisfied customers would not tell anyone about the dissatisfaction. But the few exceptions would each tell about twenty-eight others. A satisfied customer told ten to sixteen others. Subsequent research such as the 2013 Customer Rage Study[69] tells a similar and worsening story, but with a twist. Back in the 1970s, there was no Amazon, Angie's List, Facebook, Twitter, travel sites, or other online place where millions of potential prospects could find out about one person's experience with a product or service. The anger expressed by dissatisfied customers who report and fail to get an agreeable response is rising. The Internet can function to significantly leverage the power of a single customer.

The point here is that we can give ourselves all kinds of reasons why not to ask customers about what they want or how satisfied they are with what they got. Assume their message will and is getting out to uncounted others. We should seek to be the first to know and the first to act, preferably for prevention and product/service design. Asking for and understanding desired outcomes is the critical first step for doing so.

It's one thing for hotels to mistakenly or purposefully avoid asking questions about their customers' desired outcomes. What can be a shocking revelation is to discover that our own organization, in a totally different industry, has the same blind spot. A computer company discovered that the most important outcome for one of its major client companies was not percentage of uptime, a traditional industry metric. It was that the payroll checks they produced for their customers were deposited on-time.

Similarly a truck builder had always thought its customers wanted to maximize the percentage (or hours per day) of time trucks were available to use. This was often specified in purchase agreements. But we discovered a higher outcome priority was tonnage moved per day, not similarly specified. Supervisors at the customer's sites received production bonuses based on that number. Is it possible for the truck to be available but not haul the desired tonnage? You bet, leading the truck producer to believe they are satisfying the customers when the reverse may be true, and the causes for low production are unknown and unmet.

A company decided that answering the phone by the second ring was a priority goal to improve customer satisfaction. Each department displayed a chart on the wall showing the ring frequency statistics. Recognition was awarded each month to the department(s) with lowest average number of rings before pickup. Response time steadily declined, and everybody felt pretty good about his or her efforts. But general satisfaction survey results regarding response time did not improve. On close inspection, it was discovered that phones were being quickly picked up and callers were immediately put on hold. Answering the phone was confused with answering the customer. It turned out that answering the phone by the second ring was not as important as providing an understandable, accurate, and complete phone answer on the customer's first attempt.

---

[68] The original study for the White House by Technical Assistance Research Programs is out of print. However, the US Consumer Information Center in Pueblo, Colorado published a summary of the 1974–1979 study and the 1984–1986 studies for the US Office of Consumer Affairs called "Increasing Customer Satisfaction" in 1986. Contact jgoodman@tarp.com for more findings and the rest of the story.

[69] Marc Grainer and David Beinhacker, "Customer Rage," *Modern DC Business* (April 2012).

These examples may sound like common sense. They are. But only if we look at the business as an outsider and from the customer's perspective. With any new idea, there is a difference between feeling like we understand it and being able to apply it. Let's summarize the key points from case 1 and excellence-driving actions to take.

Executive Summary: Case 1

1. A good night's sleep is the customer's desired outcome (Dimension 1) for business travelers. It is his or her most important priority and can be easily identified. But nothing about it may be asked:

   - When requesting the room (before product delivery);
   - After experiencing the room (on the survey after product delivery);
   - In a manner that enables measuring the quality of the outcome experienced;
   - To identify obstacles to achieving satisfaction;
   - To prioritize individual element(s) of the experience; or
   - That could drive excellence, innovation, or differentiation.

2. Customers can tell us their most important priority if we ask the right question(s). But they won't if we don't.

3. Dimension 1 is the only one of the eight that does not change over time. When will a hotel business customer not want a good night's sleep?

4. Surveys often ask questions that fail to address customers' top priorities, potentially leading to Vital Lie 8.

5. If we don't ask about and don't know what the customer-desired outcomes are, we will likely work on topics of less importance. We might not be seeking excellence on what customers care most about.

6. It is tempting to give excuses for not asking customers the right questions at the right time, such as invoking Vital Lies 7 and 8.

7. We may be recognizing/rewarding the wrong behaviors to achieve optimum positive impact on customer experience.

8. Believing we cannot control something a customer experiences is likely to be Vital Lie 1 and can become a self-fulfilling prophecy.

9. Case 1 insights show opportunity to improve your C3IQ scores for these items: 3, 13a, 14, 15b and d, and 18.

Leader's Action 10: Capturing Customer-Desired Outcomes
(See Appendix 1)

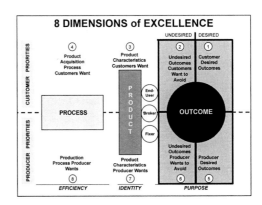

CHAPTER 10—REVEAL AND REDUCE MISSION CONFUSION

Many of us who work in a commercial business environment have likely heard an enterprise leader remind his or her followers, "We are here to make money." In government, a similar statement may be "do more with less." If those were really true, operating a profitable, if illegal, drug cartel would qualify as mission fulfillment. Likewise, being more bureaucratic with fewer resources would qualify only as a poor way to run a government agency. As discussed earlier, making money or being more frugal do not qualify as missions or purposes of an organization. There are many other instances where our stated mission is more off the mark than we may have realized. The following cases offer real examples.

CASE 2: WHEN LESS IS MORE SUCCESS

The field service division president of a major computer manufacturer asked me to set up a new initiative focused on improving quality, productivity, and customer satisfaction. They already had a formal quality assurance function in place that carried out audits and inspections to assure compliance with various specifications and procedures. That functional group was widely viewed as a kind of police officer. A visit from a QA staffer was not viewed as a happy day. The president wanted a more participative, positive, and collaborative approach to improving all of the division's functions, simultaneously reducing finger-pointing.

One of the first things I did was interview each of the six vice presidents to get their views on where improvements were most needed, how success was measured, and what actions were currently underway to achieve division success. One of the VPs told me succinctly that, if I were to be helpful to him, I needed to understand that "this business is like a fire station." When a customer had a computer malfunction, the division's mission was to get to the scene and quickly put out the figurative fire. If I could help them put out more fires per day at less cost, I would be a hero. One of their measures of success was the average number of daily "calls per field engineer." The business had recently finished a competitive analysis and found its strongest competitor had about 20 percent more calls per day per engineer. Steps were underway to increase productivity, measured by more calls per day. What could possibly go wrong? We'll see shortly.

You have an advantage over this VP. He did not have the benefit of the 8DX framework. Since you do, which of the eight Dimensions (referring to the 8DX graphic) was the VP trying to change? _____. He said their improvement goals were to

1. increase the number of fires extinguished daily;
2. reduce firefighting cost; and
3. narrow the competitive call-per-day gap.

If you have concluded the VP's aim with goal 1 was Dimension 6, you would be right.[70] That first goal deals with extinguishing (not reducing the occurrence of) fires, an undesired outcome for the business. Customers did not particularly care whether the number of extinguished fires per day (computer repairs) goes up or down, as long as their own computer doesn't quit at all. If it does, the duration and cost should be small. But none of the three goals directly address that customer experience. Goal 1 also aims at improved productivity, Dimension 8.

The way reduced cost is stated in goal 2 is a producer concern. Again it emphasizes Dimension 6. Cost would only matter to the customer if it showed up as a reduction in the repair price, Dimension 2. Arguably, customers paying for repairs based on actual time and materials could benefit. That would be an improvement in the undesired outcome of high price, Dimension 2. In practice, most customers were not charged that way. Most paid standard prices that did not vary due to unique circumstances, or they paid a monthly maintenance contract fee for a given computer or related device. We can see in this discussion that it really does matter how a specific performance element is defined in detail.

Goal 2 is also related to the firefighting process, Dimension 8. Further insight can be gained by examining how it was measured. The measure for downtime began when the complaint call came in and ended when the repair ticket was closed out. That was assumed to mean the problem was fixed. If another downtime complaint from the same customer regarding the same machine was received later in the week, it was counted as a new problem. That would be like your car repair garage telling you the problem with your car not starting is a bad battery and sending you home with a new one for $200. Then when you bring the car back a week later with the same starting problem, they tell you the problem is the alternator and charge you $1,500 to replace it. This scenario could cause many customers to conclude the problem was misdiagnosed the first time. They might easily feel they had been potentially charged more than they should have been. It also instills doubt concerning the trust they had bestowed on the repair organization. In the mind of the customer, the problem remained unchanged, that is, the car won't start. The repair organization counts it as two problems and charges accordingly. Looking at this from the customer's perspective suggests there is a problem with the quality of the initial repair. It had to be done over.

Goals 1 and 3 aimed to increase the number of calls (fires) per day per engineer. If you were an engineer, you might be able to break up a repair into two repairs on your paperwork. That could make you look twice as productive. This was exactly what some did to achieve the VP's new productivity goal (without the VP's knowledge). Goal 3 is a producer-desired outcome of improved competitiveness, Dimension 5.

In no case was the VP in question using any customer-desired outcome, Dimension 1, to drive performance improvement. The division president had clearly said he wanted three things improved:

---

[70] The relevant Vital Lies here are 2 and 5 (listed before Leader's Action 8).

quality, productivity, and customer satisfaction. Of the three, our VP was attending almost entirely to productivity. He was also unaware his definition of quality could be problematic. If the VP defines two related repairs as separate and each is done completely and correctly the first time, repair quality could be called good. But if the customer defines the repairs in terms of a single problem that had to be addressed twice, quality and satisfaction are not so good. It is possible the VP's objectives for the business are not identical with the president's or the customer's. In fact, the VP and the president may have competing objectives and not even know it!

The Master of Excellence is alert to the potential conflict between strategic direction and operational matters and looks for a way to create alignment. In this case, it was helpful to consider the analogy the VP himself used to describe the business. He said the division's function was to be a firefighter. He continued the analogy by suggesting they would be more productive if they put out more fires per day.

It was possible to redefine the business in terms of desired outcomes that customers wanted: fire-free days. That would be a Dimension 1 focus and applied to both an individual customer as well as being applicable across all customers. It would fundamentally change, add, or eliminate several key measures of success.

When the concept of fire-free days was suggested to the leadership team, one immediate discovery they made was that no measure of fire-free days existed. The data did exist once one dug around for it. Before we had the measure created, there was intuitive insight that customer satisfaction was likely to improve as (1) the number of fire-free days per period increased, and (2) the number of days between fires increased[71] for a given customer.

Another key discovery was that there was no uniform definition for a repair; nor were they all counted. Actual unit cost, cycle time, yield (fixed right the first time), and other key measures were largely not captured per repair. There were codes for problems, parts, and labor, but this data was not necessarily connected up and organized by repair. In other words, was it possible to have a problem for which parts and labor were applied but no repair resulted? You bet.

I want to resist getting ahead of ourselves, but it is important to note that repairs were the division's core products. That was definitely not how they thought of the organization's work when we began looking at improving strategic performance. This is in contrast to the way Midas Muffler[72] defined its products and differentiated itself from car-dealer service departments, starting in 1956. If you had asked the typical dealer's service department back then what a new exhaust system would cost, the most common answer would have been, "That depends." That scenario continues to exist today. Naturally, you would want to know what it depends on. The repair advisor would tell you he or she has to first find out exactly what needs to be replaced, estimate how long it will take to remove the defective parts, find out what those parts will cost, and then calculate the time it will take to install the few parts.

That kind of answer could easily cause you to (1) wonder how many times they've done this work before and (2) rightly assume you will effectively be giving them a blank check and inviting them to write in an

---

[71] This is related to the concept of mean time between failures. However, MTBF is a producer measure and is usually shown as an average across all customers for a given product. The fire-free (or trouble-free) days measure is a customer-centered measure, calculated across all products provided to each specific customer. It can also be aggregated across all customers.

[72] Midas is an acronym: Muffler Installation Dealers' Associated Service. Most people think Midas is in the muffler business. They aren't. As the acronym says, they are in the installations (repairs) business. They sell muffler repairs at a bundled price that includes all labor and parts. That repair is guaranteed for the life of your car.

amount that is yet to be determined. In contrast, Midas simply gives you a fixed price that includes everything and guarantees the repair for the life of your car. That continues to be their practice for muffler, brake, shock, and all other repairs. The traditional auto service department typically makes no such promise.

These observations about computer and auto repairs are relevant for virtually all kinds of repair. We could apply the same questions and answers for repairs related to the following: home appliances, diets, roads, medical transplants of joints and organs, computers, financial investment losses, personal identity and reputation, online accounts, and educational failures and omissions.

CASE 3: A HEALTHY DOSE OF CLARITY

It has been my great pleasure to work with some wonderful leaders throughout the health-care industry. The talent, extensive education, dedication to customers, and selflessness they and their colleagues demonstrate has been impressive. Despite those assets, it was extremely rare over the first twenty-five years of my career to find a health-care organization that routinely asked customers questions about the outcomes they were seeking, that defined and recorded those outcomes, that measured the degree to which they were obtained, and that had numerical improvement objectives. At least, that hadn't been done prior to our first day working together.

That first-day experience remains common for those not yet using the 8DX framework. We can easily see the problem when viewing much of the health-care industry from the customer's perspective. Think of yourself as the customer. What is the ultimate outcome you hope to achieve, the purpose you have as a customer when seeking help? Getting well is one outcome. But the ultimate outcome most of us say we want is good health. Health-care providers will readily agree this is important to customers. Some will argue that good health is not a realistic or relevant expectation. Could this be a Vital Lie? For customers of a hospice, it may very well be true that a priority outcome they want is pain-free death with dignity. Isn't that reasonable to want? In any event, let's start with the proposition that we should understand the expectation before we jump to discredit it as unreasonable. It has been my undeniable experience that few health-care institutions have a written definition for good health either in a generic form applicable to all customers or in a customer-specific way derived from actually asking individuals.

A definition of good health has actually been written. The World Health Organization (WHO) developed the following one in 1946, "Health is a state of complete physical, mental and social well-being and not merely the absence of disease or infirmity."[73]

Does this sound like a description you would consider relevant to yourself as a health care customer? The vast majority we've asked think this is nicely succinct and personally relevant. It clearly suggests that "absence of disease or infirmity" is not the low bar to reach. That low bar actually refers to undesired outcomes, the focus of Dimension 2. Let's examine the difference and why it might matter.

Dimensions 1 and 2 are often confused. Leaders of customer-centered excellence must be totally clear about the difference between the two. We generally make sure there are policies in place that cover all the core values and practices held dear by the leaders of the organization. If the matter is important, we've usually got at least one policy on the topic. It is common to have written policies on hiring for diversity, compensation to attract and retain talent, supplier selection for low costs with acceptable

---

[73] This definition has been unchanged since its adoption by the United Nations in its Universal Declaration of Human Rights in 1948.

quality, access to corporate information, technical quality, money management, and so on.

Such policies are intended to confirm in writing our most important values. It can therefore be surprising to discover that a priority value is unsupported by a policy. This situation can also create ambiguity. If there is no policy or no measure on something purported to be of high value, how important can it really be? If we aim to create good health (or safety, wealth, satisfaction, and other customer-desired outcomes), surely it should be reflected in governance documents.

It has been my experience that many organizations are locked into Dimension 2 thinking. This has certainly been true within the health-care industry. That means people in the organization believe their mission is successful if the customer doesn't end up worse off than when he or she came in. That is what the Hippocratic Oath is all about, to do no harm. Thinking of yourself as a health-care customer, what are the most important undesired outcomes you would hope to avoid? Put another way, what is the very worst thing that could happen after you check in to the hospital?

The supreme undesired outcome to avoid, and the one most identified, is death. You will be happy to know our health-care friends have this unambiguously defined as no electrical activity in the brain and heart. Once upon a time, death was not always an unambiguous conclusion. Families with the means could have a string or rope attached to their loved one before burial with the other end attached to a bell above ground. This was a feature of what were called safety coffins in the mid-nineteenth century. If the loved one woke up and moved, the bell would ring, and they could be unearthed to rejoin the living. This is one source of the expression "saved by the bell." Fortunately we've advanced beyond that state of ambiguity.

Death occurring in hospitals is now defined and measured, and there are numerical goals for improvement (meaning the frequency of its occurrence after a patient checks in). The same cannot be said for good health.

Morbidity is a second undesired outcome customers wish to avoid. The health-care industry has done well to define it. Simply put, morbidity refers to incidence of illness in a population. Related to the population in a hospital, it refers to the rate at which patients go in for a procedure such as an appendectomy and, while in the hospital, contract an infection such as Legionnaire's disease, a virus, or some other preventable ailment. In the United States, "preventable errors" by health-care institutions are the third leading cause of death.[74] Prior to 2008, patients requiring treatment for that new ailment after admission to the hospital would often be charged extra. Perhaps that is because their expectations were being exceeded, just not in a way they had really wanted.

Effective October 1, 2008, such "hospital-acquired conditions" are no longer being reimbursed by our federal government for Medicare customers. Insurers can't be billed for them either. Such costs for poor quality must now be borne by the producer. This change is an excellent example of how to align the definition of an undesired outcome to measurement, goal-setting, consequences, and compensation. It makes accountability much easier to obtain. Couldn't we apply this same kind of alignment to achieving Dimension 1 results?

---

[74] On May 3, 2016, British Medical Journal (BMJ) reported on research conducted by Martin Makary and Michael Daniel at Johns Hopkins University's School of Medicine, based on data from 1999 to 2013. Their finding that medical errors account for more than 9.5 percent of all fatalities in the United States is hotly contested by others in health care. What is generally agreed is that patient data quality is ambiguous and error-related mortality is higher than it should be.

Our focus on Dimensions 1 or 2 determines how we define customer success. We might easily and reasonably conclude that the absence of death or morbidity is a clear sign of success and cause for celebration. The theme song for this version of success might be the Bee Gees hit, "Stayin' Alive." But wait just a minute. Is it possible for customers to avoid death and greater illness yet still not be in good health? You bet.

One might think that the Patient Centered Outcomes Research Institute, established in 2010, would have some answers. A visit to www.pcori.org in 2015 would leave you hard-pressed to find measures that clearly speak to the patient's good health. To be sure, many in the industry are working to distinguish good health (outcome) from good health care (process). My hope is that we take renewed action to move the target and increase the pace of getting there. Not just in health care but everywhere.

The reduction or absence of an undesired outcome (death) is not the same as achieving a desired outcome (good health). Admittedly, staying alive is a desired outcome. It is a low-level, minimum outcome. Our challenge as a Master of Excellence is to prevent the organization from confusing minimum with optimum outcomes. Each industry has its own language for minimum outcomes. In health care, we might call them clinical outcomes. The customer gets a hip replaced. The clinical outcome is that the patient can now walk with little or no pain and there are no complications (preventable errors). This is good. Is it possible that the clinical outcome is different from the customer's desired outcome? That outcome might have been to regain the ability to play on the winning soccer team and go back to climbing mountains. Have we actually asked customers and recorded their answers?

When we are the customer, those kinds of outcomes seem entirely reasonable and may be the true definition of a successful outcome. When we are the producer, it is amazing how easy it is for us to use terms such as unrealistic, fanciful, unreasonable, or even delusional when a customer says such things. Masters of Excellence are a lot like those customers. They regularly seek what others think is impossible. We could call that leadership vision. It is good to remember there are some who will observe there is a fine line between vision and hallucination.

Speaking of vision, this would be a good time to check out how clearly our own organization has defined what customers want. As we have seen so far in the discussion above, we tend to be fairly specific about undesired outcomes customers want to avoid. Our definition of their desired outcomes are often vague, ambiguous, and not measured. Maybe your situation is different. If you did not complete Leader's Action 10, find the written statement (see the strategic plan, policy manual, or other major guiding document) that describes the most important desired purpose or outcome customers are known (not assumed) to want when working with your organization.

Write it below:

_____

_____

- Is the statement unambiguous and clearly understood by all employees? Y N
- Is there at least one objective measure that reveals the degree to which the outcome is achieved by each customer? Y N
- What would you do or say to improve this statement?

_____

Glenn Cunningham was injured in a fire when he was seven years old. His left toes were nearly burned off his foot, and his right leg shrank three inches shorter than the left. Doctors wanted to amputate his leg, believing he would be better off as a healthy invalid without infection-prone burned legs. He certainly would never walk again, no matter what. Their focus was on preventing an undesired outcome. There is no evidence they asked or were receptive to hearing about Glenn's desired outcome. Glenn stubbornly resisted the experts' advice. He unreasonably sought a desired outcome, believing he could learn how to at least walk unassisted again. With the support of his parents, the experts reluctantly acquiesced.

He did learn to walk and run, and then he proceeded to win his high school's track race. He was in the fourth grade at the time! The desired outcome he sought at seven was equally outrageous when he was twenty-four. His passion to run resulted in him becoming the world's fastest mile runner. He went on to break numerous other national and world track records for several years. That focus on desired outcomes is the norm for customers as well as leaders.

The head of cardiothoracic surgery at a major health care center in New England learned of my ideas and asked me to come visit and introduce customer-centered thinking to his colleagues and staff. Bill was very proud of their new facility, designed to feel more like a small shopping mall than a medical facility. One key aim was to remove the cold, impersonal feel often characteristic of health facilities and reduce the fear patients with heart ailments can feel. I asked him to tell me what cardiology patients were most concerned about when they checked in. What were the top three questions he and his staff were asked? Bill said patients asked:

1. Will I make it (survive)?
2. Can I afford it?
3. When can I go home?

We can see that these are all questions related to desired outcomes. I asked Bill what the answers would typically be. He said the physician always discussed the answer to the first question in terms of potential risks, possible alternatives, and intended benefits expected. The patient was referred to the business office to get answers for the second question and learn about possible financing options if insurance didn't fully cover the procedure. Bill said he and his staff were repeatedly asked the third question after a heart operation. He wished they had a better answer than what the patient perceived to be a version of, "We'll just have to wait and see." Patients wanted to get back home as quickly as possible and get a more predictable response on when that would be.

I asked Bill why patients were not getting a more satisfactory answer. He said every patient's situation was different, but there were a number of clinical indicators the physician and nursing staff looked for that told them the patient was ready to be released. I asked if those indicators were shared with the patient. He said they were not. I asked if they could be. He didn't think so, or it wouldn't matter if they did. In separate discussions with nurses, they tended to agree, saying they didn't think it was a good idea to discuss a patient's chart and clinical indicators of health because it might increase patient anxiety. Nurses also mentioned that they had enough on their hands just getting patients out of bed after procedures such as open-heart surgery.

I asked why that was a problem and what they were trying to accomplish. They said the patient would struggle and often be in discomfort getting out of bed but preventing pneumonia and building strength and energy were all dependent on getting up and walking around. Until the patient could walk around without overtaxing his or her heart, he or she wouldn't be ready to go home. When I asked if that were explained to patients, they said no. That was not the protocol.

I suggested to Bill that we work with nurses to identify what I called behavioral markers of health. Those could be shared with patients and might enable them to get their own sense for how close they were to being able to go home. We did that, providing the information before surgery was performed and then again afterward. An immediate change was observed. Instead of nurses feeling like they had to beg and cajole patients out of bed, the patients themselves would press their buzzers to the nursing station and ask to have help and supervision getting out of bed and walking around. The nurses began feeling they had lost control of the ward. The patients were taking charge, and it was driving the nurses nuts. But they stuck to the plan.

When Bill talked with me several weeks later, he said things had gone well, but some other issues had come up and asked me to come back and meet with staff. He said there seemed to be a morale issue and wanted me to see what the problem was. Nursing staff told me in the subsequent meeting that there had indeed been some success with the new approach of informing patients what they could do or observe in their own healing that could predict their discharge from the hospital. It had taken some adjustments for them to get used to the patients asking frequently to get out of bed, walk down the hall, and otherwise demonstrate their progress and readiness to go home. In fact, the length of time from surgery to discharge had dropped by about 50 percent!

I congratulated them and then asked if there were something bothering nurses about this change. After a pause of people looking around the table at each other, one nurse said she and others had been feeling really badly about what had happened. She said she had worked there for a number of years and never thought to consider whether patients should or could take control of their discharge process. She said nursing staff felt bad because they could have taken these measures long ago. That would have helped many other patients begin resuming their lives much earlier. They truly cared for the well-being of their patients and were chagrined to discover such a simple change that empowered customers could have such an obvious benefit.

We shifted the conversation to how we could celebrate the discoveries made. Everyone was encouraged to recognize they had done the best they knew how at the time. They now knew something new that strengthened what they had previously done well.

Staff had focused on understanding the desired outcomes customers wanted after surgery. They had provided a practical guide customers could use to see how they were progressing toward that outcome and personally take action to accelerate the pace. The result was a win-win. Patients went home earlier. The facility benefited by reducing costs, increasing capacity, and improving employee satisfaction.

Consider the fact that eight of the Ten Commandments start with "Thou shall not."[75] In a more secular vein, one of the most important guiding documents in the mental-health profession is the American Psychiatric Association's bible, the Diagnostic and Statistical Manual (DSM 5). The fifth version of this book, last revised in 2013, covers the description of over twenty categories of mental illness. The definition of mental illness is an abnormal pattern of thoughts, emotion, and behavior that causes diminished function or increased suffering to the patient and/or others. What, you may ask, would be the "normal" pattern of thought and behavior? Good luck finding the answer.

---

[75] This is also true for comparable guidance in the Torah and Quran.

You won't find a description of normal in the DSM. This manual was a handy tool used during the Cold War to send Soviet dissidents to the gulag for so-called treatment. It has not been uncommon to find innovators, explorers, and nontraditionalists referred to as crazy or heretical. This has been true for centuries, long before the DSM, as Galileo could attest when the pope had him locked up in 1610 for claiming the Earth orbits the Sun, as Copernicus had done a hundred years previously and for which Filippo Bruno[76] had been burned at the stake in 1600. Galileo even provided the astronomical and mathematical evidence. Too bad for him, the normal view at the time was that the Earth was the center of the universe. To be fair, he did get a papal apology later from John Paul II…in 1992. It didn't do much for Copernicus, Bruno, or Galileo.

Executive Summary: Cases 2 and 3

1. Customers, such as those in the health-care case 3, often do communicate their expectations regarding desired outcomes. They could be volunteered without solicitation, given in response to questions asked of them, or stated as questions, such as the three that Bill highlighted. The hidden opportunity is to recognize those as outcome statements, capture them in an organized way, incorporate them into our written strategic guidance, and have practices in place so they are likely to be satisfied.

2. Traditional guiding references used by an industry or profession are likely to put more emphasis on undesired than on desired outcomes.

3. Shifting from an undesired outcome focus (Dimension 2 or 6) to Dimension 1 could require rethinking what the enterprise's purpose and product should be. If repair-free days were a desired outcome customers wanted, then a repair could be a product customers never want to experience. This is exactly what many software producers understand when they enable fixes to occur overnight or otherwise without the user being aware of it. Likewise, if good health is the outcome wanted, is it possible customers would like to have that without experiencing the open-heart quadruple bypass?

4. It is important to define the intended, desired outcome at least as well as we've described what is undesired. Changing that focus will necessarily make prevention the target, not just detection and correction.

5. Measures of success reveal which Dimension(s) the organization is actually aimed at satisfying. Going to a repair-free outcome would mean reducing, not increasing, the number of daily repairs. In case 2, it resulted in a marked effort with product (computer) design to reduce frequency of repair, improve ease of remote repair, and build in redundancy of key components to make failures invisible to the user. This emphasis on design is exactly the approach taken by Apple, Tesla, and other leaders.

6. The producer may define its product differently than the way the customer does or in a way different from how a customer wants to experience it. The definitions of product quality can also be vastly different, depending on viewpoint.

7. An enterprise that sees its core product as repairs and is compensated for them will naturally seek to increase the volume produced. This can put it in direct opposition to the repair-free experience its customers want. The innovator will create a new business model that enables it to be compensated for the customer-desired outcome.

8. Understanding the 8DX framework can help create consensus for unity of purpose and priority for action.

9. As a Master of Excellence, we can expect to make others feel uncomfortable with our notions of what is possible and the rapid pace at which we expect to achieve it, perhaps being called

---

[76] He is also known as Giordano Bruno (1548–1600), who was a Dominican friar, mathematician, astrologer, and philosopher.

unrealistic or deranged (though we know ourselves to be visionaries).

10. Having the data to support our case is helpful but not necessarily sufficient to convince others. Consider that a significant number of early twenty-first-century American political leaders refused to accept significant scientific evidence of the strong correlation between human activity (such as carbon emissions and deforestation) and global warming.

11. Cases 2 and 3 insights show opportunity to improve our C3IQ scores for items 1–5, 8, 13a, 15a–d, and 17.

Leader's Action 11: Differentiate Desired and Undesired Outcomes
(See Appendix 1)

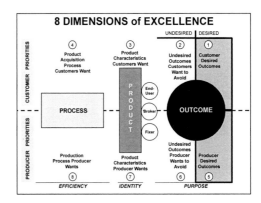

CHAPTER 11—WHY, OH WHY?

It can be a surprise to discover that we often put more energy into analyzing the past and codifying what is wrong and undesired than we do to design and articulate the future we want. This may be perfectly appropriate when responding to a crisis, but not as a habit. Fixation on the rearview mirror can distract us from looking out the windshield to find a better path forward and avoid an otherwise inevitable crash down the road.

The good news is that we do have the desire to learn from our mistakes. This can manifest itself in a natural bias to look backward at visible failures and attempt to minimize them in the future. Beyond moral and social imperatives, one of the motivators to do this is that some financial penalty is often connected directly to undesired outcomes. Can we identify the financial rewards that flow from better desired outcomes?

We humans and our works are rarely perfect so we will appropriately continue to see the need for problem-driven improvement methods. This is true across all industries. When a world-class company like Toyota has quality problems prompting recalls of millions of vehicles, there are clear and undeniably bad economic consequences for the producer, its investors, and customers. The reason Toyota has sophisticated quality management systems and practices in place is to minimize or eliminate such undesired outcomes.

One of the simplest and most widely used quality improvement tools at Toyota and other modern manufacturers is called the 5 Whys. It is used when a problem (an undesired outcome) is observed, and the goal is to identify the root cause. Using the example of a worst-case scenario where a customer leaves for a competitor, the 5 Whys user asks a series of why questions to identify what to change or fix. The graphic below is an illustration of how this might work, going from upper right to bottom left. Notice the sequence goes backward from final undesired result to potential root cause.

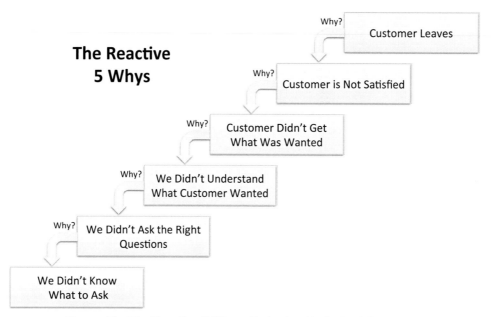

Figure 12—The Reactive 5 Whys, Reducing Undesired Outcomes

This illustration shows what answer might have been discovered to each why question. I call this the Reactive 5 Whys. In this particular example, we very frequently find that customer dissatisfaction and defection are correlated with our not knowing what to ask or observe about customers and therefore not uncovering what they want. We discussed this failure-to-ask issue in Chapter 9 and Leader's Action 10. Formal methods for uncovering customer wants are sometimes called the VOC.

Toyota is known for broadly applying the pioneering VOC methodology developed by their consultant in the 1960s, Yoji Akao. The system Akao developed was published in his 1978 book on Quality Function Deployment (QFD). Many world-class manufacturers have used Akao's methods in product design, sometimes referring to its various parts as making up the House of Quality. This highly complex system is far beyond what non-engineers and those outside of manufacturing generally find useful. One reason is the assumption that the product is a manufactured widget. It is worth noting that there are also several key omissions that could otherwise make it more broadly applicable. One of those omissions is the distinction between desired and undesired outcomes.[77]

Various industries have their own version of the Reactive 5 Whys analysis. In the army, it is the after-action report. Health-care professionals have theirs. It's called the postmortem, analysis of causes "after death." Whether it is the Toyota recall, the army, or health-care preventable errors cases, we are looking for the reason why some undesired outcome or failure occurred. Our assumption is that, by understanding the root cause, we can eliminate the problem. It's a nice idea, and sometimes it works. Do we get to bring the health-care customer back to life? So sorry, not happening. At best, we can prevent a repeat of that undesired outcome for other customers. With medical errors accounting for the third most common cause of death for several years in the United States, the evidence is that this approach to excellence has some major failings. In the real world of health care, it turns out that unwashed hands and contaminated instruments are the root cause of many preventable errors. Do washed hands and sterile instruments lead to customer-desired outcomes? Not necessarily. Remember that the absence of an undesired outcome does not assure a desired outcome.

---

[77] Despite QFD's thoroughness, there are three additional omissions of critical importance: (a) how to define all work, not just widgets, as tangible products; (b) how to determine who the customer is in every context; and (c) how to define and separate customer-desired outcomes from product performance, perception, functions, and features. We will complete the fix for these shortcomings in Volume 2.

There is an alternative approach to the traditional 5 Whys, aimed at uncovering, defining, and achieving desired outcomes. We can call this the future-oriented or Strategic 5 Whys, shown in the figure below. This method encourages divergent thinking. Each why in the series of questions helps us get to a broader, more inclusive, more strategic, higher purpose or outcome. Once we understand the ultimate outcomes wanted, we can consider alternatives, not just improvements, to the current product(s) or service(s). The objective is not traditional problem-solving. It can be particularly helpful in uncovering what a customer truly wants, beyond the problem he or she may initially state he or she wants solved.

You would think that defining the customer's ultimate outcome would be routinely done in every business. If your own business submits proposals to prospective customers, their desired outcomes ought to be clearly and prominently spelled out in the proposal. In practice, we often find specific answers to product criteria specified in the prospect's request for proposal (RFP), rarely describing the desired outcomes. Adding them, even when they are not specified, has made the winning difference for a number of my clients. We'll see at least one spectacular example in the VOC section of this book of a firm that lost a $400 billion contract by not getting this customer understanding right. The losing bidder went on to complain that the customer was at fault by not specifying everything they wanted.

A simple, powerful technique for getting new data and insights of strategic importance is the Strategic 5 Whys tool. Notice the contrast between the figure below and the traditional 5 Whys in figure 12. Rather than going backward in time, we want to ask successive whys to uncover a broader, more inclusive future purpose than the answer first given by a customer.

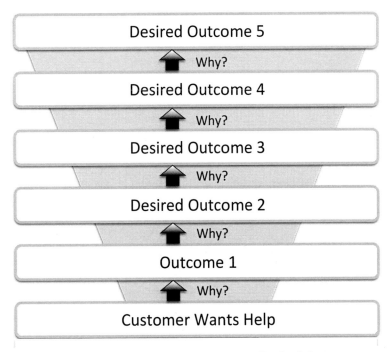

Figure 13—Strategic 5 Whys to Uncover Desired Outcomes

CASE 4: FINANCIAL SERVICES SPIN MEASURES INTO GOLD

Let's illustrate how the Strategic 5 Whys method could work for a bank and its customers. Recall your own experience as a customer applying for a bank loan. The process generally involves the loan officer asking a number of at least moderately invasive questions about your assets, legal and financial liabilities, sources of income, what you spend money on, and so on. Answering those can be about as enjoyable as having a root canal.

Suppose you have a child in her senior year of college. If she is especially gifted, perhaps she is on a full scholarship. Congratulations. On the other hand, if your situation is more like the average family's, she is likely on the parental scholarship plan. That is where you are the primary or sole source of educational funding. You are naturally looking forward to graduation day in the hope she will go and begin her productive work life.

But before that happens, she comes to you one day and tells you she has concluded that her four-year degree in psychology will probably not be enough to land a good job. You consider the competing desires to help her get to a stronger career platform with the fact you would like to continue paying the mortgage, keep the car, and otherwise attend to your current financial obligations. You suggest the two of you go to the bank and inquire about a student loan. She agrees, and off you go.

Let's suppose the loan officer at the financial institution uses outcome-oriented questions during your meeting. The dialogue upon entering his office could go something like this:

> He: Why are you interested in seeing me?
> You: *We would like help getting a loan.*
>
> He: Why? What purpose do you have for the loan?
> Daughter: *To obtain a master's degree in psychology.*
>
> He: Why have you decided on that degree?
> Daughter: *To get a great, rewarding job.*
>
> He: Why do you want such a job?
> Daughter: *To help others and positively affect my financial independence.*
>
> He: Why is that important to you?
> Daughter: *So I can have a high quality of life like my mom and dad.*

You will notice the loan officer has asked the Strategic 5 Whys questions. The flow of questions and answers is shown in the graphic below.

Figure 14—An Example of Strategic 5 Whys

Before we discuss the potential benefit of this questioning, please reflect for a moment on past experiences you've had with banks when seeking a loan (car, mortgage, home improvement, and so on). Has it been your experience that the loan officer asks at least moderately invasive questions regarding your income, liabilities, assets, work history, credit card debt, past addresses, how much you owe others, where all your assets are stashed, and so on? In comparison, these simple future-oriented why questions are pretty benign. Has your past loan officer asked 5 Whys such as shown in the above figure? If not, which whys were asked, considering the one at the bottom as #1? _____

If your experience is like the majority of bank customers in this situation, the loan officer rarely, if ever, asked more than the first two Whys (at the bottom). This might cause us to wonder whether there is a bank regulation or internal rule that forbids asking more than two Whys. We have no evidence of such a constraint. Why should the general practice be limited to just two Whys? Many observers have concluded that the bank and its personnel simply don't care what you are ultimately trying to achieve. The bank is only interested in limiting their risk and making sure you don't default on the loan. Those are both undesired outcomes for the bank. Before we accept that as the final explanation for the loan officer's typical behavior, let's test a slightly different scenario than the two-question one.

The daughter replies that she wants a great job in a psychology-related field. The loan officer asks if he might take a moment to see what the job market demand is for recent master's graduates in psychology. Your daughter agrees. He spends a couple minutes to do a quick search on Monster.com. He reports that one job category involves counseling and another is in industrial psychology, and the demand is different for the two areas. For every counseling job opening, there are about 350 applicants. For industrial psychology, there are about 225 applicants, and he asks if she has a preference on the kind of job. She says it doesn't matter too much, but hearing the different competitive situations, she would probably seek a position in the latter field.

Being a particularly astute loan officer, he reflects back to her that it appears she wants to improve her odds of finding work, which he acknowledges is a wise path. He asks if she speaks any other languages, to which she answers no. He suggests checking to see if that would make a difference in the job marketplace. His quick search reveals that, for those who also speak Spanish, every opening has about twenty-five applicants. He asks if your daughter would be willing to add a few courses in Spanish to her graduate program. She eagerly agrees. The loan is approved.

Now let's consider who all the possible winners could be by the loan officer asking just those three why questions. We began this example with a reflection on our previous observations and experiences with banks. By asking just one more why than the norm, which of the following parties could have benefited if your daughter got the loan and some extra classes to learn Spanish?

- Your daughter
- The college she attends
- The organization that employs your daughter
- The customers your daughter can satisfy
- The community where your daughter resides and pay taxes
- You and your spouse
- Friends you and your daughter tell, who then go to the bank that has gone the extra mile for you
- The bank
- The loan officer
- Shareholders of the bank

Some who hear this scenario get stuck on the idea that the loan officer has gone beyond the mission of the bank. If the bank gets its loan repaid on-time (maybe even ahead of time if your daughter gets a job right out of school) and its customer experiences enhanced success, isn't that consistent with the bank's mission? It is, but the route there is slightly different than the norm. The risk of making the loan is reduced by thinking about how to increase the likelihood of being repaid and, in this case, suggesting action be taken by the customer. Your daughter has self-interest working when she commits to become more qualified in the job market, raising her chances of getting a job offer she wants.

There are at least ten possible winners in this scenario. They include your daughter, who gets the loan and possibly a faster job offer. The college where she graduates gets to claim her as another success and thereby improve their competitive ranking among colleges. Your daughter's employer gets a better qualified candidate, more capable of satisfying the customers (within the firm, in this case) she serves. So her customers win. She will be a new taxpayer so her community gains financially. You and your spouse get to put money into paying off the house and car instead of incurring new liabilities. As much as you love your daughter, you get to help her move to her own place for good and reclaim the spare bedroom. The bank gets repaid and, if a pay-for-performance system is in place, the loan officer could get a bonus for another quality loan produced. It is quite possible your daughter may tell her friends about the uniquely positive experience she had at the bank, prompting them to become new bank customers. That word-of-mouth referral is better than any marketing campaign. Over time, the profitability of the bank could increase, along with its stock share price. Bottom line is that the simple act of asking whys to reveal the customer's desired outcomes enables responses and results benefiting all the parties shown on the list above.

You might be thinking, *Wait just a minute! It's not the bank's job to do career counseling.* This is what we might easily believe. We just might be falling into the Vital Lie 5 trap. We know what business we are in, especially if we think of the bank as a purveyor of commodity products like loans. The following standard industry practice is to adopt commodity and followership thinking where pricing is king. But the mission of this bank is, thinking more strategically, to achieve customer success and profit by it. Leadership in that bank where the whys are asked tied success to customer outcome without limiting its comparison to other banks and their traditional practices. The outcome wanted by the customer was a good job that would lead to a high quality of life. In this scenario, spending a few extra minutes to achieve that success also brought returns to the bank. This is the proverbial win-win. Yes, the bank has more broadly redefined its business mission. I'll bet this slight change was entirely consistent with at least one of its core values. Could you do this for your organization and its customers?

It is easy to consider this example a handy theoretical exercise but perhaps not be so useful in the real world. So let's look at two related real-world banking examples to see if there is any practical value to be obtained.

Kyle, the CEO of a major credit union based in the Midwest, brought his executive staff to a public seminar I conducted. I called him a few weeks later and asked what impact the experience had on his team. He said he and his staff left with mixed feelings. On the one hand, they felt much of what we had covered was very supportive of the strategic direction they were taking with the firm. But they were surprised to discover that they were not as customer-focused as they had thought they were. More than that, he had recently released his new strategic plan to the entire organization and was now thinking that its focus was more producer-centered than he wanted. His concern was the train had left the station, and he was doubtful whether anything could be done right away to redirect it.

I suggested Kyle have me take a look at his new strategic plan and offer observations. He agreed, and I sent him my comments on what I saw were both its strengths and weaknesses. A few major disconnects I saw were:

- One of the issues was that KPIs intended to address customer success really were more relevant for enterprise priorities.

- Definitions of a couple key terms, such as "share of wallet," were ambiguous and could lead to falsely concluding success was occurring when the opposite might be true.

- Assumptions were routinely being made about customer priorities without a method for validating or uncovering what those priorities were.

In our subsequent phone conversation, Kyle admitted my observations confirmed his own recent insights, but he didn't see what could be done about it until he updated the plan at least a year in the future. I told him one of the things I had really liked in his plan were the statements about key values. The employees saw the firm as a learning organization, committed to continuous improvement, operating collaboratively, and striving to be one of best performers in their industry. He said all of that was true. I suggested that perhaps he could view this moment as an opportunity to personally model those values. When he asked what I had in mind, I asked Kyle if he were willing to demonstrate the organization's core values by communicating to his direct staff the following:

- He had learned some new insights on how to be more customer-focused.
- The strategic plan could be strengthened by making it subject to the same continuous improvement values he expected everyone to share.
- With the collaborative help of representatives across the business, necessary improvements could be achieved in a very short time.
- It seemed possible that, with a few changes, they could attain an even higher standing in their market. Were there volunteers willing to help him?

He said he hadn't thought about closing the gap that way, but now was intrigued. But it had taken months to get the new strategic plan developed, and he just couldn't see repeating that lengthy process. I asked how he would feel about taking two days to handle the changes in a session with all those he wanted to include. Surprised that improvement might be achieved with such speed, he chose the dates, and we held a revision session with key management, rank-and-file employees, and invited customers.

The 8DX concepts and key tools, including the Strategic 5 Whys, were introduced and immediately applied to eliminate strategic plan weaknesses. Five of the seven measures that had been intended to address customer-desired outcomes, Dimension 1, were replaced. Several new questions, along with guidelines on how staff was to respond to customer answers, were developed and designed into core customer interaction processes (in line with the discussion we had in Chapter 9 and Leader's Action 10). A deployment plan was created with implementation set to begin the following week. This doesn't sound too complicated, does it? Here are a few of the results Kyle observed over the next six months:

- Customer answers to questions such as "What are your passions in life?" were connected to products the credit union could offer to help fulfill those passions.

- Customers for loans and other products were asked about their desired outcomes, which often involved saving money, rapid repayment, sustained or improved credit ratings, and improved quality of life. Each of these factors began being measured and showed significant improvement for customers.

- Managers and employees used a new vocabulary about outcomes, products, customer roles, and expectations that seemed to improve overall communication.

- Loans closed per week jumped more than 120 percent.

- Loan utilization rate went from about 50 percent to 75 percent. This means that customers approved for loans had previously only used the loans about half the time. By more fully understanding the purposes customers had when applying for a loan (including obtaining it at least total cost), the design or structure of loans could be changed to better match those purposes.

- Quantified customer savings resulted in their migration from other institutions with higher fees; market share increased for the institution.

- Revenue increased over $8 million per month from new business created. None of this was due to mortgages, meaning the general mortgage implosion occurring in the broader economy shortly after this had no impact on this institution.

There was gold in the new language, measures, and practices. This is one example of what can happen when senior leaders respond to my admonition, "Don't tell me what you value; show me what you measure." Kyle's dedication to improving that alignment made it possible to observe "all our performance measures significantly improved during the first six months of deployment." His personal standing with employees, already high when we started, went up as they realized he was personally practicing the core enterprise values held by them all. None of this could have happened without his courage to personally practice his business's core values, pursuing a level of excellence that had not yet been achieved.

We have just seen how redefining a few key words and measures can have profound effect. Sometimes our local leadership efforts can have a global impact. Consider the case of Bangladesh and Dr. Muhammad Yunus. Dr. Yunus was teaching economics in 1974 when his country experienced widespread famine where thousands of people starved to death. He was pained to observe that "nothing in the economic theories I taught reflected the life around me. How could I go on telling my students make believe stories in the name of economics?" Searching for a way to be relevant to the urgent needs of the poorest citizens, he tried a number of ideas and discovered one worked better than the rest. But it would require a rethinking of the way banks operated and would go counter to conventional wisdom.

To make a long story short, Dr. Yunus created Grameen Bank and offered small loans to a group that had no assets available as collateral and would never qualify for loans anywhere else, poor village women. In a society where a woman might never have ownership in her name of any physical property, the definitions of asset and collateral had to be rewritten. Grameen Bank did that. Dr. Yunus counted the social standing of women and the presence of her social network that would stand up for her trustworthiness as sufficient to grant a loan. Although Dr. Yunus's bank provided loans to men as well, there became overwhelming evidence that women receiving small economic development loans had the lowest risk and the biggest economic impact on their communities. Dr. Yunus pioneered the concept of micro-credit loans, distributing them through over fourteen hundred in fifty-one thousand villages. The impact was so phenomenal that thousands of other micro-credit lending programs in about a hundred countries now follow his lead. His impact on eliminating poverty for over 4.4 million families in rural Bangladesh earned him the 2006 Nobel Peace Prize. Strategic focus on desired outcomes customers want is relevant for change leaders everywhere. We might not end up being Nobel Prize recipients, but we can succeed in other ways that create the win-win.

One last example from the financial world is worth looking at. This one is chosen to show how an enterprise can prosper when leadership elects to consciously set aside some industry practices, minimize compensation weighted to achieve producer-desired outcomes, and instead favor satisfying customer-desired outcomes.

At the end of 2012, over seventy-two hundred mutual funds were available to US investors, more than tripling in number since 1990.[78] This suggests there is plenty of competition between fund managers and lots of choice for customers. What exactly is it that we investors want to achieve as an outcome? An investment firm using the Strategic 5 Whys in Leader's Action 12 would reveal one of our top priorities is to optimally increase our net worth. Simultaneously doing so at least risk would be nice too. Just when you think you've found a winner of a fund, you see the large font disclaimer, "Past performance is no guarantee of future results."[79] How would you feel to see that at the boarding gate for your next flight? How about as you are about to enter surgery? Not a confidence builder. But then the relevant regulating agency is the Securities and Exchange Commission (SEC), not the FAA or the Joint Commission on Health Care. All three agencies are concerned with customer safety. The FAA requires all airline passengers be told how to operate the safety equipment in case of an emergency. The underlying assumption is that passengers have a higher likelihood of survival when belted in and folded over in their seats. That is, there is some predictive data being used for passenger safety.

What is the predictive data investors of mutual funds should know? According to many academic studies, there is little to no correlation between a fund's past and future performance. Flipping a coin would be about as effective in choosing a winner. Another piece of evidence is that, according to Morningstar, "only 16.9 percent of active funds beat their passive counterparts over ten years."[80] That means a comparable index fund did better about 83 percent of the time. Then there is the extra cost to active investing. To put

---

[78] Rob Silverblatt, "Are There Too Many Mutual Funds?", *U.S. News & World Report*, June 10, 2013.

[79] The Securities and Exchange Commission (SEC) requires this disclaimer to be communicated to all mutual fund investors (http://www.sec.gov/answers/mperf.htm).

[80] Jeff Brown, "Do Actively Managed Funds Really Off For Investors?" *U.S. News.* April 14, 2016.

this in perspective, the S&P 500 gained about 15.4 percent during 2014. If you invested in an indexed fund such as the Vanguard 500 Index Fund, performance would have been similar, and your costs would be among the lowest out there. Maybe that's why investment wizards such as Warren Buffett advocate doing just that. It might also be why Vanguard had over $3 trillion in assets that year, with about $31 billion of inflows in December alone.

One of the themes in this section is that our measures can be very revealing concerning which of the eight Dimensions we care most about. Investors are familiar with the term "total return" and may have thought it a useful way to compare similar kinds of funds. What many may not realize is that the rating firm Morningstar does not adjust total returns for sales charges, such as front-end loads, deferred loads, and redemption fees.[81]

The point here is that Vanguard's index fund success is directly related to how well it delivers the desired outcome customers want, despite high uncertainty in the market and standard industry measures that may hide the truth about performance. Vanguard leadership also puts a very high priority on listening to and satisfying its customers. One key element of the culture established by founder John Bogle is that there has long been a concerted effort to avoid a focus on sales and related growth goals that could compete with customer focus, letting fund results do the heavy lifting work of marketing the firm. It has worked well since its founding in 1974 for everyone but its competitors.

The US Department of Labor introduced a rule change on April 6, 2016, intended to require such customer-centered behavior already practiced at firms like Vanguard and Blackrock. The fact that these are two of the largest such investment advisors is probably just a fluke. If the rule goes into effect as intended in 2018, firms that give advice on investments in retirement, pension plans, and similar funds must do so with the customer's interest foremost. Brokerage and other fees to be earned cannot be the driver for investment recommendations. The Obama administration based this new rule on research that found bad advice benefiting the advisor (we would call it "producer-centered behavior") cost retirees about $17 billion annually. While it is sad to see the necessity to actually regulate behavior so that customers win, those who are already customer-centered will continue to reap their rewards.

All three examples in this chapter show a clear relationship between how changing enterprise language and measures for the purpose of better satisfying customer outcomes can benefit the broader society as well as the providing enterprise. This is exactly what we look to achieve as Masters of Excellence.

Most of the Leader's Actions prior to this point may have been fine to work on by yourself. This next one requires teamwork. Invite at least three—but no more than six—other colleagues to join you. It will be helpful if they all share the same organizational focus and related responsibilities. That can mean they share responsibility for the performance of the enterprise, a business unit within the enterprise, a department, or a functional group. Refer to the work you did in Leader's Action 9 (item 3) and Leader's Action 10 (item 5a). Provide a copy of the Strategic 5 Whys worksheet to all team members.

Leader's Action 12: Strategic 5 Whys
(See Appendix 1)

---

[81] http://www.morningstar.com/InvGlossary/total-return.aspx

Executive Summary: Chapter 11

1. We tend to identify and work to correct undesired outcomes more readily than define and pursue desired outcomes that customers want.

2. Common tools, such as the traditional 5 Whys in manufacturing and postmortem in health care support that search for things gone wrong, analyze past practices in the hope of eliminating the root causes of failures.

3. Formal methods for defining what customers want, such as QFD, can be highly complex and dependent on assumptions that do not make application in a nonmanufacturing context either easy or relevant.

4. An alternate approach, looking to the future rather than the past, is called the Strategic 5 Whys.

5. The tool is universally applicable to every context and can be applied to outcomes wanted from an organization or outcomes wanted from a product or service.

6. Unless we use a tool such as the Strategic 5 Whys or other repeatable method, we are likely to ask and get answers for only the first two Why questions. These cause us to address tactical or lower-level outcomes. Answers to Why questions 4 or 5 often reveal strategic priorities we would otherwise have missed.

7. In case 4, a scenario describing a student loan acquisition at a bank showed how simply asking a third Why question revealed an opportunity to engage the customer and achieve a better outcome for her, the bank, and a number of other players.

8. Using the question sequence can also cause us to reconsider the mission of our enterprise or organization. It can shift our view from a traditional one that results in our offering of commodity products and services to one more closely aligned with innovative alternatives that create great differentiation and positive outcomes for us while better satisfying customers. Such was the case for the Midwest credit union and Grameen Bank, including revenue increases of $8 million per month and winning the Nobel Peace Prize. Roadblocks to achieving such results can be Vital Lies 1, 5, and 8.

9. Changing the outcomes we choose to pursue naturally alters our definition of success and what we will measure. In general, our measures will shift from producer-centered and tactical (Dimension 5, what we likely do well) to customer-centered and strategic (Dimension 1, what we may not do so well).

10. Insights from this chapter should reinforce priority issues we saw with cases 2 and 3, opportunity to improve our C3IQ scores for items 3 and 15b.

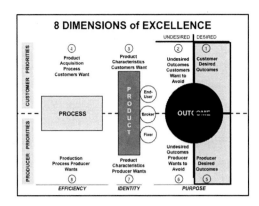

CHAPTER 12—CONNECTING THE STRATEGIC DOTS

Everything we have addressed in the last half-dozen chapters has been done to help us identify and remedy key constraints while articulating main elements in our strategic path to excellence. We should now be ready to pull all the pieces together into one document. Our Strategy Map will help us describe and communicate our purpose and intent, define success, balance priorities we and our customers have, and get ourselves ready to begin deployment.

CASE 5—50 WAYS TO HAVE THEM LOVE YOU

The CEO for a public water utility, PCU, wanted a new strategic plan that put emphasis on satisfying his customers' priorities. He was enthusiastic about the idea that a good plan would be one that is

1. understandable and personally relevant to all employees;

2. developed with the collaborative engagement of customers and a cross-section of employees;

3. a linked integration of outcomes (customer and producer), measures, key products, management accountability, and numerical goals reflecting excellence;

4. capable of being succinctly summarized in no more than two pages;

5. actively used at the department and personal level after development, not put on the shelf and ignored as in the past; and

6. linked to performance reviews and bonus criteria for all managers.

Customers including homeowners, retailers, restaurants, and industry were invited to attend the first day of a multiday planning workshop. Participants were organized into teams. Each team used the Strategic 5 Whys method. Having gotten the hang of how to think about outcomes (as opposed to process, service, problems, and any other issue), teams were asked to identify all the outcomes they could think of that customers and the enterprise wanted. They were given a time limit and the goal to brainstorm at least a dozen outcomes they believed customers wanted. Since customers were actually in the room, the outcomes identified were not guesses. They repeated the process for enterprise priorities. As we can see, their assignment was to address Dimensions 1 and 5. As each outcome was identified, it was recorded on a sticky note and put on the wall. Considering all the outcomes described by all the teams, redundancies were removed.

The participants identified about fifty unique outcomes. Teams were then asked to organize the outcomes into affinity groups, that is, to put those outcomes together that seemed to share a common theme or topic. Once grouped, they organized the outcomes vertically to show any dependent relationships. Outcomes were to be placed so those dependent on others were shown above them on the list. No more than five affinity groups could be created, and no more than ten outcomes could be included in a group. As we learned in Leader's Action 12, a desired outcome fits the phrase, "An excellent, high-performance PCU will result in..." The superordinate outcomes succinctly described each affinity group and functioned as group labels. The following figure shows what they came up with.

The strategic, superordinate outcomes are in the top three boxes. It is important to note these statements are not intended as simply topic labels, though they easily function that way. The statements in all the boxes are outcomes in their own right and must fit this word formula, "An excellent (insert organization name) will result in..."[82] _____.

Notice that two of the three top strategic outcomes are shared by both the enterprise and its customers. When that occurs, we improve alignment. Economic growth, in this case, is a producer-desired outcome. The subordinate outcomes within each column are arranged to show relative sequence and/or dependency. Customers as fans is an outcome dependent on them saving time, having confidence with products, and experiencing the other subordinate outcomes in that affinity group.

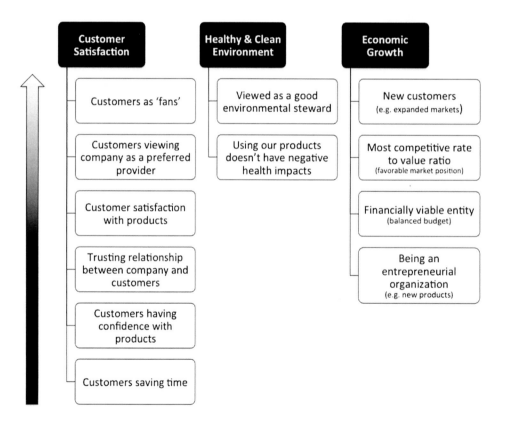

Figure 15—Strategic Outcomes in Affinity Groups Showing Dependencies

As is often discovered, there were very few measures in place for many of the outcomes. The data may have been available, but it was not captured, regularly reported, used for goal-setting, applied to guide the selection and prioritization of strategic projects, or used to strengthen the accountability of functional

---

[82] This is one of several phrases we will refer to as "word formulas." They are a set of linguistic techniques that are highly effective in uncovering what customers want, the VOC. Details are covered in volume 2.

groups and leadership within the enterprise. Otherwise, everything was just wonderful. The following are excerpts from their draft plan that made up the strategy map (and new balanced scorecard) that emerged.

STRATEGY MAP WORKSHEET, Part 1: Mission, Values, Outcomes, Measures

Rev. Date												

STEP 1
ORGANIZATION NAME: PCU

STEP 2
MISSION: Satisfy the water-related needs of residential and commercial customers through innovative leadership.

STEP 3 STRATEGIC OUTCOMES	STEP 4 SUBORDINATE OUTCOMES (Enablers/constraints on Strategic Outcomes)	STEP 5 MEASURE ID	STEP 6 Areas of Alignment with 8 Dimensions	STEP 7 RESPECT Treating others with the understanding, dignity and courtesy they value.	INTEGRITY Behaving in a correct and proper way, consistent with ethical principles.	COMMITMENT Actively engaged in supporting an organizational cause or action.	HONESTY Being truthful, accurate, forthcoming. Telling it like it is.	FAIRNESS Opportunities and constraints are equitably available and applied.	INDIVIDUAL WORTH Individuals are treated as capable of contributing to organizational priorities.	TRUST Engendering the confidence of others.
				A	B	C	D	E	F	G
CUSTOMER SATISFACTION	Customers as "fans"	1, 4, 7	1, 5	O		O		O		O
	Customers viewing PCU as a preferred provider among local utilities	1, 4, 5, 6, 13	1, 4, 8,	O	O			O		O
	Customer satisfaction with PCU products	1, 4, 5, 6, 14	1, 4, 8,	O		O		O		O
	A partnership between the PCU and the public	1	1	O			O	O		
	Trusting relationship between PCU and customers	1, 4, 5, 6	1, 4, 8,	O	O	O	O	O		O
	Customers have confidence in PCU products	1, 5, 6, 13	1, 4, 8,	O		O	O	O	O	O
	Customers save time	1	1	O		O				
HEALTHY & CLEAN ENVIRONMENT	PCU viewed as a good environmental steward	1, 3, 8, 9	1, 2, 5		O	O	O		O	O
	PCU products have no adverse health impact	1, 10, 11	1, 2, 6		O	O			O	O
ECONOMIC GROWTH	New customers (Expanded Markets)	12	5	O						O
	Most competitive rate to value ratio (Favorable market position)	1, 3, 14, 18	1					O		
	Financially viable entity (Balanced budget)	14, 16, 17, 18	1, 3, 5, 7				O		O	O
	PCU is an entrepreneurial organization (New products)	2, 3, 12, 15	3, 7, 5						O	

Figure 16—PCU Strategy Map

We can see in the strategy map above that outcomes, outcome measures, and core values are all connected. The Measure ID column refers to the descriptions of the measures, numbered 1 through 23 in the table below, labeled PCU Key Measures Summary. The measures were created to assess outcome-related performance. A single measure can be seen supporting more than one outcome. This tends to indicate the strength and utility of a single measure. We would like to have the fewest possible measures that cover all the outcomes. We also want to make sure no outcome goes unmeasured.

The Os under a core value in the strategy map show that it supports specific subordinate outcomes. If we viewed this as a cause-effect relationship, we would say the core value contributes to causing the outcome. The evidence of that support is shown in the Key Measures Summary table. The Related to Core Value column there indicates the letter for the related core value(s) shown in the strategy map. We can quickly observe any of the following:

- Almost half the measures (nine of twenty-three) appear unrelated to any of the core values. This is not necessarily a bad thing. After all, we created the measures to address specific subordinate outcomes. But it does suggest there may be a value that is unstated and driving the existence of the measure(s). For example, measures such as 7, 9, 19, 20, 22, and 23 appear related to a producer-centered value. That value might be efficiency, cost-effectiveness, competitiveness, or something else. It is unstated. If it is true that measures tell us what we value, unstated values that contribute to a significant portion of our KPIs could compete with stated values. Ambiguity and conflict could result. As Master of Excellence, we could work with leadership to label and define that value and add it to the stated core values in the strategy map. We would then want to get clarification on how that value ranks in comparison to the others. The objective is to make sure everyone understands which value, when found to compete with another, is the dominant value to follow.

- About half of the measures (eleven of twenty-three) are related to more than one of the eight Dimensions. We were working on outcome measures but can now see what we've come up with might address more than that.

- It is possible to find that all the outcomes are measured but not all core values are. It is helpful but not essential that we see in our strategy map that all core values are measured. They do need to be measured but do not have to be identified here. When they exist and are visually connected to strategic outcomes, that alignment is strengthened. If we saw that a core value had no related measures, we would want to close that gap. That could be done elsewhere. A core value with no measures at all can cause us to conclude the value exists only as an intent and has not been actualized.

Organization	PCU		Rev Date		TARGETS		8DX Alignment	Related to Core Values
ID #	**KEY PERFORMANCE MEASURES**				Baseline Year	Year 1		
1	Percent of key products that meet customer's performance, perception, and outcome expectations						1	A, C, G
2	Percent of products that are considered best in class						3, 7	A, C
3	Percent of core processes that are best in class						8	A
4	Hours of interruption for residential and commercial customers and dollars of direct cost customer incurs (through dollar value of claims paid)						2	A, B, C, G
5	Percent of original estimated completion dates that are changed						4, 8	B, C, D, G
6	Number of days deviation between first estimated completion date and actual date received						4, 8	B, C, D, G
7	Percent of customers participating in conservation initiatives						5	
8	Number of utility-related beach closings						2	G
9	Number of GD of water consumption/capita						5	
10	Number of reported utility-related health concerns						2, 6	A, B, C, G
11	Number of boil water notices						2, 6	A, B, C, G
12	Number of GD of reclaimed water to increase						4, 7	
13	Number of PCU violations						6	A, B, C, K
14	Dollar cost of fines						6	B, C, D, G
15	Number of publications that use PCU as a model of how things should be						5	B, C
16	Moody's bond rating						1, 5	B
17	Percent of key products whose unit cost is at or below industry average						3, 7	
18	Percent of potable water unaccounted for						7	D, G
19	Percent of revenue from new sources						5	
20	Percent of products generating below average market fees declines						5	
21	Percent increase in customer bill that is discretionary						1, 5	
22	Plant availability/total hours						4, 8	
23	Net megawatts sold						7	

Figure 17—PCU Key Measures Summary

Leader's Action 13: The Strategy Map, Part 1
(See Appendix 1)

Executive Summary: Building The Strategy Map

A major objective up to this point, especially from chapters 6 through 12, has been to build our Strategy Map. That completes much of what is needed in steps 1 through 4 of the Ten Steps in our Road Map to Excellence, described in chapter 2 and shown below.

---

10 STEPS TO CUSTOMER-CENTERED EXCELLENCE

1. Establish the conditions for excellence, transformation, and leadership.

2. Articulate strategic and customer-desired outcomes.

3. Determine how each outcome will be measured.

4. Set numerical goals and due dates.

5. Select the few products and owners most likely to impact outcome success.

6. Identify end user, broker, and fixer customers for key products.

7. Uncover and measure customers' priority outcome, product, and process expectations.

8. Innovate or redesign products to achieve best outcomes.

9. Cut the time to produce, acquire, and use products by 80 percent.

10. Integrate cultural change levers to sustain, celebrate, and broaden success.

Figure 18—10 Steps to Customer-Centered Excellence

A second big objective has been to start applying at least the first four of our six levers of cultural change, discussed in Chapter 6: language, values, measures, and assumptions. We have been careful to uncover and understand what desired outcomes for customer are, differentiated from topics easily confused with them, including outcomes we want from our organization's point of view; undesired outcomes and problems; backward-looking root cause analysis versus future-oriented aspirations; and activities (process) and products.

We have used carefully structured phrases, called "word formulas," to define both desired and undesired outcomes and construct potential measures where none may have existed. The main reasons for using these linguistic methods include removing some of the inherent ambiguity of language and fostering certainty, repeatability, consistency, and alignment. We discussed the fact that our core values may have been easy to state and hard to execute. That becomes evident when we find that a core value such as customer satisfaction has no policy or other universally relevant vehicle to deploy it. When we have policies covering other priorities, but not such a core value, it can create doubt about our sincerity. So we provided an example of a customer satisfaction policy and showed how it could be pragmatically used to deploy several other core values as well.

Related to the issue of core values was the story about Lumber Liquidators. One of the key points was that leadership had core values that could be interpreted as conflicting. Business financial growth was at odds with sustainability and environmental stewardship. When management was confronted with the conflict, they chose the value most likely to be tied to key measures of personal success, such as their compensation. Resolving this potential for conflict is why we strongly advocate the ranking of core values. The top-ranked value must always guide behavior. But the reality is that, without alignment among all six levers, we invite ambiguity and leave ourselves open to unanticipated and undesired outcomes.

A potential conflict could arise if parts of the enterprise differ in their priorities. The Strategy Map should be developed for the enterprise as well as for all the business units below it. Usually the core values at the enterprise level are identical to what all the various business units have and in the same priority rank. There can be exceptions to this pattern. It is quite possible that a core value, desired outcome, or KPI articulated by one business unit may actually conflict with those of another business unit. For example, one unit may put on-time delivery as its highest priority, but another group puts product quality first. Could those conflict? You bet, and they often do. The Master of Excellence will avoid the resulting problems by emphasizing that any instance of conflict at the business unit or department level will always yield to the priorities stated at the enterprise level. The goal is zero ambiguity!

Sometimes a major obstacle to achieving excellence is not ambiguity but clarity about and focus on the wrong things. View this as an important exception to our general rule that alignment is to be sought. We discussed the problem when the mission of the enterprise is erroneously stated as "to make a profit." The case of Chainsaw Al Dunlap in Chapter 6 was related to this, and the misconception that alignment of such a mission with the measure of profit proves we are headed toward excellence. In Dunlap's situation, outstanding increase in shareholder value and profit led to Sunbeam's demise and the loss of thousands of jobs. Others have embraced Dunlap's warped view of success. The Master of Excellence will be severely challenged to intervene and redirect the ship.

The last objective was to identify how to raise less than stellar C3IQ scores (Leader's Action 4). Take a look at where you were when we started and see if you now have a path to advance your score on the following C3IQ items: 1, 2, 14, and 15a–c.

We have worked on purpose, ambiguity, and our personal and organizational integrity related to strategic intent. Working on the right side of the 8DX framework required us to start with the end in mind, answering questions about why. Strategic direction has been articulated, simplified, and more easily communicated when we have defined Dimensions 1, 2, 5, and 6; have established measures of success; and set numerical goals for improvement. We have now completed the answer to why we exist, from the balanced perspective of both customers and producer. My hope is that the following statement does not describe how you now feel. Nonetheless, we will work to quickly eliminate any remaining ambiguity.

> We have not succeeded in solving all your problems. The answers we have found only
> serve to raise a whole set of new questions. In some ways we feel we are as confused as
> ever, but we believe we are confused on a higher level and about more important things.[83]

Broad understanding of our strategic intent is essential. Sadly it is not sufficient for effective deployment. Our next leadership challenge closes the gap. We will describe and prioritize the products (the whats) we

---

[83] Earl C. Kelley, *The Workshop Way of Learning* (New York: Harper, 1951).

create that enable our purpose to be achieved. The excellence of those products is addressed by dimensions 3 and 7. Our job will be simpler and ambiguity reduced with the ability to answer four practical questions personally relevant for everyone in the organization. We begin answering the first of those in the next chapter.

CHAPTER 13—TWO KEY QUESTIONS

Everyone in the high-performance, customer-centered enterprise must be able to answer two key questions, applied to themselves and the organization:

1. What is our product?
2. Who are the customers?

These questions are not remarkable. The process of answering them is what produces insights leading to transformation. These are the first two of four questions we will answer. Volume 2 answers the last two. The not-so-simple answers will establish a basis for new thinking. It would be a mistake to view the anticipated answers to be just common sense and, therefore, be perceived as not particularly enlightening. It can be tempting for us to think, "So what? I already know this." Therein lies the problem for anyone wishing to actually deploy and sustain a culture of excellence. It is not as easy as it would first appear, and the devil (or eternal joy) is certainly in the details. The details associated with the first two questions are the last main topics to be addressed here in volume 1.

It Should Be Easy

The practical path to finding succinct answers is momentarily obstructed by devilish extra questions:

a. Are employees to focus on "our product" at the enterprise, business unit, functional group, or personal level?

b. Is our product singular, or are there many products an employee or the organization might have? If there are many, how does one prioritize which are most important?

c. How does someone who does not personally create widgets such as cars, computers, and phones, who views his or her work in terms of service or knowledge (roughly 89 percent of today's postindustrial workforce), define his or her product?

d. If our product could refer to something produced at one of several levels (suggested in question "a" above), would the customer be the same party for each product?[84]

e. Once we identify a specific product, are we to focus on the end users for that product or others? Does it matter?

f. Are customer expectations the same as their requirements, needs, and hopes? If not, is it possible to meet all the agreed-upon requirements but still end up with unhappy customers?

g. When seeking to understand customer priorities, is it sufficient to understand how the product will objectively perform? If not, what else do we need to know, and how would we find out?

---

[84] See the prior discussion on who "the customer" refers to in Chapter 6, Levers and Ambiguity.

h. Quality is often defined in terms of defects, deficiencies, and risks. If we minimize things gone wrong, would that be proof our products and culture are excellent?

i. How would one create metrics for squishy expectations that customers may insist upon having satisfied, such as easy to use, appealing, and innovative?

The figure below shows that the goal is to be able to answer question number 4, how we can excel. But if excellence is believed to be defined by customers, then we will need to uncover and understand what they want, answering question number 3. Doing that requires us to unambiguously agree on who the customer really is, answering question number 2. Recall that C3IQ items 11 and 12 ask about this. Take a look at what your response was. If it were like that of many, you may not have earned the maximum score of five on each of those items. That may very well be due to the fact we cannot truly know who the customer is without being clear about what the specific product is for which they are a customer. This is why we have to start the entire sequence with a clear understanding of how to answer question number 1. Without doing that, all other answers will be based on assumptions that are hidden, not shared, and/or wrong.

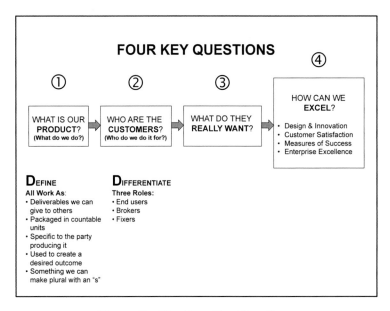

Figure 19—The Four Key Questions

The succinct answers to the first two questions are shown in this figure. The Master of Excellence will find that the correct answer can be easily communicated to others. But they are not guaranteed to understand or even accept the answers when first told. The insight gained from arriving at the answers themselves is really important. That is where the sometimes subtle benefits of doing this become clear, unambiguous, and transformative. Once we've experienced those insights, we'll wonder why everyone doesn't already think this way.

Just to make sure we don't leave our list of questions above without resolution, here are brief answers:

a. Yes. The different products identified with the enterprise are most likely to be the ones employees (and especially managers) tend to easily name. In a complex organization, there is generally no one person who personally produces those. So a product's ownership is diffused across many people, limiting accountability. On the other hand, a specific product produced by an individual has, by definition, just one owner.

b. An individual employee, his or her functional group, the department or business unit he or she works in, and the enterprise all will have multiple products. The scope or complexity of each product will generally increase the further up the organization structural chart we go. They are not all equally important. Selecting which of the many products (possibly hundreds or thousands) to choose for improvement is achieved by using the Target Product Selection Matrix, which we'll apply in Leader's Action 16.

c. Few readers of this book personally produce manufactured products. All of us produce knowledge products. Exactly what that means, and its significance, is the subject of the next four chapters.

d. While it is possible for the same individual to be a customer of multiple products, the exact role he or she plays with each product is likely to vary in significant ways and can change over time.

e. Our bias will intentionally be in favor of thoroughly understanding end users. To do so will require us to distinguish them from the other two kinds of customers, which will be addressed in Chapter 20. It matters, as we will see with examples illustrating the consequences of not getting this right.

f. This question requires several different routes to uncovering what customers may want. Which of these we attend to will determine the constraints or scope involved with our pursuit of excellence. On one end of the continuum is the use of convergent thinking to make improvement. On the other end, divergent thinking will drive innovation. The answers are in volume 2.

g. It is definitely not sufficient to understand simply the objective performance wanted of a product. At least two other characteristics are more important. Our discussion concerning the VOC in volume 2 will identify the other characteristics to understand and how to uncover them, even if no customer volunteers those priorities.

h. Seeking excellence defined as defect-free products is pursuit of a mirage. It is not sufficient. Would the leaders making perfect buggy whips, typewriters, or oil lamps be considered examples of excellence today?

i. How to easily measure the seemingly immeasurable, such as imprecise subjective perceptions, will be one of our secrets to unravel in volume 2.

The first of the key questions can be answered at three levels: for the enterprise, for the department or functional group, and by each individual within that functional group. For a very small enterprise, the way we answer these questions personally will be very similar to how we do it with the entire organization in mind.

If you are a craftsperson making products such as custom dining tables or wedding cakes, these questions are very easy to answer. The answer for each question will be the same whether you think of yourself or your small business as the "we." Sadly those connections can become pretty muddy as the enterprise gets larger and more complex.

Leadership would be so much easier if the alignment between personal and complex enterprise work were crystal clear. Our aim is to achieve that clarity regarding the first two key questions, modeling that ability for others. The not-so-obvious answers will establish a basis for thinking like our customers and achieving dramatic, measurably improved success.

Beyond Work As A Process

We tend to hear a version of question number 1 every time we meet someone new, "What do you do?" We typically answer this in terms of our membership in a particular group, the organization we work for, our occupation, our position, our discipline, or our activity. Examples could include answers such as the following:

a. I am VP for product development at Super Cloud Computing.
b. I am a donor to the West Coast Modern Arts Society.
c. I am a help desk supervisor in the IT department at Healthy Foods, Inc. My team looks for support from me to answer questions from callers using our computer systems.
d. I am director of strategic initiatives at First Financial Futures Bank. I am working to put process improvement programs in place and build cross-department teamwork.
e. I am manager of community relations at Our Town Electric Utility. My job is to communicate utility policies and listen to the needs of our citizens and other stakeholders.

A popular exhortation among change leaders since at least the early 1990s has been to define all work as a process. The advantage to doing so is that it helps us analyze the sequence, dependencies, and responsibilities involved with all activity. It can help identify inconsistent practices, delays, inefficiencies, complexity, capacity constraints, and other detriments to organizational performance. Those opportunities for improvement explain the popularity of change initiatives such as Lean (to stamp out waste), Six Sigma (to reduce variation), the Theory of Constraints (to eliminate bottlenecks), and so on.

Another handy way to make sure we don't forget to think of our work as a process is to embed activity, in the form of verbs, in the names of our functional groups. Those include accounting, bookkeeping, engineering, inspection, marketing, production, purchasing, receiving, servicing, shipping, training, data processing, production, customer support, personnel management, supply management, inventory management, quality management, human resource management, and information technology management.

An "ing" on the end of a word is a dead giveaway for activity. Whenever a word ending with "ing" could be either a verb or a noun, assume it is being used as a verb unless it is stated unambiguously otherwise. Management, in the manner used in a functional title, is a verb. The chances are good that the title of the group you belong to and/or those of the groups that report directly to you are named as activities.

Disadvantages of the work-as-process model begin with the ambiguity of whose process or activity we should define as work. The default tendency is to assume it is ours, the producer's. In the absence of any statement to the contrary, that is what we will likely focus our energies on. It's not a bad thing, but it's Dimension 8, not the same as attending to the customer's process, Dimension 4. The most positive way to look at that might be to consider the glass half-full.

Could we gain anything by describing what we do in terms of products? You bet. For starters, we'd shift focus away from producer self-interest for a moment. The notion that we have customers is far easier and more natural to apply when we're talking about a product than when thinking about process. Do customers primarily come to us for our activity or our products? If the product isn't really what is wanted, worrying about the process puts the cart before the horse. Customers care about the products we give them, whose use creates the outcomes they want.

PRODUCT PRINCIPLES

1. Products focus our vision outward to customers; process focuses us inward.
2. A product must meet all five characteristics:
    a. It can be made plural with an "s"
    b. It is a deliverable we can give to others
    c. It is packaged in countable units
    d. It is very specific to the person or group that produces it
    e. It is used to produce a desired outcome (for the producer and/or customer)
3. The voice of leadership (VOL) is expressed in products such as strategies, policies, plans, and decisions.
4. The relative priority of our core values are reflected in the decisions we make.
5. The higher we are in an organization, the less likely we are to define our work as tangible products or measure their performance; doing so drives excellence in all other products.
6. Activity that creates no product is of questionable value.
7. Service is not a product. It is so ambiguous in meaning as to be a useless term, except to categorize certain kinds of products.
8. Service products uniquely require customer involvement in the production of the product.
9. Information products are created in anticipation of a need; service products are produced in response.
10. Leaders define their knowledge products as quantified deliverables, designed to satisfy emerging expectations of highly differentiated customers.
11. Every product is a cause of success or failure; treat it that way.
12. A product that does not create a desired outcome is of no value.
13. Organize everything by product: customers, measures, outcomes, problems, processes, and teams.
14. The unit cost, quality, yield, cycle time, rework cost, and satisfaction with every product are contributors to excellence and can be measured.
15. Enlightened leaders understand the earlier a product is created within a flow of products, the bigger its impact will be, so excellence must start there.
16. A product may be defined differently by customers than its producer.
17. We can only identify our customers by their relationships to specific products.
18. Customers may not know what the product should be, but they know the outcomes it must achieve.
19. Six major constraints characterize service. Describing work as products fix them all.
20. A product is the root cause of any problem.
21. Fix the product before the process.
22. A process is a chain of products.

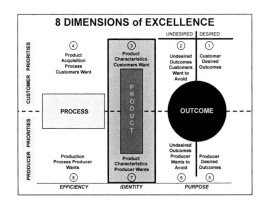

CHAPTER 14—WORK AS PRODUCTS

Define all work as products! That is our new mantra as Masters of Excellence. Outcomes are intangible. Processes are intangible. Products are tangible. They concretely connect processes and outcomes. A product must meet all five characteristics:

- It can be made plural with an "s"
- It is a deliverable we can give to others
- It is packaged in countable units
- It is very specific to the person or group that produces it
- It is used to produce a desired outcome (for the producer and/or customer)

All products must meet all five criteria. For pure simplicity, I recommend using the first criterion first, as the qualifier for whether or not something is a product. If you can't make it plural with an "s", it is probably not a product.

Not everything that satisfies that first criterion is a product, however. It's a bit like the situation where we know that all horses are four-legged animals but not all four-legged animals are horses. Salespeople, when asked what their products are, will sometimes say "dollars." Probably not. It might seem like all five criteria have been met. But you show me the salesperson creating dollars, and I'll show you a prospective inmate for a federal prison. The US Treasury Department believes they are the only group with the authority and legal capacity to make dollars. Sales folks confronted with this setback sometimes retort that they really create relationships. That may be true, but are those products that we can give to someone else? Maybe. But show me a person giving someone else a relationship, and we discover either a matchmaker or a pimp. Kind of related.

Let's face it. You could give someone a compliment but not a relationship. A relationship is an outcome obtained by giving, receiving, and using some other products. Could numerous compliments result in a good relationship? Probably not by themselves, but hey, it's not a bad idea to give them anyway. On an intimate level, a relationship between spouses is likely to be in trouble if there are no compliments exchanged.

Wait a minute. Could a compliment, a greeting, and an invitation all be products? Yup. All three meet the five criteria of a product. It turns out an eighteen-year-old started a thriving business in 1910 selling those. His name was Joyce Clyde Hall, and the company would become Hallmark.

So what would a salesperson's products be? They might include needs analyses, purchase proposals, price quotes, product presentations, and technical product answers. At a conceptual level, those aren't terribly different from what a family doctor's products might include: physical exams, examination reports, treatment plans, prescriptions, and health-improvement answers. In both situations, the cost to produce each of those products is usually unknown and unreported. The product sold by the salesperson generally has a known and reported cost (at least within the enterprise), especially if it is a manufactured product. Not so for knowledge products produced personally by the salesperson and doctor. We'll come back to this and its significance in more detail later. For now, let's identify products we personally create.

One of our six levers for cultural transformation, discussed in Chapter 6, is modeling. We can't hope to have much success shifting the thinking about work as products if we can't demonstrate to others how it applies to ourselves. The next Leader's Action will help us begin to master this or experience how challenging it can be at first. If you have understood the product concept to this point, this should not take more than five minutes to complete. Think of your current role in the enterprise as you answer. This is one of the most important Leader's Actions in the book!

Leader's Action 14: Personal Products
(See Appendix 1)

One of our objectives is to eliminate all ambiguity regarding whether something is a process, a product, or an outcome. It is also critical to complete this successfully because other key concepts, the 8DX framework, the completed Strategy Map, and the 10 Steps are all dependent on getting this right. So if you could put a check in each of the five criteria yes boxes, congratulations! You are ready to move on.

It is a surprise to many that identifying their personal products is not easy when first attempted. It represents a different way of thinking about what we do. If you had trouble or want to make certain you got this right, let's identify a few common obstacles so you can go back, try again, and be confident in your success. And when you are helping others get this right, the following guidance should be useful when anyone feels confronted by one of the following obstacles:

1. I don't have a product.
2. Some of the products I named are not countable and don't have obvious units of measure.
3. All the products I think of are really enterprise products.
4. The products I think of as mine might be claimed by those who report to me. Who is right?
5. Is it okay if some of my products look like they are also outcomes?
6. These products look trivial and don't represent all I do.
7. Some of my most important products are created collaboratively with others. Should I claim them as mine?
8. I have too many products! How do I choose the most important ones?

Response to #1. It is true that some people perform activity without producing a product. That is rare and occurs with people who are generally low wage and low skill, performing a small task for which no deliverable is created from their effort. That does not apply to you. Everyone reading this book produces products. We just need to figure out what they are. One reason it can be initially hard to do is that we have traditionally tended to think of our work in terms of activity or job role. The figure below provides a comparison of views.

WAYS OF DESCRIBING WHAT WE DO		
BY ROLE	BY ACTIVITY	BY PRODUCT
Software engineer	Programming	A software application for finding local restaurants with a phone
Medical lab technician	Drawing blood	Labeled blood specimens
Marketing manager	Market analysis	Market demographics reports
Instructor	Teaching	Project management course
VP for Quality	Quality planning	Strategic quality improvement plan

Figure 20—What We Do

Another version of this first stumbling block is to view ourselves as providing service, not products. This service issue is such a big obstacle and source of ambiguity that a whole chapter is devoted to it shortly. It is worth saying a couple of things right now. First, just because we can make service plural does not make it a product. It also fails other tests, such as being countable. There is no unit of service to count. Second, service can also be a verb, and it is usually thought of that way, as an activity. At least the first five examples of activity in the figure below are consistent with our normal concepts of service.

Our tendency to define all work as a process is the same as thinking of work as activities. There is nothing wrong with doing that, but it has many weaknesses the product concept remedies. The next figure expands on the process-product distinction with examples.

AS ACTIVITY	AS PRODUCTS
Fixing	➢ Repairs
Sending	➢ Shipments
Delivering	➢ Deliveries
Helping	➢ Answers
Communicating	➢ Emails, Presentations, Brochures
Coordinating	➢ Schedules
Leading	➢ Strategies, Policies, Decisions
Managing	➢ Plans, Reports
Auditing	➢ Audit Reports
Programming	➢ Software Applications (apps)
Selling	➢ Proposals, Quotes, Presentations

Figure 21—Defining Work as Activities and Products

Response to #2. Instructions b–e in product definition all provide examples of things sometimes named as products that are either activities or outcomes. It is not unusual to think that information is our product. Since we can't it make it plural with an "s," we know it isn't. But we also know that we give others information all the time. The problem is that information, as stated, should be considered raw material. Until that information is packaged into a form that can be counted, such as the examples in the above figure, it is not a product. The same is true with data. Just because data is a noun and is plural in Latin does not make it a product that fits our criteria. View it the same way as information. Data and information refer to the content of a knowledge product, just as rubber is the content and raw material of a tire.

Response to #3. It is very common for managers to think of the enterprise's sold products as theirs. Managers do not personally make cars, airplanes, computers, pharmaceuticals, or other commercial enterprise products. These are made by groups of people who have shared responsibility but diffused accountability. If we think an individual is the producer of a product, consider who gets blamed when the product fails in some way. If it clearly is one person, then that person is likely to be the producer. If ownership is uncertain, we either have a group that has collectively produced the product or are not sure what the product at fault really is.

Response to #4. Managers very often tend to claim the work of their people as their own. When those people are present in a workshop with their manager when this perceived land grab for others' products is discovered, a lot of snickering can occur. Of course, the manager is simply expressing a sense of ownership with his or her group. But the manager's products are clearly different. Product categories relevant for managers can include procedures, policies, work instructions, presentations, performance evaluations, and so on. Try again. Remember to make them specific.

Response to #5. A product is something we give to others. An outcome is a result they or we get by using that product. They are not the same thing. A common thought is that we create solutions. If we are chemists, that could be true. We can certainly make it plural with an "s," give it to someone, and count them. But for most of us, solutions are outcomes, not products. When we start to name specific solutions we deliver to someone else, it may very well look like an answer or proposal. Those are products, as we will address in Leader's Action 14. One of our goals as Master of Excellence is to eliminate ambiguity. This product definition cannot be considered successful if we still have confusion. See instructions c and e in Product Definition.

Response to #6. The fact that we might spend a quarter of our average day writing emails and another significant amount of time in meetings, these would have to be considered major parts of our work. In aggregate, they are not trivial. But it might seem a bit at odds with the view that our work is to inspire, direct, inform, enlighten, correct, educate, support, and otherwise help others and our organization improve performance. All those are activities. Improved performance is one of the possible outcomes. The vehicles by which we achieve the result include the kinds of products shown in the figure above. If we spend a large portion of our day producing those products but they do not create the intended outcomes, they truly could be a waste of time. That judgment about whether or not they are worth spending time to create is a separate issue. A product might be crummy, but it is still a product. On the other hand, if the product could be replaced with one that is more effective, we have just opened the door to innovation and/or the reduction of waste.

Response to #7. It is true that some products are created collaboratively with others. For the purpose of this Leader's Action, we want to identify only those we can claim as owned by just ourselves. This eliminates the ambiguity of ownership and accountability. The test is this: If there is any failing with the product, who gets blamed? Our aim is really not to affix blame, but it certainly can clarify things. For example, a strategic plan is a product often created collaboratively by the whole executive team. But if a flaw is discovered in it, the CEO is likely to be held accountable. Members of the executive team may very well view themselves in an advisory capacity to the CEO, not owners of the product. In such a case, my recommendation is to name the CEO as owner of the product.

This does not completely answer the question about ownership when a product is created by equal coproducers. We will include those when we select target products in Chapter 18. One example of a coproduced product is the American Constitution. The Founding Fathers are considered the joint producers.

The Constitution is what we will refer to as a source product. Typical source products include strategies, policies, statutes, and plans. Put bluntly, they are the source of all good and evil. They guide the creation of many other products. If they are ambiguous, contradictory, incomplete, or otherwise confusing, expect chaos and dysfunction to result. While many were celebrating the genius of the Founding Fathers during America's bicentennial celebration, Supreme Court justice Thurgood Marshall took a contrasting view:

> The focus of this celebration invites a complacent belief that the vision of those who debated and compromised in Philadelphia yielded the "more perfect Union" it is said we now enjoy. I cannot accept this invitation, for I do not believe that the meaning of the Constitution was forever "fixed" at the Philadelphia Convention. Nor do I find the wisdom, foresight, and sense of justice exhibited by the Framers particularly profound. To the contrary, the government they devised was defective from the start, requiring several amendments, a civil war, and momentous social transformation to attain the system of constitutional government, and its respect for the individual freedoms and human rights, we hold as fundamental today…We need look no further than the first three words of the document's preamble: 'We the People." When the Founding Fathers used this phrase in 1787, they did not have in mind the majority of America's citizens…On a matter so basic as the right to vote, for example,…women did not gain the right to vote for over a hundred and thirty years [when] the 19th Amendment [was] ratified in 1920…No doubt it will be said, when the unpleasant truth of the history of slavery in America is mentioned during this bicentennial year, that the Constitution was a product of its times, and embodied a compromise which, under other circumstances, would not have been made. But the effects of the Framers' compromise have remained for generations. They arose from the contradiction between guaranteeing liberty and justice to all, and denying both to Negroes.[85]

Response to #8. Great insight! Yes, we personally produce many products at work, more at home, and even more in other contexts. As I do periodically, I called a participant after she had attended one of my workshops. I asked Karen what she had gotten, if anything, out of the session. She said, "You changed my life." Thinking she had confused my workshop with something else, I reminded her that this was the customer-centered culture session a few weeks prior. Karen again said that was exactly the session she was referring to. I asked her to explain.

Karen said she had been required to attend the workshop with all the managers of her group. She had

---

[85] Remarks of Thurgood Marshall at the Annual Seminar of the San Francisco Patent and Trademark Association, Maui, Hawaii, May 6, 1987.

not been looking forward to it because she was buried with work, depressed by the constant reactive atmosphere in the company, and had been on the verge of resigning. Upon attending, one of the ideas that really took hold with her was that she had products, represented by every document she created. When Karen got back to her office and surveyed the same scene in her office she saw every day, she decided to sort the various to-dos and stacks of paper into two piles: one with the critical few products most central to her personal role and mission in the organization and the other for everything else. The second stack went into boxes in the corner. She decided to work only on the much smaller group, unless someone complained about something she hadn't given him or her.

Karen said she was surprised that not a soul seemed to notice the undone work. The key products got her full attention. She began applying some of the other C3 concepts to them. Her depression lifted, and her sense of purpose and satisfaction returned.

Karen had used an intuitive approach to determine which of her products were most important within the context of her job mission. She had considered the outcomes she had the responsibility to achieve. That approach can work surprisingly well. A more formal way is to use the Target Product Selection Matrix, addressed in Leader's Action 17.

Before we move on, please be certain to have named the products you personally create. Mastering this answer to the first of our two key questions (Chapter 13) is essential to being able to answer the others. Please Note: whenever we run into a problem completing one of the other three questions, I strongly recommend assuming we may have confusion about the product. See whether or not that is so by always double-checking that the product has not inadvertently shifted in our thinking so we are working on a different but related product. This C3 system is self-correcting if we follow that practice. We'll see examples of this product-shifting and self-correction when we discuss the second of our four key questions: Who are the customers?

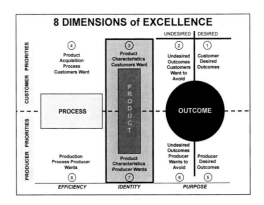

CHAPTER 15—EVOLUTION OF PRODUCTS

When we first begin thinking of work as products, we often encounter two main barriers. First, there is the baggage of history regarding that word. Second, we may view ourselves as being in the business of service, not products. Let's deal with the past first.

Humans are thought to have practiced a mostly hunter-gatherer kind of existence prior to 10,000 BC. Then the agricultural age began. By the time 1700 rolled around, about 86 percent of the colonial workforce in the Americas personally produced agricultural products. The World Bank reports that only about 2 percent of the US work population produces agricultural products today.[86] So although we are personally not likely to produce agricultural products for a living, we certainly know a lot about them. After all, we are customers for them. Furthermore, we can name the units of measure for such products with almost no thought. Name the units of measure for each of the products below:

Apples   _____

Beans   _____

Carrots   _____

Eggs   _____

Cauliflower   _____

Strawberries   _____

Milk   _____

You probably said bushel, pound or kilo, bunch, dozen, head, quart, and gallon or liter. You would be right. Those units represent the way the economic value of the product is determined and sold. How is the economic value determined for one of your own products, say an email? Sorry, did you say it isn't done or there isn't one? Both are true? Yikes! Well, it's not an agricultural product, so I guess it doesn't fit in this discussion. We'll come back to it.

Now, we might have said "each" is the unit of measure for all but the last of the agricultural products above. We would still be right because each of those names meets the five criteria for a product given in the previous chapter. What a wonderful experience to always be right. But there is a practical reason why we package the products a certain way. In some places of the world, eggs can be and are purchased

---

[86] http://data.worldbank.org/indicator/SL.AGR.EMPL.ZS

singly. That may be highly practical when you don't make more than a dollar a day and have no refrigeration. In no case are beans purchased one at a time. Their individual economic value is insignificant. This, of course, explains the value of bean counters. You always knew it was intended as an insult, and now you know why.

If we had to pick a specific year for the start of the industrial age, it could be 1769. As discussed in Chapter 7, that is when James Watt introduced his steam engine, ushering in the industrial revolution in North America. The steam engine caused volume, yield, and market size for agricultural products to go steadily upward while the unit cost, market price, time to market, and number of labor production hours required per unit went down. These represent ideal trends unless your job is the one not needed. Of course, people tended to hang on to a lifestyle they knew, even though it became less and less worth doing so from an economic standpoint. Then we had the Civil War, almost a hundred years after the start of the industrial revolution, which accelerated the exodus from farms to industrial cities. We can see the evolution in the dominant kinds of products produced by the labor-force trend lines in the graphic below.[87]

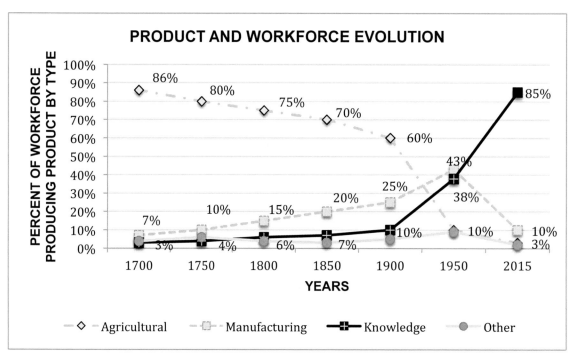

Figure 22—Product and Workforce Evolution

The chart shows changes in the US labor force in terms of the kinds of products individuals personally produced.

The peak year for the percent of the US workforce engaged in manufacturing is about 1957. The rate of decline in manufacturing employment after 1957 closely mirrors the rate of decline a hundred years previously in agricultural employment after 1857. History may not exactly repeat, but it does rhyme. In this case, we could repeat what we said about agricultural products at the advent of the industrial age: the volume, yield, and market size for manufactured products went steadily upward while the unit cost,

---

[87] The actual slope of each trend line shown represents a best estimate based on many sources since reliable data was not consistently collected or organized in this manner by any government or business entities throughout the span of time shown.

market price, time to market, and number of labor hours required per unit went down. These represent ideal trends unless your job is the one not needed.

Ross Perot, US presidential candidate in 1992, could have benefited from the chart above when he said, "If [the North American Free Trade Agreement, NAFTA] is signed as it is currently drafted, the next thing you will hear will be a giant sucking sound as the remainder of our manufacturing jobs—what's left after the two million that went to Asia in the 1980s—get pulled across our southern border."[88]

He should have realized that in 1990, farmers were only 2.6 percent of the electorate.[89] Any chance of winning a national election, even if 100 percent of the farmers and those they employed voted for you? How about if we add in the roughly 15 percent on the manufacturing labor trend line? I think not, and they didn't. The rest of the population tends to like the situation where stuff costs less. The moment US workers are willing to get paid at the same rate as Latin American agricultural workers and Asian manufacturing workers, we can expect our labor numbers in those categories to rise. Don't hold your breath.

The National Association of Manufacturers, using US Bureau of Labor Statistics data, reported in 2014 that about 9 percent of the workforce was directly employed in manufacturing.[90] Since those statistics include managers and others who are not personally engaged in the manufacture of items, that percent could reasonably be considered overstated. As in Perot's time, there are many who decry the decline in the US manufacturing workforce numbers. Yet we all love the fact that a forty-two-inch TV in 2017 costs a whole lot less than one of lower resolution and more bulk than in 2005. Heck, we haven't made any TVs at all in the United States for decades. Over ninety US companies were making TVs in the early 1950s. The Zenith Electronics company was the last, selling out to Korean rival LG Electronics on July 7, 1995.[91] Before its sale, most of its picture tubes (remember those?) were made in Mexico. It is so tempting to blame something or someone as the reason things don't go the way we might like. It's fruitless too. One would be hard-pressed to claim NAFTA had any impact on that shift since it didn't go into effect until 1994.

We've been talking about the shift in labor and kinds of products produced in the United States, but the same trends can be seen in many other places of the world. A key difference between what has happened in the United States and what is happening elsewhere is the pace of the transformation. A look at China is highly revealing. The agricultural workforce was 69 percent in 1980 and 35 percent in 2011. It took thirty years to achieve a 50 percent reduction in the proportion of agricultural jobs. The United States took a hundred years to make that change. Manufacturing's share of China's GDP lately dropped almost 25 percent in five years, from 42 percent in 2005 to slightly above 32 percent in 2010. Remember that we're talking about jobs here. The volume of manufactured products, in both the United States and China, has gone up dramatically during those same periods of job decline. If you love productivity improvement, this is heaven. If you liked the job you lost, it's hell.

The significant Chinese manufacturing workforce will hit a wall by 2030. The number of working-age Chinese dropped for the first time in 2012. The country's one-child policy adopted in 1979 has reduced

[88] "The 1992 Campaign; Transcript of 2d TV Debate Between Bush, Clinton and Perot." *The New York Times. New York Times Company,* October 16, 1992.

[89] https://www.agclassroom.org/gan/timeline/farmers_land.htm

[90] http://www.nam.org/Newsroom/Facts-About-Manufacturing/

[91] Barnaby Feder, "Last U.S. TV maker will sell control to the Koreans," *New York Times,* July 18, 1995.

the number of new entrants to the workforce. There will shortly be more leaving the workforce than entering it. The well-known economic concept related to supply and demand predicts fewer qualified workers will successfully demand higher pay.[92] Rising costs are already leading to planning, which anticipates a shrinking manufacturing labor pool. In 2011, Chairman Guo of major manufacturer Foxconn announced that it planned to install a million robots to automate sections of assembly lines. By the end of 2013, already twenty thousand robots were in place.[93]

If we don't produce agricultural or manufactured products, what the heck is it that we do? Some claim we are living in the service economy. We'll see about that.

---

[92] Unqualified, meaning unskilled, workers are not necessarily included in the rising tide of higher pay. On the contrary, job loss among those of low education and skill has been clearly shown to result in lower standards of living for them. The social and political ramifications are significant and beyond our scope in this book.

[93] Christina Larson, "Scrapping Its One-Child Policy Won't Solve China's Worker Shortage," *Bloomberg Business*, November 19, 2013.

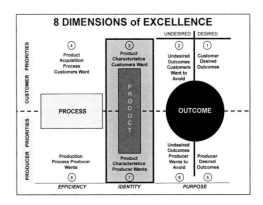

CHAPTER 16—WHAT'S SERVICE GOT TO DO WITH THIS?

We really don't need the previous chart on product evolution to know that most of us don't work on the farm or make widgets. We might consider ourselves in the service sector of the economy. We could be right. It depends on what we mean by service. You completed the six-minute C3IQ back in Leader's Action 4. What was the one word you wrote down in item 10?_____. That was what you said service means. My bet is that you did not check the "totally" box for the second half of that item. The reason I can say that is not because I'm a mind reader but because there is very little agreement on what service means. Of the thousands of answers that others have given, the following is the alphabetized short list of most common responses.

SERVICE CAN MEAN

1. Accommodating	16. Deliver	30. Partnering
2. Answering	17. Effort	31. Personalized
3. Anticipate	18. Excellence	32. Protection
4. Appropriate	19. Experience	33. Provide
5. Assist	20. Fix	34. Quality
6. Attend	21. Follow-through	35. Repair
7. Attentive	22. Fulfill	36. Responsiveness
8. Available	23. Giving	37. Results
9. Care	24. Happiness	38. Satisfaction
10. Cater	25. Help	39. Satisfy
11. Communication	26. Helpful	40. Success
12. Cooperation	27. Listening	41. Supply
13. Correct	28. Meaningful	42. Support
14. Customer	29. Meet Customer	43. Value
15. Delight	Expectations	

Figure 23—What Service Means

Before we begin analyzing the list, which response shows that some folks weren't following the instructions? The idea was to simply write one word. The twenty-ninth response above doesn't fit. Perhaps that's neither here nor there. On the other hand, many give this response. There are many more than forty-three unique definitions offered for service. We see here examples that are generic, coming from all kinds of work settings. The moment we add a specific industry to the context, we'll see even more ideas. Some observers will say that many of these words are similar. That's true, and that is really what we were asking for, synonyms. But being similar will not be good enough to avoid ambiguity and confusion. One of the patterns we can see in the responses is that at least half of the definitions describe activity. That means that about half the time we think of service as related to a process and half the time as something else. We've been working hard to distinguish process, product, and outcome. With service, we have an obvious cause of confusion among the three, as illustrated by the words in the figure above. Does it matter, and who should care if there are dozens of possible meanings?

The Master of Excellence should care. Some will say these differences in words are simply a matter of semantics and are of no consequence. Those who do that reveal their ignorance on at least two levels. First is the issue of whether there is any consequence when we use one word instead of another that seems similar. If the use of one word creates chaos, confusion, and conflict and a similar one does not, there is a clear consequence. We addressed this to some degree in Chapter 6.

Second, linguistics is the umbrella field of study under which semantics and semiotics fit. Most of us have had extensive education in math; few of us have had similar immersion in linguistics. Referring to word choice as simply semantics is commonly meant to suggest that using one word instead of another is merely arbitrary and superficial. One of the disciplines creating a foundation for C3 is linguistics. If you really want to dig into that (which is helpful but not essential for us to be effective as Masters of Excellence), please take a little time to research the area. Semantics refers to the meaning of words. The above figure clearly demonstrates there are at least forty-three different meanings for service. We could let that stand as sufficient proof this is something that matters. But let's totally put the issue to bed.

Ambiguity surrounding service is rooted in history. Folks who grew up on a farm raising livestock or those who visited such family farmers frequently enough are familiar with the term "servicing." While it could refer to maintaining equipment, that is not its most common meaning on a cattle, horse, or hog farm. Servicing there refers to mating. In another industry, sailors docked in port have historically been greeted by all manners of entrepreneurs wishing to augment their income. Such has been the case with ladies of the night, known to service the fleet. Meanwhile, back in the office environment of the twenty-first century, many of us have heard our colleagues and leaders talk about servicing the customer. Talk about ambiguity. Yikes! Is it possible our customers think that is exactly what is happening to them? Is that what we meant? Of course not. It's one more reason to ditch that term. And please, no servicing customers.[94]

Item 9 of the C3IQ asked if good service were viewed as a top priority. Take a look at how you answered that. The vast majority of responses indicates it is at least partially important. That means that we say something is important but don't agree on what it means. Under those conditions, how likely is it that we will know how to measure or improve it? We've agreed we want to hit the bull's-eye but don't know where the target is. Ouch! This is one of those situations where ambiguity is our enemy. If there is good news, it is that many others are in the same boat with us. Getting out of that boat of ambiguity will definitely help our push for excellence.

Starting with the most macro view of the so-called service sector of the economy, much can be said but not with much certainty from traditional experts. The US government is totally thorough in its knowledge about the agriculture sector. We know a lot about cows, such as how much milk the average one produced last month (about 1,888 pounds). Not so much about service. That part of the economy is estimated to account for 77 percent of private sector output. We have only six main economic indicators

---

[94] See appendices 4 and 6 for guidance on fixes for ambiguity.

for service versus seventeen for agriculture, mining, manufacturing, energy, and construction.[95] So we know a lot about what we used to do but not so much about what we now do. Lumped into the service sector are baristas toward one end (paid around $10/hour) and barristers (attorneys) on the other (average of $66/hour in 2013).

There is little evidence that the service labor number is truly known because there is no agreed definition for what service includes. Furthermore, we can make a strong case that the manufacturing labor sector is overstated. An enterprise such as Ford is considered a manufacturing firm. Are all of Ford's 224,000 employees in 2016 counted as part of manufacturing labor? Do you think the head of world marketing at Ford makes cars? How about the hundreds of software programmers, product engineers, procurement specialists, and thousands of other professionals? No, no, no on all counts. In fact, the portion of a typical medium or larger manufacturer's workforce that actually makes widgets is rarely more than 25 percent. The hourly wage of those personally making the widgets is far smaller per person (and in aggregate) than the pay rate for those working in the office. Taking things one more step, for which kind of worker do we measure the performance most thoroughly?

We measure all sorts of things related to each production line worker: the volume of product produced, the unit cost of each product, the time (both duration and work time) spent to produce each product, the yield or quality of each product, the revenue value, and a host of other variables. Which of those do we measure for those of us in the manufacturing enterprise's offices in service? Not so much. It is clear that the further we are in that enterprise from making something a customer would buy, the more we get paid (in per-hour equivalent). The reason we can do this is that the profit produced from production-line widgets is so great that we can afford to pay a lot of other folks without counting or measuring much about what they do.

A good example of a pure service enterprise is a performing-arts company. We see the same relationships regarding work definition, measurement, pay, and position there as we do in old-line manufacturing. Do we measure the work of a dancer or choreographer most thoroughly? The choreographer gets paid most, and his or her work is measured least. The underlying principle is this: we describe and measure most thoroughly the kind of work performed by those who are paid the least. The work we know about and measure least is that which we pay the most for. I am not advocating this relationship; merely pointing out that it is so. If we assume that measurement of work is somehow intended to help enhance excellence, perhaps it makes sense to apply that assumption to everyone. Doing that would cause transformation on many fronts!

SO WHAT?

If there is a "so what" here, a big one is that the opportunity to achieve improvement, let alone excellence, is greatest in the areas we know least about. The good news is we know a lot about those directly involved in producing manufactured products. We also believe we know quite a bit about those line employees who answer phones. After all, every call may be recorded. Not so much is known about work by the rest of us.

---

[95] Peter Coy, "Solving the Mystery of the Service Sector," *Bloomberg Business*, July 28, 2014.

Where does all this discussion leave us with a pure service business such as financial services, medicine, education, government, and nonprofits? We might sum it up this way:

- Service is very important to our enterprise and our customers.

- We aren't quite sure what service means so we're uncertain about what we do.

- At a macro level, we measure best the kinds of work our nation used to do.

- We are more likely to measure the cost of work performed by the lowest-level employees and those closest to external customers than those closer to the top of the pay scale and furthest from customers.

- We have defined and measured the kind of work we do least of, both at a macroeconomic level and within the enterprise.

- When we measure work, it is mostly the activity of low-level employees that is measured.

- The more intangible the work, the more costly it is, but we don't really know what it actually costs.

- The discipline required to design manufactured products is not similarly imposed on the design of service or knowledge products.

What's a Master of Excellence to do? This could be the right moment to take that antidepressant. Or we could identify the causes of confusion and eliminate them. Service contains six major constraints. The absence of any of the following six characteristics is a constraint on achieving excellence for products and service, related to Dimensions 3 and 7:

- **Repeatability:** The same desired characteristics are present every time, to the same degree.

- **Measurability:** You can count it, and the desired characteristics of each unit are measured.

- **Tangibility:** A tangible deliverable is given and received.

- **Responsibility:** The producer can be identified and held accountable.

- **Storability:** It can be stored, inventoried, and retrieved.

- **Ambiguity-free:** Consensus is easily reached on what it is, whom it's for, what they want, and what happens when they use it. Notice the nice alignment with the two key questions in Chapter 13.

Our concepts of service, reflected in our definitions or synonyms for it, contain few to none of these six characteristics. Conversely, virtually all of the characteristics are present for every product all the time. Six major constraints characterize service. Describing work as products fixes them all. Let's check it out for your situation.

Leader's Action 15: Constraints on Service Excellence
(See Appendix 1)

FIXING SERVICE CONSTRAINTS

Repeatability

For Gertrude Stein, a rose is a rose is a rose. Literary critics and scholars debate what Stein really meant. Dr. Deming drilled into the heads of his students and clients the notion that there is variability in everything. No two roses are identical, but if that is our business, then our aim may still be to produce roses with repeatable perfection. Business critics and experts on excellence find Deming's idea a bit more accessible and easy to apply to practical challenges than Stein's. Statistical analysis can be used to measure and control the characteristics of a rose that are desired. The commercial horticulturalist will attempt, through careful genetic selection and plant husbandry, to minimize rose differences within a specific strain. Sometimes we mess up by not reaching agreement first on which variables to control. You may have noticed over the years that commercial rose growers have been exceedingly successful in producing flowers that are beautiful to behold. But where did the rose scent go? Oops. Guess we missed an important characteristic of excellence.

Repeatability for roses is just as important as managing the size of the gap between the frame of the car door and the door itself. If it's too small a gap, the door will bind when it closes. If it's too big a gap, we'll get leaks and road noise. It also won't look so good. Repeatable consistency is a fundamental concept of quality in the industrial age.

Eli Whitney (1765–1825) pioneered the mass production of muskets with interchangeable parts. The precision and reduced variability of parts made this possible. Rifles produced before the industrial revolution were almost twice the unit cost of a standard musket. The next leap forward (some would claim one of the greatest of the industrial revolution) was the cylindro-conoidal bullet invention in 1823 by Captain Norton of the British Thirty-Fourth Regiment. While in India, he studied blowpipe arrows and found that their base was formed of elastic material. It expanded against the inner surface of the tube and prevented any air from escaping.[96] His bullet was made with such precision, subsequently improved many times, so that military tactics were significantly altered. By that time, the day of the craftsman building rifles was over.

The repeatability of service is about where rifle craftsmanship was in 1800. No two service experiences will be alike. This is one of the reasons many in nonmanufacturing enterprises and internal functional groups will conclude Dr. Deming's approach (and that of other industrial age gurus) doesn't apply to service and knowledge work. It is certainly true that we often do not have long production runs of the same thing in a nonmanufacturing environment. Much of our work is one of a kind (emails, answers, or plans) or can legitimately be considered custom. On the other hand, we also may not have any design documents for such products. With no design, how could we hope to have repeatability?

When was the last time you saw a design for producing an email a recipient would want to read and find useful? We're not talking about just the format. The format of the email is a holdover from its twentieth-century predecessor, the memo. We've simply put it into electronic form. Arguably, the quality of an email is not made superior to a memo just because we can send it to all with a single keystroke. It's good for the producer but maybe a nightmare for all the innocent recipients who have jammed inboxes with stuff they're not sure what to do with. We have a subject field, but how about purpose? Where is that field, and would having it improve email quality from the viewpoint of you, the recipient (customer)? You may have figured out, after reading the darned thing, that the purpose of many an email falls under the category of CYA.[97] What would happen if we offered that as one of the finite number of purpose fields? It might improve our collective sense of humor while simplifying the recipient's decision to immediately hit the delete key. If we're really lucky, it might cause the prospective email author to stop publishing trash. We actually did this for a client, inserting five possible purposes in the standard email heading, and created a

---

[96] Matthew Schroeder, "Warfare and the Industrial Revolution," *Atigun Media*, May 6, 2011.

[97] This is slang for "cover your ass," meaning the only reason an email was sent to recipients was to protect the writer in some way from future blame.

design-and-use document. Emails that did not meet the authorship requirements were returned to senders. Bottom line: the volume of emails dropped by over 50 percent within six weeks, recipients knew exactly what to do upon receipt without reading the entire thing, and decision-making speed and quality improved.

Honestly, can you imagine NASA and Lockheed Martin making the Orion space capsule with no designs? Space capsules are pretty close to one-of-a-kind, custom products, just like emails. Yet we rarely have designs in place for even our highest-volume knowledge products. Answers would be an example. Of course, if we are thinking about service, we may be thinking of answering as an activity. To define answers as products, as we did above, opens the door to a whole new level of discipline. We produce several different kinds of answers. Do we have designs in place for those different kinds? It is a big temptation to ask, "Who cares?"

Masters of Excellence would care for at least these reasons: (1) it will be very difficult to have excellent products when there is no design that defines how excellence will be determined, the bull's-eye to hit; (2) unsatisfactory answers are a major cause of rework, customer dissatisfaction, and defection; and (3) the cost to produce answers is huge but largely unknown and unmanaged. Let's make this concrete. Consider just the work time that goes into creating an answer:

- It includes the time it takes to understand the question and what will be needed to give a complete answer.

- It includes the time required to find the information to be included in the answer. This includes the time to solicit from others the parts of the answer they have.

- It includes the time consumed in packaging the answer (as either a verbal, written, or graphic response). Answers can be packaged as policies, brochures, website pages, proposals, emails, presentations, and so on. Many answers could be contained in one package; just as many fasteners may be contained within one car.

- It includes the time taken to communicate or distribute the answer.

How much of your personal day is spent doing this? Take three to four minutes on Leader's Action 15a to see what you discover.

Leader's Action 15a: The Value of Answers
(See Appendix 1)

Leader's Action 15b: Opportunities to Satisfy Customers
(See Appendix 1)

Measurability

If you completed Leader's Action 15a, it would be no surprise to learn that you spend at least 80 percent of your average day producing answers. Prior to actually doing the calculation, many managers would assume the time spent on answers would be far less. This can be due to their initial assumption that they spend almost all their day in meetings and asking questions, so not much time spent providing answers. But the meetings could be counted as part of the time spent (sometimes unwillingly) gathering information that will later show up in answers given to others. Ditto for the time spent asking questions.

An attorney who spends the whole day conducting a deposition of a witness is asking questions. In fact, his or her questions are products. As any attorney knows, a good question can be priceless. Well, actually, there is a significant price that someone will pay. But perhaps that's another topic. The point is that the attorney is asking all those questions to get answers regarding the credibility of the witness, the possible explanations for the incident being investigated, and so on.

Unlike attorneys, our time spent asking questions and creating answers may not be directly billable. Our organization still pays for our time, even though we don't track time spent per answer. By using the worksheet above, you've estimated the macro cost of answers incurred, but probably invisible, in your organization. If your observation is like most, the total cost is eye-popping.

Back at the beginning of our discussion in Chapter 15 on the evolution of products, we identified agricultural products and their units of measure. We recognized that, though we may not produce carrots and heads of cauliflower, we are aware there is a known or knowable dollar value for them. We refer to that as either their unit cost or price. I had asked about how much we really know about our knowledge products such as emails and answers. (There is overlap between emails and answers, isn't there?) We now can do the math to calculate the cost of our answers.

Formula for unit cost to produce answers:

$$\frac{\text{Hours spent per week x compensation rate per hour}}{\text{Number of answers created per week}} = \text{Unit Cost of Answers}$$

An example of unit cost to produce answers:

$$\frac{10 \text{ hours x } \$50}{30} \quad \text{or} \quad \frac{\$500}{30} = \$16.66$$

This gives us concrete evidence that the unit cost for producing answers (sometimes packaged as emails) is quite a bit higher than for potatoes. Which of the two do our cost accountants keep track of? You guessed it, the cheaper ones. What we could also do is quantify the cost of **using** answers. That would look at the issue from the customer's, the end user's, perspective. It's truly customer-centered thinking. The cost to read, understand, clarify, correct, and, if relevant, prepare to act on the answer can all be quantified.

Measurability And Tangibility

Before pursuing Leader's Action 15, we were discussing the six constraints on service. Those clearly showed how repeatability is dependent on design. That is certainly true for both industrial and agricultural products. Just as we can design an airplane, we can also design the genetic makeup of the rose. The first publicly announced genetically engineered sheep was Dolly in 1996. Monsanto is the company that comes to mind as a major player in genetically modified seeds. If we can design all these, we ought to be able to design service. But remember, we can't agree on what service means. The moment we can transform our thoughts about answering to consider what it is as a product, lending itself to design, we quickly hit on answers, emails, plans, policies, and more. Aha! All of those meet all of the key criteria for products because they are possible to be made plural with an "s," they are deliverables, they are packaged in countable units, they are specific to the person or group that produces it, and they are used to achieve a desired outcome.

Now that we've defined work as products, we've solved the constraints of repeatability, tangibility, and measurability. We couldn't do that with service. It is so convenient that, not only do repeatability and tangibility enable measurability, but measurement supports repeatability. We're seeing signs of how all these pieces that define work can become integrated. Isn't this exciting?

Beware The Vital Lie

One thing we may be thinking about is whether measuring answers is really worthwhile. Stated as a Vital Lie, it might be as follows: it's too hard, time-consuming, and costly to measure answers. I will agree that, if that is true, we shouldn't bother. But it's not.

Imagine that you are a leader in a company that makes fasteners. The firm makes all sorts—big ones and little ones. The biggest are bolts, two inches in diameter and thirty feet long. They are used in some kinds of bridges to keep the roadway properly suspended and level. Which of the following characteristics does your firm measure?

1. Number of bolts produced every month
2. Percent yield (done right first time) per month
3. Unit cost per bolt
4. Profit per bolt
5. Elapsed time to build each bolt
6. Labor cost per bolt
7. Material cost per bolt
8. Rework cost to fix bolts that are bent or otherwise defective
9. Rework time to fix bolts
10. Satisfaction of bolt customers

That's right. All of these are measured, plus more. Without discussing it, the legitimate reasons to measure these characteristics are pretty obvious. Not only that, we might very well conclude that a firm that did not measure these things is probably not as well-run as it could be.

Let's consider one your firm's other fasteners, thumbtacks. Wouldn't we also measure most of the same ten characteristics? Sure would, but the approach might be a little different. Whereas we might examine each and every bolt individually (or sample them), we would periodically weigh a kilo of thumbtacks, examine those individually (or sample them), and then do the math to determine the per-thumbtack values of the other measures. Perfectly reasonable and worth doing, right? After all, if the unit cost of a thumbtack is not greater than the price and if the yield is not as close as possible to 100 percent, we could be going out of business.

Let's compare the unit cost of a thumbtack to an email. Which one is likely to cost more? Not only will the email cost more than a thumbtack, but it might well cost more than a big bolt. At least five of the ten bolt characteristics, possibly as many as seven, would be relevant for an email. So why don't we measure them? Because we hadn't thought of them as products. The same thinking could be applied to every one of the products listed in the figure, Defining Work as Activities and Products. The other reason we don't yet measure these knowledge products is due to the immaturity of our organizations.

Let's take a step toward advancing our organization's maturity. If it makes sense to measure how many products we produce, it's equally valuable to measure our out-of-stock condition. Retailers do this because they know the buying customer who doesn't find what he or she wants on the shelf represents lost sales and diminished customer satisfacton. We don't have to be in a commercial enterprise to apply the principle involved.

There will be a point in time when those who don't create an inventory of their knowledge products and measure their performance will be viewed about as competent as farmers who don't measure the volume and cost of milk produced per cow. Masters of Excellence who begin now will be viewed as pioneers of high performance organizations. Damn the Vital Lies, full speed ahead!

Measures And Satisfaction

We will usually find it helpful to start any measurement effort by deciding what we want to measure. We don't quite do that when the task is to measure satisfaction. Surprisingly, we often skip right over the product or characteristics to be measured and simply run a survey asking general questions such as, How happy were you with…? If customers don't give us the top possible score,[98] do we know what characteristics to improve? Not usually. Suppose they do give us the top score. What was it they loved that we should be sure to do all the time? The answer tends toward a riddle, wrapped in a mystery, inside an enigma.[99]

Let's take an example of what gets measured. Time is a favorite. As with the hotel survey discussed in Chapter 9, we might ask if there is satisfaction with how long something took, such as check-in or checkout. Do we ask about the level of satisfaction as well as the duration? That would provide the basis for knowing what "how long" might refer to. If not, we have no way of knowing what constitutes "good" or "fast."

An airline wanted to know how satisfied customers were with their baggage handling. This tends to be an important topic of complaint, which is why it was selected for study. The airline had several hub airports and knew that its business and vacation travelers might have different expectations. Management hoped to figure out exactly where to focus improvement for the most impactful result.

How could we measure luggage handling? The repeatable aspect included bag deliveries (to the carousel). Aha! We named a product. There was evidence that waiting time at the carousel was a cause of complaint. The airline had its own data showing how long it took from the time the door of the aircraft opened upon arrival until the bag was placed on the carousel. One could say this was objective, unimpeachable data. It constituted one measure of "how long." This was the producer's measure.

The customer's version of "how long" was unknown. Following are the questions the airline asked in its survey of passengers claiming checked luggage.

---

[98] This is sometimes referred to as the "top box" score. The average score obtained from conducting a survey can be called the "net promoter" score, meaning that respondents feel good enough about us to promote us to others.

[99] This was excerpted from a quote by Winston Churchill made in a radio broadcast in October 1939.

SURVEY OF PASSENGERS CLAIMING CHECKED LUGGAGE

1 Thinking of the last time you waited for your checked luggage from an ABC Airline flight, about how long did it take from the time you reached the claim area until your bags arrived?

No wait at all	
1-5 minutes	
6-10 minutes	
11-15 minutes	
16-20 minutes	
21-25 minutes	
26-30 minutes	
31 minutes or more	

2 How would you describe this speed of delivery?

Excellent ☐ Good ☐ Fair ☐ Poor ☐

3 What was the primary purpose for your flight?

Business ☐ Pleasure ☐ Both ☐ Other ☐

4 At which airport did this occur?

Chicago	
Dallas Ft. Worth	
Nashville	
Los Angeles International	
NY- LGA	
NY-JFK	
San Francisco International	
San Jose	
San Juan	

Other _____

Figure 24—Excerpt of Survey of Passengers Claiming Checked Luggage

The airline could have asked just one question: How happy were you with the speed of delivery of your checked bags to the carousel? That would be an example of a typical survey question. Masters of Excellence will always have to fight those who argue that "we need a really short survey." Your job is to push for a really useful survey. The fear, of course, is that respondents won't answer one that is "too long." Asking just that one "how happy" question would have gotten a satisfaction rating that was virtually meaningless. We would not have known:

- Did the length of wait for the satisfied business traveler differ from that of the vacationer?

- What proportion of business/vacation travelers were checking luggage for each of the destination airports?

- At what point did the length of wait shift from excellent to good, to fair, to poor for businesspeople?

- At what point did the length of wait shift from excellent to good, to fair, to poor for vacationers?

- Did the satisfaction with wait time at a specific city differ for businesspeople?

- Did the satisfaction with wait time at a specific city differ for vacationers?

- How much shorter does the wait time have to be at each city for each kind of traveler to be ecstatic?

- At which airport(s) should improvement be made for the biggest impact on customers and the airline?

The Master of Excellence has to insist that sufficient questions are asked and asked in the right way to get information that enables the organization to advance. The purpose is not to get a high response rate (related to the reliability of the sample results). It is to pursue excellence (related to validity, the thing you want to measure).

The structure of these questions is very helpful because we have clearly identified the traveler's purpose (Dimension 1), the specific product that is to be excellent (delivered bags at a specific airport) (Dimension 3), and the customer's definition of timeliness (Dimension 4). We are now in great position to take targeted action for optimum impact.

Vacation travelers going to San Juan could be happy with bags delivered in sixteen to twenty minutes, but business travelers going to NY-JFK could give a poor rating if they wait over ten minutes. If you were the ABC Airline executive in charge, where would you put your improvement dollars? Not at all the airports. That could be a waste of money at San Juan if delivery time is currently and consistently twenty minutes or less, especially if the volume of travelers is lower there than elsewhere and the proportion of business travelers is also lower. If total volume and proportion of business travelers (who spend the most per ticket) is highest at NY-JFK, that's the place to invest in improvement. Even if our performance is best there, it still isn't good enough for the specific customers landing there.

Responsibility

Call-center management is famous for measuring the duration of calls. Phone systems can do it automatically so it's nice and easy. If we can say that whatever call centers do qualifies as service, maybe we can also say the length of the call matters. Is a longer or shorter call the thing to do? One thing we know for sure is that the duration of the call matters to the producer. You know, time is money. Generally, less is better. Is that the most important characteristic the caller wants met? Not usually. The caller typically wants an accurate answer to his or her question(s) on his or her first attempt. That is understandable and achieves the outcome he or she had in mind. It turns out that an answer fits all five criteria for a product. We can make it plural with an "s," it is a deliverable, we can count how many are given, and we can determine if the answer produces the desired outcome.

The next big thing (maybe it should really be the first thing) to address would be the key characteristics that ought to be designed into each kind of answer. A caller who is crying might appreciate a somewhat different answer than one who is asking where to find some information on your website. The Master of Excellence will make sure the unique kinds of answers are identified, defined, and delivered in a manner that satisfies the requestor. The time it takes to deliver the right answer is of secondary importance.

We've just identified two distinct but related products: the answer and the design. Would the person responsible for the design be the same person who is responsible for delivering the answer? Probably not. If the design is faulty, when will we likely discover it? Probably the same way most bad designs are found out, when the product the design is for fails to perform. The reality, in this case, is that the caller will undoubtedly blame the poor customer-service person when the answer doesn't satisfy. Who will the enterprise hold accountable?

As a Master of Excellence, you can now put the focus where it belongs and work first with the designer (or find someone who could become the designer) to identify what the designs for different kinds of answers should include, make sure the customer-service person understands and can apply the design, and then hold the various parties accountable for the specific products for which they are really responsible.

Maybe you are already doing these things. If so, congratulations! There are many who should follow in your footsteps.

Storability

Service is not storable or retrievable. Answers are. The ones we generally store most religiously are the ones delivered by folks at the lowest levels of the organization, those in customer service. All the warnings we give callers about the call being recorded remind us of that.

Remember that we always want to be proficient in modeling the behavior we want from others. At this point, I am going to assume you are already convinced that talking about service is highly ambiguous and it will be a good thing to shift toward the thinking about work as products. That means you are going to ask everyone who reports to you to define his or her work as products and then prioritize them so we can work on achieving excellence at least on the critical few. The first version of a pushback (as this is something new after all) could be in the form of a harmless-sounding question: How do you apply that to your work? If you can't immediately answer that question, you risk an immediate loss of credibility and the judgment that you don't know what you're talking about. We can't let that happen. That is one reason your success with Leader's Action 14 is so critical.

The two columns in figure, Defining Work, showed typical activities (all verbs) and their comparable products (all nouns made plural with an "s"). Are any of the activities listed on the left storable and retrievable? Nope. Not only are most of the related products very quickly seen to be storable in quantifiable units, some can easily be associated with companies that have built significant businesses by producing them. All we have to do is think about specific kinds of products within the categories named.

For example, when we think of deliveries, FedEx and UPS used to be first on our mind. It's probably Amazon now. For software applications, we might think of Microsoft, Apple, Uber, AirBNB, and many others. For auto repairs, think Midas Muffler. For computer repairs, think Geek Squad. For reports, consider tax returns (a specific kind of report) by H&R Block or TurboTax. The point is that naming our work as products enables us to store and retrieve products in a manner not possible when we think of work as activity, service, and process. Now let's finish the process of modeling, for those following us, on how to define our personal work as products.

Many who start defining their own work as products discover it is not as easy as they had thought. Some find themselves trapped in the naming of activities. The worst-case scenario is if you find yourself exclaiming that you don't really know what you do. Yikes! This is where a buddy system could come in handy. Share the five rules for defining work as products, share what your activity is, and ask if you buddy can name your related product. I don't think you'll have too much trouble, in part because you can always refer to examples in the figure in Chapter 14, Defining Work as Activities and Products. Some are surely yours once you add the necessary specificity.

When you are satisfied you've got the task licked, see which of the following characteristics you've met for each of your named products in Leader's Action 14:

1. Repeatability
2. Measurability
3. Tangibility
4. Responsibility
5. Storability
6. Ambiguity-free

We said early in the discussion about service that the absence of any of these six characteristics is a constraint on achieving excellence. Our last point about ambiguity hasn't even been covered yet, but I bet all your products passed the test. If so, you are about to finish a key step in becoming a Master of Excellence.

Ambiguity-Free

You know, there is an historical connection to be made between the agricultural age and service. Recalling what we know about cows could make it clear. Have you had family with a livestock farm that you worked on as a kid? If so, you have special insights. If not, ask someone who did about what the term "servicing" means on the farm. They might say it regards repairing equipment. Maybe. But for those who raised cattle, hogs, horses, and other animals, "servicing" refers to mating. We may have forgotten about that when we talk today about servicing our customers. On the other hand, many of us may feel that is exactly what has happened to us at unhappy times when we were a customer. We may have had to deal with, of all things, the customer-service department. What is their department name trying to tell us? It puts a new slant on things. Please, no servicing of customers!

So one more disadvantage of service is the unintended meanings it can carry. We don't need the grief that can come from that ambiguity. The cure is simple. Eliminate the word from our vocabulary. The exception would be when we use it as an adjective, referring to service products. A service product is fundamentally different from the other products we've discussed in one essential way. They require the customer's involvement in the production of the product. Examples of service products include appendectomies, workshops, amusement rides, root canals, trips, excursions, adventures, eye exams, mortgage loans, car repairs, software installations, depositions, contracts, building permits, licenses (driving, fishing, hunting, flying, and so forth), meals, and call-center answers. As customers, we aren't involved in the production of carrots, cars, or computers.

But for the service product examples above, we must be present during the production of the product, whether we want to be or not.

We can sum up with four main observations:

1. We are all over the map regarding what we think service is (activity, personal qualities, outcomes, and more).
2. There are six characteristics that could be absent, related to much of what we consider service, acting as constraints on achieving excellence.

3. Answers and emails are examples of products that can seem invisible or inconsequential to excellence, until we start applying measures to them that would be relevant for producers and customers of any other product.

4. The closer we are to defining service as a product, the fewer constraints stand in our way to purposeful improvement.

We should be feeling better already.

LEMONADE

We've all heard the admonition to, when life throws us lemons, make lemonade. It is meant as encouragement to take the initiative to turn a bad situation around. It's good advice. But it seems best suited to salvage a bad situation. How might we take what I call the lemon principle and actually find an opportunity for improvement that leaves us better off than we were before the lemon? I believe we might reflect on our restaurant experiences to gain some insight.

If there is one time we all tend to talk about service, it's when going out to eat at a restaurant. Everyone talks about whether the service was good or not. That service thing could be broken down into some of its component parts to discover opportunities for improvement that are relevant, not only to the restaurant but to our own very different enterprise.

Once we are seated and have a menu, the server will typically ask what my guests and I would like to drink. My preference is fresh lemonade, so I ask for that. Well over half the time, the server will tell me some version of, "We don't have fresh lemonade." So I calmly ask (because I have heard this many times before), "What part of the lemonade don't we have?" At this point, the usual server looks momentarily like deer in the headlights. He or she is expecting me to simply accept that response. Instead, it sounds like I've ignored what was said and have asked a probing question. The poor server was not expecting a quiz.

Not wishing to extend the server's potential discomfort, I ask if there is water. The answer is yes. I ask if there is sugar available. The answer is yes. I note there are lemon slices put on the lips of glasses and ask if it is possible to get a full lemon simply cut in half. The answer is yes. So I ask if I might have a glass of ice water, some sugar, and the lemon, and I say I'll squeeze it myself. It never fails to get me what I want. And it's the best lemonade I could ask for.

When the bill comes after the meal, what has the restaurant charged for the lemonade? Nothing. It was not on the menu, so there is no charge. Furthermore, there is no tracking on the bill of the lemon taken from inventory. If it's only one lemon, maybe they shouldn't worry about it. But how often could this happen? No data is collected, so the answer is unknown. No counting of the number of such requests, no accounting for lost inventory, and no accounting for revenue lost by not charging me four dollars or more for the wonderful lemonade. All point to lost opportunity. It gets worse. One scenario I've seen or experienced umpteen times is the request for caffeine-free tea, lactose-free creamer, and other items. Yet the servers will often volunteer, "We get a lot of those requests, but we don't have x." Wouldn't this information be valuable for the restaurant so they could adjust their menu and product offering, increase revenue per meal, and improve customer experience?

This version of the lemon principle applies to every organization. How many times do searchers fail to find what they were looking for on your website? If you don't plan to count the opportunities to satisfy, you've got guaranteed loss in several dimensions. If you'd like to fix this, a simple tool organized around answers as products is worth using. That would be Leader's Action 15b, Opportunities to Satisfy Customers. Please consider accepting my challenge to apply the tool to any of the important knowledge products produced by your enterprise or business unit.

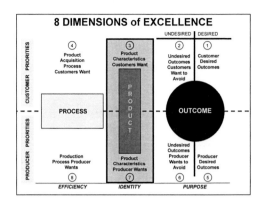

CHAPTER 17—KNOWLEDGE AGE PRODUCTS

We've probably had our fill of the agricultural age at this point. And we know that precious few of us personally produce manufactured products. We have referred to specific dates when each kind of product began being produced by a large segment of the workforce. The agricultural age began around 10,000 BC. The industrial age began with James Watt's steam engine in 1769. You may have heard of those dates before you began reading this book. You are highly unlikely to have heard anyone say when the knowledge age began. It was 1969.

It happens that 1969 saw several events that ushered in a new period of what we could call dramatic mind expansion. Think about what you may remember happened that year. You probably know exactly what occurred on July 20 at 4:18 p.m. (EDT). Neil Armstrong had just landed Apollo 11's moon lander, the *Eagle*, in the Sea of Tranquility. A tranquil experience it was not. Armstrong was attempting to find an open space in a sea of boulders when the cockpit erupted in all sorts of alarms and flashing lights. One was telling him he had only thirty seconds of fuel left. Not a Zen moment. Everyone at Houston control had stopped breathing. All the adrenaline valves were open to the max. Then there was touchdown and jubilation. At 10:56 p.m., Armstrong steps off the ladder with, "That's one small step for a man, one giant leap for mankind." If you heard this transpire on the radio, you probably remember exactly what you were doing at the time. I was working all that evening with my car radio on, delivering pizzas. What could be more mind expanding than seeing the Earth through the spaceship window on the way to the moon and back?

Quite a bit less drama but no less dramatic was the introduction of the solid-state microprocessor by Intel in 1969. This was the equivalent in modern times of the steam engine. The solid-state microprocessor, as the steam engine before, created seismic change in the culture and economy. It transformed the way information was created, stored, and transmitted. The steam engine had reduced the unit cost, cycle time, yield, and capacity and increased the volume and market size of agricultural products. Intel's new computer components (and those made by others) had similar impacts on manufactured products. It was truly mind expanding.

The US Defense Department's Advanced Research Projects Agency (DARPA) funded a project called ARPANET. The project was the first to demonstrate in 1969 how four computers in geographically distant locations could connect, share, send, and receive information. Where did the Internet originate? At DARPA. Who were the specific individuals who contributed materially to that effort? Men such as Bob Taylor, Robert Kahn, Vint Cerf, Bob Metcalfe, Douglas Engelbart, Tim Berners-Lee, Ted Nelson, Marc Andreessen, and Eric Bina. Most of them are around today, though you may not have heard of them. The Internet daily demonstrates the ability to connect up all the world's minds, great and small.

Just shy of a month after the first moon landing was another pivotal event. From August 15 through 18 saw a huge outdoor concert known as Woodstock occur in upstate New York. Called the Woodstock Music and Art Fair, around 400,000 people attended. It actually took place closer to White Lake than Woodstock, but that is another story. Considering the wealth of recreational drugs present, if you had attended the event it would be understandable if you don't remember being there. It makes our list of critical events welcoming the knowledge age for two reasons. First is its mind-expanding, some might say mind-altering, character. The second is that it is arguably the pivotal moment we can say the entertainment age began. It was joyful and remarkably peaceful.

One of the first publications to announce the new age was *Newsweek,* in 2004.[100] Yes, there was a little delay in getting out the announcement. Most folks missed the news. It is essential for our pursuit of excellence that we catch up with the times. By that year, which of the following kinds of products was the biggest contributor to the US GDP and the dollar value of exports?

1. Agriculture
2. Autos
3. Computers/technology
4. Heavy manufacturing
5. Oil
6. Services
7. Other _____
8. Don't know

You'll be forgiven if you selected "don't know." Or you'd be awarded recognition as willing to admit some ignorance. Most people choose the wrong answer, so saying up front that we don't really know at least admits our current state of insight. The correct answer is other. Without looking at the footnotes, let's see if we can get more definitive focus by considering a few facts, organized by their sequence over time:

1. Movie sales in 2003 (theaters, DVDs, and videos) exceeded total sales of steel.[101]

2. Apple Computer changed its name to Apple in 2007 to communicate it was no longer to be considered just a hardware or software producer. iTunes had already been introduced six years earlier on January 9, 2001.

3. What was a key differentiator for Southwest Airlines flights prior to its merger with AirTran in 2011? (Hint: Disregard fuel hedging and standardization on a single plane type.)[102]

4. By 2011, the $25 billion video-game industry generated twice as much as Hollywood's box office.[103]

---

[100] "Factory of the Future?" *Newsweek*, November 21, 2004.

[101] "Factory of the Future?" *Newsweek*, November 21, 2004.

[102] The answer is entertaining safety announcements and other communications to passengers. SWA's secret weapon (remember our earlier discussion) is not, as many business analysts have claimed, strictly their standardization on a single aircraft and super- smart fuel hedging practices. It's all about entertainment. It costs nothing, employees and customers love it, and competitors seem incapable of copying it. It's typical of a culture of excellence.

[103] Devin Leonard, "Master of the Game," *Bloomberg BusinessWeek*, July 4, 2011.

5. YouTube had $5.6 billion in 2013 ad revenue, $1.96 billion net, up 66 percent.[104]

6. Growth of iTunes revenue had reached $23.5 billion per quarter by 4Q13, greater than Xerox, CBS, and US Steel.

7. $4 billion was spent on video streaming in 2014, expected to be $10.1 in 2018.[105]

8. JD Powers & Associates found in 2014 that customers wanted better entertainment technology in their next new vehicle, more than any other feature.

9. The US monthly box-office receipts of $640 million were surpassed by China's $650 million in 2015, expected to reach annual revenues of $10.2 vs. $10.4 billion in 2017.[106]

10. In what industry would you put the biggest global seller, by revenue, of books (printed and online)? What is the company?[107]

11. In what industry would you put the biggest purveyor, by sales revenue, of recorded music? What company is that, and where did it rank globally in 2015 total capitalization value?[108]

12. What industry would you say Amazon, Disney, Netflix, and Nintendo are in?

If you have concluded that Other means entertainment, you just won a gold star. Some traditional experts who should know this don't. One such group of experts includes Wall Street investment advisors, where Schwab, as of 2015, still failed to identify firms named in point twelve above as in entertainment. These are the folks you might have wanted to consult around 2005 about growth industries and the related businesses that could be good investments. The first step for them would have been to know what companies are in the entertainment industry. Such companies could include Disney, Netflix, Amazon, Electronic Arts, Google, Microsoft, and Apple. Sadly not a single one is considered an entertainment firm by the experts.[109] No kidding! To paraphrase a famous singer, you don't have to be a weatherman to know which way the wind is blowing.

We have discussed how the US government does a superb job of studying and knowing all aspects of agriculture, a middling job of understanding all things manufactured and a poor job of accounting for the so-called service sector of the economy and workforce. I'd like to suggest that both our government and various private industry business and research experts have an exceedingly weak grasp of the true role of entertainment in our society. That situation is likely to remain for some time. We won't fix that here, but perhaps we can advance our understanding in some useful ways. You, dear reader, should get a big leg up over those who don't know these secrets.

Nolan Bushnell and Ted Dabney met in 1969 and soon thereafter formed Syzygy to create a computer game known as Computer Space. They also discovered the name for their company had been previously claimed. So they started up a second version of the enterprise in 1972, calling it Atari. It was one of the biggest names in computer games. Which of their early employees do we know about today? Steve Jobs. What business is Apple in? You might have said computers. After all, the first name of Jobs' cofounded company with Steve Wozniak was called Apple Computer. Jobs dropped "computer" from the name for a reason, consistent with his emphasis on entertainment. As to serial innovator Nolan Bushnell,

---

[104] Tim Peterson, "YouTube Expected to Channel $5.6 Billion In Revenue This Year," *eMarketer*, December 11, 2013.

[105] Amelia Josephson, "The Economics of Video Streaming Services," *Smartasset*, January 6, 2016.

[106] Nancy Tartaglione, "China Box Office Still On Track to Overtake U.S." *Deadline*, August 18, 2016.

[107] The answers are entertainment and Amazon.com.

[108] The answer is entertainment: Apple was number one in capitalization value in the United States.

[109] Schwab and others in 2015 said these firms are, respectively, in the media, Internet, and catalog retail; Internet and catalog retail; software, Internet software, software, and technology hardware.

he was still highly active and successful in 2016 with the development of electronic games and their use in education.

Nintendo developed the Beam Gun in 1969, which it released for sale in 1970. This was a light-based pointing device that had been used in arcade games. They did not really catch on in the home video game market until Nintendo brought out their NES Zapper, the most popular example of the light gun. The worldwide video game market grew to $93 billion by 2013. They blew the doors off the mobile game market in 2016 with Pokémon Go. All this from a company that started off in card games.

The themes of information, entertainment, and games create a very powerful and convergent force in our world economy and society. Its dominant impact has gone largely unrecognized by mainstream media and experts in fields such as business and economics. One such impact in the United States has been on the workforce. Anyone born after 1969 was born into the information and entertainment age, with emphasis on entertainment. Understanding this should matter to Masters of Excellence. Simply put, the later one was born after 1969, the greater the likelihood he or she believes work should be fun. Not sure this is true? Take a look at the core values espoused by those entrepreneurs and organizational leaders with birth dates after 1969. You will find the fun quotient is a verbalized value, accompanied by games, play rooms, and other physical signs that work and play should go together. Not so with organizations led and populated by folks born a lot earlier. Consider the kinds of organizations and the demographics of their workforce we are most likely to associate with innovation and new product development.

There was one TV in the typical US household in 1969. It was black and white. The typical US household now has over three, more than the average number of residents. Screens surround us today. Every electronic device with a screen provides a potential portal for entertainment. Thinking of your own home, how many unique screen-equipped devices are there? Count multiples of the same device only once so that three TVs are only counted as one. Don't consider what's in the car, on the bike and boat, in the office, or elsewhere. Your answer: _____.

Many of us, particularly if born before 1969, are surprised to discover the answer is not ten or fifteen. It's over twenty.[110] The dominant role of entertainment has, for some time, been part of the natural home environment for kids in most postindustrial societies. We should have been able to predict that the so-called trouble with the youth today is they want to play at work. Let's embrace their demands.

As a Master of Excellence, let's purposefully look into how to make work fun. Employee engagement is something every leader wants to improve. Is it possible that an entertaining workplace could enhance effort? How entertaining are internally consumed products such as websites, policies, procedures, strategic plans, and standards? Not so much. The executive director of one organization communicated his team's new strategic plan to all employees with a cover email containing graphics and cartoons. The response was overwhelmingly positive with employees responding that they were excited to see the new direction. This had never happened before. Thinking of its impact on our customers, we might conclude, "In the end, the fun you make is equal to the fun they get."

Let me suggest a general principle. Those who incorporate entertainment as part of their product offering will be viewed as more excellent and satisfying than those who don't. It can be helpful to take a field of endeavor that is as far from the commercial mainstream as possible to test the validity of this principle.

---

[110] Devices with screens in the home include TV, clock, radio, thermostat, computer, phone, iPad/tablet, game console, coffee maker, refrigerator, intercom, security system, entertainment system, microwave, range, dryer, dish washer, watch, portable music player, picture frame, and/or augmented/virtual reality system.

Try politics. To be fair, we ought to include the right and left sides of the political spectrum. I don't think it is too much of a stretch, considering US presidential candidates from 1970 through 2012, to say that Ronald Reagan was the darling of the conservatives. His start in radio, continuing on into movies, certainly made him one of the most formally experienced in entertainment. Liberals loved Clinton. His saxophone work on the late-night TV show circuit probably expanded his considerable political base. When we think of the predecessors and opponents for each of them (Jimmy Carter and George H. W. Bush), Ronald Reagan and Bill Clinton clearly had an advantage in the charm department. Maybe this was just coincidence.

Consider Donald Trump, a master of reality TV entertainment and expert at garnering media attention. By some estimates, his presidential primary bid of 2015–2016, up to his getting his party's nomination, had a value of $55 million[111] to $2 billion[112] in terms of media coverage, depending on your source. Either way, he paid only a teeny weeny (excuse my technical jargon) amount of that. His dominating entertainment expertise kept millions of Americans and all the media outlets riveted to his provocative communications, whether they were supporters or not.

Trump's winning result was arguably more dependent on his ability to tap the emotions of his supporters than on his governmental experience or proven qualifications for the highest political office in the land. In contrast, the absence of personal entertainment qualities (often the case with us who are introverts) likely contributed to depress Hillary Clinton's poorer emotional connection with voters, despite being perhaps the most qualified for the job.

The idea is to excite, not sedate. Steve Wozniak created great products that required an entertaining Steve Jobs to sell them to the world. So whether you are planning to run for public office, revolutionize an industry, or cause others to follow as a Master of Excellence, being able to entertain as you transform is a skill worth developing. Being fun to listen to is learnable, as graduates of Toast Masters and comedy clubs can attest.

Entertainment has likely existed since humans began to hum and drum. It has only recently become the economic powerhouse it is today. The economic dividing line for those organizations that harnessed entertainment as a core characteristic of their products to drive growth and satisfaction was 1969. Furthermore, a compelling argument can be made that excellence, innovation, satisfaction, and entertainment go hand in hand. There is lots of evidence for this conclusion.

Hunter "Patch" Adams is a renowned doctor who has brought entertaining medicine to seriously ill children around the world through his Gesundheit! Institute. Their health and recovery was enhanced, though the rest of the medical industry largely shunned his innovative approach as not serious enough.

A government agency incorporated cartoons and graphics into one of its core products. The result was that users of the product made far fewer errors and agency employees spent far less time and expense fixing things afterward. In our discussion regarding Southwest Airlines (Chapter 6), entertaining safety announcements and other products created passenger engagement, contributed to a distinctive culture employees love, strengthened the alignment of core values, and added no cost.

We have the opportunity to differentiate ourselves from other entities with a mission similar to ours. It is to

---

[111] Mathew Ingram, "Here's Proof That the Media Helped Create Donald Trump," *Fortune*, June 14, 2016.

[112] Nicholas Confessore and Karen Yourish, "$2 Billion Worth of Free Media for Donald Trump," *New York Times*, March 15, 2016.

our mutual benefit to improve the experience of those we seek to satisfy and incorporate a fun component to work that our people perform and the products they create. This can be done without diminishing the seriousness of the work. The question is not if we can, but where to do it. We will find the answer to that when we get to Leader's Action 18.

Entertainment products are one of three classes of knowledge products, contrasted in the following figure. The reason to understand the difference is so we can purposefully design the kind of product best suited to the specific context, customer characteristics, competitors, producer capacity, and so on.

KNOWLEDGE PRODUCTS		
COMMODITY PRODUCTS	EXPERIENTIAL PRODUCTS	
INFORMATION PRODUCTS	SERVICE PRODUCTS	ENTERTAINMENT PRODUCTS
CHARACTERISTICS • Customer wants are optional • Anticipatory, assumed to be wanted • Built to stock, limited variety • Large batches • Low variability in production and unit cost	CHARACTERISTICS • Requires customer involvement in production • Reactive or responsive • Built to order, infinite variety • Batch size of one • Highly variable unit cost	CHARACTERISTICS • Emotionally involves user by design • Creates sense of connection with others • Assumed to be a discretionary buy • Stimulates multiple senses • Perceived as fun by user
PRODUCTS • Answers, prepackaged • Designs • Directories • Manuals • Maps, traditional printed • Plans • Policies • Prepackaged answers • Procedures • Reports • Schedules • Websites	PRODUCTS • Answers, responsive • Appendectomies • Contracts • Courses, traditional classroom • Deliveries • Installations • Orders • Presentations • Questions • Repairs • Shipments	PRODUCTS • Announcements (e.g., by SWA) • Courses, interactive, humorous • Games • Interactive answers • Jokes • Movies • Plays • Presentations • Shows • Songs • Videos • Websites

Figure 25—Knowledge Products

A few explanatory comments, which are by no means exhaustive, are in order regarding this organization of knowledge products above. Not all the characteristics shown for a given class of products need be present for all products. We are looking for the dominant characteristics of those shown as examples. You will notice some of the products appear under more than one of the three headings. That is because a product's design or form of delivery can be changed. For example, many information products can be redesigned as entertainment products. A manual is often perceived as boring by users, produced without any thought of the diversity of readers and their contexts for use. The Japanese government discovered its citizens were not very familiar with some government policies regarding national security. Part of the solution was to create manga comic books, which were highly popular and entertaining. Citizen security awareness went up. Ditto for websites. We routinely see new websites aimed at young, urban customers to be augmented with entertaining video clips. Compare that to a website created by a defense contractor, oil exploration company, or large government agency. The example of MODOR's dramatic successes in satisfying taxpayers while saving millions of dollars resulted in a big way by making the tax-preparation booklets entertaining. Mistakes went down, processing speed of refunds was accelerated, and everybody got happy.

Despite all the emphasis we've put on the importance of eliminating ambiguous words like service, here we have a whole product category related to it. The big difference is that service is used as an adjective in "service products." Service products are unique in that they require involvement by the end user in the product's production process. We buy cars, computers, phones, bicycles, gallons of milk, and countless other products without ever being required to participate in the production of those products. And you probably like it that way.

A service product is different. You cannot have an appendectomy without being involved. You may not want to be involved, but that is the only way you get to receive the product. When you get a ride (the product) on the Matterhorn or other terrifying roller coaster at Disney, you have to be there and somewhat involved in its production to get it. Service products, like other knowledge products, are not necessarily fun to receive or use. If you view that ride as fun, then it is a hybrid, an entertaining service product. A driver's license is also a service product. It cannot be produced without you being involved in its production, at least to have your picture taken. Considering the last time you got that license, you might not have called it an entertaining experience. How entertaining was that last filling you received at the dentist's?

The reason to identify and distinguish these different classes of products is to enable us to identify which of our most important products are in the class both we and our customers want them in. If the alignment is off, the Master of Excellence will work for improvement. Using the dentist's product of a filling as an example makes me think of a new dentist. I took my young daughter to him for a filling. When he was done, he told her she now had a bright silver star on her tooth. He showed her what it looked like. His hygienist came over with a box of colored stickers with pictures or cartoon characters on them. She invited my daughter to choose whichever one she liked. Upon leaving the dentist's office, my daughter asked when she could come back to get another star and sticker. All I recall about this experience when I was a kid was the terrifying high squeal of that drill. Or maybe it was the kid in the next room. The point is, we can transform an otherwise painful experience into one that is equally memorable, but this time entertaining.

The Master of Excellence who is seriously going to consider ways to transform the organization and its products can use the following guidelines to redefine it as an entertaining enterprise:

1. Create products intended to be experienced as fun, amusing, enjoyable, or entertaining by the user.
2. Use entertainment strategically as a differentiating feature in what would otherwise be a commodity or boring.
3. Engage at least 20 percent of the user's time with the entity's main product(s) in a manner perceived as recreation, fun, enjoyment, diversion, or amusement.
4. Sell, rent, or deliver entertaining products worth at least 20 percent of the enterprise's total revenue.

When we understand who the customer is, we will naturally begin to think about what he or she might want with the product. We will know for sure when we ask. How to ask the right questions is the province of volume 2. Before we get there, we will figure out which products to work on first and then determine who the heck the customer really is.

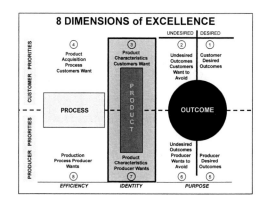

CHAPTER 18—PRIORITIZING PRODUCTS

We have used the 8DX framework to articulate in Dimensions 1, 2, 5, and 6 the strategic outcomes we and our customers want to experience. Desired outcomes have been differentiated from undesired outcomes. Measures of outcome success have been identified or created, along with the dates by which that success should occur. This work has been summarized with part 1 of our Strategy Map in Leader's Action 13. The question now confronting the Master of Excellence is which buttons to push to move the needle with least effort.

Working from right to left in the 8DX framework, we now want to clearly envision the relationship between outcomes and the critical few products on which to focus our excellence enhancement energies. Identifying those products and their owners is the last step in creating our Strategy Map. Those products form the bridge between our strategic direction and deployment to be embraced by specific individuals and groups. It is worth noting that the strategic plans, balanced scorecards, and similar guiding documents created by most organizations do not address the key products that are levers for excellence. That means they do not have these important planks in the bridge connecting strategic intent with deployment. This observation is true for Baldrige Award winners, certified ISO 9001 firms and others believed to be among the best in their field. We might conclude such a bridge isn't needed. Or we could discover that having the bridge would rapidly advance them to a whole new level of performance. Several C3-practicing organizations will tell you the latter observation is true and that the bridge speeds the pace of attaining excellence.

Recall that we discussed in Chapter 4, Leader's Actions 1 through 3, the importance of driving our transformation efforts by attending to high-potential impact, high readiness of people, and high visibility of results. Now that we've mastered the product concept, we can see that high potential refers to the critical few specific products (not amorphous issues) that, if improved, have the potential to markedly benefit both our customers and our organization.

We modeled our draft Strategy Map in Leader's Action 13 on the PCU example shown in Chapter 12. Once PCU had done that, they needed to identify the high-potential product candidates to work on. The following figure shows their short list of products, along with the owners responsible for the production of and satisfaction with the products.

151

PCU OUTCOMES, PRODUCTS AND OWNERSHIP

STRATEGIC OUTCOMES	Label	OUTCOMES	MEASURES	ALIGNMENT WITH 8 DIMENSIONS GRAPHIC AREAS	Barbara K / Contracts & Procurements	Tim W / Diagnosis	Bob M / Failure Reports	Warren S / Tons of solid waste incinerated	Warren S / Megawatts Sold	Pick T / Locates	Jim R / Wastewater Collection PM Plan	Tim W / Invoices (billing for other utilities)	Steve C / Acquisition Plan	Jim R / Home Deliveries of bottled water	Todd T / Marketing Plan	Jim R / Home Insurance Plan (for lines)	Kevin B / GMD Marketing Plan	Bob P / Laboratory Marketing Plan
Customer Satisfaction	A	Customers as "fans"	1, 4, 7	1, 5	X	X	X	X	X	X	X	X						
	B	Customers viewing PCU as a preferred provider among local utilities	1, 4, 5, 6, 13	1, 4, 8,		X			X	X		X	X	X	X	X	X	X
	C	Customer satisfaction with PCU products	1, 4, 5, 6, 14	1, 4, 8,	X	X	X	X	X	X	X	X		X				
	D	A partnership between the PCU and the public	1	1		X			X	X							X	X
	E	Trusting relationship between PCU and customers	1, 4, 5, 6	1, 4, 8,	X	X	X		X	X	X	X				X	X	
	F	Customers have confidence in PCU products	1, 5, 6, 13	1, 4, 8,	X	X	X	X	X	X	X	X	X	X	X			
	G	Customers save time	1	1	X	X	X	X		X		X	X	X	X			
Healthy & Clean Environment	A	PCU viewed as a good environmental steward	1, 3, 8, 9	1, 2, 5	X	X	X	X	X	X	X							
	B	PCU products have no adverse health impact	1, 10, 11	1, 2, 6		X	X	X	X			X		X				
Economic Growth	A	New customers (Expanded Markets)	12	5					X				X	X	X	X	X	X
	B	Most competitive rate to value ratio (Favorable market position)	1, 3, 14, 18	1	X	X	X	X	X	X			X	X	X	X	X	X
	C	Financially viable entity (Balanced budget)	14, 16, 17, 18	1, 3, 5, 7	X	X	X	X	X	X	X	X	X	X	X	X	X	X
	D	PCU is an entrepreneurial organization (New products)	2, 3, 12, 15	3, 7, 5	X	X	X	X	X	X	X	X	X	X	X	X	X	X

Figure 26—PCU Outcomes, Products, and Owners

The strategic planning workshop had identified over seventy products upon which the subordinate outcomes were thought to be dependent. We see only fourteen here, and we ended up choosing just four. The way we got from seventy to four, which you will shortly emulate, is consistent with the Pareto Principle or 80/20 rule:

1. **Create an inventory of products produced by the organization of interest.** In this case, the seventy products included those that were most central to the mission of each of the

departments. As a group, they represented enterprise-level products. It is important to note that some of the products were created solely for internal use.

2. **Apply explicit criteria to enable the ranking and selection of the critical few products.** This and following steps were taken by the executive team after the planning session. We used the Target Product Selection Matrix (TPSM), shown below as Leader's Action 17. The CEO wanted to make sure all managers reporting directly to him had at least one product on the short list so everyone would feel included at this stage, no matter what the tool told us. That got us to the fourteen products shown above.

3. **Examine the potential dependency between the subordinate outcomes and products.** The Xs in the product columns show which subordinate outcomes are expected to be either constrained or enabled by a specific product. The number of Xs in a column indicates the relative power of that product to enable or constrain multiple outcomes. The more Xs in a column, the more important that product is expected to be. This is one of the key methods for prioritizing products so that strategic projects, organized by product, can be initiated on the critical few first. It is generally used to help Masters of Excellence guide initiatives to get the biggest results that positively impact strategic direction and customers.

An outcome is likely to be dependent on more than a single product or owner. Identifying owners at the product level is highly effective since that is the unit of work that is directly controllable. We don't want to have multiple owners for a given product because that diffuses ownership and accountability. When many are perceived as owning a product, no one really owns it. An easy way to test the clarity of ownership is to ask who gets blamed when it doesn't work or is recognized as brilliant when it does. That is the owner.

4. **Test for high readiness and visibility of results.** A product identified as a potential C3 strategic project would need to be sponsored by its executive owner. That sponsor and members of his or her project team had to be intrinsically motivated to take this on (see Leader's Action 2). The product also had to be expected to create highly visible results (see Leader's Action 3). Products that did not meet those tests were omitted from consideration as first-wave efforts.

5. **Check your gut.** There is a place for gut feelings in the selection process. A product is occasionally selected that passes all the other hurdles but just doesn't feel like the best choice. This can often be due to not fully considering where that product fits in a family of related products. We can help solve this uncertainty by considering how to organize products. Before we go there, let's handle the first two steps above.

Leader's Action 16 guides you through completion of the first three steps above. You will use the last two steps here as you complete the this chapter and Leader's Actions 17 and 19.

Leader's Action 16: Target Product Selection Matrix, TPSM
(See Appendix 1)

ORGANIZING PRODUCTS

Products can be organized or prioritized in six main ways: scope, complexity, sequence, purpose, cost, and customer. Why should we care? Understanding the principles regarding their organization will help us to successfully work on the products with the greatest probability of significant impact.

Scope

The scope of products can range from the most macro to the most micro. The largest category is by economic sector, followed in descending order by industry, enterprise, business unit, functional organization, and personal. We have discussed at some length the agricultural, manufacturing, and knowledge sectors of the economy. We found that a lot is known and quantified by experts regarding the first two economic sectors. Not so much about the one we are likely to be in personally. At the other end of the continuum are the products we personally create. We discovered in Leader's Action 14 (personal products) that identifying those products was probably far more challenging than we thought. All other products are dependent on personal products. To find that we don't formally design or measure those knowledge products means excellence is resting on an uncertain or undefined foundation. Gaining mastery to at least identify and prioritize our personal products enables us to model the understanding we want our whole organization to have.

Source products are exceptionally important. They fit into this discussion of scope in the sense that they impact many other products. Enterprise leaders and Masters of Excellence are the producers of source products. They include mission statements, strategies, policies, core value statements, standards, and other documents that convey superordinate enterprise priorities and leadership's intent. That intent is the foundation under Dimensions 5 and 6 of the 8DX. This is what we, as Masters of Excellence, communicate to those within our organization regarding the values we hold, behavior we expect, and results we want, as well as problems to avoid or solve. In a very small and intimate organization, we communicate this personally, primarily through modeling and daily dialogue. In more complex organizations where we may not have the opportunity for that depth of personal interaction, we have to use source products as surrogates for that communication. We call it the voice of leadership (VOL), introduced with our values deployment discussion in Chapter 6.

Source products direct or govern the design and production of many other products. They are primarily intended for internal consumption but may also be of use with outside bodies such as financial, marketing, certification, and others with an interest in our mutual success. There are also externally produced source products. Those include statutes, industry regulations, and professional codes of conduct. In the final analysis, source products can be identified as the causes of desired and intended outcomes— or undesired and unintended outcomes— experienced by the organization or its customers. That is why we call them source products.

We use our source products to lead the organization in the direction we want. When the direction is different than what we had wished, it's past time to examine the adequacy of source products. Criteria in the TPSM that are relevant to this issue are 2, 3, 6, 9, and 12.

Procedures are not source products. Whereas a source product primarily addresses intent, procedures describe how that intent is to be executed. It is the difference between a focus on why or on how. Procedures and similar prescriptive products represent the voice of management (VOM). Products representing the VOM are commonly efforts to deploy the VOL, as contained in a VOL product. The more ambiguous the VOL, the greater will be need for translation by the VOM. That translation process very frequently narrows the scope of the related VOL and restricts the behavior of users of that procedure or similar product.

It is both possible and desirable to create understandable and unambiguous source products that are personally deployable by most of the intended audience. That minimizes the need for bureaucratic procedures and conveys to employees that they were not hired from the neck down; they can think and act creatively in alignment with source products. As Master of Excellence, we will advance our effectiveness by putting special energy into assuring source products exist and function as intended. We will also encourage the same practice among managers by modeling the behavior we want them to practice with VOM products. One technique is to provide a simple goal. Try this one— cut the number of words by at least 50 percent without reducing the intended outcome of the product. Here is an example:

- The original: "Way of exit access and the doors to exits to which they lead shall be so designed and arranged as to be clearly recognizable as such. Hangings or draperies shall not be placed over exit doors or otherwise so located as to conceal or obscure any exit. Mirrors shall not be placed on exit doors. Mirrors shall not be placed in or adjacent to any exit in such a manner as to confuse the direction of exit."

- The revision: "An exit door must be free of signs, decoration, or objects that obscure its visibility."

You might wonder if I made up the original version. No, I didn't, and many other examples could have been used. Did we achieve the goal? We did even better. When giving such as assignment, I like to make it a team effort and give a time limit to get the job done. In this case, no more than twenty minutes works well. It gets the creativity and adrenaline going, whether or not there is a competing team with the same assignment. And it's fun, making the experience memorable and transferable with very little need for further direction. I will sometimes give the goal of zero words. The creative graphics that emerge are often astounding. This is just the kind of challenge teams like the one at MODOR got, resulting in unexpected results. In the example above, the number of words in the original statement was seventy-seven. The revision has fifteen, a reduction of 80 percent. That, my friends, is simplicity and reduced ambiguity.

Complexity

We can think of the complexity of products, particularly if they are related to each other, as varying from the simplest, component-level product to system-level products. Intermediate products are in between. Why should we care? Because product excellence is typically judged by customers at the system level. The causes of excellence (or failure) start at the component level and are usually where any fix or change must occur to address limits on excellence. A component is a product that cannot be further divided into other parts by a producer of a system-level product.

A car is an example of a system-level manufactured product. It is highly complex. The collection of component and intermediate products, if working well, enable the car to function at optimum levels. Customers experience the car at the system level. If it doesn't start in the morning, it is clearly the car that is malfunctioning. The mechanic may discover that the failure to start is rooted in the ignition system, an intermediate product. A component product that failed may be the alternator that charges the battery, or the battery itself. Knowing which component to replace matters.

Notice that we said a component product cannot be further divided by the producer of the system-level product the component is in. So if Fiat is the producer of the car, the battery is a component. For the DieHard Battery Company, the battery is a system-level product. The key point here is that the complexity level of the product is determined by who the producer is.

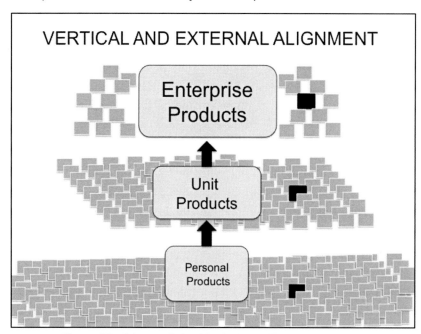

Figure 27—3-Layer Cake, Vertical and External Alignment

The intent of the figure above is to show that many individuals create specific products. Most of those products in a complex organization are component-level products. When two or more of those individual products are combined in some manner at the functional group or business unit level, an intermediate product is created. Two of more intermediate products contribute to or are combined to make a system-level product at the enterprise level. Those enterprise-level products are generally the products exchanged for money (by sale or funding) to customers external to the enterprise.

This figure shows the dependency of producers and products. We also see, by the growing size of the boxes (representing products) as we go upward, an increase in complexity and scope of products. The Master of Excellence assures that all employees have a figurative direct line of sight to the enterprise products that are dependent on their personal products. That visible relationship gives purpose to all work.

The same relationship among system, intermediate, and component products exists with knowledge products. In fact, a component-level knowledge product can cause the failure of a system-level manufactured product. Customers of a particular American-made SUV a number of years ago found themselves upside down in their recently purchased vehicle. We're not talking about financing. They were physically upside down. Vehicles were within their warranty period. A tire had blown out, causing the SUV to roll over, injuring the occupants. Vehicle owners submitted both warranty and injury claims to the auto company. The company's legal department sent rejection letters claiming tire failure was not covered by the car manufacturer; any tire failure was covered by the tire manufacturer's warranty.

During the subsequent class-action suit, investigators discovered the tires had not been badly worn. They had simply separated and fallen apart. The SUV manufacturer blamed the tire maker. The tire maker said they had manufactured the tires to the precise specification given to them by the SUV maker.

Investigators found that was true, but the tires were inflated to a pressure higher than called for in the specifications. Despite the SUV company's core value that customer satisfaction was its highest priority (published on its website), the customers were then blamed for the problem. This is always a handy defense.

But further investigation revealed the user manual in the glove box showed a higher tire inflation target pressure than the specification. The SUV manufacturer told plaintiffs that little of this mattered since the tires had their own warranty and were not covered by the vehicle warranty, though the vehicle warranty did not state that exception. There was also a separate warranty for the entertainment system, but it was found that the vehicle manufacturer repaired or replaced it if failure occurred within the life of the vehicle warranty, at no cost to the vehicle owner. Just as would happen with a malfunctioning starter. Note that the problem was experienced by the SUV customer with the system-level product, the SUV.

If we have fully understood the relationships among knowledge and manufactured products and among component, intermediate, and system-level products, we should be prepared to answer at least two questions:

- Which product(s) failed?
- Who was responsible for the crash?

You might wisely conclude you aren't sure what the answers are. If that is the case, you'll want to complete the next Leader's Action to solve the mystery.

Leader's Action 17: What Is the Target Product?
(See Appendix 1)

Sequence

We've examined how and why to organize products by scope and complexity. Products that are related to each other can also be organized by sequence. The reason to do this is to select the right product to work on. You may remember the example of eye-popping results experienced by MODOR (Chapter 3). One of the products that citizens in the strategic-planning session said they wanted improved was the tax refund. They specifically said tax refunds should be "paid directly into my bank account within one day of my tax return being submitted." You may also recall that some of the MODOR staff thought that request was laughable and "unrealistic." As the leader of the session, my job was to destroy such a Vital Lie by demonstrating what might be possible. My secret weapon was an understanding of product sequence.

I asked participants in the session what might be a reason that tax refunds took forty-five days instead of fewer. Someone volunteered that the problem really was that taxpayers made many errors in their returns. After we had a good laugh about the problem clearly being the fault of customers (remember they were in the room and joined in my pithy observation), I started to label sticky notes. Each sticky note represented a product. There were now two: the refund check and the completed tax return. I asked if there was any product that occurred prior to the completed return that might contribute to the issue. A taxpayer called out that the blank tax return came before the completed one. After several iterations of asking what product came before the one just mentioned, the following picture of sticky notes emerged:

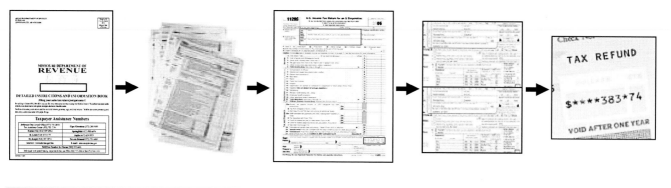

Instruction Booklet	Tax Form Package	Blank Tax Return	Submitted Tax Return	The Refund Check

Figure 28—The Product Chain

To make a long story short, everyone in the room had complaints about one or more of the products shown. The product taxpayers wanted fixed was dependent in some way on all the other products that were created or used before it. Since the instruction booklet was the first product in the chain, it was important to determine whether it was already excellent or exerting some constraint on the adequacy of the other products. Taxpayers said it was indecipherable, that only an MBA or certified accountant could make sense of it. One of the MODOR staff, with support from others, said their booklet had been evaluated by an independent body that had studied such booklets from several other states and "ours is just as good as theirs." After suggesting that the taxpayers' criteria for wonderful might be a little different than the independent evaluator's, we reached agreement to reexamine the matter. That was done, and to the chagrin of some, it was discovered that even MODOR volunteers could not all follow the instructions and produce error-free returns.

So we didn't work directly on the tax refund. The target product was changed to the instruction booklet. A team was formed with that as their focus. We had discussed the whole idea of becoming best-in-class by including entertainment characteristics. I asked them how entertaining the booklet was. Just the mere question got a lot of laughs. But they picked up the challenge. The tax booklet was redesigned, including cartoons and other graphics. It was easy to understand, easy to follow, and error-free. Millions of customers benefited, and MODOR saved piles of costs, won awards, and celebrated success. By the way, this also resulted in cutting the time for the refund 90 percent from forty-five days to under five days. That was the goal, primarily due to selecting the right product in the sequence and innovatively redesigning it with humor. So much money was saved that taxpayers got a special rebate, and the department could go shopping for an automated system.

Again and again we see the advantage of describing the flow of products over time. Our job is to pick the one that, once made excellent, positively impacts all those that follow. In other words, look upstream for the hidden opportunities to drive excellence. Most organizations would want to work on the process. The conventional view of process is that it is a flow of activity. There's nothing wrong with that. But it's not as quick, easy, or effective as describing process as a flow of products. Details and tools related to this are discussed in volume 2.

There is another really good reason for the Master of Excellence to think of process as the flow of products. Every product has specific customers for that product. In the MODOR case, the customer for the blank return was the taxpayer. For the completed return, the MODOR employee verified it and got the refund check cut. This product flow always keeps us focused on Dimensions 3 and 4 of the 8DX, customer experience with the product and process. When we work on process and activity in the conventional way, we get sucked into a focus on the producer's interests, Dimension 8. If customers define excellence, it is their objectives and experience we must keep in the crosshairs first, foremost, and forever.

This issue of product sequence can dramatically reduce ambiguity with terms such as input and output. Input can refer to activity, advice, talent, information, resources, time, money, and other considerations. Output can mean a deliverable or a result. We could have used inputs and outputs to describe the MODOR flow of products. We might have said the blank tax return is an input to the refund check. Doing so would have omitted the completed tax return from study and obscured the differing customers related to each product. If output can mean either product or outcome, it presents ambiguity. Pick one! Or live with chaos, confusion, and customer invisibility. The Master of Excellence has a passion for simplicity, certainty, and accuracy. We need only two words to achieve that, not a dozen. Replace input with product. Replace output with outcome.

We are now ready to revisit, once again, our Target Product list. This time, consider products that may be upstream from products you intuitively view as important. Criteria in the TPSM that are relevant to this issue are 6, 7, 10, 11, and 12. If there are missing products, add them to your list.

Purpose

The fourth way to organize products is by purpose or outcome. We may have saved the best until now. Chapter 9 began our discussion about desired outcomes. Our focus included all four kinds of outcomes covered by Dimensions 1, 2, 5, and 6 of the 8DX. By Leader's Action 13, we had identified strategic and subordinate outcomes that were captured in our Strategy Map. Our organizational success is dependent on achieving those outcomes. Exactly how to do that is determined by the critical few products that, if excellent, will propel us forward. On the other hand, there may be products that prevent or constrain outcome success. So we are working backward in the 8DX to find those products.

One of my favorite cases involved a city in a growing metropolitan area. A significant concern raised by the city council was how to maintain or increase their capacity in the face of an accelerating rate of employee retirements and limited budgets. In other words, just another version of how to do more with less. The desired outcome was to "improve the retention of and access to knowledge essential for running the city's business." This became the mission of a C3 project team sponsored by Cheryl, the director of human resources.

The team looked into the retirement eligibility of employees within the next five years. About 38 percent of professional and technical staff would be eligible. They also discovered that 25 percent of past retirees had been hired back as part-time consultants since their specialized expertise had not been documented in a manner easy to transfer to others. The consultation costs lasted for many months per retiree, while vacant positions were being filled. The annual rate of cost to the city per employee-turned-consultant was calculated to be $30,786. There was every reason to think that same pattern would repeat unless they took some other action.

They now knew the size of the problem (very big), the urgency (high), and the cost and critical capacity risk (significant). What they didn't know was what knowledge, when lost, would cause the city most degradation in capability. With their training in C3 concepts and practices, the team jumped at the suggestion they simplify their focus by switching from the broad, ambiguous, and squishy topic of knowledge to products. They did, working with all the departments to inventory their products, identify the ones most critical to departmental missions, then cross-reference the names of the producers on the endangered-talent list. They felt they had gripped a magic wand when public-works utility maps jumped to the top of the Target Product Selection Matrix. The magic wand was a slightly altered TPSM. They had simply modified the weighting of criteria 6 and 10 (vital to work performed by others) to be 10X, ten times more than they otherwise would have been.

The team discovered many other issues during their project. All this information resulted in the team's ability to recommend innovative changes that transformed map quality, cost, accessibility, response time, current technology use, and customer satisfaction. The first-year savings alone were found to be equal to what the costs under the old system would have incurred over five years.

Criteria in the TPSM that are especially relevant to this issue of product organization by purpose are 2, 3, 6, and 10.

Cost

A fifth and highly productive way to prioritize products is by cost. We can most easily start this at the functional group level. The objective is to identify the 20 percent of products that are believed to incur 80 percent of the functional group's budget to produce. Yes, this is done from the producer's point of view. We would have to name the specific products produced in greatest frequency during a month, identify the individuals that produce those products, know their prorated hourly labor cost, and estimate the average amount of time spent producing one of those products. Since it is highly likely these are knowledge products that we know little about, we'll be finding all this out for the first time. Once we have a good idea what the critical few most expensive products (in aggregate) are to produce, we can determine if any of them are produced based on design documents. If not, we can reasonably assume at least half the total monthly cost to produce one of those products could likely be eliminated by knowing what the end users want and then redesigning and producing those products to be as wanted. Criteria in the TPSM that are relevant to this issue are 4, 5, 8, and 9.

Customers

A sixth way to organize products is by customer. I do not recommend doing that as a normal practice because it usually has less impact than organizing products the other ways. However, one specific context is especially well-suited for this approach. That is when we have a certain customer who receives several products from our organization at different times. If those products could all be delivered at one time, the customer's experience acquiring the product, Dimension 4, can be greatly enhanced, and our producer capacity and efficiency is also likely to be improved. There is that win-win idea again. We absolutely must first be unambiguous about who the customer is for this to be successful. We will solve the customer identity conundrum in Chapter 20, providing further guidance then.

BONUS POINTS FOR FUN

We have discussed the role of entertainment in the knowledge age. Get the edge that differentiates winners from others by completing the next Leader's Action.

Leader's Action 18: Excellence Through Entertainment
(See Appendix 1)

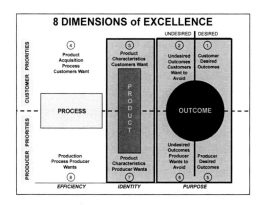

CHAPTER 19—STRATEGY MAP INTEGRATION

We can now add the last pieces to the quilt we call the Strategy Map. We've identified our core values, defined and prioritized the strategic outcomes we and customers external to our organization want to achieve, developed measures of success connected to outcomes and values, and made a major dent in prioritizing dozens or hundreds of products and identifying their owners. All this effort has been undertaken to focus our transformational leadership on the areas most likely to yield the biggest return on invested resources and effort.

The application of the six transformation levers has occurred simultaneously. When fully implemented and communicated with your Strategy Map, you will have moved the needle significantly on your C3IQ score. With the optimum you could now have earned on items 1–8, 10, 14, 15a–b, and 16, you have a score of sixty-five even if everything else were zero. It isn't, so you might be hovering close to ninety. The remaining gap will get closed by executing what we've covered, along with the final issues addressed in the next two chapters and in volume 2.

So execution is now the name of the game. The planks in the bridge between strategic intent and results consist of the critical few products, owners, and engaged employees who will drive focused excellence customers will notice. We have Leader's Action 19 to finish now. If an example can assist, please refer to the PCU strategy map excerpt shown in Chapter 18.

Leader's Action 19: The Strategy Map, Part 2
(See Appendix 1)

Considerations

Completing your strategy map has narrowed your mission from elimination of world hunger to identifying the first few bags of rice to ship. Congratulations! We want to get them to where they are needed as soon as possible. Can a single person handle the transport for each bag, or do we need a team? If a product you have selected represents a complex issue that cuts across different organizational units, a team is likely to be necessary. The team needs to have a sponsor, the ready and equipped few (usually no more than five), a guide or team leader, a charter, and a completion deadline not to exceed about five months. Focused transformation efforts with those critical resources and limited time allowed have an extremely high success rate, achieving high ROI such as the Missouri teams mentioned a few times throughout the book.

The issue of chartering and managing strategic C3 projects is a subject for another book, a note to the author or a visit to the special C3 tools that can make magic happen. One thing to note is that organizing projects by product is quite different than organizing a project to solve a problem. Is it possible to fix a problem but still create a product customers don't like? You bet. By working on a product, we have effectively grouped problems related to that product. The product and the outcomes it is intended to create are the basis for claiming success.

Assigning an owner to an outcome is, frankly, not terribly productive. Sadly, this is a common practice across organizations of all kinds. We will avoid it. An outcome is likely to be dependent on more than a single product and owner. Identifying owners at the product level is highly effective since that is the unit of work that is directly controllable by a single party and an organizational unit. What can the Master of Excellence do when the producer of a product dodges responsibility for excellence? Although I hesitate to offer simple remedies to a many-sided issue, this question occurs frequently enough to deserve a response.

By requiring all organizational units (starting with your own) to create an inventory of products, you can have a conversation with the dodger about who the producer of his or her products is. If there is acceptance of the idea that those specified products belong to him or her, follow with questions regarding who the customers are, what they have as priorities for the product, and what is known and measured about customer satisfaction. You are making the conversation about the product, not about the adequacies of the producer. If you have established a customer-satisfaction policy along the lines we discussed in Chapter 6, this would be a perfect time to pull that out for reference. Policies do, after all, describe conditions to be met for employment. C3 does not permit customer satisfaction to be an optional pursuit. A person who, in the most extreme case, does not claim ownership for any product is an employee with no connection to the strategic direction of the enterprise and its customers. What is the consequence for someone without a purpose? We can help him or her find a purpose, though it might not be with us.

For now, let's compare what you have done to this point with what you were inclined to do back in Chapter 4. You had identified what you thought were the biggest areas of opportunity for improvement, who you should enlist, and what the indicators of transformational success would be. You did this in Leader's Actions 1 through 3. If what you said then is the same as what you think now, you are clairvoyant and insightful, and we have succeeded in confirming the reason you are a talented leader. On the other hand, if you have changed your mind, that shows you are receptive to new ideas and have the persistence to get far enough on the journey to correct your course. Either way, you are a winner.

Winners do well to surround themselves with others of like mind or those who have a willingness to enthusiastically follow your lead. The product owners you have identified with your final Strategy Map may be eager to be active leaders in the customer-centered transformation. That would be best case. Sometimes they are not ready for any number of reasons. We discussed this in Chapter 4. The bottom line is that you do not need and cannot afford reluctant players as you exercise your role as Master of Excellence. We want to stack the deck in your favor so the first efforts at visible transformation are overwhelming successes. Let those not ready go do something else. Work to turn the chosen few into the heroes you know they can be.

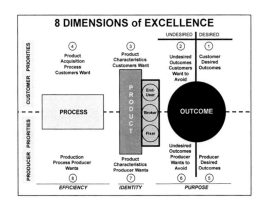

CHAPTER 20—CUSTOMERS

To say we are world citizens is to convey an enlightened attitude. It says we know and care about the welfare of people who make their home in faraway places and share similar needs and aspirations. It is an idea that fosters unity and understanding, despite our differences. But there is no world-citizen passport. To have one is dependent on having been born in a specific country or having passed certain criteria to become accepted as a citizen of that country. Otherwise, we have no vote. Our practical ability to have direct electoral power and participate fully in the direction of any country requires that passport. We aren't just a citizen of a country. We have citizenship at the state, province, county, and/or city level. Without local citizenship, we cannot qualify for a driver's license or a mortgage or otherwise have access to the privileges of citizenship. Citizenship depends on the specification of where.

To say we are customer-focused also conveys an enlightened sentiment. It means we know and care about the people we seek to satisfy. Just as being a citizen is always connected to a specific place, referring to a customer always requires us to know the specific product for which they are a customer. Otherwise, saying we are customer-focused may be a platitude with limited practical value. Customership depends on specification of the what. Ambiguity about the customer leads to uncertainty about what is wanted by whom and how to achieve excellence.

As we've repeatedly seen, language matters. Consider some of the most common labels or aliases we have for customers. Which one of the following do you wish you could use in reference to yours?

Applicant	Passenger
Buyer	Patient
Cardholder	Patron
Client	Payer
Constituent	Regulator
Consumer	Retailer
End User	Shopper
Fan	Stakeholder
Guest	Student
Homeowner	Subscriber
Investor	Taxpayer
Owner	Voter
Partner	

Figure 29—Customer Aliases

Yes, if we really wanted to have total control of those unruly customers, we might be in heaven if we could call them all prisoners. In contrast to the negative, if not violent, feelings prisoners might have about us, which of these labels conveys the most positive feelings, possibly even affection? If we are customer-centered and are successful making our end users into winners, perhaps they will feel like fans. One of the really good things about having fans for customers is that they tolerate the occasional screw up on our part. They actually like us, even when we're not perfect. But all the different labels we use for customers can create enormous confusion.

The most important first step for removing ambiguity is simple: *the product always determines the customer.* This tight alignment between product and customer has tremendous power to simplify and strengthen our relationships. It is the what that matters, not the where. A personnel policy regarding discrimination is a product. All employees are customers. An executive compensation package is a product. Executives are the customers. Both products are created for use by those within the enterprise. Other parties, such as regulators and stockholders, may care about those products, but they are not the intended users. The cell phones a company produces also are intended for specific users. A big challenge and source of ambiguity in all cases is that other parties may have interests regarding those products but not be users of them. The solution is again simple: *identify which of three roles an individual plays regarding a specific product.*

Our natural tendency is to talk about classes of products without being sufficiently specific. The licenses a government agency produces are intended for specific users. To understand who those users are requires us to know exactly which licenses are the products in question. Are we talking about fishing licenses, building licenses, driving licenses, barber licenses, liquor licenses, or what? The user of a barber license is unlikely to be the same person as the user of a commercial building license. The agency departments that produce each of these various products are likely to be different entities. We can't know who the user (or producer) is without an unambiguous specification of the product. Without certainty about the product and user, we can't know what is wanted that qualifies the product as excellent, nor who is responsible for making that happen.

Talking about internal and external customers only recognizes their location. It sounds like a helpful dichotomy on the surface. It is actually the cause of ambiguity and misdirection. Where the customer is located does not matter and is a distraction. Customer location does nothing for our drive to customer focus, with the possible exception with a logistics enterprise wishing an accurate delivery address. Even then, customer role is far more important to define and achieve excellence. The Internet age has made location even more irrelevant.

Suppose you make custom furniture. A woman comes to you and asks you to make a bedroom suite for her grade school-aged daughter. You discuss options and decide on a four-poster bed with a matching dresser made of the same wood, finish, and style. Is it clear who the customer is? If you said it is the woman, you might be a third right. The daughter is also a customer. Do we know what the daughter wants? We may rely on the mom to know what the daughter wants and not worry about her being absent from the conversation. Our hope and expectation is that the daughter will be thrilled with the high quality and uniqueness of the bed and dresser. But is it possible to create exactly what the mom requests but the daughter be unhappy with the result? Before we start assuming things about how ungrateful the daughter might be, let's examine how normal this situation is. It would seem we have a very simple business. We have direct dialogue with the customer who will be buying the two products we will make. What could go wrong?

The problem is that we have not realized that a customer can have three roles with a product and we have only talked with one. The three roles are end user, broker, and fixer. The end user, the person who will personally use the product to achieve a desired outcome, is the daughter. *The broker is an agent for the end user and/or the producer.* The broker's function is to acquire or transfer the product for the benefit of both users and producers. As an agent for the end user, the broker makes the product more accessible, easier to use, and more appealing. As an agent of the producer, the broker encourages the user to accept the product. In this case, the mom is a broker. Her primary role is to represent the interests of the end user, her daughter. A fixer is any customer who will have to repair, correct, modify, install, or adjust the product at any point in its life cycle for the benefit of the end user. In this case, that is the woman's husband. He will be the one picking up the two products, moving them into the bedroom, and setting up the bed. He was also missing from the discussion. We can now see we've only talked with one of three customers. This could have a happy ending. But we have unwittingly stacked the deck against ourselves by having no direct knowledge of the interests and needs of all three customers. Maybe our business is not so simple after all.

We follow up with the mom a week after she and her husband pick up the furniture. She tells us everything is great. We are happy, knowing another customer has been pleased. Here is what we don't know:

- The dresser was three quarters of an inch wider than the bedroom doorway. The husband had to dismantle part of the door frame to get the dresser into the room.

- A week later, the daughter put her glass of milk on the dresser top, causing a ring to form on the surface. The mom could not wipe off the ring because the surface had been damaged, not being waterproof. The husband told her he would need to sand it down and then would refinish it with a polyurethane coating impervious to liquids.

- The daughter banged her toes against the feet of the bed several times, crying and complaining the bed's feet stuck out too far.

- The mattress was a source of complaint, being too hard for the slight weight of the daughter.

What we know is that the mom had reported total satisfaction. The end user and fixer were not quite so enthused. We never talked with them. Ignorance is not bliss. Had we done so, we could have learned to include end users and fixers in all future discussions during the specification stage. We might have added new questions regarding the context in which the product would be used. Follow-up could have been done with both the daughter and husband. We might have discovered the dresser top needed your expert attention (at no charge since you stand behind your product), and changes in the surface material in the future would be a new selling point. We could have turned a near miss into a home run. Instead we fell victim to three Vital Lies (in Chapter 6):

> Vital Lie 6- We know who our customers are.
> Vital Lie 8- We know what customers want.
> Vital Lie 9- What customers say they expect is what they really do want.

It is our responsibility as a producer to always know who the end user is and how the product will be used. You'll notice this is point 1 of our customer satisfaction policy discussed in Chapter 6. It is also related to item 11 in our C3IQ assessment. Fixers know in excruciating detail what the end users experience with a less-than-perfect product, so it is to our advantage to know and love them too. To love our fixers is to treat them as experts about our products, worthy of being included in product improvement and design work on a regular basis.

It is tempting to blame the mom in some way. Absolutely do not do that. The mom may very well have assumed we have made furniture for other grade school kids and knew how to make it durable. In the same vein, she may never have considered that the width of the door frame could be a problem. The attitude we want to adopt here is consistent with all of the points in the customer-satisfaction policy. Note the fifth point: never blame the user when he or she cannot make a product or process work; provide understanding and then help. Assume they have done their best. As Master of Excellence of a far more complex enterprise than this entrepreneurial furniture maker, our challenges are magnified significantly.

Vital Lies, Power, Your Business Model, and Customer Focus

There is a connection between our business model, Vital Lies, societal changes that shift power, and how we view our customers. To see that, it helps to look at things differently than we have been familiar with. The understanding that customers have three distinct roles can reveal insights about the past and enable anticipation of the future.

The Master of Excellence will often find that, when one specific Vital Lie is operating, it is tied to another. Such is the case with Vital Lies 6 and 8. Vital Lie 6 is "We know who our customers are." If we don't realize this is not true, we are immediately vulnerable to Vital Lie 8, "We know what customers want." The trouble starts more often than not with confusion about customer roles. To prevent the potential to have the unfounded assumption supporting Vital Lie 6, always assume we do not know what end users want until we check. View this rule the same way you would when talking with your child about how to handle a gun (whether in the house or elsewhere). Always assume it is loaded until you check, for safety.

Examples of competitive advantage gained by Apple, Tesla, eBay, Google, Uber, Didi, AirBNB, and others illustrates why focus on end users is so important. It is not necessarily about how differently a technology company may work than others. Within their own fields, competitors often focused on satisfying brokers. It is good to satisfy brokers, but not at the expense of end users. Not being clear about the difference in customer roles will usually empower brokers and disenfranchise end users. Those enterprises that have capitalized on this distinction have excelled at a time when their industries were going through major changes. Those industries include automobiles, computers, retail, media, education, and medicine, to name a few. Some brief illustrations are in order.

It is easy to confuse the people who buy, fund, or regulate with those who use the product. Customers are usually a significantly more diverse group than we realize. The ones we are furthest from (figuratively, not literally) are the ones we know least well. But those end users are the most important to satisfy in the long term. An example of a nontraditional approach to customer definition has been Elon Musk's insistence that he has no need of dealers for his Tesla cars. His intent is to be as close to the end user as possible and eliminate reliance on dealers.[113] This is a differentiating strategy. As of 2014, a number of competing car manufacturers and dealer organizations lobbied their state governments (could Michigan have been one?) to outlaw Musk's practice. Did people stop buying Teslas as a result? Hardly. You can go into a Tesla showroom or test drive a car and then buy it online. Or cross the border into another state and buy it there. The car gets delivered to you. The losers in this model include the states that outlawed direct sales since they receive no sales tax revenue. The competitors got distracted by their relationship with brokers and the location of end users, as if that would matter, and gained nothing. Tesla end users did not have to pay the additional markup price for brokers. The company gained a critical advantage by establishing a direct relationship with end users, meaning they could capture changing expectations without them being filtered through third parties. What was their edge? Actually knowing who their customers are.

---

[113] Dealers are a kind of customer we'll refer to as brokers, one of three roles a customer can play.

Computer makers had good reason once upon a time to focus on businesses as customers. The cost and complexity of computers, particularly when they were large mainframes, put them out of the reach of average citizens. These were business tools. Apple started up at a time when hobbyists were the principal users of what were then called microcomputers. Business people I knew from IBM held a view typical at the time: small computers such as the Apple 2 were toys. There was some truth to that claim because they were actually used to play games. But that was not all they were capable of or used to do. The growing power of desktop computers and their commensurate ability to function as legitimate business tools failed to alter the business models of the established behemoths. They continued focus on industrial customers and firms like Apple continued to pay attention to individual users. Those divergent paths in history explain much of the demise of the firms that failed to shift to satisfy the growing power of individual buyer/users.

In tandem with changes in who the buyers of computers were, we saw the growing bottleneck within enterprises for those employees needing computer access and not getting it. If you wanted a new software application created, you put a request in to your friendly data-processing department (ancestors to IT departments) and then chewed your nails for quite a while before you got turned down. There were just too many demanding too much of a resource-constrained IT group. So users did what users do. They revolted, but not en masse. It was more like guerilla warfare. The challenge was to see how creative you could be to beat the system. Vestiges of that situation can be seen today where there can be an uneasy truce between users who bring in their own computing devices and the IT department that is trying to minimize the chaos, in their minds, of a dozen different systems that don't communicate with each other. If we could just stop, take a breath, and get clear about who the end users are for what products and how to creatively satisfy them, life would be better. We know one thing for sure. When end users of any product have the money to acquire it, their power grows.

As women became more economically independent, during the same years we were moving from mainframes to laptops, they became more powerful. Again, for those organizations that thought they knew who their customers were (men), the awakening has been punctuated with pain. This brings to mind a client company that was in the business of manufacturing cell phones and other high-tech devices. They had huge global market share. I asked their engineering, management, and other staff why their phones were black and gray. One of the common answers was, "It's just a phone." Digging deeper, it became clear management and professional personnel were convinced the color did not matter. Only the technical function and durability of the phone was important. Their claimed proof was that their customers had never asked for any other colors.

Sensing I might be hearing Vital Lie 6 and 8 (at least), I asked whom they viewed as their customers. They said it was obviously (and with some smugness) the people who buy the phones. Asked who those buyers were, they said "telcos." That meant the telephone companies of the day such as AT&T, Verizon, and so on. I asked if the buyers at those firms were also users of the phones. My client didn't know and insisted it didn't matter. If a color other than black or gray were wanted, it would have been stated in the purchasing contract. The whole point to a phone, they said, was that you could communicate with someone.

When I suggested the possibility that the phone users might have different priorities than the buyers, engineers agreed. So working with this first point of agreement, I asked what proportion of users were women. This was data they thought might be obtainable, but it wasn't something on anyone's radar and would be hard to get. This meant it didn't matter to them. In any audience I had at the time, perhaps 15 percent were women. Asking the women about whether color was a priority for them, they said, "Of course." They went on to say that a phone could be viewed as an accessory.

I asked the men what an accessory meant to them. The first thing that came to mind was that an accessory referred to someone at the scene of a crime. Talk about a communication divide. It will not be news to you that women generally have shoes, purses, sweaters, blouses, pants, and dresses that are not all black. The women explained that an outfit generally needs to have matching, or at least complementary, colors. Red, blue, teal, white, and taupe were examples of colors to account for at the time. The shoes and purses were examples of what they considered accessories. Notice the importance of a shared language begin to emerge.

The guys were pretty adamant that they were just as color-coordinated as the women. Their shoes were black, their belts were black, and their wallets were black. Or sometimes the main color would be brown. To women, what men viewed as color-coordinated was a bit narrowly defined. Heck, men weren't really sure what taupe even was. They did agree that women made up about 51 percent of the potential world market for cell phones, due simply to population statistics.

Brokers often have more power to determine the design of products than end users do. Producers who are not attentive get surprised to discover the end users always win in the long run.

The real tragedy here is that this major division of the company tolerated, if not encouraged, a culture that defined a main product as "just a phone." The thought that women could represent a different and important kind of end user had little bearing on the future of the business. The conviction remained unchanged that product users as a group were less important to satisfy than the product buyers were. They sure knew who their customers were! Excellence mattered from a purely technical perspective, but leaders never pushed back on the core Vital Lies.

The business was dislodged from its perch as number one in the world by a much smaller company that introduced color. It was probably just a fluke. Or else they fell victim to Vital Lies 3, 5, 6, 8, and 10. They certainly were convinced they knew who their customers were (Vital Lie 6) but were only partly right. If we look closely at the subsequent bloodletting at that previously dominant company, Sherlock, we can see the footprints of Apple all over this crime scene.

Another division of the same client company made two-way radios. Upon being asked the same question about black and gray, they saw it as a novel idea that color might be important. They were about to introduce a new two-way radio product that included teenagers in their target market. After some investigation involving actually asking those prospective customers what they might want, yellow radios were introduced. They were a dramatic hit. A fluke? This contrast in success can be explained in large part by the differing cultures of two divisions within the same company.

Samsung wanted to sell high-end TVs to design-enlightened Europeans in the mid-2000s. Samsung and their competitors viewed TVs as high-tech devices. As Samsung leaders looked at how to differentiate themselves, they discovered women were the main decision makers on TV purchases. Women considered TVs as furniture, not as techno wizardry. The concept of fitting in was more important than sticking out. Those insights led to a shift in Samsung's approach to design. They successfully became the world's largest TV maker with a resulting reputation in Europe for elegant design. Considering TVs as furniture rather than electronics required Samsung leaders to smash Vital Lies 5 through 6.

Vital Lie 6 is far more problematic than it often appears at first. It's not that dealers, whether for phones, cars, or anything else, are not customers. Of course they are. But they are a customer, not the customer, and the difference matters. Furthermore, all our discussion about customer roles and power is equally relevant for products we create for use solely by those within our organization.

I was coaching the top three executives at a major oil firm. They had asked what they should do to model the right behavior. They had attended my workshop with a cross-section of their organization and wanted their people to understand they were serious about transforming the business to become customer-centered. Among the things we discussed, I asked if they felt able to identify the top-five important products they personally created (as with Leader's Action 14). They said they could. I asked if they could identify who the end users were for each those products (as you are about to do with Leader's Action 20). They said they could. I asked if they could use the VOC methodology (addressed in volume 2) to uncover the end users' outcome, performance, and perception expectations with each of those products. They said they could. I asked them to give me the date they would have this done by. We agreed that the four of us would meet to review their progress.

We connected again several weeks later. I asked how their assignment had gone. There was a pause, and then one of the guys said in an unconvincing way that he guessed it had gone okay but they had been surprised. What was the surprise? They said the first surprise was that almost all their most important personal products turned out to have end users who were mostly managers within their own organizations. They had thought their priority products would have been mostly outward-looking, intended for customers of the enterprise. It turned out not to be so. The second surprise had come when they sat down with those end user employees.

When the executives explained they wanted to know what those folks wanted regarding the products the executives created, employees were reluctant to respond. With some probing, employees said they wanted to know what the executives were really looking for. In other words, what was the unstated agenda? This reaction was totally unexpected. I asked them how they interpreted that. The executives said it was clear the employees were not quite trusting about what the bosses were really going to do with whatever they heard. How did they handle that? Employees were told emphatically that, if leadership were going to create a customer-centered culture, they understood it would be up to them to practice the behaviors they wanted everyone to follow. That was why they were meeting. They truly wanted to know how to make their own products more effective and satisfying.

The third surprise came with the employees' response. Many said the products the executives were giving them were largely unwanted and not viewed as helping to get their various jobs done. Taken aback, the executives then asked why no one had told them this before. This was when they got the fourth surprise. Employees answered, "Because you never asked."

What these executives experienced with their own products and their end users created more insights than they had expected. That scenario is amazingly similar to what happens for many who begin applying C3 principles, especially when applied to products whose end users are external to the enterprise and whose satisfaction is critical to enterprise success. We can see many seismic changes that have or are in the process of changing whole industries. Having these insights about customer roles and power provide at least partial explanation for why some organizations struggle and others thrive.

It is no secret that the broad media industry has experienced tremendous turmoil in the early twenty-first century. The American Society of News Editors tracks newsroom jobs. They have found jobs held to have dropped over 40 percent from 2006 to 2015.[114] It's not just jobs that have declined. All sorts of positions no longer exist, while a number of new ones have come into existence. The *New York Times* was an early partner with Google in 2004 but failed to understand they were dealing with an emerging competitor. One of the strong dynamics in this industry, related to our discussion about who the customer is, involves the buyers of a newspaper. The old model was that advertisers were a major source of funding for the paper. Advertisers were producers of ads. Newspaper firms were brokers for them and were paid to distribute the ads. Was a traditional newspaper or magazine primarily intended to represent (as a broker) the interests of advertisers or, as producers of articles, the interests of readers? To find the most obvious of answers, do a page count of any women's magazine. Find the percentage of pages (or column inches) devoted to articles versus ads. The ratio will reveal that readers of articles are not the intended end user.

Central to this discussion is the definition of the product. The newspaper could be viewed as a package of articles. Or it could be defined as a package of ads. The definition of the product has a direct bearing on the identity of the end users. When the purpose of a product is ambiguous, we will be easily confused about who the end users are.

This funding of newspapers by advertisers is a pretty inefficient model, at least for advertisers. Depending on the item being advertised, only a small percentage of ad recipients actually buy the advertised product as a result. The new model is far more efficient. Instead of a shotgun approach, companies like Google, Amazon, and Facebook look for those folks searching for a topic on the Internet and then use a rifle to target ads for that specific product to the searcher. Who needs a newspaper? When advertisers shift to a more targeted marketing model with Google, the newspaper is left with the actual value of the news articles to the reader. That value is now exposed to be far less than previously believed. The seriously declining newspaper revenues and profits from 2004 through 2015 are proof. Another element in this media upheaval is the power of do-it-yourself (DIY). In this case, the photographer of a newsworthy scene is your average citizen who happens by with a cell phone camera. A writer of articles can soon become the proud owner of a blog. If you get enough visitors, all sorts of previous TV show sponsors will ask if they can host their products on your blog, paying you for the privilege. These are the new competitors for newspapers.

It is always amusing, if not terribly frustrating, to experience the pervasiveness of Vital Lie 6 every November. Major retailers such as L. L. Bean, Lands' End, Pendleton, Talbots, and countless others send out their big printed catalogues and promote their online versions in time for the holiday season. What jumps out at me is the heavy promotion of parkas, fleece-lined boots, and other foul weather gear. But millions of prospective customers like me live in Arizona, California, Florida, Nevada, New Mexico, Texas, or other states that have balmy or hot weather year-round. Where are the swimsuits, tropical shirts, flip-flops, and other apparel appropriate for us?

This blindness to the obvious has equally afflicted traditional brick-and-mortar firms like Macy's, Nordstrom, Sears, and others. It is unthinkable that such big firms that reputedly rely on big data regarding their markets could miss the disconnect. Any fifth grader could easily just look at the address of the store or the zip code on the catalog cover and tell you that snow boots and Disney don't go together. The buyers for these large outfits clearly live in places like New York and have become distracted by the location of customers close to them. Like a stopped clock that's right twice a day, such buyers (brokers)

---

[114] Ken Doctor, "Newsonomics: The Halving of America's Daily Newsrooms," www.niemanlab.org, July 28, 2015.

are possibly right two seasons out of four. Amazon doesn't care where end users are located and treats all as if they could be anywhere. How has that worked out for them? A lot better than for Macy's, which announced in January of 2017 massive store closings and 10,000 jobs eliminated.[115] This is in addition to the thirty-six stores previously closed.

The four most dangerous words in investing are, "This time it's different."[116] The closely related version of this statement I've heard from leaders of a variety of enterprises when discussing the necessity to pursue customer-centered cultural transformation is, "our organization is different." That would be true if we don't have products and end users with changing expectations. Otherwise, it is a deadly Vital Lie.

The Uber and Didi Disruption

Failure to understand what the product is and who plays what role with it obscures what the Uber business model really involves. Didi is a Chinese version of Uber, so we can apply the discussion here to it as well. Arguably, the first industry directly impacted by Uber's presence in an urban area concerns taxis. Comparing the taxi and Uber business models is an exercise in product and customer clarity. The revelation comes from answering two questions we first saw in Chapter 13: What is the product? Who is the customer?

It may be a surprise to know that the key product for a taxi company is not a ride. The company has two main products: a car rental and a work order. The cab company rents cars to taxi drivers, the end users. When you call for a ride, you reach the dispatcher who issues an order to available drivers in the vicinity. The one who accepts the order first gets to pick you up. You have no say in the matter. The ride is produced by the driver, and you, the end user, pay the driver. In this situation, the taxi company is a broker for the ride. Depending on the taxi company and whether or not you pay with cash, the driver may split some of the fare with the company. So far, this scenario may very well be what you are familiar with.

Is Uber's product the ride? It might seem intuitively that way. Just like the taxi company, Uber's product is not the ride. Uber's product is a free software application that enables you to create a work order to your desired destination; determine the wait time you are willing to tolerate to get picked up; find out, in advance, what the ride will cost; pay for the ride from the credit or debit card connected to your account; evaluate the driver's performance; get an automatically emailed receipt; and be evaluated as a customer by the driver.

That last point is of great importance since it recognizes that all ride end users are not equally desirable. If you are the driver and a customer throws up in your car, how eager will you be to drive him or her home from the next party? Of course, you could accept the order at a much higher rate than what you might offer to a quiet teetotaler. Customers do have some responsibility to use a product with reasonable care, and they are not always right.

The Uber ride is produced by the owner/driver of the car used to pick you up. Uber and Didi, through their apps, are brokers for the ride. You are the end user. Unlike the taxi company, Uber has no capital tied up in cars (though this may change shortly with autonomous vehicles). Although some have contested the idea that Uber drivers are independent contractors, they are just like taxi drivers who control the tools and schedule of their work. That is usually what determines whether someone is an employee or not. On the

---

[115] Barbara Farfan, "Macy's Announces Store Closings for 2017," *The Balance*, January 5, 2017.
[116] "Every Crisis is Different," *Money*, January, 2017.

other hand, someone at Uber sees the driver evaluations and may disqualify a poorly performing driver from receiving any orders from you or anyone else. Gee, I wonder how many taxi drivers we would lose if this idea were applied universally to them.

Compared with the taxi company, Uber has a very low fixed cost structure (cars, employee labor, facilities, and maintenance), can expand or contract the suppliers (drivers) it works with based on local demand and quality performance, can vary ride pricing based on demand and weather conditions, and is highly agile in every way. It has also given power to both the rider and ride producer via pricing, responsiveness, and satisfaction.

Five Ps of Power

Speaking of power, the role a customer plays with a product is often not the key determinant in who has it. Power refers to the ability to direct or change the design of the product before it is delivered to the end user. Because power is one of the six levers to transform organizational culture, it is our Master of Excellence responsibility to understand the sources and appropriately manage the expression of power.

There are five common sources, what we can call the Five Ps of Power:

- Position, the level of authority within an organization or group
- Purse strings, the one with the money who funds or buys the product
- Proximity, the one who is closest to the producer (literally and/or figuratively)
- Personality, the one we like most, is most threatening or is otherwise most persuasive
- Presence, the one with whom we most frequently and recently had contact

To be customer-centered with C3 means we are end user-centered, *independent of the Five Ps*. Our natural inclination is to bend to the will of those endowed with one or more of the Five Ps. The greater the number of Ps in one's favor, the more power they will have. In our furniture example, Mom had the purse strings and the proximity to us. She was most present and maybe had the personality that effectively persuaded us to invest all the available power in her. She came to us with four of the Five Ps. Risky as this might be, it is hardly the worst scenario. That would be when the producer makes all the design decisions about the product with zero direct knowledge or understanding about the prospective end users. When such behavior is the norm in an enterprise, we call it a producer-centered culture. Sometimes the behavior is industry-wide.

At this point, we may think the end user always has the most power because he or she can walk away, rejecting the product. Reexamine our definition of power. It specifically says that power is exercised before the product is delivered. The walking-away action generally occurs after product delivery. Furthermore, customer defection does not necessarily result in any direct change to the product. The producer usually does not know the reason(s) why the customer left. What the research by many parties does show is defecting customers may not tell us anything but they may tell many others of their bad experience. And when once gone, they are unlikely to return unless there is no other choice, as with a monopoly. In our furniture example, the end user is the daughter. She did not have the option of walking away, even if she had wanted to. Wait until she becomes a teenager.

Fixers very well know what causes customer distress. It is common practice to put fixers together in groups we call "customer service." You remember what we said in Chapter 16 about servicing customers. Unfortunately fixers often have a low rank, may hold entry-level positions, are given constraining scripts on how to handle complaints, operate outside of the producer organization, and/or otherwise have low power within the enterprise. They are frequently omitted from formal product development and improvement discussions and teams, despite their great knowledge of end users. The Master of Excellence will aggressively move to empower fixers by making sure they have a formal voice and can speak without fear to those with greater power.

David, the director of the customer-service group in a larger organization, was on the leadership team, working to transform their monopoly enterprise to become a customer-centered culture. Aware of the unintended meanings of service, he asked if he should call it the customer assistance group or the information desk. David understood their role was often as fixers for a variety of products that external end users encountered. This may seem like a tiny speck of an issue, hardly worth a leader's consideration. If all we did was change the group's name, this could certainly be a great example of how to waste time on minutiae. But this simple question is surprisingly common, so maybe we should see where we can go with it. A little context to consider was that this group had contact with a huge number of customers. Many interactions occurred because customers didn't know who else to contact or how to find information on the organization's website, and high employee turnover meant it was a challenge to keep knowledgeable staff.

I told David both names were fine, but we might consider the group as the answers desk. The name suggests the mission. The folks there should track questions received, creating and cataloging the answers given. Then anyone at the desk in the future could give the predesigned answers. Of course, those answers could also be used on the organization's website, organized by topic or in other relevant ways.

The beauty about answers versus the other options is that answers are products. The others are not. So the answers can be inventoried, counted, and even designed with different variations for several end users, should the urge arise. It is a great way to think of designing some answers in a humorous vein. You could also offer simple awards for anyone who asks a question that the answers desk can't answer. This can engage customers in finding gaps in the organization's communication products, much like a company such as Microsoft offers bounties to helpful hackers who find failures in software applications.

With answers, you could create a tally board at the desk to chronicle the number of questions asked each day, the number not answered (representing answers out of stock), the questions asked most often, and so forth. In fact, Leader's Action 15b, opportunities to satisfy customers, in the appendix, might be just the ticket. You could also award recognition to individual staff who create new answers that the team accepts into the catalog of stock answers. This might add an element of fun to a job that can be stressful to some. This is a simple example of how we can turn reactive response into product design and improved satisfaction for customers and employees. Whether we do this at help desks or check-in desks of other places where customers pose questions, we empower fixers.

We can consider the US Supreme Court for a bit more gravitas on customer roles. Thurgood Marshall wrote about the Constitution as a less-than-perfect product of the country's founders (see Chapter 14). We can now see that, in that context, the Supreme Court is a fixer.

> And so we must be careful, when focusing on the events which took place in Philadelphia two centuries ago, that we not overlook the momentous events which followed, and thereby lose our proper sense of perspective. Otherwise, the odds are that for many Americans the bicentennial celebration will be little more than a blind pilgrimage to the shrine of the original document now stored in a vault in the National Archives. If we seek,

instead, a sensitive understanding of the Constitution's inherent defects, and its promising evolution through 200 years of history, the celebration of the "Miracle at Philadelphia" *will, in my view, be a far more meaningful and humbling experience.*

Thus, in this bicentennial year, we may not all participate in the festivities with flag-waving fervor. Some may more quietly commemorate the suffering, struggle, and sacrifice that has triumphed over much of what was wrong with the original document, and observe the anniversary with hopes not realized and promises not fulfilled. I plan to celebrate the bicentennial of the Constitution as a living document, including the Bill of Rights and the other amendments protecting individual freedoms and human rights.[117]

In the context of all our work on products and customers, we can summarize Justice Marshall's observations consistent with C3 principles. The Founding Fathers were the coproducers of the Constitution, a source product. The values expressed therein were in the VOL. The Supreme Court is the fixer of last resort. Congress also holds that role. When executing on their responsibility to reduce ambiguity, Congress becomes a producer of amendments (repairs).

The American public-school system has been the target of many attempts at transformation for decades. The World Economic Forum rated American schools seventeenth in science and twenty-fourth in math of fifty-seven industrialized countries. Finland is number one, despite the fact students start later to school at age seven and use very limited standardized testing. We will not dwell on all the reasons for the relatively poor showing of the United States, regardless of all the resources invested to improve its effectiveness and global ranking. What we can do is point out a few contributors related to power within the American public school system.

Most parents have participated in some way with their child's parent-teacher association, which may go by slightly different names around the country. The thing to notice is its general structure and role. What is missing from the PTA? The tip-off is in the name. If courses are the main enterprise products of the school, what role do parents play? Parents are not end users; they are brokers. They would say they represent the interests of their kids so they are brokers for the end users.

What role do the teachers play with the courses? Teachers are producers if they created the content for the class. If a third party created that content, teachers are brokers. Are they representing the interests of the producers or the end user students? It may be hard to tell. Where is the student in the title of the PTA? Missing.

We talked earlier about the fact we are in the entertainment age. If students had an equal voice in the PTA and other such groups, would they be more or less likely than their parents and teachers to demand classes be entertaining? If you have had a child in public school, you might remember where the attribute "entertaining" fit in the course design for math. Probably missing too. Kids can memorize the lyrics to songs but not their multiplication or periodic elements tables. Any message here? It just might be that the kids have the least power in course and school building design according to the Five Ps. To connect the dots, we might conclude the producers and brokers have acted in collusion to the disadvantage of end users. Ouch! We haven't even considered the convoluted flow of money to fund the schools and reward (or not) teachers in accordance with their proven ability to advance the learning of their students.

---

[117] Bowen, Miracle at Philadelphia: The Story of the Constitutional Convention May to September 1787 (Boston, 1966).

Products Determine Roles

Issues regarding customer roles, power, product flow, and entertainment can be seen with the MODOR case.[118] The final product was the tax refund. The first product in the chain of products was the instruction booklet. The figure below shows the customer roles with each of the products.

**THE PRODUCT CHAIN &
CUSTOMER ROLES: MISSOURI DOR**

Instruction Booklet	Tax Form Package	Blank Tax Return	Submitted Tax Return	The Refund Check
End-Users - Tax Payer - Tax Preparer	End-Users - Tax Payer	End-Users - Tax Payer - Tax Preparer	End-Users - Data Entry Staff - Auditors	End-Users - Tax Payer
	Brokers - Tax Preparer - Branch Bank	Fixers -Tax Preparer - Customer Service	Fixers - Tax Preparer - Error Correction Staff - Customer Service	

Figure 30—The Product Chain and Customer Roles

You may recall that this C3 project team had a mission to significantly accelerate the speed of delivering refunds. The tax return preparation booklet of instructions was believed to be the source of errors, complexity, ambiguity, rework, and delay impacting every product following it. The MODOR director and I had decided we would not invite tax preparers to our focus groups. He communicated the rationale to the team by saying such folks were engaged by end users of the tax booklet as fixers and brokers. If the tax booklet were truly easy to use, there should be no need for most individual taxpayers to pay others to figure out what was owed or due back. This was a conscious effort to empower end users and disempower brokers and fixers in the design of the new booklet. One of the characteristics of the new booklet was that the team, despite their initial resistance to the idea, actually built in graphics and cartoons for entertainment. True, to say the booklet was as much fun to read as a comic book would be a stretch. But it worked to fulfill the team's mission and create satisfied, excited customers.

Among the things we can do to improve the power balance as Masters of Excellence is identify all the products our enterprise produces. It is not our task to personally do that. Just make sure every business unit, department, and/or functional group does it. That means they would create an inventory of products, which we now know how to do. For each product, identify the producer, end users, brokers, and fixers. Determine the power ranking of all the players with each specific product. Decide whether end users ought to have more power than currently. If so, empower them by putting in place a simple but effective way to uncover their priorities. That method is precisely what we will do to uncover the heart, mind, and VOC in volume 2. Before doing that, we have to be clear who are and who are not end users.

---

[118] This was introduced in Chapter 3.

To be customer-centered means we purposefully seek to make end users winners. This would be a good time to apply what we've learned about customer roles and power. Notice, with the examples in the figure below, that the products always determine customer roles and the same individual may have more than one role. Sometimes the producer also has a customer role. Then proceed with the following Leader's Action.

PRODUCTS DETERMINE CUSTOMER ROLES

PRODUCT	PRODUCER	POSSIBLE CUSTOMERS		
		End-users	Brokers	Fixers
Appendectomy	Surgeon	Patient	Referring Physician Insurance Administrator	Patient Advocate Customer Service Agent Attorney Surgeon
Business Tax Regulation	Tax Agency	Chief Fin. Officer Bus. Accountant	Tax Advisor Tax Specialist Chief Fin. Officer	Tax Auditor
Car	Production	Driver Passenger	Dealer Passenger	Mechanic Customer Service Agent Owner
Insurance Policy	Underwriter	Policy Holder Beneficiary	Salesperson Financial Planner	Customer Service Agent
Departmental Budget	Finance Manager	Department Manager	Mail Room Personnel Financial Analyst	Department Manager Secretary
Equipment Requisition	Requestor	Order Fulfillment Person at Supplier Purchasing Agent	Approving Managers(s)	Originator Purchasing Agent
Training Course	Course Designer Developer	Participant	Instructor Participant Registrar Participant's Manager Salesperson	Participant Instructor Participant's Manager Course Designer
Mortgage	Lender	Borrower Builder/Contractor	Mortgage Banker Processor Mortgage Consolidator	Collector
Prescription	Prescribing Physician	Pharmacist	Nurse Patient Insurer	Prescribing Physician
X-ray	Technician	Radiologist	Technician	Radiologist Referring
Invoice	Billing Clerk	Purchaser Payables Clerk Insurer	Patient	Auditor Customer Service Agent

Figure 31—Products Determine Customer Roles

Leader's Action 20: Customer Roles and Power
(See Appendix 1)

Debriefing and Executive Summary

- The power a customer has in his or her role of broker or fixer is different from his or her power as an end user. Special effort is often needed to appropriately balance the interests of the different roles to counteract the Five Ps of Power. These Five Ps can exceed the power a customer may otherwise have by virtue of their role with a product.

- The Five Ps reveal power concerning the relationship with you or your organization, not with a product.

- An individual customer can play multiple roles with the same product, especially at different points in the life cycle of the product. A person can create a specification (as a producer), be one of its end users, pass it to others who may review but not use it (as a broker), modify it for ease of understanding (as a fixer), or correct errors in it (as a fixer).

- It is easy to confuse two different but related products. The producer of a specification is usually not the producer of the product the specification characterizes. The solution is to always be sure the product we have in mind does not change as we examine roles.

- What happens when we satisfy brokers but not end users is illustrated by the fate of major players in industries such as cell phones, cars, TVs, and media outlets.

- An example of a good broker, putting end users and producers close together, is eBay.

- Brokers can be an asset when bilingual, speaking the languages of both the producer and end user.

- The more brokers are involved with a product, the less power the end users are likely to have.

- The role of brokers in health care, education, and news media (taken over by blogs) reveals a possible (undesired) future for those not intensely focused on end users.

- We now know how to simplify the seventeen roles identified in Chapter 6 under language (as a source of ambiguity), how they are related to the Five Ps, and how we can reduce roles to three.

- By revisiting Leader's Action 5, we can now confirm or correct who the end user customer is in the identified documents named as potential sources of ambiguity.

- Consider the impact of demographics of the producers versus the end users of public restrooms for women. The evidence for lack of alignment is the long line outside those restrooms at theaters, ballparks, entertainment arenas, and other public venues. Some see this as a process issue. I see it as a product design problem and a lack of attentiveness to end users.

- Just as citizens have responsibilities, so do customers. They, as all other humans, are not always right!

- Here is a condensed version of how to make customers a lever for change: it is the responsibility of the producer to know what is unique about end user interests and focus on satisfying them. Referring to customers without specifying their role invites ambiguity and loss of appropriate focus.

CUSTOMER PRINCIPLES

1. Tolerating ambiguity in defining who the customer is permits confusion and reduced enterprise performance.

2. We cannot meaningfully talk about who the customers are without specifying each of the products for which they are customers.

3. There are only three roles a customer can play with any product: end user, broker, or fixer.

4. A customer may play multiple roles with a single product.

5. The more specific the product, the easier it is to identify a customer's role.

6. Clarity about the customer leads to certainty about what is wanted by whom and how to achieve excellence.

7. To call a customer a case or other such label effectively depersonalizes them.

8. End users for a product are rarely a homogeneous group.

9. End users often have less power than brokers do.

10. Eliminate, consolidate, and then automate the broker role to build end user empowerment.

11. Ability to directly change the design of a product is often based on the Five Ps of Power: position, purse strings, proximity, personality, and presence, not the role of the customer as it should be.

12. Brokers add value for producers and end users when reducing the time, cost, error, and complexity incurred in producing, delivering, and acquiring desired products.

13. Brokers foster understanding by being bilingual, speaking the languages of end users and producers.

14. Brokers may represent the interests of end users, the interests of producers, or their own interests, independent of any others.

15. A broker can be said to act as an agent for the end users of a product only if the end users think so and the priorities of end users direct broker behavior.

16. The more brokers are involved with a product, the less power the end users are likely to have.

17. The end users' knowledge of and feelings about the producer and its brokers will color their satisfaction with the product.

18. Just as citizens have responsibilities, so do customers. They, as all other humans, are not always right! But start with the assumption they could be.

19. End users always win in the long run.

CHAPTER 21—SIGNIFICANCE, INSIGHTS, AND CONNECTIONS

We have been following a fairly linear, additive path toward excellence. Whether we consider the 8DX framework, the 10 Steps to Customer-Centered Excellence, or the Six Levers for Transformation as marking the milestones along the road taken, each step has built upon previous ones. This is helpful when learning something new. Seeing how all the pieces fit together should have brought you to a new level of competence and insight as Master of Excellence. This represents just the first level of mastery.

There are two additional levels of mastery to be achieved. Both use nonlinear thinking and experience. The second is based on understanding and applying the C3 principles. Steps and tools are not required. The impact of doing this is broad and greater than one would imagine when we first begin.

The third level of mastery is based on unintended discovery. Consider the analogy I offered at the start of our journey concerning our exploration of Yellowstone National Park. We have visited the main sights, hiked the most important trails, and seen the geysers, prismatic springs, and special animals that give us an appreciation of the park's diversity and grandeur. But there is always the magic of discovery when we go down an unmarked path and stumble upon a startling vista or something new that we hadn't noticed on the map or in the guidebook. We may have had no intent to find it, but now will include this unexpected experience in our most important memories and tales shared with others about the park.

You probably had some specific questions for which you wanted answers when you began this book. I hope you have the answers now, plus answers to questions you didn't know you had. There are more surprising finds coming in volume 2. Before we get there, you may encounter other challenges that suggest a connection to what we've already covered. If you continue down those unmarked trails, you may very well continue to find answers you hadn't sought. I'd like to share a few of those with you now.

Seeing work as products has many more implications than are immediately obvious. We are likely to experience a form of progressive revelation as we apply this powerful concept as Masters of Excellence. Many benefits will be unanticipated. The following are a few briefly described actions worth pursuing.

Failure to Launch/Improve the Success of New Business. Some readers may think the ideas and methods addressed are primarily suited for large, complex enterprises. It is true that complex organizations require approaches for achieving excellence that may be more formal than what a small or new business needs. But I have learned in over thirty years of applying C3 methods that there is more in common across all kinds of organizations than different. When the five-year average survival rate of new businesses of under five hundred employees is 50 percent,[119] there is certainly room for improvement. Remember that this is an average. The definition of "success" is also highly variable, with many businesses operating at a loss before they finally go under. While undercapitalization (not having enough money on hand to survive start-up costs) is a large contributor to failure, the four main contributors related to our excellence conversation are (a) a poorly defined product, (b) inadequate identification of the intended end users, (c) inadequate understanding of end user outcome expectations, and (d) missing or inappropriate measures of success. These issues are as relevant to new product development in a large enterprise as to a brand-new business.

I have seen countless cases of entrepreneurs who approach their new venture with an attitude similar to those who climb mountains. When asked why they do it, the answer is often a version of "Because I can" or "If others can, I can too." They're nice sentiments but not sufficient for success. It is not just my own experience that has revealed that technology-oriented enterprises, as merely one business category, often get obsessed with their technical abilities but end up producing products only a mother would love. Others will tell you what the market is for the product but be unable to describe the specific target end users, their characteristics (gender, age, and so forth), their unique contexts within which the product will be used, or the outcomes to be achieved by using the product. You now have the method and means to bring such an organization success.

Improve the design and operation of enterprise systems such as Customer Relationship Management (CRM) and data warehousing systems to better fulfill their missions. Corporations can spend a fortune on enterprise information systems. Many of those will not work right out of the box. Considerable customization at great expense is required beyond the product purchase or license. If the intended purpose of a CRM system is stated in its name, the enterprise installing such a system would reasonably expect its relationships with customers to improve. Good luck with that. What I have observed is that these systems often do not include a basic template to do assure some essential tasks get done:

- Identify the primary role a customer plays with a specific enterprise product;

- Designate fields or locations to capture the performance, perception, and outcome expectations of a given customer for each of the relevant products;

- Capture demographic information at a sufficiently detailed level to assist in product corrections as well as future product design and delivery; and

- Ensure that all information on a customer's product needs, comments, requests, and results are easily accessible by whoever in the enterprise interacts with customers.

Either this information should routinely be collected and used, or we should call a CRM system something that is more accurate.

A Fortune 100 firm had spent a fortune on a new data warehousing system. The important intended end users included plant managers and production managers at the company's various manufacturing facilities. These individuals were not included in the discussion about the system characteristics prior to its purchase. It did not take long for the IT folks to hear that the production folks could not use the information housed in the system because it was not in a format compatible with existing plant systems, was not able to be combined with related data in a manner to predict demand or assess capacity, and had other deficiencies. As one group observed, the company had confused a data-housing system with a data-using system. The difference was just two letters, but the result was catastrophic.

---

[119] According to the US Department of Labor Statistics, 50 percent of new businesses survive the first five years, and 33 percent survive at least ten years.

Capitalize on the growth of entertainment products when you don't create them yourself. If you had been sufficiently clairvoyant early in the twentieth century to realize the automobile was going to be a huge new product category, you might have wondered how your bicycle business could benefit. One way could have been to leverage your knowledge of bike tires. You didn't have to build cars to profit by providing at least four tires to every car made by any car producer.

Using similar thinking, two brothers in Chicago transformed their 1928 purchase of a bankrupt company. That firm made devices that enabled battery-powered radios to run on household current. They decided to see if they could make radios for cars. The gambit paid off, and in 1930, the Galvin brothers renamed their firm Motorola. The name was a convenient contraction of motorcar and Victrola. Their subsequent introduction of walkie-talkies and other mobile radios used by police, the military, and similar enterprises led to their 1940 rank in the top one hundred military suppliers.

We've made the case that entertainment surrounds us, and the growth in the industry, as we've redefined it, has been significant since the beginning of this century. One of the transformations that has taken place is the desire by customers to have wireless access to all knowledge products. Where is this headed? Look up. Revenue in the global satellite industry was $208 billion in 2015, according to the Satellite Industry Association. Half came from consumer products such as streaming programs, broadband transmissions, and cell phone calls. Growth is strong. There were 107 launches in 2013 and 208 in 2014. A 200 percent growth rate appears capable of continuing for some time.[120] You don't have to be Elon Musk to benefit from providing products to companies like Space X, others who support them, and customers of all of them.

Another industry that ought to have a direct connection to entertainment and knowledge is education. Research over the past fifteen years has found that video games can positively impact cognitive skills that carry over into work and other areas. Improvement in perception, cognitive flexibility, strategy, social behavior, empathy, persistence, problem-solving, and spatial skills are some of the benefits. All of these are relevant to the world of work.[121]

Many educators have rightly pushed for strong emphasis on science, technology, engineering, and math (STEM) curriculum in public schools. Despite that, we find that digital literacy among American high school graduates is weak, and courses in programming are woefully underrepresented in high-school curricula. The demand for those skills is evident from the length of time job postings go unfilled, and it's twice as long if any coding skills are required.

According to 2013–2014 government survey data, 30 percent of Zambia girls become pregnant before their eighteenth birthday.[122] It has been hard to entice them to come to clinics for information about their reproductive health options. Ideo.org found that culture, semantics, and religious barriers were contributors. They set up Diva Centres, which are designed more like spas than clinics, using a relaxed and entertaining club atmosphere to attract girls and address lifestyle aspirations that get tied to contraceptive approaches. Of those who visited, 75 percent now use contraception.

---

[120] 2016 State of the Satellite Industry Report, Satellite Industry Association, June, 2016.

[121] Daphne Bavelier and C. Shawn Green, "The Brain-Boosting Power of Video Games," *Scientific American* (July 2016).

[122] How IDEO's Diva Centres Are Using Nail Polish to Promote Sexual Health in Zambia, *Impact Design Hub*. October 21, 2016.

Avoid changing organizational structure (so tempting for new leaders), which is of limited effectiveness in improving enterprise performance. Many of us have witnessed, been on the receiving end, or been the instigators of a wholesale reorganization. That experience has often been equated with rearranging the deck chairs on the *Titanic* after impact with the iceberg. In fairness, reorganization can be a necessary and effective course when two enterprises merge. Even when that is so, the resulting chaos and confusion generally causes huge frustrations and disruptions in carrying out productive work.

Reorganizations often occur when a new leader arrives and/or major enterprise dysfunctions or irregularities are observed. Admittedly such reorganizations may be effective in removing poor performers and elevating stars. But the main weakness of shuffling people around is that the poor products they produce may not change. If their products were deficient and now new people are going to produce them unchanged, how will performance improve?

There is ample research on the failings of mergers and other versions of reorganizations to change the performance of an enterprise. Of the many reasons for this poor result is that product ownership (and therefore capability and accountability) is torn away from the relevant products. Institutional knowledge about how things are done and why can be lost. A less destructive alternative can be to carry out the reorganization in a manner where the producers stay with their products. This can make any organization structure as effective as any other. Making it better than it was calls for intervention by the Master of Excellence to transform the culture, not just the structure.

Transform the adverse experience and impact of the normal personnel performance review systems, universally viewed with the same enthusiasm as having a tooth pulled. Another area that has been researched to death involves performance reviews. Both those who conduct the reviews and those who receive the reviews hate them. We have found there is another way to provide feedback and direct improvement without the conventional pain. The story of the three oil-company executives (Chapter 20) who asked how they could model the new C3 behaviors is consistent with the new way. The essence is this:

- All employees at every level identify up to five of their most important products. (The Target Product Selection Matrix can be used.)

- The end users for each product are identified.

- Priority performance, perception, and outcome expectations each end user (or, if there is a large number, a sample of end users) has for the product are solicited.

- Measures of product and outcome success are established.

- End user satisfaction, tied to their priorities, is solicited upon receipt, not necessarily every time and not just once a year.

- That level of satisfaction and its subsequent improvement (or not) is the basis for the performance review.

What is now being reviewed is satisfaction with the product, not satisfaction with the producer. Accountability is still maintained without the unnecessary heat of confrontation and personal evaluation. A producer who has low satisfaction across all his or her products, however, does invite some personal assessment concerning capability. The power for assessing performance shifts from the manager of the producing employee to the end users of the products received.

Accelerate, simplify, and leverage process improvement by looking at products, not activity. Please refer to the MODOR discussion in chapters 3 and 20.

Identify diminished or constrained excellence due to missing products. We've repeatedly pointed out the role source products such as policies play in values deployment. When employees don't know what is expected of them, arriving at excellence may be just chance. A source product such as a policy provides a bridge between core values and daily work.

Break down parochial silo thinking and improve cross-functional performance. Silo thinking is the epitome of producer-centered thinking. Turf warfare or more passive-aggressive internal conflict is a sure sign that producers of internally consumed products are not attentive to their customers. Since everyone knows that what goes around comes around, it is easy to develop reciprocal one-upmanship behavior, feuds, and the opposite of teamwork. The correction for this starts with a clear articulation of core values related to satisfying customers. A next step is to require all functions and all departments to create their target product inventories. Since every product has customers, identifying exactly who they are and what they want related to each target product is the next task. Of course, appropriate rewards and penalties should be in place to encourage responses that improve total customer satisfaction.

Eat the proverbial elephant one bite at a time. This was the whole purpose to completing the Target Product Selection Matrix. Not everything is equally important. The job of the Master of Excellence is made a bit more manageable and joyful when the critical few products can be addressed with speed, simplicity, and eye-popping impact. That is one of our goals in creating the Strategy Map.

Create a common language that drives and sustains transformation to customer focus. Start by replacing ambiguous words such as input, output, supplier, customer, and service. Replace them with product, outcome, producer or broker, end user, and product, respectively. Apply the new language and related knowledge by assuring everyone understands how his or her products connect with the Strategy Map at both their organizational unit and the enterprise.

Integrate current change initiatives with C3. We identified twenty change initiatives or major methods for improvement that have been popular over the recent decades. There is a good chance you are familiar with, and possibly engaged with, one or more of these. All of them are capable of bringing benefits to an organization. Expert practitioners of several of the most current offer their highly insightful observations of how C3 principles and practices connect and contrast with more traditional approaches in the next chapters. There is no conflict between traditional improvement efforts and the transformation toward excellence brought by C3. They will compliment and support each other, increasing the effects.

In Summary

Some practitioners of the C3 system have referred to it as the Swiss Army knife of transformational thinking and practice for organizations or every size and type. The range of material we've covered together in-depth, plus what has been touched on above and throughout the book, may offer some explanation for that analogy. Our leadership challenges as Master of Excellence can include the disparate topics of strategic planning, product design, innovation, personnel performance management, information systems, enterprise agility, workforce development, and many other issues that can leverage enterprise performance. Each of these is one element in your multi-tool survival knife.

If a picture could summarize what customer-centered thinking is all about, maybe two pictures are even better.

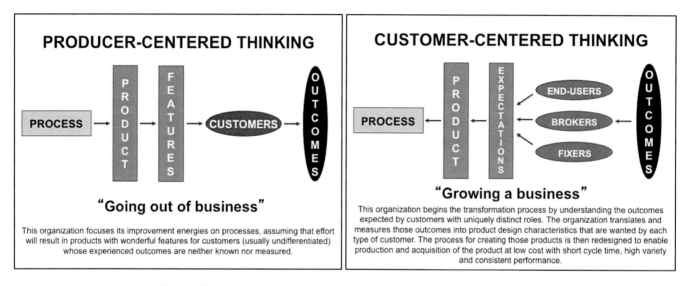

Figure 32—Producer-Centered versus Customer-Centered Thinking

In every case, your persistent injection of customer focus the way we have addressed it will change the paradigms and behavior of everyone you engage. My hope is that you will now find success more exciting to pursue and easier to achieve. I would be honored to hear of your experiences and invite you to tell me about them at MasteringExcellence@icloud.com.

The difference between the winning Olympic skier and the one who comes in second may only be a 2 percent difference. It is that 2 percent edge I hope this book has given you.

GUEST AUTHOR

Baldrige National Quality Award Expert
Brian Lassiter, President
Performance Excellence Network, Minnesota

CHAPTER 22—BALDRIGE AND C3: DIAGNOSIS AND TREATMENT PLAN

Setting the Context: The History of Baldrige-Based Performance Excellence

In the wake of the last Great Recession (though we didn't call it that back then) in the 1980s, America was in trouble. The country suffered a two-phase recession from 1980 to 1982 that left unemployment high and interest rates even higher. (Recall credit cards and mortgages well beyond 20 percent!) A fragile banking and savings and loan system caused the economic challenges, but one of the other root causes that's not as frequently discussed is quite simple and fundamental: America had stopped focusing on the customer.

To give you just a little context, post–World War II, America was productive and economically vibrant. To rebuild infrastructure left dormant during the war—and to begin to create more modern luxuries like televisions, automobiles, and appliances—manufacturing produced at nearly full capacity. As a result, except for a few minor blips, the United States enjoyed one of its longest periods of economic expansion from 1950 to 1975. So much so, I would argue, that there was little incentive for US manufacturers to pay much attention to product quality or the needs of the customer. Businesses would just keep making stuff, and people would keep buying the stuff.

But the often untold story behind the story was this: a gentleman by the name of W. Edwards Deming, often credited for creating the modern quality movement, was imploring US manufacturers to use his principles to improve processes and product quality and focus on the worker and the customer. He could see the waste in most American enterprises, but he couldn't get their attention to address it. When the perception was "it ain't broke," there was no incentive to fix it.

So he went to Japan in the early 1950s, espousing the principles of quality, and the rest, as they say, is history. Japanese products, processes, and companies quietly but significantly improved in the 1950s and 1960s, creating what would be a competitive force to the United States in the 1970s and 1980s. Companies like Toyota, Datsun (now Nissan), Sony, and others flourished and started taking market share from US companies who had become complacent and possibly a bit arrogant.

When those forces collided—a major US economic correction in the late 1970s and early 1980s coupled with the rise of postwar Japan—public- and private- sector US leaders realized that businesses needed to operate in a different way to stay competitive in an emerging world market. The now seminal NBC television episode "If Japan Can, Why Can't We?"—which aired on the *NBC White Paper* series in the early 1980s—is now credited for creating the US quality movement. The show outlined many of the principles that Japanese manufacturers used to optimize resources, engage workers, focus on customers, and drive quality, principles that Deming had taught Japan some thirty years earlier. America was playing catch-up and needed to galvanize US manufacturers to improve performance or risk becoming the number two economy to Japan.

In 1987, the US Congress approved the creation of the Malcolm Baldrige National Quality Award, named after the Secretary of Commerce Mac Baldrige, who had suffered an untimely death by falling off a horse in a rodeo accident. The program was to be managed by the Department of Commerce, specifically the National Bureau of Standards (now called the National Institute of Standards and Technology), where it still resides today. The legislation created an award program to recognize those organizations that have demonstrated superior quality and other performance results (such as financial, customer-related, workforce-related, and leadership). But more importantly, the Baldrige Program attempts to shine a light on best practices that advance the principles of excellence and improve organizational results.

What is Baldrige?

Today the Baldrige Framework has become the *de facto* definition of performance excellence not only in the United States, but throughout the world. More than eighty countries have similar frameworks and award programs based on Baldrige. Also, today thousands of organizations across the country are using the Baldrige Framework. There are many practitioners in all sectors: manufacturing, service businesses, health care systems and hospitals, educational institutions (both K–12 and higher education), nonprofits of all types, and governmental agencies. Why? Because the principles of quality not only work in making widgets but have also been proven to work in every type of organization. And the principles of quality have proven scalable, from the large, complex multinational businesses to the small mom-and-pop shops and rural school districts and everything in between.

The Baldrige Framework has become a management system to help leaders better understand how their enterprise is working, of what processes might be considered strengths that need to be maintained or leveraged, and what might be considered opportunities for improvement. In other words, Baldrige has become a diagnostic system to help leaders identify strengths and improvement opportunities, so they focus their precious resources on improving the right things that create the most value for customers, workers, shareholders, and other stakeholders. In many ways, Baldrige can be viewed as the annual physical for your organization. It provides an opportunity to check its pulse and to systematically improve those things that matter the most to organizational health.

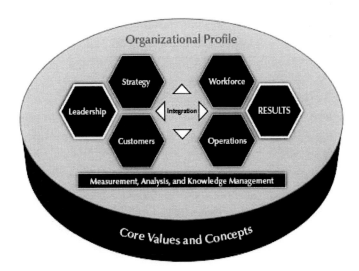

The Baldrige Framework has seven categories, six of which represent a collection of processes and the seventh that represents outcomes that an organization is trying to achieve. Under categories 1 through 6 sit a collection of about 270 high-level, open-ended, nonprescriptive questions that each imply a process.

Some of the questions include the following:

- How do senior leaders communicate with and engage the entire workforce and key customers?
- How does your strategy development process stimulate and incorporate innovation?
- How do you build and manage customer relationships?
- How do you determine key drivers of workforce engagement?
- How does your day-to-day operation of work processes ensure they meet key process requirements?

For each question, organizations should have a systematic approach (a well-ordered, repeatable, data-based process) that's widely deployed (across organizational locations, units/departments, shifts, and so forth), systematically evaluated and improved (the closed-loop refinement cycle that ensures processes are kept current with organizational needs), and are aligned (and, in some cases, integrated) with other organizational processes.

The Baldrige questions (the Criteria for Performance Excellence) change every couple years by studying and understanding what high-performing organizations are doing to achieve excellence, vetting those practices, and then including them in future versions of the criteria. In this way, the Baldrige Framework has become what's now called the "leading edge of validated management practice." It is truly a set of best practices against which any organization can gauge its performance, identify gaps, optimize resources, and rapidly improve and sustain outcomes. This makes the framework powerful. It's not theory or someone's good ideas, but rather it's an evidence-based system that includes processes and management principles that truly drive outcomes.

The Alignment with C3

But here's the deal: Baldrige is intentionally nonprescriptive. It doesn't tell leaders how to manage their enterprises. That's probably appropriate, as no two organizations are alike. They operate in different environments (even in the same industry). They are pursuing multiple strategies. They have several core competencies, and they are addressing different strategic challenges. As an example of the nonprescriptive nature of the framework, Baldrige does not declare that you must use Lean or Six Sigma to achieve superior operational results. You may, of course, but you don't have to. There are other appropriate tools that help organizations achieve superior operational outcomes.

So this is where C3 comes in. At its core, the purpose of C3 is to change the culture of an organization so that its strategy, the design of its products and services, and its daily operations are all aligned with customer priorities. It sounds simple. And I think it sounds appropriate. Most organizations would say that they want their enterprise to be aligned with, perhaps driven by, customer priorities. But saying and doing are two very different things. And being truly customer-focused is challenging because so many organizations are self-centered. Rob Lawton, the architect behind C3, would claim that most organizations are producer-centered, not customer-centered. And his C3 method is the prescriptive answer to the critical questions Baldrige asks about being customer-focused.

The similarities of intent and philosophy between Baldrige and C3 are many:

- Both have as a central goal total customer satisfaction. In fact, Baldrige encourages organizations to have processes to measure customer satisfaction, dissatisfaction, and engagement, the latter meaning that customers are willing to make an investment in or commitment to the organization's brand and product offerings.

- Both believe quality can and should be designed into service, not only addressed after the fact as an outcome of the service.

- Both require organizations to determine customer groups and segments because both realize that no two customers are created equal. Customers have different needs, priorities, roles, and behaviors. Segmenting them helps organizations sort through those differences, aligning products and services to address varying needs. The alternative is whitewashing customers all the same, which rarely produces satisfying customer outcomes.

- Both state that customer requirements should drive product, service, and process requirements. And both declare that organizations should have measures to ensure that products and processes are delivering against those requirements.

- Both state that organizations should make not only continuous improvements (to its products, services, and processes) but also develop breakthrough improvements that create new value for customers. Baldrige defines this as innovation, and it's a theme throughout the framework. C3 refers to this as pursuit of excellence, going beyond what is required.

- Both focus on outcomes. C3 states that many organizations focus too much on features and functions of a product, not the outcomes that the product is trying to create for the customer. I tend to agree. And if you focus on desired outcomes first, then you can work backward into the features and functions that support a better customer experience.

- Both offer a systems perspective of the organization, meaning both believe that all components of the organization should be understood, managed, and aligned as a unified whole to fully achieve the organization's mission, to maximize value for customers, and to achieve and sustain performance excellence. Most improvement approaches only consider part of the system, which almost by definition will suboptimize the system. To its credit, C3 focuses on the interconnected nature between customer and producer, helping organizations, much like Baldrige does, to improve alignment across various processes.

C3 has a few other prescriptive suggestions that Baldrige doesn't address, which makes it useful. Some of these include:

- A fundament principle of C3 is that there is a difference between being producer-focused (the organization putting its own needs first) and being customer-focused. To fully achieve a customer-centered culture, organizations should view their enterprise through the lens of their customers. Their strategy should be framed through the perspective of the customer. Their products and services should obviously be designed to satisfy customer needs. Their processes should be designed to achieve positive customer outcomes. Their workers should be trained and equipped to fully satisfy customer needs.

- C3 suggests that organizations should define services in terms of products. Why? Because defining service is ambiguous, which makes it extremely difficult for organizations to know when they've fully satisfied customer requirements. Instead, if services are defined as products, the organization can think in more concrete terms and can better define and deliver against customer needs. The trick, C3 says, is to call services by a noun. Examples include a plan, a speech, a report, or a meeting. Once a service is defined as a product, more concrete outcomes can be identified, measured, and achieved.

- When segmenting customers, organizations should think in terms of end user, broker, and fixer and should always first try to satisfy end user customers. End users are individuals (or organizations) who use the product to achieve a desired outcome. While it is often assumed they are the ones who write the check, so to speak, the reality is that another kind of customer does that— the broker. The adage "follow the money" reveals that brokers may have very different priorities than end users, but their grip on the money creates distraction. Brokers transfer the product to someone else who will use it, either as an agent of the end user or an agent of the producer. And fixers transform, repair, or adjust the product at any point in its life cycle for the benefit of end users. These distinctions are helpful in considering how organizations should segment customers and also prioritizing which customers are more important than others. C3 makes clear the frequent lack of alignment between importance and power when it comes to customers.

- C3 suggests that organizations should strive to significantly reduce time in their processes. In fact, it suggests that the redesign of processes be aimed for zero time or at least to strive for cutting out 80 percent of the time of any given process. Time as a requirement is fairly universal across products and customer segments. While traditional quality systems strive to reduce process variability, cost, and defects (which are important), time is a customer requirement often overlooked by organizational producers.

Summary

The need to improve your organization's performance has perhaps never been greater. Today, customers expect more, competent workers are growing scarce, competition is intensifying, technology and information are accelerating, and business models are changing at increasing speeds. But with the complexity of today's organizations, making random improvements is no longer enough. Organizations need a system, and they need a way to better understand how processes are currently working and a systematic pathway to make change to create new value for customers. The Baldrige Framework provides an excellent lens through which to diagnose and set priorities for improvement, and C3 provides a useful approach to significantly transform an organization's culture to focus on the customer. Making that change may be more important today than ever. As Deming once said, "It is not necessary to change. Survival is not mandatory."

GUEST AUTHOR

Six Sigma Expert
Michael Mosby
Tides, San Francisco Bay Area

CHAPTER 23—SIX SIGMA AND C3

At first blush, the comparison between C3 and Six Sigma (6s) seems logical. Both include a set of methodologies, concepts, and tools focused on delivering customer satisfaction. Both require active management support to be successful. Both rely on the training and deployment of teams to drive visible improvement. With a deeper examination of the methodologies, the comparison loses its binary nature. It's more than "either/or" or "this one or that one." The comparison becomes a relationship of components in the Business Success System (see graphic).

Taking a look at a comparison of topic areas helps to understand the relationship and interface of the methodologies.

Comparison Topic	C3	Six Sigma
Purpose	Cultural change	Strive for perfection
Strategy	Five Key Questions	Solve Y=f(x)
Road Maps	10 Steps to Alignment Customer-desired outcomes as the basis for product and process design	DMAIC for existing processes DMADV for new processes
Primary Focus	Voice of the customer (VOC) Voice of leadership (VOL)	Voice of the process (VOP)
Natural Approach	Proactive	Reactive
Business Success System	Strategy circle	Process circle
Approach/Thinking	Divergent	Convergent
Deployment	Six Levers for Transformation Teams	Teams

PURPOSE

C3: The purpose of C3 is to change the culture of an organization so its strategic direction, product/service design, and daily operations are aligned with customer priorities.

Six Sigma: The purpose of Six Sigma is to drive organizations to design and produce products or services that meet customer requirements. This drive is characterized as a strive for perfection in the form of a process that must not produce more than 3.4 defects per million opportunities (6 sigma, sigma level = 6).

A comparison of the purposes begins to clarify the breadth and depth of the results each attempts to achieve. C3 reaches for a strategic level result of cultural change. C3's purpose is based on principles, divergent thinking, transformation, paradigm shifts, and innovation. 6s focuses on a tactical-level result of marching toward process performance perfection. 6s's purpose is based on convergent thinking, incremental improvement, and root-cause analysis.

STRATEGY

C3: The strategy of C3 is to ask and answer Five Key Questions: What do you do? Who do you do it for? What do they want? How can we dramatically improve their satisfaction and our performance? What is the strategy and process for transforming the culture?

Six Sigma: The strategy of Six Sigma is to solve for the equation $Y=f(x)$ through the implementation of a measurement-based strategy that focuses on process improvement and variation reduction through the application of Six Sigma improvement projects.

A comparison of the strategies leads one to depict the application of art versus science in each of the strategies. The C3 strategy feels like it applies more art than science. While the underlying foundation of C3 concepts is very definitely rooted in science, multiple disciplines, and widely accepted research, the execution of asking and answering the Five Key Questions utilizes an extensive understanding of communication, behavior, and motivation.

Another way to consider the science contrast between the two approaches is more a matter of comparing hard science to social science. Whereas 6s, Lean, and other approaches use statistics and math, C3 uses linguistics as math. C3 uses word rules that enable language to be predictive, like math. The rigorous scientific method used by C3 relies on linguistics, psychology, anthropology, sociology, even religion, and other social sciences. It is unconventional. More traditional, manufacturing-oriented approaches use the engineering-friendly statistics. Magic can happen both ways. C3 speaks more emphatically for customers, applying the scientific method to the squishy area of customer perceptions, translating the subjective into the objective. Of course, the entire focus on products and customers applies the same level of linguistic discipline.

Another issue, for what it's worth, is that statistics typically used by Lean/6s tend to be inferential statistics. Reliability and confidence of the sample findings is of paramount importance. With C3, population statistics and validity get more emphasis. When Rob talks about how inadequate surveys tend to be, he is really lamenting the neglect of validity in composing survey questions. It is true that repeated use of a survey may yield very comparable results. But if we don't ask the right questions, we only find out answers to the often producer-centered and irrelevant things we do ask. This latter issue in not a 6s problem. Both the 6s and C3 approaches to the use of statistical data produce compelling, unimpeachable results leaders can act upon.

One last comment is that statistically based 6s improvement tends to focus on what goes wrong. C3 is aspirational, driving toward what could be. These are merely biases that do not diminish their effectiveness to achieve improvement. The glass half-full versus half-empty are perhaps the divergent ways of thinking of the two.

So the strategy of 6s seems to apply more science than art. Because 6s is, by its very nature, based on statistical analysis and the scientific method, the solution for the $Y=f(x)$ equation is usually characterized by a regression expression defining the relationship of causal factors (x) to process output (Y).

ROAD MAPS

C3 Road Map

Outcome Definition—Product Identification—Customer Role Definition—Expectation Identification—Process Design—Measurement

Six Sigma Road Map

- Improvement system for existing processes: Define—Measure—Analyze—Improve—Control (DMAIC)
- Improvement system for used to develop new processes or products: Define—Measure—Analyze—Design—Verify (DMADV)

A comparison of the road maps further exemplifies the divergent and convergent approaches of the methodologies. C3 begins with an outward gaze to customers in determining their desired outcomes. C3 then works backward and aligns organizational systems and processes with customer-desired outcomes. 6s begins with the definition of a problem to solve and the process within which the problem exists. 6s then utilizes data and root-cause analysis to pinpoint critical causal factors impacting the output of the identified process.

PRIMARY FOCUS

C3: The primary focus of C3 is VOC. Because of this focus, C3 cuts through the confusion and multiple definitions of customers by defining a customer based on the role he or she plays in relation to the product. C3 customer roles are end user, broker, and fixer. The VOC is paired with VOL. The emphasis is to assure the VOC and VOL are both articulated, visibly aligned, and consciously deployed. The Six Levers are the means by which the VOL is deployed and the culture is changed. C3 specifically addresses how customer focus is to permeate all internal relationships within the organization, not just those with external customers.

Six Sigma: The primary focus of Six Sigma is voice of the process (VOP). Because of this focus, 6s identifies critical causal factors causing process variation and defects. However, the ability of 6s to identify customers is weak and can easily mislead a project team to solve problems for the wrong people.

Based on C3 and 6s purposes, strategies, and road maps, it is evident that C3's primary focus is VOC and 6s's primary focus is VOP. Inherent in these foci is each methodology's understanding of delivering customer satisfaction. Both share the goal to deliver customer satisfaction, albeit from different viewpoints. C3 focuses on determining customer-desired outcomes and how those outcomes are achieved through using process outputs (products). C3 operates under the assumption that utilizing reverse engineering to create effective and efficient processes based on customer-desired outcomes will achieve customer satisfaction. One of the main tools C3 uses is linguistics, whose purpose is to reduce or eliminate ambiguity inherent in understanding customers and communicating VOL. 6s focuses on improving process performance to entitlement through reduction of variation and elimination of defects. 6s operates under the assumption that determining the optimal levels to set critical causal factors will result in optimal process outputs production that will result in customer satisfaction.

NATURAL APPROACH

C3: The natural approach of C3 is proactive. It begins with the end in mind. C3 is about defining desired outcomes.

Six Sigma: The natural approach of Six Sigma is reactive. Poor process performance triggers process improvement projects. Six Sigma is about fixing problems.

DEPLOYMENT

C3 and 6s: Both methodologies rely on trained teams for deployment. C3 uses teams for big wins but relies on the VOL for pervasive cultural transformation that is not strictly dependent on team projects.

Fundamentally Different and Exist in Harmony

At this point, one may have formed an opinion of value for C3 versus 6s. In reality, that value judgment would be an unfair and likely inaccurate lens. Upon zooming out and looking at the Business Success System (graphic), C3 lives in the Strategy circle. Six Sigma lives in the Process circle. In this context, the comparison between C3 and 6s has less meaning than the interface of C3 and 6s. The strengths of C3 address the gaps in 6s, and the rigor of 6s augments the ability of C3 to prove the achievement of customer-desired outcomes.

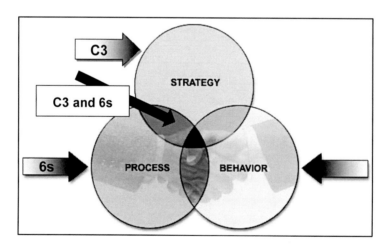

Figure 33—Business Success System

A PRACTICAL EXAMPLE…GO FIX HR

One of my first projects as a Master Black Belt came from the director of operations of a large institution. The director of operations called me into his office and said, "Go fix HR (human resources department)."

Logically, I asked, "What would you like me to fix?"

He simply repeated the directive, "Go fix HR!"

The following is a synopsis of how I answered my boss's call.

Using C3, I formed a team to identify a list of desired outcomes for HR end user (hiring managers), broker (senior leadership, compensation, and security), and fixer (recruiting and employment) customers. The team identified the primary product of HR to be a qualified new hire. The most important (and most underserved) end user expectation was a quick hire decision from a streamlined hiring process.

Once the process was defined, the team used 6s to determine the critical causal factors to the long hiring cycle time. Once identified, the team created process-improvement initiatives to reduce hiring cycle time while hiring high-quality new hires. As a result, I was able to report to the director of operations that hiring cycle time was reduced by 70 percent and hiring-manager satisfaction increased to 98 percent.

So the question for me isn't "How does C3 compare with Six Sigma?" The question is "How do I leverage these two powerful methodologies to satisfy customers?"

GUEST AUTHOR

Cost of Quality Expert
Douglas Wood
DC Wood Consulting, LLC, Kansas

CHAPTER 24—COST OF QUALITY AND C3

How many managers would be pleased with a return on investment of eight to one? In other words, investing $125,000 and gaining a $1,000,000 return? The technique is not a high-risk one; it is an approach that has been applied for thirty-five years. It is called "cost of quality."

Cost of Quality or Quality Costs Defined

"Quality costs represent the difference between the actual cost to produce a product or service and what the reduced cost would be if there were no possibility of inadequate or defective products, or defects in their manufacture."[123]

This definition does not include the cost of doing it right the first time. That is the cost of doing business. In other words, cost of quality counts the unusual activities, not the usual ones.

Quality costs are broken down into four categories: prevention, appraisal, internal failure, and external failure. While this terminology reflects the language of thirty years ago, better labels describing these four categories in today's terms are investment, monitoring, waste, and downstream consequences.

Older Terminology	Current Terminology
Prevention	Investment
Appraisal	Monitoring
Internal failure	Waste
External failure	Downstream consequences

Figure 34—Terminology of Cost of Quality Categories

---

[123] D. C. Wood, *Principles of Quality costs: Financial Measures for Strategic Implementation of Quality Management*, 4th ed. (Milwaukee: ASQ Press, 2013).

Prevention Costs Are Investments

"The costs of all activities specifically designed to prevent poor quality in products or services."[124]

In this category, we keep the focus on activities that are associated with designing, installing, and maintaining plans of control. This category of quality cost is usually small relative to downstream wastes. Almost all design activities may be related to prevention unless they are redesigning something that was done poorly the first time. Redesign is considered waste.

Appraisal Costs Monitor Expenses

"Costs associated with measuring, evaluating, or auditing products or services to assure conformance to quality standards and performance requirements."

In this category, we focus on assuring conformance by the measurement of process quality and product quality. Conformance is meeting the standard. While these costs may be larger or smaller depending on the sophistication of the organization and the complexity of the workflow, these are necessary expenditures to know what is happening in the processes. As controls become embedded in the processes, there may be less need for these monitoring activities.

Internal Failure Costs Are Waste

"Failure costs occurring prior to delivery or shipment of the product, or the furnishing of a service, to the customer."[125]

Any cost that does not reflect value added to the customer can be considered waste. We break the waste costs into "before delivery" and "after delivery" as a way to identify approaches to reducing them. C3 focuses directly on the quality of process as demonstrated by products in the eye of the customer. A process that does not produce something the customer wishes is a poor-quality process and likely to be fraught with waste. Put another way, a product not wanted by a customer is a waste, as is the process that created and delivered it.

External Failure Costs Are Downstream Consequences

"Failure costs occurring after delivery or shipment of the product, and during or after furnishing of a service, to the customer"[126]

The newer phrase, downstream consequences, helps by showing that these problems go beyond the immediate experience when the product is delivered. To sort out an organization's costs into these new categories may seem difficult, but the next figure makes it a straightforward process.

With these definitions, we begin to see that cost of quality is more than "poor quality cost" and more than just finding defects. It is proactive by seeking to place preventative investments and monitoring activities in place as "good quality costs." Measuring only wastes and downstream consequences (internal and external failure costs) is like steering a ship by watching the wake.

---

[124] Ibid.

[125] Ibid.

[126] Suhansa Rodchua, "Quality Costs and Enterprise Size in the Manufacturing Industry: A Study of American Society for Quality (ASQ) Members," PhD dissertation, Indiana State University, 2005.

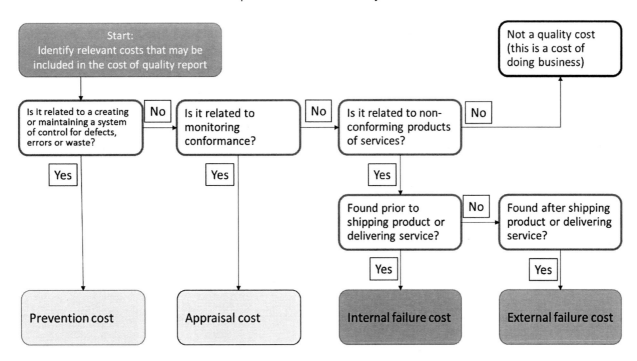

Figure 35—Cost of Quality Decision Tree

The Core Principle Of Quality Costs

Now we can substantiate the eight-to-one ROI statement: the core principle of quality costs is that investing a relatively small amount of money in prevention produces a large reduction in cost of failure and eventually a reduction in cost of appraisal.

Most organizations are not spending enough on prevention and design. Well-run organizations today often display a proportion of quality costs between prevention: appraisal: failure of $1:$4:$9. That is, each dollar of prevention is matched by $4 of appraisal and $9 of failure or waste. Organizations with greater difficulties may see this proportion as $1:$5:$30, even $50. In a 2005 study,[127] the self-identified average cost of quality (P, A, and F) was found to be approximately 6 percent of revenue. The population of organizations in this study were already measuring cost of quality, so presumably had been working for some time to reduce it. Other firms who do not measure it are likely to have a higher cost of quality relative to their revenue.

I have a further note on ROI. On average, the increase in prevention expense drives a reduction of failure cost in the proportion of $1:$8 within one year. Of course, the added prevention expense needs to be invested in the areas of significant failure expense.

You can see by these proportions that there is ample opportunity even in an already well-run organization to reduce costs by placing investments (more prevention expense) in the proper places. Finding the proper places is difficult. C3 provides a framework for identifying the proper prevention investments to drive out waste.

C3 looks at three activities that need to occur in order for an organization to truly excel. First, the business needs to be designed in a specific manner to be able to achieve both product and process

---

[127] Ibid.

excellence based on customer needs. We may call these three activities business design, product development, and process development.

The elements of cost of quality can be found in each of these three activities. If we build a matrix to show these and include descriptions of the contents, it may look like the next figure.

12-way costs	Prevention costs (Investments)	Appraisal costs (Monitoring)	Failure costs (internal waste and downstream consequences)	Cost of business
Business design	Gain knowledge, experience of tools and psychology, and build independent quality structure	Plan aligned measures of results, controls, and inputs	Resulting from clumsy evolved knowledge workflows, distractions, and rework	Embedded costs of doing it right the first time
Product development	Gain deep understanding of customer needs, design for customers, and process	Obtain good qualitative and quantitative market data and create internal metrics of customer value	Resulting from unsold products, missed opportunities, and customer flight	Expense of meeting customers' deep needs; good materials and quality labor expenses
Process development	Quality systems design and apply house of quality tools	Promote efficiency of resource use with input, process, and output metrics	Resulting from internal wastes and inefficiencies	Operating costs from Lean enterprises with zero waste

Figure 36—Matrix of Cost of Quality and C3 Business Activities

The Language of Money

The cost categories above are almost never seen in cost accounting or common management reporting schemes. Many improvement programs measure process characteristics to demonstrate improvement. Lean programs typically measure cycle-time reduction; Six Sigma programs measure defects per million opportunities.

While many process characteristics could be used as an overall metric of improvement, the above cost measures have one significant benefit compared to the others. All strategic planning involves money: costs, investments, ROI, increased revenue, and decreased costs. If you can't measure it in dollar terms, it is not strategic! Without measuring dollars, you are not speaking the language of leadership, either for profit-based organizations or not-for-profit organizations.

Leadership makes the choice of which action plans will best carry out strategy by measuring ROI. Resources are allocated to the most important areas and top priorities by looking at the planned ROI. Whether or not a strategic plan is successful will be measured via ROI. This is what makes quality cost **the strategic measure of improvement**. Consider two kinds of ROI: to design a product customers love and to fix a product they don't. The first reflects an increase of money coming in to the enterprise; the second involves reducing money going out. This is one way to understand the two sides of the money coin both C3 and COQ seek to give the well-run enterprise.

C3 and quality cost both focus on alignment with the organization's strategy. No improvement program will succeed unless the senior levels of an organization are behind the key drivers of implementation. Time is limited, so what is most important is to be dealt with first. This alignment is shown best by using the language of money.

Purposes of Cost of Quality and C3

Cost of quality has three primary purposes: (1) guide improvement programs, (2) raise awareness of the strategic nature of quality management, and (3) calculate the ROI of improvement programs. All three of these purposes are focused on change and improvement. These three purposes are relatively narrow and focused. This suggests they have a specific aim and are best for focused situations.

C3 has a broader and more simply stated purpose— to link customer needs to products and business processes. A broader purpose makes it a more powerful tool applicable in many areas of human work. Quality cost is a more focused tool, suitable for use within a broader C3 framework. Cost of quality thinking is procedural, and C3 thinking is transformational. In addition, C3 expressly targets knowledge products, making its application potential universal and weighted to work upstream from any delivered product, whether manufactured or not. Since every manufactured or sold product is at the end of a stream of knowledge products, C3 has a powerful effect on all the products that could contribute to final product excellence.

The Constraint of Inertia

Why don't more organizations embrace these concepts? Simply put, everyone likes to think things are going well now, they are a successful organization simply due to profitability or meeting their budget, and rocking the boat is uncomfortable. Just look at measuring the cost of all waste and downstream consequences. Would you want your cost of failure made public? Would you share it with the board of directors without them asking for it? If you have a publicly held organization, how would your shareholders react if they knew 6 to 10 percent of your revenue was spent on waste?

The best argument to measuring the cost of quality is how it will pinpoint process weaknesses while measuring the investments to fix these issues. You do not have to share these figures with shareholders or outsiders. Most firms will not share, as they consider cost of quality a competitive advantage tool.

C3 is like cost of quality in that few know about it to embrace it, but those who do see it as invaluable. C3 helps to find the pain points in product delivery from concept to customer acquisition. Cost of quality looks at internal processes, optimizing resource allocation.

No process improvement effort is ideal without taking into account the humans who direct and execute the processes of the organization. Cost of quality may be prone to missing this human element since it focuses on monetary metrics. At its core, C3 is a human-centric approach, starting with the customer and his or her needs. This focus may prevent a misapplication of approaches, avoiding alienation of the people we rely on to make our organizations succeed. Consider the fact that everybody wants improvements but no one likes to have improvement done to him or her.

What to Do

Cost of quality assumes that the process to produce the product has been designed. What is a designed process? It is one where thought has been applied to the overall flow as well as the various steps in the flow. The entire flow is optimized for overall efficiency (use of resources) and effectiveness (applicability of output to end users or customers). C3 helps with this design. It starts by describing a flow of products. This flow of products describes a process. By obtaining and using a careful description of results expected from and characteristics of products to be used by customers, C3 proceeds to the receipt of that product by the customer.

Stream-based process thinking is uncommon with knowledge work in many industries such as in financial- services and health-care delivery. Both of these industries are ripe for change and exhibit significant and costly wastes in their present form. Both of these industries also resist change for improved customer quality. But what is end-to-end process thinking?

End-To-End Process Design

There is significant waste in most office work systems. (Think of poor meetings, bad workflow, communications waste such as email overkill, distractions, and lack of engagement.) It is tempting to accept these negatives as simply our lot in life within complex organizations. Resist that temptation and examine the overriding cause. Much of the waste in offices is due to nondesigned systems. These office systems have evolved over time. Unlike offices, factories use mechanical/electrical/industrial engineers to design their work systems. Who designs the work system in offices? Most likely no one, but if there is an office manager who has designed the workflow, do they have an equivalent education to the plant engineers? There is rarely the same rigor applied in office work design.

The waste in office environments is partly due to not having clear and useful product specifications. In a factory, the design of the work process uses product specifications as rigid guides. How can office work be designed well if the products have missing or weak specifications?

Furthermore, product specifications must be based on customer needs, not on past practice. If the design does not start with insight of customer needs at sufficient depth and precision, the specifications will be weak, the process will be sloppy, and waste will run rampant.

Many firms are seeking to automate their office work process. But what kind of flow is being designed? Simply buying a packaged flow is unlikely to fit every office situation. And few packages address the product specification issue from the customer's view. Most office work requires a larger portion of flexibility than factory work, so prepackaged solutions are likely to be rigid and not robust.

One example is that of automated pharmacy refills. The phone rings, and you get a recorded voice telling you that your refill is due, but your prescription is out of refills, and there may be a delay while the pharmacist gets your doctor to send in a new one. If you are changing doctors or locations, you don't get the chance to talk to someone and make the fixes right away. Such an automated system is unlikely to allow for special situations, such as you are on vacation and so on. No one asked you what kind of service product you would like.

Many of our more mature manufacturing industries have long understood that someone needs to design the process. Furthermore, someone needs to supervise and maintain the end-to-end process. Financial, health care, and other knowledge industries (mentioned above) also lag in the effective application of quality cost principles. A big contributor to this situation is the fact that such industries do not generally think of their work as definable products. This is even more pronounced regarding products created for strictly internal use. Application of C3 facilitates creating an end-to-end process that is effective; cost of quality is a tool designed to help with maintenance and efficiency.

Successful applications of quality cost have been within a framework where end-to-end process management is well understood. Industries where end-to-end process design and management is not commonplace will have a hard time applying or visualizing the value of cost of quality. By beginning with a flow model describing the relationships of all relevant products, C3 enables visualization of the end-to-end process. This may be needed before a cost of quality metric is contemplated.

Good work processes do not just happen; they are designed. Sometimes they're not designed well. Sometimes a design looks good on paper but does not actually work well. We know what happens when we begin work without a design and a design without customer specifications. There will be significant confusion, ambiguity, and waste. In new situations or processes, we are often tempted to live with this confusion, ambiguity, and waste. But there is no reason when dealing with existing and well-defined processes that we should live with these problems.

C3 helps with end-to-end flow design by providing customer-based guidelines. Even if the customer does not know or need to know the internal work processes, those designing the internal processes need to know exactly what the customer expects in the product and how the process impacts that product.

Let's set up an example to illustrate cost of quality in a flow situation. Department A passes its product to department B. A measures their waste and monitoring expense and begins prevention efforts to improve their cost of quality. With this investment, A reduces internal defects. Department B may see little change if department A has been routinely monitoring and doing rework (waste), not passing these defects downstream. The quality costs generated in department A have improved. B has no reason to be concerned with this aspect of their supplier department, A, unless a few defects occasionally have sneaked by department A's rigorous cleanup squad.

When allocating resources across all departments for improvement projects, a comparison of quality costs between department A and department B is invaluable. Allocating equal investment for unequal waste is another waste. This example shows how quality costs may support overall efforts even if issues are mostly contained to local organizational units. Of course, waste may spill downstream when a deficiency is not completely remedied, increasing the importance of a higher-level cost of quality measure. If wastes leave department A, the causes in A need to be related to effects in department B.

C3 and quality cost start at different ends of the workflow. C3 starts with a customer perspective and moves back up the supply chain. C3 links diverse organizational silos with the overarching needs of the customer. Quality costs start inside and focus on metrics of waste, monitoring, and investment for prevention. These two approaches complement each other, providing multidimensional drivers of improvement.

Quality costs take an insider view of the organization and measure cause and effects of waste. This may result in a relatively negative view, exaggerating the misconception of quality personnel as police or continual naysayers. The ability of quality personnel to identify issues before they are apparent to customers is critical, but this ability can be discounted when more influential personnel in the organization see quality in a negative light. This issue is exaggerated when quality is understood by influential personnel as "catching things gone wrong."

C3 takes an outsider approach to the organization and helps to bring to light aspects that may not be evident to operational personnel and leadership. C3 is a more positive approach, one that emphasizes the better way to align the organization with customer desires.

How Large Is Office Waste?

A recent study[128] has shown the average total dollar cost of office waste to be over $17,000 per person per year. With thirty-five people in an office, that is over a half-million dollars each year. Just like in the case with factory cost of quality at 6 percent of revenue, the actual costs are staggering. This total office waste breaks down into major categories of poor workflow, messaging issues (phone calls, emails, and instant messaging), distractions, and motivation issues. Much of this is due to poor work design, unclear product specifications, and missing insights of customer need.

C3 and Cost of Quality: Two Approaches That Complement Each Other

There is much to gain by combining these two approaches. First, C3 helps make sure the customer needs (via outcomes and products) drive the internal process. All quality processes and products start with the customer. Second, C3 and quality cost differ in pacing. In today's culture we seek fast answers. It is not always the best product that wins the race to acceptance, but often the fastest one. C3 emphasizes fast action using rules to ensure effective results. Quality cost is a slow-thinking tool. It is formulated by teams and implemented in stages. To make a difference, quality-cost measures often take months. C3 can produce results much more quickly.

Change can come quickly and slowly. C3 has repeatedly shown that change can occur faster than expected. Quality costs suggest a slower pace is necessary, one that uses tracked expenses to understand the degree of change process improvers have actually implemented in organizational processes. Also cost of quality tends to focus on specific situations, while C3 seeks to address broader cultural issues wherever a customer is involved. The scope of the two approaches is quite different, like using a fishing rod versus a net.

Some change is needed quickly, or employees will tire of the effort. At the same time, keeping the effort in place needs a sustaining hand. C3 can make initial change felt, and quality costs can provide a longer-term strategic change driver.

Quality costs are focused on accounting and numeric measures and start with the idea that metrics guide behavior. To get behavior A, you need to show the costs of B and C. Quality-cost measures assume that by measuring a thing, improvements will occur. This requires that fact-based improvement thinking be in place in an organization. You measure the costs using selected categories, read the ratios, make comparisons over time, and use these measures to drive decisions. We assume that quality costs are focused on what is important and designed to achieve the best results. This is analytical thinking.

Of course, there is also creative thinking. C3 provides a framework for productive application of creativity and innovation.

---

[128] D. Wood, "Types of Waste in the Office and Their Relative Magnitudes," master's thesis.

Summary

- Cost of quality can create a measure of the ROI for improvement. Large financial improvements are possible, even for organizations for which high expenses do not appear to be a problem.

- Cost of quality is an underutilized tool for alignment of improvement efforts.

- The size of quality costs may be painful to face, especially in a profitable organization.

- Cost of quality uses the language of leadership, the language of strategy, and the language of money.

- C3 and cost of quality have different purposes. Cost of quality is narrower and internally focused and primarily looks at efficiency. C3 is broader and more externally focused (at least at the start) and primarily drives effectiveness.

- A designed work process is essential to measure cost of quality, and C3 will make for a good process design.

- C3 and cost of quality complement each other. Cost of quality is a fishing rod-like tool, and C3 is a broader cultural, net-like system.

GUEST AUTHOR

Balanced Scorecard Expert
Michael Melton
The Liebherr Group

CHAPTER 25—BALANCED SCORECARD AND C3

Three questions I have found the need to answer repeatedly for management include these: Where does the quality management system (QMS) begin? Is the strategic plan included in the QMS? What is leadership's role with both?

My answer is that top management produce products that represent the VOL. These include specific statements (mission vision, values, strategy, directives, and core policies) that establish the direction and the culture of the organization. So, yes, the strategic plan is in the QMS. The quality of the VOL products along with top management's participation and application of those products establishes the quality of the culture.

Effective Leadership Products

It is common practice for organizations to evaluate their products and core process for effectiveness. However, evaluating VOL products and the culture that results from them is uncommon. One of leadership's jobs is to eliminate ambiguity in strategy and clearly communicate VOL. I've used various strategic planning, deployment, and evaluation methods over the years. Of all methodologies, two are structured and at a glance seem to offer a comprehensive and robust framework. The methodologies are the Balanced Scorecard (BSC) and C3. The differences become evident with deeper review.

A Brief Comparison of BSC and C3

	BSC	C3
INTENT	Capture, communicate, and deploy the company strategy top-down in report cards used for performance management	Transform the culture of the enterprise to achieve excellence and satisfaction for customers throughout and external to the enterprise
FOCUS	Strategic map, objectives, initiatives, and measures in scorecards that are cascaded from top down into the origination	Align the strategic direction and operational practices of the enterprise with customer outcome, perception, and performance priorities for all its internally and externally used products
APPROACH	Top-down table and tier handover format; identifying how to measure performance before capturing either what or why to measure	Requires definition of customer-desired outcomes first and then work backward from that purpose to product and process performance
DIFFERENCES	Various terms for goals Process focus Assumed customer identification Satisfaction assessment occurs after product delivery Success is internally defined with no requirement for an articulated connection to customer priorities	Unambiguous language Outcome, product, and process excellence are pursued in that order with appropriate measures tied to each Measures are balanced for both customers and the producer with all 8 Dimensions related to outcome, product, and process Methodology is universally applicable at every level of the enterprise from individual contributor through leadership Process improvement follows outcome and product definition and design
SIMILARITIES	Success requires engaged leadership	Success requires engaged leadership

The Balanced Scorecard (BSC) Strategic Planning Process

The BSC is a methodology that is intended to link strategy with operational performance. BSC is a tool, not a system. It is a series of report cards that show areas or processes that an organization determines relevant for performance management. The term "balance" suggests that objectives and measures, assembled together on one sheet or scorecard, offer a comprehensive view of organizational direction.

Scorecards typically focus only on subjects of internal interest. The customers' interest areas are inadequately integrated into the grand scheme. The BSC can sometimes suffer from identifying how to measure performance before defining either what or why to measure. The BSC linearly cascades top-management objectives to mid-management and then to the individual contributors. The BSC linear approach typically assigns customer satisfaction to a specific department. That silo then owns it, and other departments may or may not have customer satisfaction as a focus. Internal customer outcomes are not included in planning with this approach.

The BSC top management (Tier 1) scorecard cascades to department (Tier 2) scorecard that immediately narrows into process (not outcome) focus. Process focus fails to determine what the internal produced products or the desired outcomes are. BSC doesn't require subordination or alignment to VOL directives such as mission, vision, and values. Objectives can exist that conflict with company values and conflict with other objectives. As a default, BSC may consider your customers but does not factor in other key performance indicators, such as your competitors or changes to your business environment. This may lead to an overemphasis on internal processes instead of outcomes.

Scorecards can be developed tier-by-tier in silos. If something is incorrect or ambiguous in Tier 1, it gets processed in Tier 2 without validation or correction. This forces departments to address only handed-down topics. Customers, internal and external, can be completely ignored. The BSC terms of pillars, themes, imperatives, objectives, and initiatives are confusing and routinely morph and appear differently in the various tier documents. This easily creates confusion.

C3 Strategic Plan Methodology

C3 is an integrated system. The purpose of C3 is to change the culture so strategic direction is aligned with customer priorities. The strategy of C3 is to ask and answer:

- What do you do?
- Who do you do it for?
- What do they want?
- How can we dramatically improve their satisfaction and our performance?
- What is the strategy and process for transforming the culture?

C3 uses an 8DX framework to ensure the business matrix and the customer are in scope at all times. Said another way, C3 is respectful that corporate goals and customer outcomes exist and must be considered simultaneously. C3 clarifies a path that begins with outcomes and products before focusing on processes. C3 captures customer expectations, mission, vision, and values prior to cascading goals into the organization. C3 defines the critical products and success measures for those products. It connects and weighs the company mission, vision, values, and customers' outcomes in each product and KPI decision. VOL commitments are included in evaluating success. This is a major difference between C3 and BSC.

C3 creates superordinate and subordinate outcomes, thus enabling prioritization. C3 has simultaneous external and internal vision. C3 uses unambiguous terms such as outcome instead of BSC terms of pillars, themes, imperatives, objectives, and initiatives. Outcomes are relevant to all products, including VOL products. C3 front-loads the strategic planning process, connecting customer expectations and prioritizing corporate goals. It requires that the organization defines success for the products they produce both internally and externally. C3 seamlessly and consistently references and cross-checks outcomes and products so alignment remains true and robust.

Conclusion

Comparing C3 and the BSC may seem peculiar at first glance. One is a system; the other is a methodology of measurement categories. C3 methodologies, concepts, and tools focus on outcomes and customer satisfaction. The BSC focus is on a set of tables (cards) to capture strategic objectives and initiatives.

The C3 methodology applies cultural behavior, while BSC is more of a hand-over process approach. A Tier 1 BSC can be developed by top management and handed off in a form that is ambiguous and not aligned with customer-desired outcomes. The company mission and values may not be aligned with outcomes or included in a planned evaluation methodology. The Tier 2 will follow within the parameters set forth by the VOL Tier 1. Hence, Tier 2 doesn't include VOL. A C3 strategic plan results in VOL quality (shared C3 strategy). C3 includes VOL commitments in evaluating success.

GUEST AUTHOR

ISO 9001 Expert
Dr. Bruce Laviolette
New Bern, North Carolina

CHAPTER 26—ISO 9001 AND C3

I am an ISO 9001 practitioner and implement that standard in organizations. I am also very enthused by C3. I believe in its concepts and fully recognize that C3 is implemented in organizations as a stand-alone system. My purpose in this Chapter is to discuss the interface of these two systems. Since this is a chapter on ISO 9001, I chose to look at how C3 can support ISO 9001. The heart and the brain work in tandem. The heart beats to a regular and predictable rhythm sustaining life by delivering oxygen, nutrients, and fuel wherever needed within the entire system. The brain orchestrates movement that propels the entire body to take direction, compensate for uneven terrain, consume calories, and perform the endless series of tasks and motions that accompany life. A nurtured heart will beat efficiently and effectively, maintaining the system and thereby feeding the health of the brain. A brain attuned to the needs of the body will make choices that benefit the system and support the life span of the heart. These powers of a healthy body are what C3 and ISO 9001 bring to an organization.

ISO 9001:2015 (ISO 9001) is arguably the world's most used management system standard. ISO 9001 is a standard specifically designed for a quality management system (QMS). Its precise title is "Quality Management Systems—Requirements." The parent organization of the ISO 9001 Standard is the International Organization for Standardization (ISO) in Geneva, Switzerland. ISO 9001 applies only to a QMS and is only one of thousands of internationally accepted standards that ISO has published. It is currently the world's most required registration to demonstrate maintenance of a QMS that assures adherence to quality requirements for customers. It is used heavily in the supply-chain world of manufacturing.

The United States DOD MIL-Q-9858 standard and the British standard BS5179 are the roots of ISO 9001. Today ISO 9001 is applied to all types of businesses, government, educational institutions, the health-care industry, and nonprofit organizations, with over a million organizations maintaining the ISO 9001 Registration. At the very foundation of consideration, a primary difference between C3 and ISO 9001 is that C3 is not a QMS. ISO 9001's primary focus is quality management, while C3 distinguishes itself by providing a system of cultural change that ensures an organization's strategy aligns customer priorities with the design of its products and services and its day-to-day operations.

The portfolio of ISO quality management standards has two kinds of quality management standards:

requirements and guidelines. Together these two kinds of quality standards make up what is known as the ISO portfolio of quality management standards. Requirements are the formal expectations that an organization must meet if it wishes to be officially certified or registered. ISO 9001 is compulsory. ISO's current quality guidelines include ISO 9000 2015, ISO 9004 2009, and ISO 19011. They are supportive in nature and are not compulsory. Together they provide a QMS on adrenaline!

The first publication of the ISO 9001 standard was in 1987. The first revision followed in 1994. The standard has been revised numerous times since then, and the current version is ISO 9001:2015. Current users of ISO 9001 must update their systems to the ISO 9001:2015 version by September 2018. New revisions designed to address the changing needs of the users are loosely scheduled for publication every seven years. Teams of quality experts from nearly two hundred countries recommend and select the included changes for the next publication. This process brings me to a distinction between ISO 9001 and C3. The ISO 9001 is a system that is largely a compromise among those members who contribute to it. Even the wording is often a compromise, since the standard must be translated into about 150 languages and mean the same in all of them.

C3 is the well-conceived creation of Mr. Lawton, and revisions occur as he develops the system over time. As regards the changes to ISO 9001, I fear that supply-chain management represented by mid- to large-sized manufacturers often have more influence on the ISO 9001 system than smaller organizations. That could skew the future changes. As it stands now, I believe it can be applied to any organization, large or small, as intended by ISO.

ISO 9001 purports to align itself closely with the concepts of TQM. Strangely though, Dr. Edwards Deming, the father of TQM, never recognized ISO 9001 nor other systems or awards as a system that followed his philosophies and principles. Those systems did not embrace Dr. Deming's fourteen points of management or meet the needs of the Deming philosophy. ISO 9001 has changed significantly since that time. However, knowing Dr. Deming as I did, I feel it is likely that he would not change his mind even today. Nevertheless, there is much association with TQM by many systems. C3 was not around during Dr. Deming's lifetime, so of course, there were no Deming comments regarding C3.

By design, the ISO 9001 standard is descriptive in nature and does not prescribe solutions or methods of application. ISO 9001 recognizes that every organization operates in a different fashion. All organizations have different environments and core competencies that they feel are related to addressing their challenges. So the tools that support implementation are not specified, though ISO does provide some complementary noncompulsory support documents for ISO 9001. The decision for appropriate implementation tool selection is left solely up to the individual organization's leadership. The basic concept is that the organization should identify which method of implementation would best benefit its needs. In my experience, that is where the responsibility should reside, but improper tool selection might hamper the ISO 9001 implementation process.

A summary of the contrasts between ISO 9001 and C3 is offered at the end of this chapter. One of the differences is between the general and descriptive nature of ISO 9001 and the fact C3 is highly prescriptive. C3 starts with the assumption that all organizations have customers and all producers must understand and align customer priorities with the organization's strategic direction and practices. C3 does not suggest what must be done to satisfy customer priorities. It provides clear instruction on how to do that, from creating the strategic plan down through deployment at the line-work level. A specific road map and tools are provided to accomplish this, applicable to all organizations.

Any organization can use the ISO 9001 standard and not seek registration. If not seeking registration, the organization is free to use the standard as desired. In this case, the organization may not claim ISO 9001 registration, and they must refrain from using the ISO 9001 designation in any organizational literature, communications, or product marketing. If the organization is seeking a registration, a certified third-party auditor must review the organization. Any errors in the implementation process identified by that third-party auditor might result in failure to attain that coveted registration. Resolutions of those errors, meeting the satisfaction of the registration agency, must occur before final registration can occur. The successful completion of the ISO 9001 results in registration, which allows the organization to feature ISO 9001 in its marketing information and to claim itself as ISO 9001 registered. A final note is that an organization can freely decide to implement ISO 9001, although many organizations require ISO 9001 registration of suppliers and support organizations as a prerequisite to establishing a business relationship.

There is no registration process for C3, and no third-party audit process oversees the C3 deployment. The structured understanding of customer wants provides the target to be hit. There is, however, a program of certification for C3 Masters of Excellence. So the focus is on individual competency of C3 practitioners. Any organization can choose to implement C3. The ISO 9001 registration purportedly guarantees the ability of an organization to meet customer needs, much the same as the successful attainment of a driver's license implies satisfactory driving skills. Recognize that the driver can be dangerous even with a license.

This analogy brings us to another difference between C3 and ISO 9001. Consider the case of the driver's license analogy. Think of the Indy 500 in this comparison. The skills and tools needed to win the Indy 500 are related but significantly different from the driver's license requirements. An Indy driver who wins the race does not need a driver's license. ISO 9001 and C3 would be in sync thus far. The intention of the C3 and ISO 9001 systems, if correctly used by the practitioner of the principles and practices, will win the Indy 500. However, the difference lies with the checkered flag.

With C3, the customer always holds the checkered flag. With the ISO 9001 standard, the producer organization itself could hold the checkered flag. The organization could also choose to allow the customer to hold the flag. There is always a danger and added risk when the producer is the sole arbiter of who wins. This latter concept is an important distinction and provides a good reason to use C3 as a guiding light during the implementation process of ISO 9001. I would pose the question, "If you control the flag, do you control the race?" If the organization itself waves the flag, will it truly be the winner? Furthermore, is it possible for the organization to conclude it is the winner while its customers think otherwise? Those implementing C3 prevent such conflicts.

The ISO 9001 standard provides a road map to a QMS, which must align itself with the established strategic plan and direction of the organization. In the ISO 9001 system, objectives are established that enhance the strategic plan and ensure customer satisfaction. Also ISO 9001 is very concerned with meeting the needs and priorities of the customer, though often the organization strategy does not apply to any customer. This is a very important point.

In comparison, C3 begins with the strategic plan. The existing strategic plan must be evaluated and modified if found to be inadequate, to ensure the organization heads in the right direction. C3's 8DX provides the framework for that assessment, requiring the organization to articulate, measure, and set numerical improvement goals for desired outcomes wanted by both customers and the enterprise. The resulting strategic plan heavily engages leadership and customer requirements in the final development of the strategic plan. I like that! The effort regarding the strategic plan is an area where C3 gives a big boost to ISO 9001. After all, if the strategic plan is not right, how can the organization expect to head in the right direction?

The purpose of C3 is to change the culture of an organization to ensure alignment with customer priorities, which, contrary to popular belief, is not an easy undertaking. I have read and observed that most organizations believe customer priorities drive them. My experience has been that this belief is incorrect as most organizations place their own needs ahead of the customer's. The truth is that they may have the best intentions, but best intentions frequently do not align with customer needs and priorities. By introducing C3 into the mix, the organization becomes customer-centered. That is where the ISO 9001 system desires to go, though no good method is provided.

C3 and ISO 9001 share the goal of customer satisfaction. ISO requires that customer satisfaction is measured and that customer perceptions be understood. Customer needs come first, but other stakeholder needs must also be considered. Further, ISO requires that customer complaints must be corrected appropriately. ISO 9001 requires that solutions be derived that prevent the recurrence of the complaint. C3 and ISO 9001 realize that no two customers are created equal and customers have different needs, priorities, roles, and behaviors.

ISO 9001 introduces the concept of recognizing that customers can be direct or indirect, anyone who receives value from the organization. A customer could be internal or external to the organization. The organization is expected and assumed to understand customers' current and future needs and expectations. The organization's goals and objectives must be linked to customer needs and expectations. Those customers' needs and expectations must be clearly communicated throughout the organization. Customer needs and expectations must be used in all phases of planning, designing, development, production, delivery, and support of the products and services. The organization must measure and monitor customer satisfaction and take appropriate actions. Finally, ISO 9001 requires organizations to actively manage relationships with customers as a basis to achieve sustained success.

C3 agrees with those requirements but enhances those functions and considerations by eliminating ambiguity about the concept and identity of the customer. C3 provides that an organization should think regarding end user, broker, and fixer and should always first try to satisfy end user customers. Though ISO 9001 recognizes the many customers that exist at all levels, giving consideration to them all becomes very complicated while trying to meet their needs. ISO also recognizes that there are numerous interested parties related to any given product. C3, on the other hand, says that end users use the product to achieve the desired outcome. There is also a distinction made between brokers and fixers. These distinctions are helpful while considering how to segment customers and prioritize customer importance. This C3 concept adds to ISO 9001 interpretation and would help any organization to overcome confusion caused by the misinterpretation of those roles. Every organization struggles with the competing interest of different customers. C3 provides the means by which those distinct customers and stakeholders, with their differing roles with a specific product and their differing interests, can be appropriately balanced.

C3 and ISO 9001 share the concepts of quality assurance that quality must be designed into a product or service. C3 and ISO 9001 agree that customer requirements should drive product, service, and process requirements. Both systems declare that organizations should have measures to ensure that products and services are meeting those requirements. The primary difference is that C3 starts the process with the customer. ISO 9001 begins by using the established strategy plan. In the C3 system, the focus is on desired outcomes for the customer from the onset. The C3 approach is a consideration that I believe should be used by all systems and would enhance any customer experience. Looking at customer satisfaction after the product is built is tantamount to asking the question "Is the road safe?" after the road is built, in use, and an accident has occurred. Certainly the question is important, and the accident that has occurred should be investigated, but waiting for a customer to satisfy action results is way too late. In C3, those are serious questions that are asked and resolved right up front. Customers are incorporated into the process from the very beginning. In the ISO 9001 world, those important questions should be asked when considering risk. However, the jury is still out on this and the effectiveness of ISO 9001 in this area. The C3 system has a means to ensure customer satisfaction before going into production. I like that certainty.

The ISO 9001 methodology emphasizes a process approach as the way to get to outcome focus. C3 uses a systems approach that starts with outcomes. I find that a systems approach is far more effective. Dr. Russell Ackoff, one of my personal mentors but, more importantly, a pioneer in systems theory thinking, advocated that systems thinking will open the door to more effective problem-solving techniques. Ackoff validated that a purposeful system is formed by linking work, people, and things and examining their social, cultural, and psychological implications. In a purposeful system, participants become dedicated to intentionally and collectively formulate objectives that are supportive of the larger system. They seek to achieve a specific ideal and objectives. In comparison with the process approach, the belief is that, when all individual processes operate well, the total system will operate well. In reality, however, that actually doesn't work well. By using the systematic approach of C3, we can act more decisively and more effectively deal with the organization's issues.

C3 and ISO 9001 understand the importance of leadership in meeting the commitments and needs of the customer. While this is a new change to the ISO 9001 standard, C3 takes it a step further. At its most elementary roots, C3 recognizes that an organization must assess itself through the lens of its customers. The use of the customer lens brings us to the importance of starting the C3 process by establishing strategic direction through the perspective of the customer. ISO 9001 does not do that. To be fair, ISO 9001 now recognizes that it is the leadership's responsibility to set the course of the organization, and its strategy is of major concern. ISO 9001 drives this through the establishment of a quality policy, goals, and objectives. C3 clearly focuses on the strategy and various policies established with the expressed intent of addressing customer needs. The intention of the ISO 9001 standard is for those issues to be covered. However, the school is still out since the standard is still very new and implementation is just starting. Not being more specific in the ISO 9001 clauses to ensure that leadership takes the lead in ensuring that core values are achieved could be a significant flaw.

Some leaders will not lead unless required or compelled to do so. ISO 9001 provides that hammer if the leadership is not demonstrating it is using ISO 9001. Understand though that most organizations work in cooperation with the registrar and find comments from the registrar as valuable. So, as the registrar observes that the leadership is not an effective partner in the process, nonconformances will be identified. C3, in contrast, uses an entirely different mechanism to entice, not coerce, leaders to lead. Perhaps a contrast, in this respect, is compliance versus aspiration. Both have their place, but they are clearly different.

ISO 9001 requires that the leadership enhance customer satisfaction by identifying and addressing risks and opportunities that may impact customers and satisfaction. No direction or details are offered for how to do this, nor which essentials must be included to carry out that responsibility. C3 provides a highly articulated approach, insisting that outcome definition is the most important customer expectation to determine before beginning anything. It is the leadership's responsibility to ensure these outcomes are identified, and here again, C3 will strengthen the ISO 9001 QMS and provide direction.

Identifying customer outcomes is a distinctive characteristic of a true leader. I recall a company with whom I worked that had not sold a product in years. Workers were being laid off, and resources were being drained. Leadership blamed the economy, yet competitors were selling the product. They were quick to let me know that they knew how to run the business. As I observed the operations, I found numerous operational problems were ignored. Leadership perceived that these problems were inconsequential. Hundreds of customer complaints were unanswered. The company was a cutting-edge manufacturer in the field, and the leaders thought they knew what customers needed. Therefore it was not necessary to respond to errant customers. Besides, there wasn't enough time.

Is this a demonstration of leadership? These leadership "Vital Lies" made the leadership feel good, which was the only value the lies served. In the end, the customers, the employees, and the owners were hurt. The leadership of the organization could not perceive the Vital Lies that seemed to soothe their wounds. These lies, though not maliciously applied, resulted in a series of poor decisions and misdirections. The self-deceptions were very costly and became a permanent part of the culture. Those Vital Lies set the tone for the future.

A properly implemented QMS would tend to pick this circumstance apart through detection of the individual problems. However, each of those problems is merely a symptom. Though correcting the symptom will help, the problem will not be cured. Only by thoughtful use of C3 can the organization come to understand their Vital Lies and hope to save the business. Vital lies is an area of supreme importance, and every company needs to address those. Recognizing the organization's Vital Lies and dealing with them is critical for an effective QMS.

Leadership must ensure that the organization is perfectly suited to do what is required of it. That is, the organization should be aligned with the outcomes that best support the customer needs. Of course, understand that this is where Vital Lies come into play, as an organization is perfectly suited to do precisely what that organization is currently doing. Meeting customer needs and doing what the organization does best are two very different situations. The burden of success lies clearly and firmly on the shoulders of the leadership and cannot be placed anywhere else. Though the individual efforts are often delegated, the responsibility for ensuring proper functioning of the organization remains with top leadership. C3 clearly stresses the importance of that formula, and there is great effort to drive out what I will call "leadership ambiguity" within the system by proper use of the C3 instruments. C3's focus on and methods for strengthening what Lawton refers to as the VOL makes a significant contribution to ISO 9001, capable of producing a healthy and vigorous organization that ensures a customer remains or becomes enthusiastic.

Though the intention of the standard is to create an organization that fully supports the customer, organization operational policies often do not represent those needs in spite of best efforts. Here is where Mark Twain's statement, "It's not what we don't know that gets us into trouble. It's what we know for sure that just ain't so" becomes so enlightening. Organizations develop these various policies in isolation from customer involvement, using their best efforts. As Dr. Edwards Deming said, "We are being ruined by best efforts." Mr. Lawton suggests it is necessary to have a customer satisfaction policy. The ISO 9001 quality policy is intended to ensure customer satisfaction, though in practice it may not. Remember, in the ISO 9001 world these policies are often determined in isolation by the producer through best efforts. The C3 insistence that additional policies are needed is supported by observable fact.

Planning is a major focus within the ISO 9001 standard and C3. Planning, in general, should be thought of like the big P: planning of product, planning of production, planning of delivery, planning of customer satisfaction, planning of support after sales, and planning of all points in between those vital planning areas. Both risks and opportunities should be identified and planned. From an ISO 9001 perspective, planning should ensure that an organization focuses its energy on matters that impact quality and customer satisfaction. Successful planning ensures that stakeholders of the organization are working toward the same goals, to assess and adjust the organization's direction in response to changing environments. The outcome of planning should produce decisions and actions that shape and guide the organization's future. Planning will define what an organization does and why it does it. Planning should be effective and bring value to the system and customers, and good planning will keep the organization relevant. Who can argue with that? These are concepts that ISO 9001 and C3 share.

C3 provides specific methods to ensure thorough planning. While ISO 9001 requires good planning and points to the use of PDCA, it does not specify what or how.

Few would argue with the importance of planning. The complication comes in the execution. Most ISO 9001 organizations that I work with spend a great deal of time planning. As I observe an organization's planning, I always ask, "Are the right things being planned?" The answer is, sadly, not always yes! To be sure, most organizations are using their best efforts. You can understand the problems that best efforts can bring.

My wife and I like to travel. When we decide to go on a trip, we determine where we want to go, our mode of transportation, and budget. Typically that results in a road trip to a specific location. A good map or a GPS are very beneficial in defining the route we must take. Thanks to these technological advancements, we are normally very successful in arriving at our travel spot. On the other hand, had we not determined our desired outcome in the first place, any route would have gotten us there. My concern is that organizations approach planning in a similar fashion, without identifying where they want to go. Often planning begins with what they know or perceive, which might not be the desired destination. If organizations do not know where they want to go, then it is simple. Any road will get them there.

C3 and ISO 9001 agree that organizations must make continuous improvements to its products, services, and processes. C3 names those improvements as "breakthrough improvements." This is the intention of the ISO 9001 concept of continual improvement. C3 refers to this as the pursuit of excellence. Both systems recognize the necessity that going beyond what is required is imperative. ISO 9001 implies it, but C3 is explicit. For example, C3 meaningfully advocates that organizations should strive to significantly reduce time in its processes by as much as 80 percent. The ISO 9001 model strives to reduce process variability, cost, and defects, and time can be a part of that. C3 adds time to that mix. Time is a universal customer requirement that is often overlooked. The idea of time is a C3 distinction.

ISO 9001 requires that an organization determine and identify opportunities for improvement by actively soliciting opportunities to improve processes, products, and services and through the scrutiny of the QMS and its customer evaluations, complaints, and suggestions. Nonconformities—including those arising from customer, government, and stakeholder complaints; faulty production or execution of processes; or negative internal audit findings—require actions to deal with the consequences and prevent recurrence. Often these actions are taken in isolation, solely from the producer's view. The proper execution of corrective actions are another point in the system where C3 can ensure that the nonconformances are properly corrected. Further, C3 provides the system and methods that ensure that corrective and continual improvement actions remain connected to the customer. Remaining connected to the customer is a point that cannot be overstated.

C3 and ISO 9001 emphasize that all areas of the organization should be understood, managed, and properly aligned to assure the greatest value for customers. Each part of the organization should be cognizant of its impact on the entire organization and the customers' needs. Dr. Ackoff observed that a system is more than the sum of its parts; it is an indivisible whole. It loses its essential properties when it is taken apart. The elements of a system may themselves be systems, and every system may be part of a larger system.

ISO 9001 and C3 share the intent of enterprise success. Among the ways the approaches differ is in how they define success and seek to achieve it. While it is true that any enterprise could use the standard, only about 15 to 20 percent of the registered companies are service-type organizations. Today there are approximately five thousand hospitals; schools; local, state, and federal government; and nonprofit organizations that are ISO 9001 registered in the United States. There are another six thousand companies related to the logistics industry, including trucking, shipping, warehousing, transportation, and wholesale providers.

The fact that there are fewer service organizations registered to ISO 9001 is greatly attributed to the fact that the original standard was derived from a manufacturing standard and therefore was more difficult to apply in a service environment. A service provided by a service organization was considered the product of the organization. This language proved to be a difficult concept to understand. The last several revisions have worked to make the language more appropriate for service organizations, but the ISO 9001:2015 version was in part rewritten to ensure inclusion of service organization needs. The jury is still out as to whether efforts in this version to make services more inclusive will be successful. On the other hand, more than half of all C3 users are made up of nonmanufacturers. There is no question that the C3 focus is on customers and the redefinition of all work as products that meet five specific criteria. Without a product, there can be no customer. There is no service to be addressed because C3 specifically identifies this as an ambiguous term that cannot be meaningfully defined.

ISO 9001 and C3 agree that the goal is to satisfy customer requirements. Customer requirements are often assumed to be stated specifically and completely. This assumption typically is not the reality. C3 makes a reverse assumption. Customer-defined excellence is hidden, and it is the duty of the producer to uncover the customer's definition of excellence along four dimensions (the global view) and along three classes of characteristics at the product level. This assumption necessitates the use of divergent thinking, in addition to convergent thinking focused on outcomes and aspirations. C3 assumes it is necessary but insufficient to hit the customer's voluntarily stated target. ISO 9001 requires that the organization determine and satisfy customer requirements, but the method of determining that important information is left up to leadership. We must also hit the target not stated, and that is usually of equal or greater importance.

A C3 requirement that ISO 9001 doesn't address is the fundamental concept that there is a difference between being producer-focused and being customer-focused. This difference is a significant point and, I believe, of great value. The consideration of the differences between producer-focused and customer-focused is one of those issues that I believe is intended between the lines in ISO 9001 but gets lost in the process approach.

A significant consideration that ISO 9001 brings to the table in its latest version is the requirement for risk-based thinking, something we all do automatically in everyday life. For example, when I start my electric lawnmower, I look to make sure my toes are not under the mower body. I do not desire to suffer the potential consequences. ISO 9001 requires the use of risk-based thinking in all aspects of the system. Risk-based thinking establishes a systematic approach to considering risk rather than treating prevention as a separate component of a QMS, as was the case in previous versions of the standard. From an ISO 9001 perspective, risk-based thinking is essential for achieving an effective QMS. The risk is inherent in all aspects of a QMS. There are risks in all systems, processes, and functions. Risk-based thinking ensures these risks are identified, considered, and controlled throughout the design and use of the QMS. Though the concept of risk-based thinking has been unspoken in previous editions, it had some basis within the system through processes such as carrying out preventive actions to eliminate potential nonconformities, analyzing nonconformities, and taking action to prevent recurrence of customer complaints and other effects of nonconformities.

An organization needs to plan and implement actions to address risks and opportunities. The addressing of risk is an area that does not receive specific attention from within C3, yet I would suggest that any properly implemented C3 system reduces risk. For example, is risk reduced when an organization understands what matters most to customers and has achieved their satisfaction? Absolutely. C3 assumes that achieving desired outcomes means the organization automatically reduces or eliminates undesired outcomes. The reverse is not true. Just reducing undesired outcomes does not assure desired outcomes have been achieved. This focus on the positive is one of C3's hallmarks and differentiators.

ISO 9001 includes requirements for monitoring, measurement, analysis, and evaluation. Organizations must consider what needs to be measured, which methods need to be employed, when data should be analyzed and reported on, and at what intervals it should happen. Performance evaluation includes all work processes, technical and operational systems, organizational activities that can affect quality in any way, and the QMS. ISO 9001 requires that organizations must actively seek out and analyze information on customer perception. An organization is required to ensure improvement occurs on customer perceptions. **ISO 9001 does not provide the method to accomplish any of this.** That decision is left to leadership to determine. C3 provides a highly accessible and robust means to capture and deal with those perceptions.

Internal audits and management reviews must be conducted. The audits must be conducted in a manner such that no part of the organization is auditing itself. The standard requires correction of any deficiencies identified during those audits. The correction of audit findings provides an avenue to ensure that there is continued concentration on the requirements of the standard. The registrar reviews the audits during its annual review to ensure they are properly conducted and that appropriate actions are being taken to correct the findings. Audits are expected to evaluate performance in the context of the customer or customer perspective. Auditing performance regarding dealing with customer perspective is new to the standard, so it is not clear how this will be accomplished. However, this is an area where C3 offers exceedingly powerful tools to aid and ensure performance.

C3 is an excellent system that does offer many benefits, as you have learned, and is very worthy of implementation within any organization. It is a stand-alone system, but it can be applied along with numerous other systems. An organization will benefit greatly by applying the concepts of C3 either with or without ISO 9001. As regards to ISO 9001 specifically, I fully support the implementation of C3 in any organization that has already applied ISO 9001. C3 will add new dimensions to any ISO 9001 system.

A system that is not fully implemented is not the system that was intended by its originators. So when you choose to implement a system, in this case ISO 9001 or C3, one cannot cherry-pick parts of the system and still have the system. Doing it all is doing it properly. Cherry-picking might be appropriate if you are looking for auto parts in a junkyard. However, what happens when data in a survey is cherry-picked? The data's resulting integrity becomes questionable, and the resulting report becomes skewed and valueless other than to mislead. What happens when a doctor cherry-picks patients based on the ability to pay? Some form and level of human suffering will result. Certainly, the Hippocratic Oath might be violated. What would happen if the telephone company cherry-picked who you are allowed to call? Individual rights would certainly be violated. You as the customer could not conduct your business as needed. Each of these scenarios results in very serious problems that impact the customers when one chooses or neglects aspects of either of these systems. Partial implementation of a system, though some gain might be realized, will result in something other than the system had intended. Serious problems will result, and customers will be adversely impacted. Especially in the case of ISO 9001, partial implementation could create considerable chaos. In the case of C3, partial implementation of its important features will produce something less than C3.

I would be less than honest if I did not state that, if not properly implemented, ISO 9001 will not bring its potential improvement and positive change to the organization, product, or customer. I believe strongly in the value of a properly implemented ISO 9001 system. In my mind, the term "properly implemented ISO 9001 system" is a very different scenario than a system acquired from a minimally applied use of the standard. Proper implementation requires that the implementer goes beyond the written words of the standard. C3 is one of those systems that I strongly recommend for that support. Other methods are very helpful for specific aspects of the organization's systems such as TOC, 5S, Six Sigma, calibration management systems, Lean, and so forth.

Customers expect and deserve a higher level of quality than ever before. All of this demand is at a time when resources are being stretched, competition is escalating, technology is changing at a rapid pace, and the business world is changing daily. Companies that meet those challenges will be the winners. Many executives will step up and say they believe providing quality products will secure loyal customers. They say that loyal customers are a key to business success. But what are those executives doing about it? Some will point to their monthly newsletter, perhaps a discount program, or the eight hours of customer-support training the employees had to demonstrate their efforts. I wish the answer were so simple, but those responses are not the needed ones.

The abyss between minimally satisfied and completely satisfied customers grows ever deeper and can totally overcome a business. The complexity of today's world requires significant support that can help an organization survive and thrive. ISO 9001 is a QMS that an organization strategically selects to deliver that assistance. ISO 9001 helps improve an organization's overall performance and provides a sound basis for sustainable development initiatives. Organizations that apply ISO 9001 develop the ability to consistently provide products and services that meet customer and legal and regulatory requirements. The ISO 9001 standard is intended to enable opportunities to enhance customer satisfaction and address risks. Finally, ISO 9001 increases the ability to demonstrate conformity to specified quality requirements.

C3 transforms an organization's culture to focus on customer needs and requirements at every level. Transformation for the customer is a key that will unlock the door to today's true success. After all, an organization earns very little from its past. A lasting organization is only as good as it makes of itself in the future. C3 and ISO 9001 can be major contributors to that future!

COMPARISON OF ISO 9001 AND C3 METHODOLOGY

	ISO 9001	C3
INTENT	Establish and/or improve the quality management system used by the enterprise to improve its success, minimize risk, and satisfy its customers	Transform the culture of the enterprise, aligning strategic direction and operational practices to satisfy customer priorities and engage employees to excel Create convergence of the VOL (intent and direction) with the VOC (expectations about outcomes, products, and processes) to guide excellence desired by both parties
FOCUS	Achieve certification based on meeting ten criteria minimums, spelled out in numbered clauses Satisfy customers internal and external to the enterprise Process improvement Principle application by industries that manufacture goods or process materials	Achieve optimum performance throughout the enterprise as defined by 8DX Satisfy the outcome, performance, and perception expectations of end users (primarily), brokers, and fixers for every product produced for use within or external to the enterprise Outcome definition and measurement followed by product characterization and measurement, followed by process description and measurement, with all performance aimed at optimums driving innovation Application to all knowledge-intensive enterprises, commercial, private, and nonprofit Reduction or elimination of ambiguity in leadership practices regarding language, values, measures, power, assumptions, and modeling
APPROACH	No prescription or methodology specified to enable the enterprise to satisfy certification criteria Correction of deficiencies (things gone wrong) Provides guidelines for a process-driven approach that seeks to manage or reduce risk	Provides a specific road map and tools set to align strategic objectives, culture, measures, and daily work with customer priorities Pursuit of aspirational objectives (ways to excel) Requires all work to be defined as products, meeting five criteria Requires definition of customer-desired outcomes first and then works backward from that purpose to product and process performance
UNIQUE BENEFITS	ISO-certified enterprise meets internationally agreed-upon standards Third-party audits and identification of needed corrective actions tied to guidelines of a QMS to reduce enterprise risk Creation of a continual improvement culture	Verification of excellence directly linked to customer priorities for all products produced for external or internal use Robust methodology relevant to all industries, especially knowledge-intensive organizations in fields such as government, nonprofits, education, health care, and other nonmanufacturers. Scalable C3 system, applicable from the individual person to the largest of global enterprises Creates organizational culture based on universal and articulated moral principles, deployed with emphasis on easy, rapid deployment

NOTABLE DIFFERENCES	Certification criteria Process and risk management focus with special attention to correcting deficiencies Assumed customer identification Satisfaction assessment occurs after product delivery	Customer-centered culture determined by the degree to which the organization practices a set of articulated principles and deployment practices Desired-outcome focus with the recognition that its achievement reduces undesired outcomes and risk and the reduction of undesired outcomes does not assure desired outcomes are met, not that excellence is achieved Customer identity unambiguously defined regarding the three roles they can play with specific products Emphasis on leadership's role to reduce ambiguity as it projects the VOL using six levers for transformation Description of an easy-to-use, universally applicable method for uncovering, translating, and satisfying the VOC through design and innovation Outcome, performance, and perception expectations uncovered before design and development
SIMILILARTIES	Meeting standards' practices is based on ten principles or clauses in the standard Success requires active leadership	Rapid and sustainable culture transformation directed by over sixty principles under the topics of leadership, product, customer, satisfaction, culture, measurement, innovation, and process Success requires active leadership

CHAPTER 27—PREVIEW: THE VOC METHOD

The main topics of volume 1 were the six change levers, outcomes, products, customers and measures. We integrated them all with the Strategy Map. All were discussed in relation to the 8DX framework. Having stopped with how to determine customer roles and why it matters, we are now prepared to find out what customers want. We call those wants the VOC. There's only one little problem. Customers don't always voice their wants until after we've given them a product that falls short. Oops! That's a bad time to find out. So we are going to use a bit of mind-reading to discover their wants. We'll still refer to the methods for doing that as VOC. But it will involve more than just close listening to what they say. Let's face it, if everything an end user had as top priorities for a product were captured in orders, contracts, intake exams, CRM systems, and other such vehicles, we might have a decent chance of getting things right more often. Sadly that is far from how the world works.

We Masters of Excellence are going to beat the system that has so far hidden those customer priorities. We'll beat it by changing it. That is done in volume 2 by continuing down our Road Map with steps 7 through 10 of the 10 Steps to Alignment:

   7. Uncover and measure customers' priority outcome, product, and process expectations.
   8. Innovate or redesign products to achieve best outcomes.
   9. Cut the time to produce, acquire, and use products by 80 percent.
   10. Integrate cultural change levers to sustain, celebrate, and broaden success.

The moment we have uncovered the mind, heart, and VOC, we can proceed to develop measures that can be used for product (re)design, innovation, the assessment of satisfaction with and without surveys, and goal-setting. Applying the VOC system to end users means we can also use it with brokers, fixers, and producers. Yup, we can actually figure out and document what we, as producers, want from the products we create. After all, we are seeking the proverbial win-win.

Finally we will address process issues that are near and dear to customers and producers. Those are reflected in Dimensions 4 and 8. All our work prior to that will enable us to make process design and execution changes much more quickly and easily than would otherwise have been possible. The results we discussed regarding several cases occurred at lightning speed because of this sequence of steps and application of the foundation C3 principles.

We will end volume 2 by revisiting the cultural transformation process, the role of strategic projects, and the immortal role of the Master of Excellence and all the heroes that will follow your lead.

Our mission at the moment is to succinctly introduce a few key elements of the C3 VOC method that is explored in-depth in volume 2. In short, we use word formulas and linguistic rules that enable us to apply language with as much rigor as we presently do with math. And we do so with greater simplicity. We will use the context of four main questions, shown below. The first two were covered at length in volume 1. We will address only the third in this preview. This method works equally well in business-to-business, customer-to-business, industry, health care, government, and every other environment where one party is seeking to satisfy another. It even works at home.

FOUR KEY QUESTIONS			
1	2	3	4
What is the product?	**Who are the customers?**	**What do they really want?**	**How can we excel?**
DEFINE	DIFFERENTIATE	REVEAL	TRANSFORM THE CULTURE
As: • Deliverables • Plural with an "s" • Countable • Specific • Used to produce a desired outcome	**Roles:** • End users • Brokers • Fixers	**Expectations Regarding:** • Outcomes (desired and undesired) • Product (functions and features) • Process (product acquisition)	• **Translate** subjective perceptions into objective performance measures • **Apply** the 10 Steps • **Align** VOC, VOL, and new practices with strategic and operational priorities • **Innovate** or redesign products and processes that best achieve desired outcomes • **Celebrate** success on all 8 Dimensions of Excellence

Figure 37—Four Key Questions

The ultimate reason to understand the VOC is to prepare ourselves to answer question number 4: How can we excel? That enables the Master of Excellence to anchor all efforts to transform the culture, design superb products that satisfy customers, engage employees, and fully deploy the VOL. But those big goals are dependent on first determining the answer to question number 3, uncovering what customers want. We've already answered the first two questions. Correctly answering question number 1 makes everything else possible; failure to do so leads to ambiguity, conflict, chaos, confusion, and dysfunction.

It helps to understand the relationships among the four questions, four rules, and eight formulas shown in the figure below. All four rules applied to questions 1 and 2 are ones we can answer by ourselves without necessarily having any dialogue with customers. But the first four formulas (related to question 3) must be asked of the correct customers, especially end users. Their answers are the heart of the VOC inquiry. See you in volume 2 for the rest of the story.

QUESTION	HOW TO FIND THE ANSWER
	WORD RULES

1- What is the product?	1. Define all work as products (not service, activities, or results).
	
	2. Every product named must meet all five characteristics:
	
	    a. It can be made plural with an "s."
	    b. It is a deliverable, something you can give to others.
	    c. It is packaged in countable units.
	    d. It is very specific to the person or group that produces it (avoid naming groups, kinds, or types of product).
	    e. It is used to create a desired outcome (for the producer or customer.
	
	3. Determine the critical target product(s) you will focus on.

2- Who are the customers?	4. Describe customers by their role(s) with a specific product as:
	
	    a. End user
	    b. Broker (for either the end user or the producer)
	    c. Fixer

3- What do they really want?[129]	**WORD FORMULAS TO REVEAL the VOC**[130]
a. Desired outcomes customers want to achieve	1. A satisfying (insert product name) is one that will result in (insert expectation).
b. Undesired outcomes customers want to avoid	2. A satisfying (insert product name) is one that will not result in (insert expectation).
c. Function expectations of the product (usually expressed as subjective perceptions)	3. A satisfying (insert product name) is one that is (insert expectation).
d. Feature expectations (expressed as objective, ambiguity-free criteria)	4. A satisfying (insert product name) is one that has (insert expectation).
4- How can we excel?	**WORD FORMULAS FOR EXCELLENCE BY DESIGN**
a. Translate subjective perceptions into objective design criteria for the new or improved product b. Examine innovative alternatives to the current product c. Set goals to create the biggest impact on satisfaction and success	5. The number of _____ could indicate that the (insert product name) is/is not (insert VOC priority answers to formulas 3 and 4). 6. The percent of _____ could indicate that the (insert product name) is/is not (insert VOC priority answers to formulas 3 and 4). 7. The dollar amount of/for/to _____ could indicate that the (insert product name) is/is not (insert VOC priority answer to formula 4). 8. What is the numerical target to achieve, by when, by whom, and for each measure of success?

Figure 38—The C3 VOC Method

---

[129] The terms "needs," "wants," "expectations," and "requirements" have different meanings that can be critically important. In general, needs and requirements are the most basic (often the minimum acceptable). Wants are the most inclusive and optimal desires to be satisfied. The name of the popular TV program *Who Wants to Be a Millionaire?* could be a desire many people share. Not many would resonate with "Who Needs to Be a Millionaire?" For our purposes here, we will use expectations as a sort of shorthand, as if the different meanings are of no consequence.

[130] The word formulas shown and described here are core to all VOC work, whether pursued through focus groups, interviews, surveys, or otherwise. But the unique circumstances of a specific project can require adding a few more word formulas. Please view the word formulas discussed here as essential, but not necessarily sufficient.

APPENDIX 1—LEADER'S ACTIONS

(These are also available in the optional Excel-based electronic Mastering Excellence Workbook in the store at http://www.C3Excellence.com.)

Leader's Action 1: Opportunities with High Potential

Objective: Identify three problems or opportunities that, if successfully addressed, would dramatically improve success for both your customers and organization.

1. _____

2. _____

3. _____

Leader's Action 2: The Ready, Reluctant, and Powerful
Objective: Identify potential allies to support your transformation efforts.

1. The three most ready:

   _____ _____ _____

2. The three with potential but not eager:

   _____ _____ _____

3. The two most powerful people you need as allies:

   _____   _____

Leader's Action 3: Indicators of Highly Visible Results

Objective: Identify potential results from your leadership efforts that would be highly visible to many external customers and/or employees.

1. _____

2. _____

3. _____

Leader's Action 4: C3IQ, a Self-Assessment

CUSTOMER-CENTERED EXCELLENCE ASSESSMENT

Your Name		Title	
Enterprise		Date	
Department or Function		Phone	
Email		State/ Province	

Please put a 5, 3, 1 or 0 in one of the columns at the right of each item to indicate your level of agreement with each statement below.	Totally 5 Points	Partially 3 Points	Hardly 1 Point	Disagree/ Unknown 0
STRATEGIC DIRECTION 1. Your enterprise has a current strategic plan.	5	3	1	0
2. The plan articulates outcomes (results) the enterprise seeks to achieve.	5	3	1	0
3. The plan defines outcomes customers want to achieve from the enterprise.	5	3	1	0
4. All managers and supervisors have seen the strategic plan.	5	3	1	0
5. All line employees have seen the strategic plan.	5	3	1	0
6. Business unit and/or department plans are written to enable execution of the strategic plan at that level.	5	3	1	0
7. Personnel reviews address contribution to strategic plan outcomes.	5	3	1	0
CUSTOMERS & SATISFACTION 8. The enterprise has written policies covering critical priorities.	5	3	1	0
9. "Good service" is viewed as one of the enterprise's top priorities.	5	3	1	0
10. Using only **one** word, define what "service" means to you: _____	5	3	1	0
Would everyone on the management team give the same definition?	5	3	1	0
11. There is consensus on who "the customer" is.	5	3	1	0
12. There is a defined and applied method for determining who "the customer" is at the department, functional and work group level.	5	3	1	0
13. There is a defined and practiced method for uncovering customer priorities: a) For products and services used by those outside the enterprise.	5	3	1	0
b) For department or functional group product and services used by those within the enterprise.	5	3	1	0
14. There is a written customer satisfaction policy.	5	3	1	0
EXCELLENCE 15. "Success" is defined and measured in terms of the degree to which:	5	3	1	0
a) The enterprise achieves its self-defined desired outcomes.	5	3	1	0
b) Customers achieve their desired outcomes (ultimate results).	5	3	1	0
c) Customers' undesired outcomes are avoided or reduced.	5	3	1	0
d) Customers get their most desired characteristics in enterprise products and services.	5	3	1	0
e) Internal processes are consistent, efficient and error free.	5	3	1	0
f) The customers' experience acquiring products and services is satisfying: (1) For those produced by the enterprise.	5	3	1	0
(2) For those produced by your functional group.	5	3	1	0
16. Employees in your department or functional group agree on the top 3 priority products/services produced by that group.	5	3	1	0
17. Verbal management commitments to make specific improvement actions are executed in a timely, effective manner.	5	3	1	0
18. Recognition and consequences are consistently applied when success or failure to achieve priorities occurs.	5	3	1	0

	Totally	Partially	Hardly	TOTAL SCORE
OPPORTUNITY 19. Please TOTAL the points in each checked column for questions 1-17. (Total possible = 125)				
20. Which statement above do you **most** wish you could have said "Totally" to?				
21. Which **one** of the items in Question #15 have been the principal focus of your enterprise improvement or innovation efforts in the past 3 years? (a, b, c, d, e, f1 or f2)				

Leader's Action 5: Confusion Regarding the Customer

Objective: Identify sources of ambiguity about who the customer is.

1. Based on the previous discussion about language, is it possible there is ambiguity in your enterprise about who the customer refers to? Yes _____ No _____.

   - If your answer is no, congratulations! You are in a very rare minority of leaders and will likely find the average C3IQ assessment score, for the group you have asked to take it, is five on items 11, 12, 14, 15b–d, and f.

   - By answering yes, you have lots of company and have just identified a major hidden obstacle to achieving excellence. It is likely the scores on assessment items named above by your group average three or less.

2. Name at least three specific guiding documents (such as a strategy, mission statement, policy, plan, or other directive) that refer to how we will treat customers:

   _____   _____

   _____   _____

   _____   _____

3. Put a yes or no next to each named document above to indicate if it is possible for readers of each one to disagree about who the mentioned customers actually are.

   - If no, congratulations! You are in the exceptional minority that has established customer clarity.

   - If yes, you will want to become an active Master of Excellence by removing all ambiguity regarding customer identity, described in Chapter 20. Reference this page number at the beginning of that chapter to remind you of this pending Leader's Action.

Leader's Action 6: Core Values Ambiguity

Objective: Identify any ambiguity of or conflict among stated values, policy, and behavior.

1. List five stated core values of your enterprise. Indicate the name of at least one written policy or comparable leadership document(s) that (a) defines and (b) deploys each value well.

Core Value	Defined By	Deployed By
a.		
b.		
c.		
d.		
e.		

2. Considering each core value named above, what reward or formal recognition is consistently provided when it or its related policy is practiced?

    a.

    b.

    c.

    d.

    e.

3. What consequence or penalty is consistently delivered when a core value or its related policy is violated?

    a.

    b.

    c.

    d.

    e.

4. If a value is not clearly defined, provide unambiguous definition here.

    a. _____

    b. _____

    c. _____

    d. _____

e. _____

5. Which of your core values could the six-point customer satisfaction policy help deploy?

a. b. c. d. e. None All

If none, what would you change in the policy to improve the deployment of values?

_____

_____

6. What discoveries have you made?

_____

_____

_____

_____

7. What action should you take now?

_____

_____

Leader's Action 7: Alignment of Values with Measures (KPIs)

Objective: Determine how well core values are aligned with measures.

1. Considering each core value named in Leader's Action 6, record a critical measure and numerical goal currently in place that verifies the value is practiced.

Core Value	Measure	Goal to Achieve in One Year
a.		
b.		
c.		
d.		
e.		

2. Which of the core values, if any, appear to have weak measures? _____

3. What action should you take to align values, measures, and goals?

_____

_____

Leader's Action 8: Crush Vital Lies

Objective: Identify Vital Lies in your organization and determine how to eliminate them.

1. Which of the ten common Vital Lies have you heard in your organization? _____

2. What Vital Lie not on this list is repeatedly stated in your organization and should be added?

   _____

3. For the Vital Lie you believe could be the most constraining or destructive, what could you now do to stamp it out? (Circle all that apply.)

   a. Get it stated aloud so it can be critically examined.

   b. Empower and encourage everyone hearing a Vital Lie to name it as such.

   c. Ask for data that unambiguously supports the assumption.

   d. Ask for or provide evidence and illustrations demonstrating the Vital Lie is unsupported by fact.

   e. Ask what the consequences might be (to the enterprise, its customers, and potential competitors) if the assumption is false.

   f. Recognize and reward the truth-tellers.

   g. Promote the new finding wherever possible to supplant the old Vital Lie.

   h. Other _____

4. Who defines "the leading edge" in reference to your organization? _____

   a. What is the criterion for it? _____

   b. What other enterprise(s) claim to be on that leading edge? _____

   c. Do customers agree with that determination? Yes No Unknown

5. Is there evidence customers are less satisfied than our internal sources suggest? Yes No

   a. Beyond surveys, what do referrals, social media, observable customer behavior, litigation, contract disputes, formal complaints, and other customer-initiated actions suggest about satisfaction? _____

   b. Is it possible that coercion or the absence of alternatives is cause for customer retention? Yes No

6. What evidence suggests it is possible customers want something more than you think you are in the business to give? (Consider that no slide-rule user asked for a four-function electronic calculator to be developed; no typewriter user asked for word-processing software.)

   _____

7. When you hear a colleague say, "Our customers want…" which question(s) do you ask to eliminate confusion about who the customers are? (Circle all that apply.)

    a. Customers for what product?[131]

    b. Which role[132] does that customer have with the product you just named?

    c. Are you referring to:

        i. all demographics for that customer role

        ii. only a specific one? (For example, are we thinking of both men and women, working or unemployed, highly educated or not, multilingual or not, seniors or youth, and so on?)

    d. Other (specify) _____

    e. No clarifying questions are routinely asked.

8. Are customer priorities truly known? Yes No

    a. If yes, where is the defined and repeatable method described that is used to uncover what customers want? _____

    b. Is the absence of articulated customer priorities assumed to mean they (a) don't know, (b) don't care, or (c) other? A B C (explain) _____

    c. Have we heard what they (a) have wanted or (b) what they will want? A B

    d. Is it an (a) expectation, (b) anticipation, (c) minimum requirement, or (d) hope? A B C D

    e. Does it matter? _____ (Prospective customers said they loved the Edsel and New Coke but didn't buy those.)

9. Do the topics and manner in which we measure our excellence reflect (a) the intent we have or (b) the intent our customers have? A B Both Neither Don't know

10. What action should you take?

    _____

    _____

---

[131] How to determine what a product is (beyond what is sold) is discussed in Chapter 14.

[132] See Chapter 20 for customer definitions that are unambiguous.

Leader's Action 9: Connect Initiatives and Measures with the 8 Dimensions

Objective: Determine which of the 8 Dimensions currently get most attention and identify any corrective action needed. Refer to and use your work in Leader's Actions (LA) 6 and 7.

1. If your enterprise has current improvement initiatives in place, name up to two of them here:

   _____   _____

2. Considering the enterprise's investment of money and/or time in those initiatives and related meetings, written communications, training, and formal improvement projects:

   a. Which two of the 8 Dimensions are likely getting the most attention? _____ _____

   b. Which two of the 8 Dimensions are likely getting the least attention? _____ _____

   If Dimension 1 is not among them, shifting that emphasis will be necessary to balance and enhance excellence.

3. Use the Key Performance Measures table on the following page to complete these steps:

   a. Identify at least eight, but no more than sixteen, of your top KPIs and record one on each numbered line below. Please note: If you believe it is important to have a balanced scorecard at least at the enterprise level, the key KPIs you list here will confirm (or redirect) that balance. Dimensions without KPIs indicate imbalance.

   b. Referring to the graphic here or descriptions for the 8 Dimensions, record the Dimension number (1–8) in the 8DX Alignment column next to each measure.

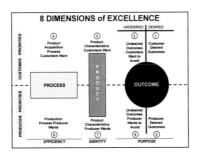

   c. Referring to LA 6 and 7, identify the core values (by their letter) that each measure supports.

   d. It is critical to have measures for both Dimensions 1 and 2. If you don't or the measures look in any way inadequate, complete Leader's Action 9a before proceeding.

4. Refer to your answers recorded in the Key Performance Measures table. Which Dimensions, as measured by current KPIs, have numerical goals for excellence? 1 2 3 4 5 6 7 8 (Circle all that apply.) Discard from consideration any goals that are already being achieved since such goals merely communicate that no improvement is possible or wanted.

5. What you have discovered regarding:

	Great	Fair	Poor
a. The strength of alignment between core values and key initiatives?			
b. The strength of alignment between core values and KPIs?			
c. The strength of alignment between key initiatives and KPIs?			
d. The importance of Dimensions 1 and 2 to the organization?			
e. The degree to which all eight Dimensions get balanced attention?			
f. The current balance among initiatives, core values, and KPIs?			

6. What do the top KPIs for the enterprise reveal about which Dimension is most valued?

    _____

7. Leader's Action 9 can be applied to any other department within the enterprise. Doing so may reveal a pattern similar to what you have seen here.

8. Based on everything you have done in LA 9, what are your most important discoveries?

    _____

    _____

    _____

9. Who should take what action?

    _____

    _____

    _____

| Organization | | | Rev Date | | TARGETS | | 8DX Alignment | Related to Core Values |
ID #	**KEY PERFORMANCE MEASURES**				Baseline Year	Year 1		
1								
2								
3								
4								
5								
6								
7								
8								
9								
10								
11								
12								
13								
14								
15								
16								
17								
18								
19								
20								
21								
22								
23								

Leader's Action 9a: Create Missing Measures

Objective: Create measures that are missing for Dimensions 1 and 2 (if relevant).

1. Define the desired outcomes, the ultimate results that customers want to achieve by working with your organization. Record those here:

   * _____

   * _____

   * _____

2. Define the undesired outcomes customers want to avoid or minimize by working with your organization:

   * _____

   * _____

   * _____

3. Use any of the following phrases to structure your new measures. Record them in the Key Performance Measures table above. Be sure you have at least two unambiguous measures (omitting any subjectivity) for each desired and undesired outcome.

   * The number of _____ could indicate how well this outcome is (or is not) experienced by customers.

   * The percent of _____ could indicate how well this outcome is (or is not) experienced by customers.

   * The dollar amount of, for, or to _____ could indicate how well this outcome is (or is not) experienced by customers.

   This would be a great time to celebrate your achievement if you currently have Dimension 1 defined, measured, and attached to numerical goals. If not, you may feel differently now about what you initially answered in C3IQ items 15a–f. You should find it helpful to see how Dimension 1 gets addressed in the cases to follow in chapters 9–11. They provide guidance on defining desired outcomes. Please note it is possible for a single KPI to address more than one dimension. But a measure for Dimension 2, undesired outcomes customers want to avoid, is often erroneously used as a measure for Dimension 1. Consider that failure to drown does not mean you know how to swim.

   Return to and complete Leader's Action 9.

Leader's Action 10: Capturing Customer-Desired Outcomes

Objective: Identify how customer outcomes are uncovered and acted upon.

1. Name your enterprise or organizational unit for which we should understand customer-desired outcomes:

    _____

    Important Note: This organization is the one we will consistently refer to, unless stated otherwise, throughout all subsequent Leader's Actions. You may choose the enterprise, or a business or functional unit within it for your focus.

2. Is there unambiguous responsibility for:	Yes	No	None/ Don't Know
Uncovering your customers' desired outcomes before and after delivery of core products/services?			
Routinely capturing those priorities in formal ways that are easily accessed from your databases/systems?			
Guiding behavior to achieve satisfaction?			
Measuring and improving success?			

3. What is the earliest point in the process of communicating with new or prospective customers that their desired outcomes could be discovered? _____

    _____ Is this when it usually does happen? Y N Don't Know

4. What are up to two specific questions routinely asked of customers to uncover their desired outcomes?

    _____

    _____

    Which of these methods are used to ask these questions? (Check all that apply.)

a. Survey	
b. Website	
c. Phone or in-person	
d. Other (specify)	

5. What are the two most frequent answers customers give to the outcome questions above?

    _____

    _____

    a. If you are unsure about customer outcomes or no questions routinely capture customer-desired outcomes, what are the ultimate results you would expect them to say they want? Those outcomes must fit this phrase, "An excellent (insert organization name) will result in…"

    _____

    _____

An example: An excellent hotel will result in a good night's sleep.

b. What would an appropriate KPI be for each of the outcomes customers say they want (or you have said they want) above?

_____

_____

Refer to Leader's Action 9a for guidance on constructing KPIs.

6. What is done with the information collected? (Check all that apply.)

a. Routinely forwarded to those involved in assuring the result(s)	
b. Captured in a database or other central file accessible to those who will need to know	
c. Analyzed to make product/service design changes	
d. Analyzed to make process changes	
e. Analyzed to make organization structure or responsibility changes	
f. Used to measure satisfaction with outcomes experienced	
g. Other (specify)	
h. Nothing	
i. Don't know	

7. If questions to uncover customer-desired outcomes are not being asked as intended, which Vital Lies or excuses are given most often for not capturing, knowing, measuring, and using that information as the basis for driving excellence? _____ See Leader's Action 8. How can you eliminate them (especially 1, 7, and 8)?

_____

_____

8. What are the names of strategic initiatives, if any, in place to improve the satisfaction of customer-desired outcomes? Refer to your answers for item 1 of Leader's Action 9.

_____

_____

9. Satisfaction Policy

	Yes	No	Don't Know
Is there is a written satisfaction policy in place?			
Is it being implemented as intended?			

10. Based on your answers and insights, what issues should you take to improve understanding and satisfaction of customer-desired outcomes?

_____

_____

Leader's Action 11: Differentiate Desired and Undesired Outcomes

Objective: Clarify understanding of and emphasis on desired outcomes.

1. Based on patterns in cases 2 and 3:

	Des.	Undes.
Is most formal change driven by desired or undesired outcomes?		
Is there a defined method used for uncovering desired outcomes? (If no, we will close that gap with Leader's Action 12.)	Yes	No
Do we currently measure the degree to which desired outcomes are achieved as a result of our actions?	Yes	No

2. Are personal consequence(s) experienced by your management (see Leader's Action 6) when:

	Des.	Undes.
An improvement of a customer-desired outcome is not achieved as planned		
An improvement of a producer-desired outcome is not achieved as planned	Yes	No
A reduction of an undesired customer outcome is not achieved as planned	Yes	No
A reduction of an undesired producer outcome is not achieved as planned	Yes	No

3. Identify outcomes for Dimensions 2, 5 and 6 after recording here the name of your organization identified in Leader's Action 10, item 1:

    _____

    a. In contrast to the customer-desired outcomes you identified in LA 10 (item 5), what are two undesired outcomes customers would most want to avoid (Dimension 2) by working with your organization? Complete this phrase, "An excellent (insert organization name) will not result in…"

    _____

    _____

    For example, "An excellent overnight stay at hotel XYZ will not result in next-day fatigue."

    b. What are two desired outcomes your own producer organization most wants to achieve (Dimension 5)? Answer by completing this phrase, "An excellent (insert organization name) will result in…"

    _____

    _____

    c. What are two undesired outcomes your organization most wants to avoid (Dimension 6)? Complete this phrase, "An excellent (insert organization name) will not result in…"

    _____

    _____

4. Which of Dimensions 1, 2, 5, or 6 is most clearly the priority of the following?

REFERENCE DOCUMENTS	1	2	5	6
Strategic plan				
Core policies (see Leader's Action 6, item1)				
Key initiatives (see Leader's Action 9, item 1)				
Balanced scorecard/top KPIs (see Leader's Action 7 and Leader's Action 9, item 3)				
New product development road map				
Formal employee recognition and reward system (refer to Leader's Action 6, item 2)				
Management's performance review criteria (refer to Leader's Action 6)				

5. Discoveries you have made:

_____

_____

_____

_____

Leader's Action 12: Strategic 5 Whys (with your team)

Objective: Uncover the ultimate desired outcomes wanted by customers.

Instructions Assign each of the following roles to different members of your team before you begin. These roles are in addition to functioning as a fully participating team member. When finished, discuss the debriefing guidelines below.

- **Rules coach.** Make sure the team reads and follows the instructions. Pay careful attention, especially to step 3. The team's job is to describe desired outcomes that customers of the named organization want. It will be easy for the team to inadvertently describe problems, likely to be undesired outcomes. You can constructively stop that by redirecting them to the instruction and the need to identify desired outcomes. If the team gets focused on undesired outcomes, it will get into a problem-solving mode. That is definitely not the purpose of this application.

- **Timekeeper.** Decide at the beginning how much time the team will allow itself to finish. The minimum time should be thirty minutes, the maximum sixty. When done, allow a minimum of an additional five minutes to summarize the team's findings and discoveries.

- **Recorder.** Although it is always a good idea for all team members to record your work, designating a formal recorder makes a single version official. The recorder should show or verbalize the results after completing each step in the instructions to make sure all are in agreement. This person will also have responsibility for sending out the final version to all team members and filing it in a designated location for easy retrieval whenever it is needed later.

1. Name your organization for focus (enterprise, business unit, department, function, or other). You may wish to continue with the organization you named in Leader's Action 10, item 1:

   _____

2. Brainstorm at least three different purposes or desired results your customers have in coming to your organization. State these outcomes in the voice of the customer as they would say them.

   _____

   _____

   _____

   _____

   _____

3. Eliminate from your list any undesired outcomes that may have crept in. For example, if you run a fire station, you may have said your community wants fires extinguished. While this may be true, it states an <u>un</u>desired outcome they want to avoid or minimize. Continuing the series of whys is likely to drive you to problem-solving. That is not the purpose of this version of 5 Whys. Perhaps the community really wants fire-free days.

4. Select one of the remaining desired outcomes that customers are likely to say is most important. Write this in the **bottom** box below. Ask the successive whys until you have uncovered what the customer would consider the ultimate reason why they would see working with you as a success. Fill in the outcomes from bottom box (tactical) to top box (strategic).

Y or N

(5)

STRATEGIC

Why? ↑

(4)

Why? ↑

(3)

Why? ↑

(2)

TACTICAL

Why? ↑

(1)

5. In the five boxes on the right, indicate with yes or no which, if any, of these outcomes you are currently measuring. ↗

6. What have you discovered?

(Optional) Summarize your work using the Team Summary.

Instructions for Team Summary

1. What is the name of your organization (enterprise, division, department, or function)?

    _____

2. Name the outcomes identified in step 4 of the 5 Whys instructions

	Customer-Desired Outcomes	In Strategic Business Plan? (Y/N)	Currently Measured? (Y/N)	Name of document in which outcome performance is measured or reported
5				
4				
3				
2				
1				

3. How many outcomes are currently measured? _____

4. How many of the outcomes identified above are named or described in your organization's strategic business plan? _____

5. How many customer-desired outcomes, other than those above, are in that strategic business plan?

    _____

6. What have you discovered?

    _____

    _____

    _____

7. What action, if any, should occur?

    _____

    _____

    _____

Leader's Action 13: The Strategy Map, Part 1

Objective: Draft the Strategy Map and related KPIs, connecting seven key elements that will communicate strategic priorities and how success will be measured.

Instructions: Refer to figures 16 and 17 as models. Complete the steps below, using any answers you have already developed or discussed in the referenced sources. (For an optional electronic version, see the Mastering Excellence Workbook in the store at http://www.C3Excellence.com.)

Step	Source	Done
1. Your organization's name	Leader's Action 10	
2. Organization mission	Insert or create this now	
3. Strategic outcomes	Leader's Actions 10, 12	
4. Subordinate outcomes, listed as shown in your affinity group	Leader's Action 12	
5. Measures of success (no more than thirty) with first-year goals	Leader's Actions 7, 9	
6. The Dimension(s) of the 8DX related to each measure	Leader's Action 9	
7. Core values, using the discussion following figure 16 regarding how to show the relationship between outcomes, values and measures.	Leader's Actions 6, 7	

When you believe you are done with this stage, put a check next to each step in the matrix above to indicate you are satisfied that the clarity, completeness, and alignment of strategic direction with customer priorities would be easily understood by your employees. If you now see conflicts, ambiguity or omissions likely to diminish the potential for optimum success, capture key actions you should take now:

_____

_____

_____

_____

You will finish building the Strategy Map (Part 2) with emphasis on deployment with Leader's Action 19. You may find it helpful to review those objectives briefly now, before going on.

STRATEGY MAP WORKSHEET, Part 1: Mission, Values, Outcomes, Measures

Rev. Date	
STEP 1	

ORGANIZATION NAME:

STEP 2

MISSION:

			CORE VALUES						
		STEP 7	A	B	C	D	E	F	G
	STEP 6	**Areas of Alignment with 8 Dimensions**							
	STEP 5	**MEASURE ID**							
STEP 4	**SUBORDINATE OUTCOMES (Enablers/constraints on Strategic Outcomes)**								
STEP 3	**STRATEGIC OUTCOMES**								

258

KEY MEASURES SUMMARY

Organization			Rev Date		TARGETS		8DX Alignment	Related to Core Values
ID	KEY PERFORMANCE MEASURES				Baseline Year	Year 1		
1								
2								
3								
4								
5								
6								
7								
8								
9								
10								
11								
12								
13								
14								
15								
16								
17								
18								
19								
20								
21								
22								
23								
24								
25								
26								
27								
28								
29								
30								

Figure 39—Key Measures Summary—Blank

Leader's Action 14: Personal Products

Objective: Demonstrate understanding of the product concept with the ability to personally model it, differentiating process, product, and outcome.

What are at least four of the most important products you personally create?

_____ _____

_____ _____

_____ _____

_____ _____

If you can answer yes to the following questions about each of the product names listed above, you've mastered the first step in customer-centered thinking. Correct the product names as necessary before proceeding, using the instructions below.

	Yes	No
a. Is the product specific and something only you can claim as yours? For example, a product name of "policy, "plan," or "report" isn't specific enough to claim ownership. These are product groups. Others could also claim those products as theirs. Be specific. A "market plan for product xyz," "cycle time reduction plan," or "departmental budget report" are examples of specific names of products only you or your immediate work group might claim as yours.		
b. Can you make the product plural with an "s"? Products are nouns. If the label you wrote is followed by "ing," it is an activity (a verb), not a product. The product is the tangible result of activity. Words like "satisfaction," "assurance," and "security" are also not products. They are outcomes (intangible results or conditions) obtained by using the product.		
c. Is the product a deliverable you can give to someone else? A "relationship" might seem like a product because we can make it plural with an "s", relationships. This is one of a very small number of exceptions to the plural-with-an-s rule. A relationship is not a deliverable, something we can give to someone else. It is an outcome.		
d. Does the product, as named, occur in countable units? Information can only be considered as a product by the various packaged forms it may take. Reports, graphs, answers, plans, and manuals would be examples of informational products. Information is the raw material that is delivered to others in some organized or packaged form.		
e. Is the product intended to create a desired outcome or result for a customer? Satisfaction, security, fun, health, productivity, and understanding are outcomes the product might create. Some people confuse outcomes with the product itself. Executives sometimes think their products are "leadership" or "vision." Their true products may consist of mission statements, policies, strategies, guidelines, and assignments that, when used by others, propel the organization in a desired direction. These kinds of products include what we call source products (policies, strategies, and plans) and will be addressed in Chapter 17. Leadership is either a skill or an outcome, not a product. Vision is also an outcome, a desired future condition. A vision statement is a product.		

Leader's Action 15: Constraints on Service Excellence

Objective: Determine which of the six constraints exist for service as understood in your own organization.

1. On line 1 in the matrix below, copy what your answer was to question 10 in the C3IQ, Leader's Action 4. Make sure it fits the one-word rule. Put a P or A in that row for each of the six columns to indicate whether the characteristic defined above is currently *present* or *absent*.

	What Service Means	Repeatability	Measurability	Tangibility	Responsibility	Storability	Ambiguity-Free
1							
2	Accommodating						
3	Answering						
4	Anticipate						
5	Appropriate						
6	Assist						
7							
8							
9							
10							

2. Repeat the P/A designation for the four synonyms below yours, taken from the first four shown in the What Service Means list in chapter 16. Or take any other four from the list that you believe represent the most common definitions any random sample of your employees would give. Put those on lines 7 through 10 and apply the P/A designation.

3. What pattern, if any, do you see? _____

4. What action should you take? _____

Debriefing

The more Ps there are, the easier it will be to achieve sustainable excellence. The more As there are, the greater is the necessity to stamp out these constraints. Identify each word that has three or more Ps next to it. Could the word be altered slightly so you can make it plural with an "s"? If so, you are close to defining service as a specific product. The closer to a product name it is, the more likely it will be that some of the six characteristics are in place. Examples are answering, deliver, fix, and repair. As they are currently stated, they look like activities and verbs. We could restate them as products, retaining their core meaning, by using our plural-with-an-s rule for defining work as products. We then have answers, deliveries, fixes, and repairs. We've just redefined service as products. Pretty cool, huh? By doing this restatement, we've taken the first step in removing all six constraints that apply to service.

For words with only As, some will be activities that are too vague to easily identify a related product without knowing the context. Examples include accommodating, anticipate, assist, attend, cater, fulfill, provide, and supply.

Other words with only As next to them may actually refer to characteristics of a person. Examples include attentive, available, care, helpful, and responsiveness. Just so we're clear, a person is not a service. But when we present such characteristics in satisfaction surveys, we are asking respondents to evaluate individuals. That may not have been our intent. It is also possible that the person who gets evaluated may actually be performing in a manner proscribed by or constrained by the system he or she is working within. This means an individual is being held accountable for the design of a system over which he or she may have absolutely no control. Is that appropriate or fair? But maybe this is something we really don't want to get into at the moment, even though it just might have something to do with excellence. I will say that, once we can routinely identify all work in terms of products, the ability of individual producers to exercise control and improvement is greatly empowered.

Some of the A words that reflect an absence of at least one of the six characteristics are outcomes. Examples include delight, experience, happiness, protection, results, satisfaction, and success.

We can sum up with four main observations:

1. We are all over the map regarding what we think service is (activity, personal qualities, outcomes, and more).

2. There are six characteristics that could be absent, related to much of what we consider service, acting as constraints on achieving excellence.

3. Answers and emails are examples of products that can seem invisible or inconsequential to excellence, until we start applying measures to them that would be relevant for producers and customers of any other product.

4. The closer we are to defining service as a product, the fewer constraints stand in our way to purposeful improvement.

We should be feeling better already. To dig deeper into the constraints related to service and how to eliminate them, see the related Leader's Actions 15a and 15b.

Leader's Action 15a: The Value of Answers

THE VALUE OF ANSWERS

NAME
DEPARTMENT

1. What percent of your average day is spent producing answers? % ☐
   Include time spent on these activities:
   - Understanding either proactively or reactively the need for the answer(s)
   - Obtaining information required to assemble the answer(s)
   - Packaging/organizing the answers(s) in understandable form
   - Distributing/communicating the answer(s)
   Do you currently measure this time spent producing answers? Yes/No ☐

2. If you estimated 80% or more for question 1, please go to question 3.
   If your estimate was less than 80%, how is your time spent for the rest of the day?

   _____

   If any of this time can be considered as one of the four activities named in question 1, please go
   back and adjust your initial estimate.

3. What percent of answers do you produce reactively, in response to questions? % ☐
   Do you currently measure this? Yes/No ☐

4. How many questions are you typically asked in a week? % ☐
   Do you currently measure this? Yes/No ☐

5. Consider any answer which **the asker would perceive** to be incomplete, untimely or inaccurate as
   an "I don't know" (IDK). What percent of the questions you answer could be viewed as IDKs? % ☐
   Do you currently measure this? Yes/No ☐

   Questions 6-9 refer to your enterprise or business unit. What is the name of this enterprise or
   business unit?

   _____

6. What would you estimate is the total annual payroll of this organization? $ ☐

7. Estimate the average percent of time spent per day by all employees of this organization to create
   answers, as defined in #1 above. % ☐

8. Estimate this organization's total cost to produce answers by multiplying the dollar amount in #6 by
   the percent in #7. $ ☐

9. Is this cost specifically accounted for in current department budgets? Yes/No ☐
   If yes, indicate how: A) By line item   B) By individual   C) By a stated percentage of "overhead"
   D) Other (specify):

   _____

10. What conclusions or discoveries have you made?

    _____
    | |
    | |
    |_____|

11. What actions should be taken, if any, and by whom?

    _____
    | |
    | |
    |_____|

12. What obstacles to these actions exist?

    _____
    | |
    | |
    |_____|

Leader's Action 15b: Opportunities to Satisfy Customers

Objectives

- Organize and prioritize customer requests for help and improve the quality of our answers

- Identify ways to eliminate customers' need to ask questions

- Eliminate opinions/guesses; work with facts

- Identify patterns, trends, and opportunities to create a win-win outcome with our customers

- Establish a baseline for deficiencies in the current (or test pilot) product. Any question someone has about the current product represents a deficiency. (For example, in the case of a cost estimate, any question someone has about it represents ambiguity or incompleteness.)

Definitions

- An answer is a product that everyone produces.

- An answer is a complete, accurate response that satisfies the customer's question on the first attempt. Answers are products.

- An "I don't know" (IDK) is a question perceived by the requestor to be not answered accurately, completely, or at the time first asked. An IDK does not necessarily mean "I don't know" was explicitly stated.

Instructions

Any data collection should be quick, easy, unambiguous, and enable improvement. Use these steps with the following Opportunities to Satisfy Customers worksheet:

1. Select the time period to collect pilot data. One to two weeks is recommended. This will give enough time to assure the topic categories are right.

2. Identify who the people are who get questions from your target customers. Meet with them to identify the most commonly asked questions.

3. Write in the questions asked or abbreviate them by topic.

For instance, suppose you work in the purchasing department and get a question such as, "When is my order going to arrive?" You could write in the whole question. Or you could write "Order ETA" (where ETA stands for "estimated time of arrival.") You may want to differentiate the various kinds of orders you get questions about. You could list those different questions, which could require different levels of effort, time, and expertise to answer, like this:

Computer Equipment ETA
Cleaning Supplies ETA
Office Supplies ETA

4. You are now ready to test your data collection method for a brief pilot period (one to two weeks). The purpose of this step is to learn enough about the questions you really get to modify this tool for a more complete data collection period.

5. If using a hard copy, instruct the users of this check sheet to place a tick "/" next to each question. Count in groups of five (for example, ⫙). The users should be encouraged to add additional topics or questions that they hear repeatedly and tally the frequency of those questions during the target period.

6. When the brief pilot data-collection period ends, you will want to take three actions. First, compare all of the lists of questions developed by each data gathering period to determine what questions should be on the revised sheet you are going to use. Next, even though this was a pilot period, follow the steps below to identify patterns and opportunities. Finally, if using a hard copy template, total up all the answers and IDKs by topic.

   When your data sheet has been designed reflecting what you have learned during the brief pilot period, repeat the process above for a long enough period to establish clear patterns.

7. Record the sum of all answers and IDKs, then calculate the satisfaction index.

   Total questions asked = Total 1 + Total 2. If fifty questions were asked during a week and you accurately and completely answered forty at the time asked but could not answer ten, your satisfaction index would be:

$$\frac{40}{10 + 40} = \frac{40}{50} = .80 \times 100 = 80\%$$

Notes

The goal is to proactively satisfy all your customers all the time. To raise the satisfaction index to 100 percent, first circle the item numbers for the five topics where the ratio of IDKs to answers was highest. These topic categories offer the best opportunity for improvement so you'll want to create an action plan to reduce these IDKs.

It is possible for a category of question to receive a relatively infrequent (or least) number of IDKs but cause relatively serious consequences. These consequences might include the loss of a customer, inability of someone to perform his or her job in a timely way, high costs to your business or failure to meet an important objective for you, or a customer. Work on eliminating the occurrence of this kind of IDK first, independent of whether it occurs most often.

Eliminating the five priority categories of IDKs is the short-term objective. The longer-term goal is to remove the causes of questions needing to be asked or, alternatively, eliminating the need to ask the questions that are most easily answered.

When you have finished, what were your biggest discoveries?

_____

_____

_____

_____

OPPORTUNITIES TO SATISFY CUSTOMERS

Start Date:	Department/Function:
End Date:	Send To:
Collected By:	

	TOPICS OF QUESTIONS ASKED	QUANTITY	
		ANSWERS given completely on first attempt	IDKs: I don't know
1			
2			
3			
4			
5			
6			
7			
8			
9			
10			
11			
12			
13			
14			
15			
16			
17			
18			
19			
20	Other/Miscellaneous		
		1	**2**

SATISFACTION INDEX =

$$\text{SATISFACTION INDEX} \quad = \quad \frac{\text{TOTAL 1}}{\text{TOTAL 1 + TOTAL 2}} \quad = \quad \underline{\hspace{2cm}} \quad \text{x } 100 = \boxed{\qquad \%}$$

269

Leader's Action 16: Target Product Selection Matrix (TPSM)

Objective: Determine the critical few products that, if improved or reinvented, will have the greatest impact on advancing the outcomes and values captured in the Strategy Map.

The Process: Completing this action is a team effort. The folks you had involved with Leader's Action 12 could be good candidates. Use this sequence for greatest simplicity, effectiveness, and insight:

A. Complete just steps 1 through 3 of the TPSM instructions. Then review your work in Leader's Actions 1 and 14 to see if products identified or inferred there should be included in the product inventory.

B. Read the Organizing Products section that follows the TPSM worksheet. That will help you edit and amend your product inventory.

C. Complete the remaining steps in the TPSM instructions to prioritize the critical few products.

Time estimates are merely suggestions. The product selection criteria are generic and frequently used as is, but they are not set in stone. Feel free to replace or add criteria, and adjust the weighting to reflect your own circumstances after completing the product inventory. The weighting currently shown in a column under each stated criterion is indicated with a 2X or 10X. That simply means the points shown in cells under that criterion should be multiplied two or ten times.

INSTRUCTIONS	Estimated Time (Minutes)
1. Name the specific organization you will focus on. This could be your enterprise, division, agency, department, functional group, or special interest group. A separate Target Product Selection Matrix must be used for each organizational unit considered. Recommendation: Choose a department or functional group as your organization of focus, not the enterprise, the first time you time you use this tool. Narrow scope aids simplicity and speed.	2
2. Identify at least the top three outcomes (A, B, and C) that best describe this organization's mission or purpose. Be sure customers' outcomes are included. (See your Strategy Map in Leader's Action 13.)	3
3. Brainstorm to create an inventory of products produced by the organization you have named. Focus especially on naming all the products that could enable or constrain achievement of the priority outcomes named in step 2. Don't be limited by the number of lines on the page. The minimum number of products to consider is thirty.	30
4. There are twelve selection criteria in the matrix. Record information next to each product. a. In Criteria column 1 put a Y (yes) or N (no) in the row next to each product that meets this selection criteria. Discard from further consideration any product marked with an N.	5
b. In Criteria column 2, rank all the remaining products with regard to how well they meet the criteria. The quickest way to do this as a team is to give each person five votes. The products with the most votes have the highest rank. If thirty products are identified, the product that best meets a specific criteria could be given a rank score of 30, the next best 29, and so on, in descending order. (A high rank is given a high number with this tool.) Enter that score in the appropriate row. When a criteria description includes several alternative subcriteria, you may find that only one of the subcriteria is most relevant for your listed products. If so, circle the subcriteria most applicable before applying the selection criteria to the products.	10
c. Repeat the previous step for Criteria 3 through 12.	20
5. Add up the row score for each product, and record the sum in the Total column. The most important products have the highest scores. The most important one is not necessarily the one with greatest improvement potential. In other words, a product may be very important but already be close to perfection in the eyes of customers and competitors.	5
6. Prioritize products with greatest improvement potential named in step 3. You can use the same multi-voting technique you used in step 4b. Notice that Criteria 1 through 4 address producer interests, Criteria 5 through 7 concern internal end users, and Criteria 8 through 12 impact end users external to this organization. (See the discussion about customer roles in Chapter 20, if desired. The emphasis here is on end users. End users will vary by product. The tool can also be applied to other customers: brokers or fixers.)	10

a. Apply a second weighting to only the top twelve important products (as scored). Multiply their rank two times or ten times, as indicated by the 2x or 10x for the respective Criteria descriptions. Record these weighted scores in the row of boxes for each of the relevant products. Add up all the final rank scores for each product. Record the sum in the Total column for the row. Rank the twelve products with the highest scores. These are most likely to have high-potential impact on both customer satisfaction and organizational performance. Record their total weighted ranking in the Rank column and consider the top-ranked products your best candidates for improvement or replacement with an innovative alternative.	10
b. Determine which of these high-potential products are best to address first for immediate results and greatest long-term results.	15
7. Now name the individuals who would sponsor a project addressing each priority product. A sponsor has control over the people and resources likely to be involved in amending, correcting, or redesigning a product.	10
Total Estimated Time	120

TARGET PRODUCT SELECTION MATRIX

1 ORGANIZATION NAME

_____

2 PRIORITY OUTCOMES

A. _____

B. _____

C. _____

4 Products with the most importance and/or improvement potential are...

		PRODUCER			INTERNAL END-USERS			EXTERNAL END-USERS				
	1	2	3	4	5	6	7	8	9	10	11	12
3 PRODUCTS	Possible for this organization to change	Enablers of priority outcomes	Constraints on priority outcomes	The greatest time consumer to create, fix, maintain or sell (if relevant)	A source of error, complexity, cost or dissatisfaction within this organization	Vital to work performed by others internal to this organization	Created earliest in a process which impacts internal customers	A cause of time consumption and cost to use/own for others external to organization	A source of error, complexity, cost or dissatisfaction outside this organization	Vital to work performed by others external to this organization	Created earliest in the relationship with customers external to this organization	A potential cause of dissatisfaction, defection or complaints of final end-user customers	**5** TOTAL / **6** RANK
	Y or N	(2x)	(2x)	(2x)	(2x)			(2x)	(2x)			(10x)	TOTAL / RANK
1													
2													
3													
4													
5													
6													
7													
8													
9													
10													
11													
12													
13													
14													
15													

TARGET PRODUCT SELECTION MATRIX

4						PRODUCER			INTERNAL END-USERS			EXTERNAL END-USERS						
					| Products with the most importance and/or improvement potential are…												**5**	**6**
					1	2	3	4	5	6	7	8	9	10	11	12		
3	PRODUCTS				Possible for this organization to change	Enablers of priority outcomes	Constraints on priority outcomes	The greatest time consumer to create, fix, maintain or sell (if relevant)	A source of error, complexity, cost or dissatisfaction within this organization	Vital to work performed by others internal to this organization	Created earliest in a process which impacts internal customers	A cause of time consumption and cost to use/own for others external to organization	A source of error, complexity, cost or dissatisfaction outside this organization	Vital to work performed by others external to this organization	Created earliest in the relationship with customers external to this organization	A potential cause of dissatisfaction, defection or complaints of final end-user customers	TOTAL	RANK
					Y or N	(2x)	(2x)	(2x)	(2x)			(2x)	(2x)			(10x)		
16																		
17																		
18																		
19																		
20																		
21																		
22																		
23																		
24																		
25																		
26																		
27																		
28																		
29																		
30																		

TARGET PRODUCT SELECTION MATRIX

3 PRODUCTS		PRODUCER			INTERNAL END-USERS			EXTERNAL END-USERS						5	6
	1 Possible for this organization to change	2 Enablers of priority outcomes	3 Constraints on priority outcomes	4 The greatest time consumer to create, fix, maintain or sell (if relevant)	5 A source of error, complexity, cost or dissatisfaction within this organization	6 Vital to work performed by others internal to this organization	7 Created earliest in a process which impacts internal customers	8 A cause of time consumption and cost to use/own for others external to organization	9 A source of error, complexity, cost or dissatisfaction outside this organization	10 Vital to work performed by others external to this organization	11 Created earliest in the relationship with customers external to this organization	12 A potential cause of dissatisfaction, defection or complaints of final end-user customers			
	Y or N	(2x)	(2x)	(2x)	(2x)			(2x)	(2x)			(10x)	TOTAL	RANK
31														
32														
33														
34														
35														
36														
37														
38														
39														
40														
41														
42														
43														
44														
45														

4 Products with the most importance and/or improvement potential are…

Leader's Action 17: What Is the Target Product?

Objective: As the Master of Excellence (AKA Sherlock), you are brought in as an impartial expert to advise the court on the following:
1. Identify all the products mentioned which are relevant in this case.
2. Name the producers of each product, identifying who had responsibility for what.
3. Determine which one or two products were the likely cause(s) of SUV crashes.
4. Name the party or parties with greatest responsibility for crashes.
5. Advise the court on the role or culpability of the SUV customer.

To prepare for your testimony, Sherlock, you have drafted the following list of products (shown in the order in which they were introduced in the case) and their producers. Consider each product an exhibit.

1. Make sure there is nothing missing or in error before proceeding. If you think a fact correction is needed, correct the list or add any omission to the list.

PRODUCT	PRODUCER	CAUSE OF CRASH
SUV	Auto Company	
Vehicle warranty	Legal Department, Auto Company	
Tire	Tire Company	
Tire Specifications	Engineering Department, Auto Company	
User Manual	Technical Publications Department, Auto Company	
Tire Warranty	Legal Department, Tire Company	

2. Put a check in the Cause of Crash column next to the product(s) you believe at fault.

3. What party or person is responsible for SUV crashes in this case and why?

_____

4. Does the SUV driver have culpability? Yes No Why or why not?

_____

5. What are your discoveries?

_____

Debriefing

Six products are shown on the draft list. If you read the case closely, you would have noticed that eight others are missing and would have added them and their producers to the list. They are the two claims submitted (and produced) by owners, the rejection letters by the auto company's legal department, the auto company's core values statement, their website, the entertainment system, and its warranty. Fourteen products were named. How many did you catch? _____.

There are two problems. One is on the human relations side; the other is technical. Had the auto company's legal department demonstrated compassion and regret and taken responsibility for the failure of the SUV to function safely, there might have been no class-action suit. A published core value should have guided the department's behavior. A breakdown in alignment between stated core values and actual practice is evident.

The technical problem is the lack of alignment between the target tire pressure contained in the specification and the higher pressure contained in the vehicle user manual. The auto company is responsible for both products. The two departments producing those products should have coordinated their work. Had that occurred, the tires would likely not have been overinflated by drivers.

The auto company attempted to blame first the tire manufacturer and then the customer. The fact that the tires were the only component of the SUV for which the automaker claimed no responsibility was clearly a convenient attempt to shield itself from responsibility. After all, other components such as the entertainment system and the starter were all treated as integral parts of the SUV. Were the tires optional equipment? Can you imagine buying a new car without tires? We think not. The SUV drivers had no responsibility or culpability for this exploding tire case. The SUV maker bears full responsibility for its multiple product failures.

This case was simplified for our purposes here, but it was not fiction. That is the true tragedy. If we looked deeper, we would find that the tires were subject to all sorts of quality tests and inspections before they were ever shipped to the SUV maker. This is normal for manufactured products. What comparable quality examination occurs with all the knowledge products involved in this case? Sadly the typical answer is, little to none. As a Master of Excellence, we have the challenge to create and deploy the same level of discipline with knowledge products as is done with manufacturing work. If a culture of excellence is the goal, this is not optional. Understanding the relationships of knowledge products is key to our success.

How is this complexity of products issue related to our target product selection? We saw in our SUV story the failure of a system-level product. But getting at the root cause included consideration of more than a dozen others. Eleven of those were knowledge products! This ratio of knowledge to manufactured system products is a major reason I recommend keeping manufactured products off the Target Product list. Ditto for sold products. It is not that they are unimportant. They are too complex for us to tackle and get fast results. And they are always dependent on component and knowledge products. In our story, it would be faster, cheaper, and more effective to fix the user manual, specifications—or even others among the knowledge products—than to fix the tires. There is no evidence they needed fixing anyway.

So looking for specific component-level products is smart. This would be a good time to revisit your Target Product list and add any you might have missed. Don't be constrained by the lines on the page. It is not uncommon for an organization to identify over a hundred products that seem reasonable candidates to put into the top of the funnel. When we are done prioritizing, we still want to have only a handful to focus on first. But don't winnow the list prematurely, or we'll miss opportunity. Criteria in the TPSM that are relevant to this issue are 5, 6, 9, 10, and 12.

Leader's Action 18: Excellence Through Entertainment

Objective: Identify possible products that, if made more entertaining, could improve enterprise differentiation, employee engagement, or customer satisfaction.

1. Identify ten specific products.[133] Choose those from your personal products (Leader's Action 14), those created by the enterprise (whether sold or not), and/or those created by your business unit (department, function, or division named in Leader's Actions 10 and 12).

2. Rank the products to indicate which few could have the biggest impact on improvement or excellence. A rank of 1 equals biggest expected impact.

	PRODUCT	RANK
1		
2		
3		
4		
5		
6		
7		
8		
9		
10		

3. Name the key individuals you want on your team to confirm your choice and explore how to proceed.

   _____   _____   _____

4. Include any of these products in your Target Product Selection Matrix, which you are now ready to complete. This enables us to assemble all the pieces of your Strategy Map in the next chapter.

---

[133] Make sure they fit the five criteria for a product: expressed as plural with an "s," a deliverable, countable, very specific, and used to produce a desired outcome (for the producer and/or customer).

Leader's Action 19: The Strategy Map, Part 2

Objectives (with your team)

1. Demonstrate the alignment of mission, values, outcomes, products, owners, and measures.
2. Further reduce the number of target products to match available resources and readiness.
3. Combine Leader's Action 13 (Strategy Map, part 1) with top products from Leader's Action 16 (TPSM).
4. Identify the critical few who will be engaged in the first wave of transformation efforts.
5. Determine whether change will be driven by strategic projects (organized by product) or some other means.

Instructions

1. The first table below is a blank version of the final strategy map you are going to create. Each area in the table includes a step number from 1 to 9. Use this table simply as a visual reference for what the final version will look like.

2. The second table below (from steps 1 through 7 shown there) is identical to the blank Strategy Map, part 1, you completed in Leader's Action 13. The only difference is its rotation 90 degrees here to make the next steps easier.

3. Using either your map from Leader's Action 13 or the version shown in the second table below, you will be connecting target products with the third table below.

4. Transfer your top-twelve ranked products from Leader's Action 16 to the third table below. Record the names of the individuals who are considered the owners of those products. In other words, name the person ultimately responsible for assuring the specific product is error-free and has control of the resources necessary to fix or improve it. This completes Map steps 8 through 9.

5. Look at the two tables side by side so the horizontal lines on the two can be matched. Going down the first product column, put an X in the box where the Product column intersects with the row for the first subordinate outcome if you believe the product could be acting as a constraint on achieving that outcome. Leave the box blank if you believe there is no correlation or those on your team cannot agree. Continue the process down the Product column, considering each outcome.

6. Repeat step 5 for all the products.

7. Count up all the Xs in each column, recording the total at the bottom in the row labeled Priority. Identify the six products with the highest scores.

8. The products with the highest priority score are the critical few you believe are exerting the biggest constraints on achieving the strategic outcomes.

9. Identify any outcomes you believe need improvement but for which none of the top six products appear to be related as a constraint. Determine which of the other six is/are most likely to be constraints which, if changed, could enable improvement. Add/amend your critical few products.

Considerations

Congratulations on narrowing your mission from elimination of world hunger to identifying the first few bags of rice to ship. We want to get them to where they are needed as soon as possible. Can a single person handle the transport for each bag, or do we need a team? If a product you have selected represents a complex issue that cuts across different organizational units, a team is likely to be necessary. The team needs to have a sponsor, the ready and equipped few (usually no more than five), a guide or team leader, a charter, and a completion deadline not to exceed about five months. Focused transformation efforts with those critical resources and limited time allowed have an extremely high success rate, achieving high ROI such as the Missouri teams mentioned a few times throughout the book.

The issue of chartering and managing strategic C3 projects is a subject for another book, a note to the author or a visit to the special C3 tools that can make magic happen. One thing to note is that organizing projects by product is quite different than organizing a project to solve a problem. Is it possible to fix a problem but still create a product customers don't like? You bet. By working on a product, we have effectively grouped problems related to that product. The product and the outcomes it is intended to create are the basis for claiming success.

Assigning an owner to an outcome is, frankly, not terribly productive. Sadly, this is a common practice across organizations of all kinds. We will avoid it. An outcome is likely to be dependent on more than a single product and owner. Identifying owners at the product level is highly effective since that is the unit of work that is directly controllable by a single party and an organizational unit. What can the Master of Excellence do when the producer of a product dodges responsibility for excellence? Although I hesitate to offer simple remedies to a many-sided issue, this question occurs frequently enough to deserve a response.

By requiring all organizational units (starting with your own) to create an inventory of products, you can have a conversation with the dodger about who the producer of his or her products is. If there is acceptance of the idea that those specified products belong to him or her, follow with questions regarding who the customers are, what they have as priorities for the product, and what is known and measured about customer satisfaction. You are making the conversation about the product, not about the adequacies of the producer. If you have established a customer-satisfaction policy along the lines we discussed in Chapter 6, this would be a perfect time to pull that out for reference. Policies do, after all, describe conditions to be met for employment. C3 does not permit customer satisfaction to be an optional pursuit. A person who, in the most extreme case, does not claim ownership for any product is an employee with no connection to the strategic direction of the enterprise and its customers. What is the consequence for someone without a purpose? We can help him or her find a purpose, though it might not be with us.

For now, let's compare what you have done to this point with what you were inclined to do back in Chapter 4. You had identified what you thought were the biggest areas of opportunity for improvement, who you should enlist, and what the indicators of transformational success would be. You did this in Leader's Actions 1 through 3. If what you said then is the same as what you think now, you are clairvoyant and insightful, and we have succeeded in confirming the reason you are a talented leader. On the other hand, if you have changed your mind, that shows you are receptive to new ideas and have the persistence to get far enough on the journey to correct your course. Either way, you are a winner.

Winners do well to surround themselves with others of like mind or those who have a willingness to enthusiastically follow your lead. The product owners you have identified with your final Strategy Map may be eager to be active leaders in the customer-centered transformation. That would be best case. Sometimes they are not ready for any number of reasons. We discussed this in Chapter 4. The bottom line is that you do not need and cannot afford reluctant players as you exercise your role as Master of Excellence. We want to stack the deck in your favor so the first efforts at visible transformation are overwhelming successes. Let those not ready go do something else. Work to turn the chosen few into the heroes you know they can be.

Leader's Action 19 (continued): The Strategy Map, Part 2

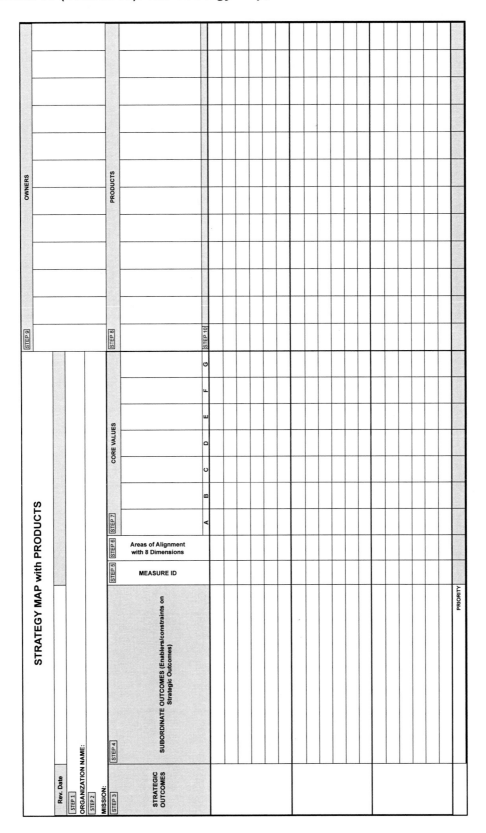

This is what your Strategy Map will look like when combined. We will break it into the two pieces shown next. (See the electronic Mastering Excellence Workbook in the store at http://www.C3Excellence.com.)

STRATEGY MAP with PRODUCTS

Rev. Date		

STEP 1
ORGANIZATION NAME:

STEP 2
MISSION:

STEP 3	STEP 4	STEP 5	STEP 6	STEP 7	CORE VALUES						
STRATEGIC OUTCOMES	SUBORDINATE OUTCOMES (Enablers/constraints on Strategic Outcomes)	MEASURE ID	Areas of Alignment with 8 Dimensions		A	B	C	D	E	F	G
PRIORITY											

Leader's Action 20: Customer Roles and Power

Objectives

1. Identify who your customers are and what role they play with the specific product you have selected.
2. Determine who currently has the most power and who should have it.
3. Decide what changes, if any, should occur.

Instructions

1. Name the specific product you want to evaluate or improve, referring to the Target Product Selection Matrix (Leader's Action 16). Focus on this target product as you answer questions 2 through 8.

2. Name the producer of this target product.

3. Name all the end users of this product. Note: Identify the roles people play with this product, using names of positions, titles, or individuals, **not organizational names**. Add lines if needed.

   a. Segment End Users. Assume end users are not a homogeneous group (nor are brokers and fixers). One size rarely fits all. Expect end user priorities to differ regarding the purpose and characteristics of a product. Identify with a check mark here which kinds of end user characteristics could lead to unique or differentiating expectations. Such end user characteristics can include the following:

Gender	Mental or physical characteristics, ability
Age	Financial resources
Cultural heritage	Geographic location
Type of job function	Tenure in group
Level of authority	Previous experience with the product
Political power or influence	Frequency of using the product
Educational, other credentials	Purpose for using the product
Kind of lifestyle	Degree of satisfaction with the product
Native language	Environmental context for using the product

   b. A large number of characteristics can differentiate end users. But life is short. Circle here three priority end user demographics you must satisfy to achieve product success.

4. Name the brokers between the producer and end user customers, if any exist.

5. Name the fixers for this product.

6. What is your primary role, if any, with this product?

7. Now go back and rank the current power of all the parties identified in numbers 2 through 5.

   Power refers to the ability to direct or change the design of the product. 1= most powerful. Write only one number 1 in this column, only one number 2, and so on, even if the same person appears in more than one place. Give every entry a unique rank. If there are twelve entries, the assigned ranks will go from 1 to 12. A customer can have more than one role with a product. Power may vary depending on the role.

8. What discoveries (insights, learning, or aha moments) did you make?

9. What action is needed now?

CUSTOMER ROLES & POWER

			7. RANK
1.	Product		
2.	Producer		
3.	End Users		
4.	Broker for End Users		
	Broker for Producers		
5.	Fixers		

6.	Your primary role with this product:		
	_____ Broker for producer	_____ Producer	
	_____ Broker for user	_____ End User	
		_____ Fixer	

8. Discoveries (insights, learning, "ah-ha's")

9. What action is needed?

Debriefing and Executive Summary

- The power a customer has in his or her role of broker or fixer is different from his or her power as an end user. Special effort is often needed to appropriately balance the interests of the different roles to counteract the Five Ps of Power. These Five Ps can exceed the power a customer may otherwise have by virtue of their role with a product.

- The Five Ps reveal power concerning the relationship with you or your organization, not with a product.

- An individual customer can play multiple roles with the same product, especially at different points in the life cycle of the product. A person can create a specification (as a producer), be one of its end users, pass it to others who may review but not use it (as a broker), modify it for ease of understanding (as a fixer), or correct errors in it (as a fixer).

- It is easy to confuse two different but related products. The producer of a specification is usually not the producer of the product the specification characterizes. The solution is to always be sure the product we have in mind does not change as we examine roles.

- What happens when we satisfy brokers but not end users is illustrated by the fate of major players in industries such as cell phones, cars, TVs, and media outlets.

- An example of a good broker, putting end users and producers close together, is eBay.

- Brokers can be an asset when bilingual, speaking the languages of both the producer and end user.

- The more brokers are involved with a product, the less power the end users are likely to have.

- The role of brokers in health care, education, and news media (taken over by blogs) reveals a possible (undesired) future for those not intensely focused on end users.

- We now know how to simplify the seventeen roles identified in Chapter 6 under language (as a source of ambiguity), how they are related to the Five Ps, and how we can reduce roles to three.

- By revisiting Leader's Action 5, we can now confirm or correct who the end user customer is in the identified documents named as potential sources of ambiguity.

- Consider the impact of demographics of the producers versus the end users of public restrooms for women. The evidence for lack of alignment is the long line outside those restrooms at theaters, ballparks, entertainment arenas, and other public venues. Some see this as a process issue. I see it as a product design problem and a lack of attentiveness to end users.

- Just as citizens have responsibilities, so do customers. They, as all other humans, are not always right!

- Here is a condensed version of how to make customers a lever for change: it is the responsibility of the producer to know what is unique about end user interests and focus on satisfying them. Referring to customers without specifying their role invites ambiguity and loss of appropriate focus.

Robin L. Lawton

APPENDIX 2—VITAL LIES

A Vital Lie is a constraining assumption, self-deception, justification, denial, rationalization, myth, or other excuse for not changing. Here are ten of the most common, along with some brief comments:

1. **We don't have control over that.**

This belief gives us permission not to seek change. The destructive beauty of such a self-fulfilling prophecy is that we can prove it true by inaction. This Vital Lie is often invoked in regard to an outcome that customers may want from an organization: a good night's rest (hotel), health (health-care provider), wealth (financial institution), or great career (university). While it is true that meteorologists don't prevent hurricanes, an accurate and timely forecast can minimize loss.

A Ford Motor Company ad, signed by CEO Bill Ford, appeared in *BusinessWeek* on September 18, 2006, and ran for several weeks. Mr. Ford, grandson of Henry Ford, was quoted as follows.

> "We know we don't control the price of gas, but we can innovate to reduce the need. That's why we're building cars that can go 500 miles on a single tank...At Ford, innovation is the guiding compass of everything we do."

At least five assumptions are embedded in that statement. As you read them below, circle T or F to indicate whether you believe the statement to be true or false:

Cars require gas	T	F
The price of fuel is beyond our control	T	F
Bigger tanks reduce the need for gas	T	F
A 500-mile gas tank equals innovation	T	F
More of this kind of innovation will create success	T	F

We can test these assumptions by considering a few facts known within the industry in 2006:

- Customers in 2006 wanted low total cost of ownership. This desired outcome was not new then and remains current today. Energy costs would be one significant component of that total cost.

- The percent of fuel-efficient, smaller car models on the market had been going up for the prior thirty years.

- The number of those cars produced by Ford had declined during that time. In 2006, Ford made a total of two small cars with ratings of thirty-two miles per gallon or better, the Focus and Escape.

- Toyota had introduced the Prius worldwide six years earlier in 2000.

Ford stock value lost over 40 percent between 2001 and 2006. Ford reported a loss of $12.6 billion for 2006. Bill Ford brought in a replacement for himself from outside the automobile industry in the same month as the ad above, September 2006. Could there be any relationship among these facts?

Admittedly you had the benefit of hindsight when you reviewed the truthfulness of Mr. Ford's assumptions above. The vast majority of people I asked in 2006 (and since) viewed all the assumptions as false. Toyota had conclusively proven cars did not require gas when it introduced the electric hybrid Prius eleven years prior at the Tokyo Motor Show, with the first available for sale in 1997 in Japan. The first million had been sold by May 2008. By the end of 2014, Toyota had over two-thirds of the world market for hybrids.

Another company to consider as a benchmark in 2006 is Honda, where I worked with Lexus leadership to support customer-centered thinking. American Honda had the Fit Sport (thirty-eight miles per gallon), Civic Hybrid (fifty-one miles per gallon) and Insight (sixty-six miles per gallon). As a side note, it also had the first motorcycle with an airbag.

Vital Lie 1 is all about leadership. Prius means "to go before" in Latin. Worth considering is that Toyota CEO Akio Toyoda, grandson of Toyota's founder, introduced the first hydrogen fuel cell mass-market cars for the US market in 2015. It is called the Mirai from the Japanese word for "future." The irony to this story is that it illustrates the insight in the adage attributed to Henry Ford, "If you think you can or think you can't, either way you're right." The price of fuel for cars is clearly within our control. Elon Musk has proven with Tesla cars that the size of the tank is irrelevant; there is none. Bill Ford himself demonstrated what was possible by introducing the Fusion Hybrid in 2010, named the North American Car of the Year at the Detroit Auto Show, Motor Trend's Car of the Year, and one of *Car and Driver* magazine's 10 Best Cars for 2010. And it was given the inaugural Hermance Vehicle Efficiency Award by the publishers of HybridCars.com.[134]

Bill Ford is no dummy and, as a major stockholder, had every reason to chart a new path. What Bill Ford is quoted as saying in the ad was consistent with cultural truths or Vital Lies within the company at the time. But it was quite different from what he was actually doing to bring out several vehicles that needed smaller, not larger, tanks. This story demonstrates what a leader can do to turn around his enterprise. Destroying key Vital Lies is part of the leader's job. He recognized he needed help and brought in Alan Mullaly from Boeing as new CEO, who was not constrained by auto-industry thinking. The two worked effectively as a team.

At a keynote presentation at Ford in the mid-1990s, I shared the observation that US auto companies had demonstrated over at least a couple of decades a lack of attentiveness to the priorities of drivers. The result of that was the strong and consistent slide in market share for US-designed cars. One of the corporate board members in attendance asked me to meet with him afterward. He insisted I had been wrong in talking about what customers wanted, saying he had been on the engineering team that heard customers say "they wanted more range." He and his team had interpreted that as a need for bigger tanks so cars could be driven farther on a fill-up, not the need for a more fuel-efficient engine that required fewer fill-ups. Tank size was also believed to be the most important, quickly changeable part of the car. When board members insist they have a grip on the truth, even when the evidence says otherwise, a leader like Bill Ford may need reinforcements from the outside to change both the belief and action demonstrating we *can* control that.

Within a decade after Bill Ford's quote, the company had nine models of cars with thirty-two miles per gallon or better, of which four were hybrids or electric. Mr. Ford had successfully destroyed Vital Lie 1 regarding the five assumptions made in his 2006 ad.

---

[134] "Ford Fusion Hybrid," HybridCars.com, January 2, 2013.

Leadership Action to Take:

- Ask for data that unambiguously supports the assumption.
- Ask for data that could prove the assumption false.
- Ask what the consequences might be (to the enterprise, its customers, and potential competitors) if the assumption is false.
- Complete Leader's Actions 10 and 11.

2. **Satisfaction will occur if dissatisfaction declines**.

This is a bit like saying customers will feel good when they stop tripping over our poor practices. We may stop inflicting pain on them, but that hardly qualifies as making them feel good. A second assumption embedded here is that we know what satisfaction is, that we have defined it. Dissatisfaction can seem obvious when we hear customers complaining about something as late. But would on-time be a source of satisfaction?

Consider the case of airlines. Airlines are all attentive to on-time departures and arrivals. There are two industry (producer) definitions for "on-time." One means the aircraft is pushed away from the gate no more than fifteen minutes after its published departure time, regardless of whether or not it then sits on the tarmac for an hour before takeoff. The other definition means the plane touches down no later than fifteen minutes after its scheduled arrival time, again independent of whether you sit there an hour or more before being allowed to get off. Airline management may believe that being on-time is a differentiator in a highly competitive industry. Like business travelers everywhere, I can say unequivocally that being late to arrive at my destination can definitely be a dissatisfier. The airline that is sufficiently late on a consistent basis will certainly succeed in differentiating itself. I'll avoid it like the plague. Truly, dissatisfaction creates differentiation.

But consider the reverse. If you arrive on time, do you jump up and down for joy? Perhaps not. You probably expect to be on time. Arriving on-time may be neither a differentiator nor a satisfier, unless, of course, your experience with that airline's on-time performance is markedly better than any other and a higher priority for you than other characteristics of the flight.

The aim to reduce dissatisfaction is not a bad thing. It may just be misguided, insufficient, and backward-looking. Satisfaction is the goal. Is it possible to eliminate dissatisfaction but not create satisfaction or loyalty? See the health-care discussion in Chapter 10, case 3.

Leadership Action to Take:

- Direct and model the consistent practice of asking questions of customers that enable the definition of their performance (objective), perception (subjective), and outcome expectations. Exactly what those questions must include is spelled out in the VOC discussion, volume 2.
- Make sure surveys and other structured forms of enquiry are asking questions about their known priorities, not simply questions concerning issues the producer is willing to improve. See the discussion on measuring satisfaction with and without surveys in volume 2.
- Ask for the evidence showing that overall satisfaction rises as dissatisfaction on each specific issue falls.

3. **We are on the leading edge in our industry**.

I once interviewed many directors of boards for the largest firms within a certain industry. Almost to a man (as there were no women on those boards), they each said they believed their firm was on the industry's leading edge. It seemed clear to me that not all of them could be right; someone had to be wrong. Unless, of course, we live in Garrison Keillor's fictitious Lake Wobegon where "all the women are strong, all the men are good-looking, and all the children are above average."[135] Believing we are the best might be the truth but can often breed complacency and arrogance. It discourages critical thinking. Intel's Andy Grove had a passion for destroying innovation-draining complacency and created a high-performance enterprise. His motto and book have the same name, "Only the paranoid survive." He wanted the assumption to be that someone else was about to overtake Intel. Running more creatively and faster was the only way to stay on top.

Leadership Action to Take:

- Clarify who it is that defines the leading edge.
- Ask what role the customer (end user, broker, or fixer) has in its definition.
- Ask for the objective evidence supporting the assumption.

4. Growth in customer demand or market share means customers are happy.

IBM was the dominant producer of personal computers, and Microsoft was king of personal computer software prior to 2000. Were their customers happy? Why did they defect in droves to a much smaller company based in Cupertino making mobile devices with an alternative operating system? Producing the biggest and best phone directory (think Yellow Pages) does not guarantee us a position in the Internet search business (think Google and Baidu). Growth in or size of market share may have nothing to do with customer satisfaction, nor with your future.

A large telecommunications company had millions of new customers sign up every month. Commission was paid for each new two-year contract sold. The same company had a loss of over a million customers per quarter over several years. No special individual or group compensation was paid on the basis of customer retention. Did new demand prove customers were happy?

Leadership Action to Take:

- Rule out the possibility that coercion, external constraints, and the absence of alternatives are causes for customer retention and market growth.
- Examine whether compensation or reward encourages capture, satisfaction, or retention of customers and whether the weight of compensation and reward is where it should be for strategic outcomes to be met.
- Seek independent verification of customer satisfaction from sources uncontrolled by the producer. Instead of reliance on surveys, examine what social media indicates about satisfaction, the effectiveness of word-of-mouth testimonials, and observation of related customer behaviors. What do legal suits, contract disputes, formal complaints, and other customer-initiated actions suggest?

5. We know what business we are in.

The popularity and growth of Southwest Airlines (SWA) from their inception in 1971 is often attributed to their lower-priced flights, their fuel-purchasing practices, or standardization on a single aircraft. Those are related to SWA's success but represent a narrow, dangerously incomplete view that is producer-biased. Does that explain how SWA, by 2014, had forty-one years of consecutive profitability and became the largest US carrier in terms of passenger miles? What few of their competitors and industry analysts did

---

[135] Garrison Keillor, radio host of the *Prairie Home Companion*, used this tagline with his stories of the fictitious northern Minnesota town of Lake Wobegon.

not understand, but could easily have discovered, is that successive SWA leaders had created and sustained a business culture that did everything possible to entertain its customers, often in unexpected ways. It's no accident their trading symbol is LUV and that flight attendants are trained and encouraged to give safety announcements by song, poetry, skit, and joke. Are they an airline or an entertainment enterprise?

Case Study 4 (Chapter 11) was about a financial-services company. Leadership had employees uncover and try hard to satisfy its customer's desired outcomes beyond simply getting a loan. That effort resulted in rethinking its student-loan business as one aimed to help some customers improve their likelihood of getting a good career that would result in a high quality of life. This an example of how we might consider that the reasons a customer comes to us may not be what we think we are in business to satisfy. Realigning our purpose with theirs can enable us to improve a higher-level outcome and put us in a much stronger competitive position.

Apple is perhaps the biggest company in the world to have been persistently misunderstood. Apple's standard industry classification (SIC) codes, a US government system for classifying industries by a four-digit code, include the following:

- 3663, Radio and Television Broadcasting and Communications Equipment
- 3571 (primary), electronic computers

Does this sound right to you? Is there any fit between Apple and the entertainment industry?

Leadership Action to Take:

- Watch for and discourage self-imposed constraints that limit our satisfaction of strategic customer outcomes.
- Help those you lead recognize that customers may be wanting from you (and maybe even getting it by chance) something more than you think you are in the business to give.

6. **We know who our customers are.**

We often confuse the people who buy, fund, or regulate with those who use the product or service. Customers are usually a significantly more diverse group than we realize. The ones we are furthest from are the ones we know least well. But those end users are most important to satisfy in the long term. An example of a nontraditional approach to customer definition was Elon Musk's insistence that he had no use of dealers for his new Tesla cars. His intent was to be as close to the end user as possible, and eliminating the need for dealers[136] was part of the strategy. As of 2014, a number of competing car manufacturers and dealer organizations lobbied their state governments to outlaw Musk's practice. His model was exactly the same as Steve Jobs', who insisted for many years on selling computers direct to end users.

This Vital Lie is far more problematic than it often appears at first. It's not that dealers, whether for phones, cars, or anything else, are not customers. Of course they are. But they are a customer, not the customer, and the difference matters. Please see the related discussion about retailers in Chapter 21, just prior to the section on Uber and Didi.

---

[136] Dealers are a kind of customer we'll refer to as brokers, one of three roles a customer can play.

Leadership Action to Take:

> Whenever you hear "our customers want…," ask:
> - Which customers for what product?
> - Which role (end user, broker, or fixer) does that customer have?
> - Is the speaker referring to all demographics for that customer role or only a specific one? For example, are we thinking of both men and women, working or not, highly educated or not, multilingual or not, and so on?

7. Customers don't know what they want.

This belief permits us to not bother asking and, instead, tell them what we think they want or act as if we know. We might call this the "father knows best" belief. It leads us easily to number 8 next.

It is true that customers may not be able to articulate what they want in a way the producer will unambiguously understand. The story of the board member at Ford thinking customers meant bigger tanks when they said they wanted more range is an example. The challenge is to ask the right questions so the answers lead us to the correct actions. It is possible to use language— whether for asking questions or giving instructions— that is as unambiguous as mathematics, used in solving a math problem. That skill can be quickly learned and applied to effectively uncover, understand, and satisfy the VOC.

Leadership Action to Take:

- Ask what defined and repeatable method was used to uncover what customers want.
- Assure the ultimate customer-desired outcomes have been articulated.
- Ask for the behavioral customer practices that support the assumption.
- Do not accept the absence of articulated customer priorities as meaning they don't know or care.

8. We know what customers want.

This may have been true yesterday. A safer bet is to assume we don't know until we check again. The following example is excerpted from Chapter 20, in the Vital Lies section.

A client company was in the business of manufacturing cell phones and other high-tech devices. They had huge market share. I asked their engineering, management, and other staff why their phones were black and gray. One of the common answers was, "It's just a phone." Asked what that meant, they said color wasn't something their customers ever said was something that mattered. I asked whom they viewed as their customers. They said it was obviously (and with some smugness) the people who buy the phones. Asked who those buyers were, they said, "The telcos." That meant the telephone companies of the day such as AT&T, Verizon, and so on. I asked if the buyers at those firms were also users of the phones. My client audiences didn't know and insisted it didn't matter. If a color other than black or gray was wanted, it would have been stated in the purchasing contract. The whole point to a phone, they said, was that you could communicate with someone.

When I suggested the possibility that the phone users might have different priorities than the buyers, engineers agreed.[137] So working with this first point of agreement, I asked what proportion of users were women. This was data they thought might be obtainable, but it wasn't something on anyone's radar and

---

[137] See Chapter 20 on customer roles.

would be hard to get. This meant it didn't matter to them. In any audience I had at the time, perhaps 10 percent were women. Asking the women about whether color was a priority for them, they said, "Of course." They went on to say that a phone could be viewed as an accessory. I asked the men what "an accessory" meant to them. The first thing that came to mind was that an accessory referred to someone at the scene of a crime. Talk about a communication divide. The women explained that an outfit generally needs to have matching or at least complementary colors. Red, blue, teal, white, and taupe were examples of colors to account for at the time. That explained why they would have purses and shoes of multiple colors that went together. The shoes and purses were examples of what they considered accessories. We can see the importance of a shared language start to emerge.

The guys were pretty adamant that they were just as color-coordinated as the women. Their shoes were black, their belts were black, and their wallets were black. Or sometimes the main color would be brown. The whole idea about what color-coordinated meant was a bit narrowly defined. Heck, they weren't really sure what taupe even was. They did agree that women made up about 51 percent of the potential world market for cell phones.

The real tragedy here is that this major division of the company tolerated, if not encouraged, a culture that defined a main product as "just a phone," the view that women as customers had little bearing on the future of the business, and the conviction that product users as a group were less important to satisfy than the product buyers. Leadership said excellence mattered but never pushed back on the core Vital Lies. A much smaller company that introduced color dislodged that business from its perch as number one in the world. It was probably just a fluke. Or else they fell victim to Vital Lies 3, 5, 6, 8, and 10. They certainly were convinced they knew who their customers were (Vital Lie 6) but were only partly right.

Another division of the same client company made two-way radios. Upon being asked the same question about black and gray, they saw it as a novel idea that color might be important. They were about to introduce a new product that included teenagers in their target market. After some investigation involving actually asking those prospective customers what they might want, yellow radios were introduced. They were a dramatic hit. A fluke?

Samsung wanted to sell high-end TVs to design-enlightened Europeans in the mid-2000s. Samsung and their competitors viewed TVs as high-tech devices. As Samsung leaders looked at how to differentiate themselves, they discovered women were the main decision makers on TV purchases. Women considered TVs as furniture, not as techno wizardry. The concept of fitting in was more important than sticking out. Those insights led to a shift in Samsung's approach to design. They successfully became the world's largest TV maker with a resulting reputation in Europe for elegant design. Considering TVs as furniture rather than electronics required Samsung leaders to smash Vital Lies 5 and 6.

Leadership Action to Take:

- Repeat actions outlined for Vital Lies 5, 6, and 7.

9. **What customers say they expect is what they do want.**

This belief has caused untold frustration for leaders sincerely listening for customer priorities. There can be significant differences between what customers expect and what they want. For example, a dental customer may expect pain but not want it. Should our aim be to satisfy their expectations or their wants? We can easily shoot for the former and discover that our success does not result in their satisfaction. In addition, customers may not give us an answer to every question we ask. This may be due to their inability to understand our question or their perceived irrelevance of the question. And we may not ask every pertinent question we should have. In general, customers will easily tell us the improvements they want in a product they are already familiar with. Unless we ask, they may not tell us the outcome they are trying to achieve. Improving the product without improving the outcome inevitably leads to customers telling us they didn't get what they really wanted.

Leadership Action to Take:

- Determine if the expectation is a want or simply what has previously been experienced. Ask if we are hearing what they have wanted or what they will want. Is it an expectation, an anticipation, a minimum requirement, or a hope? Does it matter?
- Ask if it is possible the customer's expectation is incompletely articulated. Could they want something beyond what is stated? No slide-rule user asked for a four-function electronic calculator; no typewriter user asked for word-processing software; no record-buyer asked for a Walkman. Conversely, prospective customers said they loved the Edsel and New Coke but didn't buy.

10. **Our performance measures confirm our excellence.**

An organization can meet or exceed all industry standards, have no product returns, see no customer defections, nor receive any lawsuits filed against it. This does not mean customers love it. A water utility can meet all government regulations but still provide water consumers hate to drink. The danger is interpreting customer capture, retention, and even loyalty as anything close to customer ecstasy. An industry or enterprise that uses the term retention and loyalty synonymously is confused and looking at the wrong goal. Our measures of success can lead to faulty conclusions. An organization that believes it is already at the top of its game, which is especially easy for a monopoly to do, may see no reason to change a thing. See number 4 above.

Leadership Action to Take:

- Ask if the content and the manner in which we measure our excellence is how customers would.
- Ask for the criteria that define Dimensions 1 through 4, the basis for that criteria, and the measures that reveal our excellence.

Challenging Vital Lies will make some people uncomfortable. Too bad. Challenging the organization's fictions is part of our Master of Excellence job description.

APPENDIX 3—AN EXAMPLE OF CORE VALUES

Southwest's stated purpose is to "connect people to what's important in their lives through friendly, reliable, low-cost air travel." The SWA mission is "dedication to the highest quality of Customer Service delivered with a sense of warmth, friendliness, individual pride, and Company Spirit." Core values are referred to as the Southwest Way:

Warrior Spirit
  Work hard
  Desire to be the best
  Be courageous
  Display urgency
  Persevere
  Innovate

Servant's Heart
  Follow the Golden Rule
  Adhere to the Principles
  Treat others with respect
  Put others first
  Be egalitarian
  Demonstrate proactive customer service
  Embrace the SWA family

Fun-LUVing Attitude
  Have FUN
  Don't take yourself too seriously
  Maintain perspective
  Celebrate successes
  Enjoy your work
  Be a passionate team player

Work the Southwest Way
  Safety and reliability
  Friendly customer service
  Low cost

APPENDIX 4—FIVE FIXES FOR AMBIGUITY

We identified several words in Chapter 6 that were the source of much hidden ambiguity, often resulting in chaos, conflict, and confusion. I promised to show you how we could eliminate issues with at least five sources of ambiguity when we discussed levers to achieve excellence and strengthen the culture.[138] My hope is that the promise has been kept. The following are five specific words, the essence of the challenge and a synopsis of the solution.

SERVICE

Problem A: Leadership, customers, and employees all agree service is critically important but are unable to agree on what it means. Service is most frequently used as a verb to describe reactive activity (for example, help, support, assist, or fix). It can also be used as a noun (for example, legal services) or as an adjective (for example, service center). The history of the terms "service" and "servicing" can create unintended and offensive meanings. Service also suffers from constraints related to repeatability (no two experiences are alike), measurability (no units of measure), tangibility (it isn't physical), responsibility (customers may be required to participate in the production of the service product), and storability (it can't be saved, inventoried, or retrieved). What cannot be defined is difficult to manage, measure, and improve.

Solution: Replace the word "service" with "product." A product is a deliverable that can be given to someone, is highly specific, is countable, is a noun, and can be made plural with an "s."

Problem B: The customer-service department title is ambiguous. What is its purpose, role, and products?

Solution: Rename the customer-service department to better fit the outcome it is intended to create (such as customer satisfaction), its role (such as answer center, customer advocate, or customer support), or its products (such as answers, repairs, or orders). Should you apply this same rigor to other functional names? Not necessarily. You can earn a college degree in accounting, marketing, purchasing, quality assurance, human resources, engineering, IT, legal, and most other disciplines associated with functional groups within the organization. Wherever that is true, ambiguity is reduced. A marketing department creates products such as marketing plans. Books are written on how to write an excellent marketing plan. If answers are a core product of the customer-service function, has its management created a written design and measures for producing excellent answers? Purchasing produces purchase orders. Quality assurance produces audits, corrective action plans, and quality manuals.

Does Apple have a customer-service department? No! What do they call the people who answer your questions or solve problems with an Apple product? In the Apple store, you will talk with an Apple Genius. By phone, they are called technical advisors. These titles convey that the individuals holding them are important and competent. It's not an accident.

CUSTOMER

Problem: Common synonyms include client, stakeholder, partner, student, taxpayer, patient, and guest. Organizing customers simply according to location (internal or external) compounds the confusion. So what if we know where they are? The term is often used without reference to a specific product. As a

---

[138] See ambiguity in Chapter 5.

practical matter, a person can only be a customer in terms of a product.

Solution: Replace customer with end user, broker, or fixer and include a reference to the relevant product. These labels refer to the individuals who actually use the product, the person who passes the product to someone else who will use it, and the person who amends, corrects, installs, repairs, or corrects the product for the end user.

SUPPLIER

Problem: This can refer to a person or group that creates a product, transfers the product to an end user or acquires the product on behalf of someone else. As with the term "customer," we've got a bad case of role confusion.

Solution: Replace supplier with broker or producer, which clarifies the role or relationship that party has with a given product.

INPUT

Problem: This can refer to activity, verbal instruction, knowledge, talent, undefined communication, or products provided to or used by others.

Solution: Eliminate ambiguity by referring to the specific product.

OUTPUT

Problem: This can be confused with a product or an outcome.

Solution: Use product or outcome.

APPENDIX 5—LOCATION AND IMPACT OF AMBIGUITY

We can purposefully eliminate the constraints ambiguity creates by first identifying specifically where it exists. There is no better way to do that than to examine how these levers are currently used in the organization we wish to lead. We did this for the first time with the third step in Leader's Action 5. Lucky for us, it will only take a few minutes to build on that, using your C3IQ results in Chapter 5. This will help us strategically employ or destroy ambiguity to achieve specific outcomes. We are assuming the results from all the respondents to whom you gave the C3IQ assessment have been tabulated and an average has been calculated. If not, do that now or simply proceed with your own score for reference.

To recap the introduction when we started the conversation about levers, our analysis now is intended to help identify the sources of ambiguity; recognize where ambiguity exists and its probable effect on the organization and those we wish to satisfy; and adopt behaviors, mechanisms, or systems to master its presence or impact.

Seven C3IQ items call for special attention right away: 7, 10, 13a, 14, 15, 17, and 18. Scores of five on all these indicate you have done a superb job of communicating strategic intent, have deployed it all the way down through the organization to the personal level, have eliminated key sources of ambiguity regarding customer priorities, and are consistent in your follow-through and recognition practices. You have a low-ambiguity organization with clear purpose and mechanisms for excelling. The following comments and recommendations are relevant for low scores of three or less:

- Question 7 regards how well personnel reviews align with strategic outcomes. This can be dramatically improved by including in the review the top three to five products the individual produces that are most supportive of strategic outcomes, the priorities of those using those products, and the measured degree to which those customer wants are satisfied. See chapters 14 and 20 regarding the definition of work as products and customer roles. Volume 2 regarding the heart, mind, and VOC deals with uncovering and satisfying customer wants.

- Question 10 addresses one of the most ambiguous words we use and the one most likely to diffuse efforts to improve excellence that customers will experience. Other words that are frequent sources of ambiguity will be addressed shortly below. The cure for number 10 is covered in Chapter 16 on service.

- Question 13a says we have no defined and consistently used method for uncovering what customers want. Chapter 26 provides the preview for how we will do this.

- Question 14 tells us we have a major section of our deployment bridge missing. If we say customer satisfaction is a high priority for the enterprise yet have no policy on it, we are inconsistent in our intent. If we have policies on other matters but not on this, either we don't really have customer experience as such a high priority, or we have not put in place the appropriate discipline to achieve it. See the discussion under policy at the end of this section.

- Question 15 suggests we have not yet advanced to the point that our measures support one or more of the 8DX framework. Such absence reduces the confidence and trust we can expect from others that we mean what we say. Without measurement, there is limited incentive to develop the capacity for follow-through and improvement. Our leadership power is weakened.

- Question 17 is an indicator that our modeling of the behavior we want from others is inconsistent (or absent) and trust in leadership is likely low.

- Question 18 suggests we don't recognize excellence, either at the personal or group level, and don't follow through with consequences when there is failure to execute.

In general, a score of three or less on an item is considered low, needs corrective attention, and suggests ambiguity exists as a constraint on achieving excellence. The table below offers comments for low scores, addressed by each individual assessment item. Following the table, we'll address clusters of related items. An X in a Lever column indicates which lever(s) an assessment item addresses.

THEME	ITEM #	Language	Values	Measures	Power	Assumptions	Modeling	AMBIGUITY EXISTS Item average score ≤3	COMMENT & ACTIONS FOR IMPROVEMENT (When item average score is ≤3)
Strategic Direction	1		X						
	2	X	X		X				
	3	X	X		X				
	4		X		X				
	5		X		X				
	6				X		X		
	7		X	X	X		X		
Customer Satisfaction	8	X	X						
	9	X	X						
	10	X	X			X			
	11	X			X	X			
	12	X							
	13A	X	X		X		X		
	13B	X	X		X		X		
	14	X	X		X		X		
Excellence	15A	X	X	X	X				
	15B	X	X	X	X				
	15C	X		X	X				
	15D	X		X	X				
	15E	X		X	X				
	F1	X		X	X				
	F2	X		X	X				
	16	X	X			X			
	17	X	X	X	X	X	X		
	18		X	X			X		

Figure 40—C3IQ Assessment Levers Ambiguity Worksheet

INSTRUCTIONS

1. Put an X in the Ambiguity Exists column for every item with a score (or average) of three or less.
2. In the Comments column, note which action could be taken by whom to reduce ambiguity.
3. What are your general discoveries?

Debrief

As you review the notes below, put a check in the Ambiguity Exists column next to each low-scoring item. Use the Comment & Actions for Improvement column to note what you might do to raise the average score by your organization. Reflect on which lever(s) you could push.

The first objective is to identify where ambiguity exists and what its probable effects are. We can examine clusters of items to reveal the role ambiguity plays in constraining excellence and to identify which levers to push on to achieve improvement.

- Items 1–5, 7, 9–10, 14, and 15a–f tell us how well strategic objectives and the definition of success have been communicated. Low scores tell us we have ambiguity of intent.

- Items 6, 7, 8, 13, 14, and 16 tell us how clearly we have connected and deployed department and personal behavior to strategic objectives. Low scores suggest a disconnect between intent and deployment.

- Items 7 and 18 address recognition and consequences. Low scores tell us we have ambiguity. Intrinsic motivation can go a long way to creating organizational success and personal satisfaction. An effective Master of Excellence still provides occasional feeding. It should be widely understood within the organization that recognition is to be expected and given when an individual or team makes a notable contribution to a strategic outcome. We may not have the basis for knowing when that occurs if it isn't part of the normal performance review. Even when a contribution is made, recognition may be absent. An effective Master of Excellence understands the value of a simple "thank you" as a key element of recognition. Conversely, when an individual or team's performance falls short, there should be a reasonably predictable consequence. Cynicism or fear can result when there is a perception that incompetence is rewarded but working outside "the way we do it" to produce an excellent result is reprimanded. Related to this discussion is trust.

- Items 17 and 18 indicate the degree that trust in leadership exists. Low scores suggest the possibility of distrust and disrespect due to inconsistent or absent follow-through. This is relevant for commitments we make as a leader but don't honor, as well as expectations we have of others whose results or failures go unrecognized. The more consistently inconsistent we are, the less trust and respect we can expect to get from others.

- Items 15a–f specifically reveal how well we have defined and are measuring six of the 8 Dimensions of excellence. The item number and relevant Dimensions are aligned as follows:
  15a: D5, producer-desired outcomes
  15b: D1, customer-desired outcomes
  15c: D2, undesired outcomes customers want to avoid
  15d: D3, product characteristics customers want
  15e: D8, process characteristics the producer wants
  15f: D4, process characteristics the customer wants

Included in this first objective is to determine when ambiguity works to support or impede the effectiveness and efficiency of the organization. At a summary level, variation in total scores of 20 percent or more (across all those you have asked to complete the assessment) should be interpreted as an indication that ambiguity is likely impeding excellence. That score variation also shows the degree of

305

agreement among respondents. The issue of total score variation is more important the lower the average total score is. For instance, if the average total score is ninety-five with variation of 20 percent, I would not be terribly concerned about the disagreement among respondents. Your organization is way above the norm and, if you haven't considered applying for the Baldrige National Award, Global Excellence Model (GEM) or a comparable award for excellence, you should. Several of my clients have successfully done exactly that within only two years of applying C3 practices.

Low scores on item groups 8 through 10 and 11 through 14 offer specific instances of ambiguity that are very common but rarely recognized. That first item group generally reveals that policies often cover issues of high value to leadership, but that, though customer satisfaction and good service are said to be important, are actually not supported by policy. Nor is there consensus on those concepts.

The second objective is to identify what the sources of ambiguity are. Ambiguous definitions of outcomes wanted, lack of clarity on the personal relevance of those outcomes on work to be performed, absence of aligned measures of success, and inconsistent follow-through are all sources of ambiguity. Disagreement on the meaning of key terms such as service, outcome, satisfaction, and customer makes any deployment and measurement of success difficult.

Part of our leadership challenge is to establish a common language without ambiguity. We have all received extensive education in math. We know there are certain rules that must be followed to achieve the correct answer to solve a math problem. Even so, we are periodically reminded of how attentive we must be to avoid disaster. One example that comes to mind is when the Hubble Space Telescope (HST) was launched into a low Earth orbit in 1990. The HST's main mirror was found to be defective, producing blurred images. It had been ground very precisely, but to the wrong shape. Oops! The fix only took five space walks and over $150 million.[139]

Unlike with math, few of us have had much in the way of education in linguistics. Is it any wonder that communication failure within organizations is one of the perennial top complaints of both leaders and their followers? We have begun to fix that in chapters 9 to 11 by focusing on the four kinds of outcomes represented by Dimensions 1, 2, 5, and 6. We continued to apply a rigor with language as we discussed products and customer roles, comparable to what we do with math, so the optimum results we seek can be achieved with least time and effort.

---

[139] "Who pays for Hubble flaws?" *Baltimore Sun*, October 27, 1992.

The third objective is to outline ways to increase or decrease ambiguity. The wording of each C3IQ assessment statement suggests the action your leadership team can take to advance excellence. Those actions should include the following:

1. Create or revise the strategic plan so it includes customer-desired outcomes with measures of success.

2. Eliminate language that creates ambiguity. Specific words to replace with unambiguous ones include service, customers, suppliers, inputs, and outputs. Yikes! That might seem to just about gut our lexicon of key terms related to improvement and change. But if you were able to suspend your disbelief, you started to become superbly equipped by the time you finished Chapter 20 to eliminate ambiguity that causes chaos and confusion, even if it hadn't been terribly visible before. In lieu of the full explanation, a synopsis is offered now.

    a. Service: It is virtually impossible for members of an organization to agree on what this means. Service is most frequently used as a verb to describe reactive activity (for example, help, support, assist, or fix). But it can also be used as a noun (for example, legal services) or as an adjective (for example, service center). What cannot be defined is difficult to manage, measure, and improve. Replace service with product. A product is a deliverable that can be given to someone, is countable, is a noun, and can be made plural with an "s."

    b. Customer: Common synonyms include client, stakeholder, partner, student, taxpayer, patient, and guest. Organizing customers simply according to location (internal or external) compounds the confusion. The term is often used without reference to a specific product. As a practical matter, a person can only be a customer in terms of a product. Replace customer with end user, broker, or fixer and include a reference to the relevant product. These labels refer to the individuals who actually use the product, the person who passes the product to someone else who will use it, and the person who amends, corrects, installs, repairs, or corrects the product for the end user.[140]

    c. Supplier: This can refer to a person or group that gives a product to someone else. Replace supplier with broker or producer, which clarifies the relationship with a given product.

    d. Input: This can refer to activity, verbal instruction, knowledge, talent, undefined communication, or products provided to or used by others. Eliminate ambiguity by referring to the specific product.

    e. Output: This can be confused with a deliverable (see product) or a result (see outcome).

3. Identify and prioritize the specific work products that currently constrain or whose improvement could enable enhanced outcome excellence.

4. Identify the owners and work groups who produce the priority products, increasing accountability and the ability to recognize achievement or administer consequences.

5. Determine who the customers are for each of those products and uncover their priorities that will be the basis for their satisfaction.

Up to this point, we've focused on how ambiguity is bad. When could it be good? When the purpose and intent is unambiguous but the ways to execute it are numerous, we encourage others to think creatively and seek a solution they love. Ambiguity can be good when it supports your cause, so long as trust in and by leadership is not diminished.

We have already observed that many organizations will have statements to the effect that customer satisfaction is the highest priority. Actual daily behavior might reveal that cost, time to market, or other factors trump satisfaction in key decisions. The leader seeking improved customer focus will seize on any prior leadership statements that satisfaction is the priority and explicitly base decisions on those. We all

---

[140] See Chapter 20 for the full discussion.

realize that there are multiple topics an organization will say are of top priority at different times. That means ambiguity surrounds us. A winning approach is to adopt the view that ambiguity is your friend. Use it carefully to promote your leadership agenda. Just as an attorney will do to create a compelling case, you get to choose which rules, past precedent, and evidence to use to support an unimpeachable course of action.

APPENDIX 6—C3 PRINCIPLES

LEADERSHIP PRINCIPLES

1. Leaders envision and embrace as achievable what others think is impossible.

2. It is not enough for a passionate innovator to create the technically possible. Success is dependent on understanding and articulating who wants it and why.

3. Excellence is achieved and sustained when defined by customers, created by engaged employees, measured by management, and rewarded by leaders.

4. Confusion, chaos, conflict, and dysfunction are reduced as ambiguity is replaced with certainty.

5. Purposeful success will not be fully realized without continuously using all six levers of cultural transformation: language, values, measures, power, assumptions, and modeling.

6. The complexity of cultural transformation is simplified by creating explicit alignment among core values, strategic outcomes, measures of success, and product ownership.

7. The mind and fortitude of an innovator are focused on why we do what we do for specified others.

8. The differences among the four outcomes in the 8DX framework are as fundamental as differences among the four elements of earth, fire, water, and air.

9. Vital Lies are destroyed with proof the assumptions are false.

10. When we claim something is important but don't measure it, the importance is less than we claim.

11. A core value whose practice is rewarded will be more dominant than a value not tied to reward.

12. Excellence is undermined by failures that carry no consequences.

13. Internal alignment is enabled when every employee can see the relationship between his or her personal products and those at the enterprise level.

14. A core value is alive when a written policy directs and supports its active deployment and related behaviors.

15. The Master of Excellence assures that end users of all products produced everywhere within the enterprise are treated as the definers of excellence and determiners of satisfaction.

16. Those who incorporate entertainment as part of their product offering will be viewed as more excellent and satisfying than those who don't.

17. Language functions as a lever when it creates consensus of meaning and purposeful, deployable intent.

18. Power is determined by those who drive the design of products and processes, select what behavior gets rewarded, and hold both the authority and capacity to achieve or prevent a specified result.

19. Policies can make values visible, actionable, and personally relevant.

20. When you hear a Vital Lie, ask for the evidence that would prove the statement.

21. The role of a leader is to identify when there is potential conflict between strategic direction and operational matters and find a way to create consensus.

22. Leaders of customer-centered excellence are totally clear about the difference between customer-desired and undesired outcomes, Dimensions 1 and 2.

23. If pursuing excellence is the goal, we have confused activity with results.

PRODUCT PRINCIPLES

1. Products focus our vision outward to customers; process focuses us inward.
2. A product must meet all five characteristics:
   a. It can be made plural with an "s."
   b. It is a deliverable we can give to others.
   c. It is packaged in countable units.
   d. It is very specific to the person or group that produces it.
   e. It is used to produce a desired outcome (for the producer and/or customer).
3. The VOL is expressed in products such as strategies, policies, plans, and decisions.
4. The relative priority of our core values is reflected in the decisions we make.
5. The higher we are in an organization, the less likely we are to define our work as tangible products or measure their performance; doing so drives excellence in all other products.
6. Activity that creates no product is of questionable value.
7. Service is not a product. It is so ambiguous in meaning as to be a useless term, except as an adjective to describe certain kinds of products.
8. Service products uniquely require customer involvement in their production.
9. Information products are created in anticipation of a need; service products are produced in response.
10. Leaders define their knowledge products as quantified deliverables, designed to satisfy emerging expectations of highly differentiated customers.
11. Every product is a cause of success or failure; treat it that way.
12. A product that does not create a desired outcome is of no value.
13. Organize everything by product: customers, measures, outcomes, problems, processes, and teams.
14. The unit cost, quality, yield, cycle time, rework cost, and satisfaction with every product are contributors to excellence and can be measured.
15. Enlightened leaders understand the earlier a product is created within a flow of products, the bigger its impact will be, so excellence must start there.
16. A product may be defined differently by customers than its producer.
17. We can only identify our customers by their relationships to specific products.
18. Customers may not know what the product should be, but they know the outcomes it must achieve.
19. Six major constraints characterize service. Describing work as products fixes them all.
20. A product is the root cause of any problem.
21. Fix the product before the process.
22. A process is a chain of products.

CUSTOMER PRINCIPLES

1. Tolerating ambiguity in defining who the customer is permits confusion and reduced enterprise performance.

2. We cannot meaningfully talk about who the customers are without specifying each of the products for which they are customers.

3. There are only three roles a customer can play with any product: end user, broker, or fixer.

4. A customer may play multiple roles with a single product.

5. The more specific the product, the easier it is to identify a customer's role.

6. Clarity about the customer leads to certainty about what is wanted by whom and how to achieve excellence.

7. End users for a product are rarely a homogeneous group.

8. End users often have less power than brokers do.

9. Eliminate, consolidate, and then automate the broker role to build end user empowerment.

10. Ability to directly change the design of a product is often based on the Five Ps of Power: position, purse strings, proximity, personality, and presence, not the role of the customer as it should be.

11. Brokers add value for producers and end users when reducing the time, cost, error, and complexity incurred in producing, delivering, and acquiring desired products.

12. Brokers foster understanding by being bilingual, speaking the languages of end users and producers.

13. Brokers may represent the interests of end users, the interests of producers, or their own interests, independent of any others.

14. A broker can be said to act as an agent for the end users of a product only if the end users think so and the priorities of end users direct broker behavior.

15. The more brokers are involved with a product, the less power the end users are likely to have.

16. The end users' knowledge of and feelings about the producer will color their satisfaction with the product.

17. Just as citizens have responsibilities, so do customers. They, as all other humans, are not always right!

18. End users always win in the long run.

SATISFACTION PRINCIPLES

1. Reducing dissatisfaction is not the same as improving satisfaction.
2. Performance, perception, and outcome expectations are the basis of satisfaction.
3. Assume customer expectations are unmet until you check.
4. Assuming customers don't know what they want causes us to give them what we want.
5. What customers expect is not necessarily what they want.
6. End users' desired outcomes are stable over time.
7. Customers always know the outcomes they want.
8. Customers do not always know the product that will best achieve their outcome.
9. Current customer behavior is not a predictor of future expectations.
10. Customers will answer the questions we pose, so ask the right ones.
11. Favor end users of the product when their expectations compete with interests of brokers.
12. It is possible to achieve standards and specifications yet still not satisfy end users.
13. A luxury, once experienced, becomes a necessity.

MEASUREMENT PRINCIPLES

1. What we measure is what we value.
2. Anything can be measured.
3. The biggest constraints on what we measure are our Vital Lies.
4. Success is defined by the quality of measures and pace of improvement for each of the 8 Dimensions of Excellence.
5. The higher a person is in an organization, the less likely it is his or her work is measured.
6. Measure customer-desired outcomes at least as well as undesired outcomes.
7. If a product is worth producing, it is worth measuring.
8. The unit cost, quality, yield, cycle time, rework cost, and satisfaction with every product are key contributors to excellence and can be measured.
9. A measure without a numerical goal for improvement is of limited value.
10. Measurement systems and tools that emphasize reliability over validity can easily create misleading conclusions.
11. Don't tell me what you value; show me what you measure.

INNOVATION PRINCIPLES

1. Innovation depends on divergent thinking about outcomes; quality improvement uses convergent thinking about products.

2. Understand customer-desired outcomes before considering product functions or features.

3. Building a better mousetrap will not assure the world beats a path to our door. Customers don't want trapped mice. They want no mice.

4. Customers are loyal to outcomes, not products.

5. The biggest constraints on innovation include our beliefs that we are already best in class, doing more of the same will sustain our success, and "it can't be done."

PROCESS PRINCIPLES

1. Process improvement, not positively experienced by customers, is a competitive mirage.

2. The customer's process begins when an outcome is wanted and ends when satisfaction is achieved.

3. Question the value of any process that does not create a customer-valued product.

4. Mapping the flow of products simplifies and should precede mapping the flow of activities.

5. One product represents many activities.

6. Eliminate and consolidate before automating.

7. The yield of the entire process is constrained by the lowest product yield within the process.

8. Process improvement is constrained—or enabled—by source products.

PRINCIPLES FOR CREATING A CUSTOMER-CENTERED CULTURE

1. Products focus our vision outward to customers; process emphasizes introspection.

2. Customers (end users, brokers, and fixers) can only be identified by their relationship to specific products.

3. End users always win in the long run.

4. Performance, perception, and outcome are the basis for satisfaction.

5. Always assume customer wants are unmet until you check.

6. What we measure is what we value.

7. Without knowing what we do (produce knowledge products), who we do it for (end users), what they want, and why (outcomes), how we do it (process) is irrelevant.

8. Eliminate and consolidate before we automate.

9. Process improvement, not positively experienced by customers, is a competitive mirage.

10. Vital Lies are constraints on any change initiative.

11. The absence of an undesired outcome is not the same as achieving a desired outcome.

12. Failure to address desired outcomes leads to preoccupation with reducing undesired outcomes

APPENDIX 7—GLOSSARY

8DX An abbreviation used in reference to 8 Dimensions of Excellence and the related graphical framework.

ANSWERS A complete, accurate response (or proactively delivered information product) that satisfies the customer's question on the first attempt. Answers are products.

ATTRIBUTE An expectation or design characteristic of a product, process, or outcome. All attributes are measurable. Performance attributes describe objective criteria. Perception attributes describe subjective criteria.

BROKER A customer who acts as an agent for the end user and/or the producer. As an agent for the end user, the broker makes the product more accessible, easier to use, and more appealing. As an agent for the producer, the broker encourages the user to accept the product.

C3 The abbreviation for customer-centered culture. It is pronounced as "see three." C3 is a system for aligning the strategic direction and operational practices of an organization to satisfy customer priorities and engage employees to excel. It is also used as an adjective (for example, C3 model or C3 technology).

CERTAINTY A class of product or process attribute that includes accuracy, reliability, consistency, predictability, and safety. It is also the opposite of ambiguity.

CULTURE Commonly shared language, beliefs, values, relationships, and behaviors. Whether a culture is producer- or customer-centered depends on whose needs primarily direct the development, creation, and modification of products. The measures used to manage the organization reveal the culture's priorities.

CUSTOMER Anyone who receives a product to use it to achieve a desired outcome (end user); transfer it to someone else (broker); or transform, repair, correct, install, or modify it (fixer). A specific product always determines a customer's role. A customer's role may change if the product changes. A customer can have more than one role simultaneously with a single product.

CYCLE TIME The total elapsed time or duration of a process, as customer-experienced. It includes value-added time (work), delays, inspections, and rework, usually measured in days.

END USER The customer for whom the product is primarily intended. This customer will personally use the product to achieve a desired outcome. There are usually more of this type of customer than any other. This is the most important customer to satisfy.

EXCELLENCE The definition or example of best from the customer's experience and aspiration. It is not corrective in emphasis. It suggests we are elevating the target to a new level.

EXPECTATIONS The basis for determining what excellence means. Customers have expectations about the performance and perception attributes of the product as well as the outcomes to be achieved by using the product. Perception expectations are stated in the voice of the customer (VOC), which may not be directly measurable. They have to be translated by the producer into precise design criteria that are directly measurable. Producers sometimes refer to these translations as requirements, specifications, needs, or standards. None of these terms is as inclusive as expectations; they reflect the minimum to be achieved by the product and generally are focused on objective performance attributes. Expectations are

315

based on the customers' past experience with products. Wants are desires focused on optimums (versus minimums) and hopes (versus past experience) regarding a product or outcome. An experience may be personal or vicarious.

FIXER Any customer who will have to make repairs, corrections, modifications, or adjustments to the product at any point in its life cycle for the benefit of the end user.

IDK Short for "I don't know." An IDK is a question perceived by the requestor to be answered inaccurately, incompletely, or not at the time first asked. An IDK does not necessarily mean "I don't know" was explicitly stated. Since answers are products, IDK responses indicate an out-of-stock condition.

INNOVATION A reference to the process of making a desired outcome easier to achieve.

INPUT Can refer to an activity, a resource, labor, a product, or undefined communication. It is ambiguous. It can be replaced with PRODUCT.

INSPECTOR Someone who approves others' work.

LEADERSHIP Intelligence, credibility, humanity, courage, and discipline.
Sun Tzu, circa 300 BC, *The Art of War*

LINGUISTICS The meaning of words. Linguistics is used to uncover values embedded in a word or statement. Those values can influence relationships and elicit or provoke specific behaviors within a particular culture. The purposeful use of words recognizes that seemingly slight differences in word choice evoke significant differences in meaning. (See SEMANTICS.)

MISSION A statement of organizational purpose and scope.

NOMINAL MEASURE Counts of things organized by category.

ORDINAL MEASURE A measure reflecting rank, priority, sequence, or rating.

OUTCOME A purpose or result achieved or sought.

OUTPUT Often confuses results (see OUTCOME) with deliverables (see PRODUCT). Replace with PRODUCT or OUTCOME.

PERFORMANCE EXPECTATIONS Unambiguous, objective, and directly measurable attributes of a product, process, or organization. Performance expectations address specific quantity, frequency, cost, elapsed time, weight, distance, and so on.

PERCEPTION EXPECTATIONS Subjective criteria. Perception expectations are often synonymous with the voice of the customer (VOC) and include product attributes such as easy to use, timely, accurate, cheap, quick, understandable, concise, and complete.

PLAN Detailed scheme, program, or method worked out in advance for the accomplishment of an objective, task, or project.

POLICY A statement of intent regarding the manner in which decisions will be made or practices and actions will occur. (For example, "Our policy is to provide equal employment and promotional opportunity without regard to race, creed, religion, national origin, gender, sexual orientation, or age.")

POWER The ability to direct or change the design of a product.

PRECISION (of process) Degree of variation from a promised/expected delivery or completion time.

PROCESS The sequence of activities or flow of products that creates a final product. Many processes may contribute to the creation of a single product.

PROCESS OWNER The primary person responsible for the performance of the process, the internal resources used in the process, and the satisfaction of the customers who use the product produced by the process. See PRODUCER.

PRODUCER The person or group that creates a product for a customer.

PRODUCT Something created by work that can be given to someone else. It is:
- A deliverable
- A noun
- Very specific to the person or group producing it
- Packaged in countable units
- Expressed as something that can be made plural with an "s"
- Used to create a desired outcome for the producer and/or customer

PROVIDER Ambiguous term synonymous with supplier, commonly used in health care. See BROKER, PRODUCER, or SUPPLIER.

QUALITY The definition of acceptability, offered either explicitly in requirements developed by customers or as defined by current industry (producer) standards and technology. The absence or reduction of "things gone wrong" often determines the degree to which quality exists. Quality is a necessary but insufficient basis for leadership. See SATISFACTION and EXCELLENCE.

REFERENCE PRODUCTS Document used to guide the creation or production of another product. Examples are specifications, procedures, and standards. Reference products are usually technical and detailed and provide little flexibility for interpretation and application. More tactical than SOURCE PRODUCTS.

RELATIONSHIP MEASURE Expressed in its simplest form as a ratio or fraction. Others include measures of correlation, prediction, or regression.

REQUIREMENTS See EXPECTATIONS.

SATISFACTION The degree to which a product, outcome, or process meets customer expectations. What they get is what they want. It is the feeling of contentedness that occurs when an expectation is matched by an experience.

SEMANTICS Often implies an arbitrariness in word choice. The phrase "that's just semantics" refers to the choice of words used as if the words used are interchangeable. This phrase assumes the differences in word usage are of little significance. (See LINGUISTICS.)

SERVICE See PRODUCT.

SIX SIGMA A statistical term. Its nontechnical usage refers to 3.4 defects or errors per million products or process steps.

SOURCE PRODUCTS Includes strategies, plans, and policies produced by leadership to create a bridge between the organization's mission (why we are in business) and processes (how we do work). The adjective—source—suggests these documents are the ultimate source of all practices that advance or restrain excellence. Source products represent the voice of leadership (VOL) and are the directing influence on major business practices. They define the purpose or intent of an organization, process or outcome. Most source products are created exclusively for internal consumption.

SPECIFICATIONS See EXPECTATIONS.

STANDARD An ambiguous term with many meanings, such as the following:

Out in front (flagpole held by standard-bearer)   Common (standard practice)
Best (gold standard)   Average (standard cost)
Goal (highest standard)   Minimum (minimum standard)
Target (industry standard)   A document, as in ISO 9001

Given these alternatives, standards are most commonly treated as minimums, producer-defined (versus customer-desired), rigid, slow to change, and tied to objective (versus subjective) performance measures.

STRATEGY An overall plan for projecting the organization toward a goal or desired outcome.

SUPPLIER A person or group that gives a product to someone else. Remove the inherent ambiguity of this term by replacing it with BROKER or PRODUCER to unambiguously specify their relationship with a given product.

VITAL LIE A limiting assumption, self-deception, denial, or unfounded justification for continuing current practice or not changing behavior. It prevents or limits pursuit of the possible.

VOICE OF THE CUSTOMER (VOC) Refers to the priorities, preferences, and aversions customers have regarding a product, product, outcome, or the producer organization, as shown in Dimensions 1 through 4 of the 8DX. These priorities are often expressed in ways other than verbal. VOC also refers to the methods for uncovering and understanding what those priorities are.

VOICE OF LEADERSHIP (VOL) The intent, direction, and priorities leaders have of their enterprise, articulated in strategies, plans, policies, and other guiding documents.

VOICE OF MANAGEMENT (VOM) The detailed translation into procedures and processes of what managers believe leadership wants.

VOICE OF WORKERS (VOW) Expectations about the context of work, the products workers receive, and the processes they are required to use to satisfy the VOL, VOM, and VOC. Dissatisfaction expressed by the voice of workers is a good indication there is perceived conflict between what they hear from VOL, VOM, and VOC. Employee engagement is enhanced when all voices are in alignment.

APPENDIX 8—BOOKMARK: 8DX FRAMEWORK

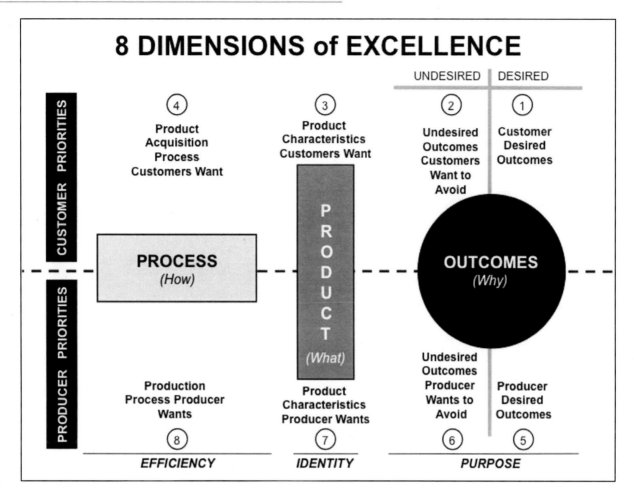

10 Steps to Customer-Centered Excellence

1. Establish the conditions for excellence, transformation, and leadership.
2. Articulate strategic and customer-desired outcomes.
3. Determine how each outcome will be measured.
4. Set numerical goals and due dates.
5. Select the few products and owners most likely to impact outcome success.
6. Identify end user, broker, and fixer customers for key products.
7. Uncover and measure customers' priority outcome, product, and process expectations.
8. Innovate or redesign products to achieve best outcomes.
9. Cut the time to produce, acquire, and use products by 80 percent.
10. Integrate cultural change levers to sustain, celebrate, and broaden success.

---

10 COMMON VITAL LIES

1. We don't have control over that.
2. Satisfaction will occur if dissatisfaction declines.
3. We are on the leading edge of our industry.
4. Growth in customer demand or market share means customers are happy.
5. We know what business we are in.
6. We know who our customers are.
7. Customers don't know what they want.
8. We know what customers want.
9. What customers say they expect is what they *do* want.
10. Our performance measures confirm our excellence.

Figure 41—10 Common Vital Lies

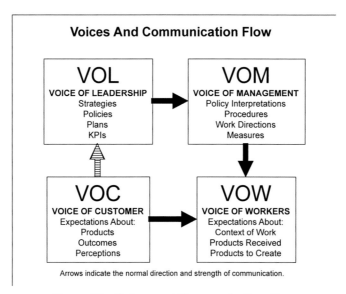

Figure 42—Voices and Communication Flow

PRINCIPLES FOR CREATING A CUSTOMER-CENTERED CULTURE

1. Products focus our vision outward to customers; process emphasizes introspection.
2. Customers (end users, brokers, or fixers) can only be identified by their relationship to specific products.
3. End users always win in the long run.
4. Performance, perception, and outcome are the basis for satisfaction.
5. Always assume customer wants are unmet until you check.
6. What we measure is what we value.
7. Without knowing what we do (produce knowledge products), who we do it for (end users), what they want, and why (outcomes), how we do it (process) is irrelevant.
8. Eliminate and consolidate before we automate.
9. Process improvement, not positively experienced by customers, is a competitive mirage.
10. Vital Lies are constraints on any change initiative.
11. The absence of an undesired outcome is not the same as achieving a desired outcome.
12. Failure to address desired outcomes leads to preoccupation with reducing undesired outcomes.

ABOUT THE AUTHOR

Robin L. Lawton
Cultural Transformation and
Voice of Customer Expert
Sarasota, Florida

Robin Lawton started his business in 1985. Prior to that, he had worked in a variety of fields, including government, computers, education, entertainment, and oil. He has lived in Latin America for several years and has traveled extensively in Europe. Rob was twice a foster parent before becoming an international adoptive parent in 1998. These diverse experiences have had a great impact on what his many colleagues and clients have referred to as "thinking different."

He coined the term "customer-centered culture" with his first book, *Creating a Customer-Centered Culture: Leadership in Quality, Innovation and Speed* (1993). Those ideas and his system for achieving excellence, now referred to as C3, are expanded upon in this book.

Rob loves to inspire, challenge, equip, and guide those leading excellence to envision and do what they never thought possible. Users say his principles, strategies, and tools have the feeling of simplicity and common sense. The principles are embedded in his technically sophisticated underlying system, making his ideas appealing and accessible to both executives and individual contributors. His thought-leading and humorous presentations excite audiences from many industries, domestic and international.

Rob enjoys working with creative, passionate, and innovative leaders who are impatient to make seismic, sustainable transformation occur in their organizations. He is honored to have been viewed as a twenty-first century thought leader, favorably compared with management giants from the last century such as Russell Ackoff, Edwards Deming, Peter Drucker, Philip Crosby, Walter Shewhart, Tom Peters, and others. Where their ideas were born of the industrial age, Rob's work is especially relevant for those immersed in knowledge age work.

Rob enjoys playing the guitar, reading, sailing, camping, hiking, and the great outdoors. He also appreciates hearing from readers, knowing he learns as much from them as they do from him.

TABLE OF FIGURES

INDEX